Understanding Autism

Understanding Autism

Parents, Doctors, and the History of a Disorder

Chloe Silverman

PRINCETON UNIVERSITY PRESS

Princeton and Oxford

Copyright © 2012 by Princeton University Press

Published by Princeton University Press, 41 William Street,
Princeton, New Jersey 08540

In the United Kingdom: Princeton University Press, 6 Oxford Street,
Woodstock, Oxfordshire OX20 1TW

press.princeton.edu

Jacket Art: Jim Dine, *Blue Clamp*, 1981; painting; acrylic on canvas with English C-clamp,
84 1/4 in. x 96 1/2 in. x 5 in. (214 cm x 245.11 cm x 12.7 cm); Collection SFMOMA, Gift of
Harry W. and Mary Margaret Anderson; © Jim Dine / Artists Rights Society (ARS), New York

ISBN 978-0-691-15046-8

Library of Congress Cataloging-in-Publication Data
Silverman, Chloe.
    Understanding autism : parents, doctors, and the history of a disorder / Chloe Silverman.
        p.   cm.
    Includes bibliographical references and index.
    1. Autism in children.   2. Parents of autistic children.   3. Autistic children—Family
relationships.   4. Autism in children—Treatment.   I. Title.
    RC553.A88S55 2012
    618.92'85882—dc23 2011013942

British Library Cataloging-in-Publication Data is available

This book has been composed in Minion Pro

Printed on acid-free paper. ∞

Printed in the United States of America

10 9 8 7 6 5 4 3 2 1

This book is dedicated to my parents,

Peter and Noele Silverman.

CONTENTS

ACKNOWLEDGMENTS

This project began with a chance meeting at an MIT workshop and an exhilarating introduction to the worlds of autism research, treatment, and advocacy. Without Martha Herbert's help and encouragement, I would never have been able to conduct this research or write this book. I hope that I have done justice to the generosity she showed in welcoming me into her life and work.

Susan Lindee, my mentor and chair of my dissertation committee, is an inspiration. She continues to teach me about what it means to be both a scholar and a good person, and her own work on emotional knowledge and biomedicine has informed every part of this project. The other members of my dissertation committee, Robert Kohler and Joe Dumit, provided invaluable input at key moments. A Jacob K. Javits Fellowship from the Department of Education supported my graduate work, and the first two years of work on this book were funded by a Mellon Foundation postdoctoral fellowship at Cornell University's Science & Technology Studies Department.

Writing this book depended on the passion, intellectual openness, and kindness of researchers, advocates, and parents who willingly shared their work. I am grateful in particular to everyone associated with ARI/Defeat Autism Now! conferences and to Jacquelyn Sanders. Researchers made time in their schedules to explain the technical details of their studies. Owners of laboratories walked me through their facilities. Physicians allowed me into their offices and homes. Librarians at the University of Chicago Special Collections and Yale University Manuscripts and Archives Collection offered guidance in navigating their collections. As this book makes clear, I am in awe of many of the parents that I met. Their devotion to their children and their intellectual creativity and resourcefulness animate this book.

I shared portions of this book at a number of institutions, workshops and conferences: the "Lively Politics" conference at UC Irvine in November 2004, the Hastings Center, the BIOS Centre at the London School of

Economics, a Society for Critical Exchange conference on "Autism and Representation" in October 2005, the Mellon Seminar and Science Studies Reading Group at Cornell, and the SUNY Center for Medical Humanities, Compassionate Care, and Bioethics. As a result of these workshops, an earlier version of one chapter was published as "Brains, Pedigrees and Promises: Lessons from the Politics of Autism Genetics," in *Biosocialities, Genetics and the Social Sciences: Making Biologies and Identities,* edited by Sahra Gibbon and Carlos Novas (Routledge, 2008), and another will be published as "Desperate and Rational: Parents and Professionals in Autism Research," in *Lively Capital: Biotechnologies, Ethics and Governance in Global Markets,* edited by Kaushik Sunder Rajan (Duke University Press, 2011).

A number of colleagues, friends, and students have taught me about the history and social studies of medicine and the life sciences, autism, and disability studies. These include Jesse Ballenger, Michael Bérubé, Sarah Birge, Paul Burnett, Alexandra Choby, Adele Clarke, Biella Coleman, Rich Doyle, Greg Eghigian, Noah Feinstein, Mike Fischer, Brendan Hart, Stephen Hilgartner, Sheila Jasanoff, Andrew Lakoff, Martine Lappe, Janet Lyon, Jonathan Marks, Aryn Martin, Pamela Moss, Esra Ozkan, Kris Peterson, Trevor Pinch, Rachel Prentice, Nikolas Rose, Erich Schienke, Jeanette Simmonds, Ilina Singh, Jennifer Singh, Olga Solomon, Susan Squier, Kaushik Sunder Rajan, and Audra Wolfe. Erik Olin Wright was a generous and encouraging reader at a critical moment. Other friends sustained me and kept my priorities straight: Ruth Ainsworth, Becky Charnas Grant, Jen Hsiung, Eric Jenson, Stephen Motika, Jeffrey Stutz, Bowie Snodgrass, John Thompson, and Kate Winchell.

My grandparents, Dot and Eliot Silverman, provided a home away from home. My Granddad did not get to see this book published, but his omnivorous intellectual curiosity and belief in getting the story right are a constant inspiration.

Bob Vitalis, my most important reader, favorite working companion, and partner in all things, edited every page of this book. In the process, he taught me a lot about writing. More important, he makes every day sweeter and brighter.

This book focuses on the unique kinds of knowledge that parents possess, and the responsibilities—and pleasures—of parental love. I am not a parent yet, and I have had to rely on the accounts of others to understand parental love and labor. I do know a great deal about what it means to be a well-loved child, and I am forever grateful for that. This book is for my parents, Peter and Noele Silverman. Thank you.

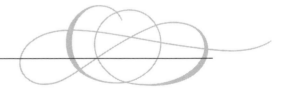

Understanding Autism

Love as an Analytic Tool

*Women's work is of a particular kind—whether menial or requir-
ing the sophisticated skills involved in child care, it always involves
personal service. Perhaps to make the nature of this caring,
intimate, emotionally demanding labor clear, we should use the
ideologically loaded term "love." For without love, without close
interpersonal relationships, human beings, and it would seem
especially small human beings, cannot survive.*[1]

*Of course, love is never innocent, often disturbing, given to
betrayal, occasionally aggressive, and regularly not reciprocated
in the ways the lovers desire. Also love is relentlessly particular,
specific, contingent, historically various, and resistant to anyone
having the last word.*[2]

If You Think My Hands Are Full . . . You Should See My Heart![3]

This is a book about love. It is a history of autism, one that pays particular
attention to the importance of affect in biomedical research during the second half of the twentieth century and the first few years of the twenty-first.
I explore the role of love as a social experience and technical discipline.
I do this for several reasons. Passions are a key part of the production of
knowledge and the identities of contemporary scientists and medical practitioners. Theories of affect, and love in particular, shape the discourses of
developmental psychology, psychiatry, and, more recently, biology. Affect
and its synonyms, including despair, anger, caring, and love, work as "good
enough" analytic tools for interpreting contemporary biomedicine. Like

1

the parents described as "good enough" by the child psychologist and autism researcher Bruno Bettelheim in one of his warmer portrayals, our analytical categories need only be up to the task of illuminating key themes and conflicts in the material. Love works pretty well. It also helps me think through the role of the social scientist and historian negotiating the thorny issues of trust, complicity, and participant observation.

Autism refers to a symptom, a disorder, and a syndrome.[4] The concept derived from the idea of negative social affect: "autistic isolation" in patients with psychiatric disorders. According to the current *Diagnostic and Statistical Manual of Mental Disorders* used by most psychiatrists and physicians in the United Sates, autism is a developmental disorder involving "qualitative impairments" in language, communication, and social relationships, alongside "restricted, repetitive and stereotyped patterns of behavior," with onset before the age of three. Any additional claim is contentious, but the standardized diagnosis obscures the complexity of the behavioral and physiological syndrome in any given individual. Autism is also commonly seen as a lifelong disorder. To focus on children is to ignore entire lifetimes of membership in families and communities. Nevertheless, this book is about childhood because those are the years when families have to wrestle with the ambiguities of the diagnosis, invest in therapies and treatments, and prepare to live with the impact of their choices on their child's future.

Understanding Autism traces the evolution of the diagnostic category of autism as people have understood it in different places and times, paying particular attention to how people have thought about autism in different ways depending on the type of work they performed. These practices included diagnostic interviews with parents, psychoanalytic milieu therapy, genetics research, and biomedical interventions. The first three chapters deal mostly with the past, the final three with the present. Because the focus is on practice, even the sections of the book that draw on archival sources read in parts like ethnography, as I describe social practices as symbolic systems and seek to illuminate how participants understood the meanings of their actions. However, unlike ethnography, my analysis depends on public statements. I focus on how people describe informal practices of nurturance and care—private activities—in journal articles, memoirs, conferences, and courtrooms.[5] I attend to the language they use to communicate insights about the affective content of practices to those outside their professional or social communities. When people work to explain those parts of biomedical care that are difficult to render in technical language, they talk about love.

Looking at autism in terms of the affective content of practices associated with it does three things. First, it illustrates the degree to which ways of representing autism depend on particular institutional and epistemological arrangements. Second, it shifts the focus from psychiatrists, epidemiologists, and geneticists to parents, counselors, diagnosticians, and lawyers, as they try to make sense of and apply systematic, authoritative knowledge in their daily lives and work. Third, and most important, in describing changes in autism over time and how expert knowledge works in practice, it highlights the centrality of love as a way of knowing about bodies, persons, and relationships in biomedicine.

I use "love" because it is the term used by the people and found in the texts that I have studied. Love is one of those terms in a conversation where expert discourses inform everyday language and where the quotidian in turn shapes biomedical knowledge. It might be more accurate at points to refer, ecumenically, to "affective commitments" or "emotional connections." I prefer the everyday term, even if it is occasionally necessary to point out the technical alternatives employed by particular actors. Freud called psychoanalysis a "cure through love," but contemporary social psychologists favor "empathy."[6] Needless to say, empathy also has a specific and localized technical meaning. Therapeutic practitioners might insist that their work involves "caring" and "help" while resisting "love" on the grounds that it does not involve a rational or intellectual component, a criticism that I will return to.

I focus less on love as an abstract concept than on the statements of participants in several domains of autism research when they talk about love as a form of labor. Love has been seen sometimes as a liability, a barrier to reliable knowledge, and sometimes as the source of specific, focused, and committed knowledge. It entered autism research as something that psychologists studied. Autism seemed to demonstrate what happened when people developed without giving or receiving affection. Love became for a while a behavior that might be encouraged or cultivated externally, before clinicians abandoned it for terms more in keeping with behavioral and cognitive models. Beyond the laboratories, however, love continues to function in normative claims about the practice of research. Parents and their allies say that emotional knowledge enables them to observe and attend to their children in the right way, guides them in medical decisions, and helps them make the right choices for the person whom they love. Those who are concerned about the actions and choices of parents say that it is love that blinds parents and incites acts of desperation. They also worry that the idea of love is used to rationalize and naturalize labor by making the hard work that parents do seem instinctive instead of intentional and sensible. There is truth in both sets of claims. These examples all show how the emotional work of science is made visible when parents and professionals interact.

People do not just talk about love in the world of research on developmental disorders like autism—they actively practice it, often because they are also parents. Clara Claiborne Park, whose daughter was diagnosed with autism in the 1960s, said that she had followed "the imperative that an eminent mathematician has given as a two-word definition of the scientific method: 'Try everything.'"[7] The approach was as appropriate for the parents of affected children as it was for scientific and medical professionals. The work of professionals and of parents is not, in the end, as different as we have been led to believe. For example, the leading journal of autism research, then called the *Journal of Autism and Childhood Schizophrenia*, ran a remarkable column between 1974 and 1985, "Parents Speak," edited by the first two presidents of the National Society for Autistic Children. Park reviewed books for the journal, arguing for the importance of reading parent memoirs not only as historical documents but as clinical evidence, "raw data in the fullest sense."[8]

To be clear, love may not protect against harm. People who love routinely commit acts of violence. Consider three apparent murders of children with autism by their parents in 2006. The editor of a daily Internet autism clipping service and father of a child with autism agonized, "I have been struggling with trying to find a response that does justice to these situations, and I don't think I've been doing such a good job of it because the subject hurts so, the heart can get too much in the way."[9] These were not isolated instances. In one, grieving relatives of the parent called a murder-suicide "an act of love."[10] Different groups interpret such acts in line with their own beliefs. Some blame the lack of support services. Others curse promised cures that fail to deliver, "[leaving] the parents of a half-million autistic children feeling like failures."[11] Some parents will admit that they have also considered violence in spite of, or perhaps alongside, their love for their children.[12] Such acts and the agony that precedes and follows them resist simple explanations.

In focusing on parental love, I am not suggesting that only parents can provide the particular kind of attentive care that I am interested in. Many parents do not love their children. They are completely absent from their children's lives. Some actively and intentionally harm their children. There are also many caregivers in residential facilities or employed by families who are more intimately involved in children's lives than are their parents.

When I discuss the love that is part of effective care and treatments, I am less concerned with biological relatedness than with attitudes of investment in and devotion to another's well-being. Counselors, nurses, and teachers are often the ones providing this care.

Clara Park listed the advantages that parents have in treating their own children, leaving one quality of parental care, "a parent's love for his child," until the very end of her list. Park's hesitant attention to the necessity of attachment and caring, even in instances where doctors and parents are expected to impartially evaluate different treatment options, points to a tension that affects medical research and treatment in general. Love is not a panacea, and "we must be aware of the ways to go wrong in loving, ways that help not the person we love but ourselves." Nevertheless, "there are millions of parents—as well as teachers, and social workers, and doctors, and ministers, and psychiatrists, and ordinary men and women—who practice this love daily, knowing that love is a technique as well as an emotion."[13]

Understanding Autism pursues Park's insight about love as a technique in biomedical knowledge and practice. It is about why love is the last item on Park's list, and why it is the most important.

Thinking about Caring: Theories of Love in Biomedicine

Research programs in autism, as in many areas of the life sciences, have been defined largely by the passions and commitments that have informed them. These commitments inform not only the broad theoretical framing of investigations but also the day-to-day practices of research. My interest in love is a consequence of taking seriously the commitment to analyze science as a social system. It is indebted to work in science studies on reason, rationality, and objectivity. If science is a culture, it should be possible to analyze the rituals and modes of behavior that enable scientists to comprehend and trust each other, and to produce facts that the community recognizes as valid. Sociologists have analyzed the behavioral norms that have allowed scientists to see their work as insulated from the pressures of politics, social aspirations, and commercial enterprise.[14] Even when those norms are not followed to the letter, they have provided models for how scientists believe they ought to behave.

In addition to observing rules of conduct, scientists have also used representational techniques to establish their distinctive identities. They have adopted styles of observation that emphasize impartiality and objectivity, extending to the way that they write up experimental results and illustrate their findings.[15] As scientific work became more collaborative, the problem of knowing whether or not to trust an individual's observations or experimental results became a crucial one. Scientists solved this problem in many ways, but one important way was by making clear distinctions between appropriate and inappropriate attitudes and behavior.[16] Because there is such a close connection between the identities of scientists and their ideas about what constitutes reliable knowledge, one way to learn about epistemology is to study scientists' own statements about acceptable behavior and attitudes. I am interested in particular about claims regarding the emotional content of scientific and biomedical practices.

Love has mattered to feminist science studies scholars for some time. It has been a focus of their work on the role of passion and commitment in maintaining careers and research programs, on the importance of both caring and pleasure in scientific work, and on the way that expectations about gender have influenced scientific investigations.[17] Love also reminds us of the gendered structures of labor in American society, including the institutions of domestic life and the division of domestic labor, as well as ideologies of motherhood and parental work. Caring labor most frequently falls to women, and because women are socialized to accept that obligation, they develop moral systems that are more attentive to matters of care and dependence.[18] Beliefs about gender and its connections to affective behavior inspire speculations into the biology of sex and cognition, as well as psychological theories about cognitive normality and typical functioning in social interactions.[19] These are especially salient in view of the brute demographic fact that boys are diagnosed with autism four times more frequently than girls. Ideas about gender color ideas about "autism moms" and dads who "fix things."

Gender runs deeper than the division of labor, to what we could call gendered economies of care—types of labor can retain their gendered associations no matter who is performing the work. Parent memoirs of autism begin and end with love, while practitioners speak of parents' diligence and devotion. In this view, commitment explains their ascent to near-professional levels of expertise. This praise is not disingenuous, but it still is worth questioning because it goes to the heart of how American society categorizes caring labor and daily commitments. The top professions for women have changed little in the past fifty years, with low-status "pink collar" jobs in elementary and secondary education, nursing, and administrative work still ranking highest.[20] In addition, women continue to provide much of the child care in the United States, although many fathers of children with autism work as hard as mothers on advocacy and treatment. However, caring labor continues to be devalued because of its associations with women, and the expertise associated with it is often considered suspect. To begin to understand the hidden forms of labor in science and medicine, we need to consider the erasure of the research, long hours of therapeutic work, and advocacy that the care of a child with autism entails. It is significant that the serious effort required to know a person well or care about them effectively is often described as a spontaneous expression of affection rather than conscious work.

The fact that caregiving is hard but also intellectually and emotionally demanding work is key to understanding the arguments that this book makes about the ethics of autism treatment. It is also important to understanding how the philosophy of disability can deepen our understanding of the affective components of biomedical practices.

Moral Personhood, Families, and Dependence

Through much of this book, I present the primary act of intervening on the bodies and behaviors of children with autism as relatively unproblematic. Specific practices draw criticism in retrospect as poorly justified, but from the 1950s through the 1980s, few questioned the idea of treating autistic children or of recovery as a goal, whether attainable or not. This has not been the case from the 1990s onward. A growing number of adults with autism have joined a self-advocacy movement modeled on gay rights and Deaf advocacy, arguing for the validity of autistic experience and autistic culture. For this reason, I want to address what treating autism can mean in terms of respecting and acknowledging the personhood and rights of people with disabilities. I return to this question in more practical terms in an interlude midway through the book.

The ethics of treating autism turns on a question of personhood: whether or not one sees it as a disabling condition, something that it would be better not to have or to be. As Evelyn Fox Keller has argued, the definition of autism as a pathology rather than a normal difference rests on the conviction that the ability to relate to other people is not only developmentally necessary but morally necessary as well. It is a component of personhood. Someone cannot be a "whole person" without it.[21] Many disabilities scholars argue in the same vein. Michael Bérubé, in a memoir about his son who has Down syndrome, suggests that it is Jamie's ability to relate to others, his sensitivity to the needs of people, and his sense of humor that reveal his intelligence and his value as a person. Eva Kittay, writing about her daughter who has multiple physical and cognitive impairments, argues that it is her membership in a network of relationships of caring, kinship, and love that grants her "personhood," the quality that makes it ethically necessary for society to protect people like her and provide for their care. One way that society can respect the personhood of people like her daughter is by providing for her caregivers, those who attend to her physical needs, but also those who care for her as a person.[22]

Autism, though, poses a problem. There is no definitive model for how cognition functions—or fails to function—in autism. The dominant psychological and neurological models continue to emphasize the absence of empathy. If Leo Kanner first framed autism in terms of a lack of affective contact, contemporary scientists describe the disorder in terms of lacking the "theory of mind" that allows people to imagine others' mental states. Neuroscientists point to malfunctioning mirror neuron systems, the part of the brain that helps us understand the behaviors of others by providing us with a mental model of their actions. In essence, we understand the behaviors of others in part by imagining ourselves doing the same things.

Although the terms may be more sophisticated, the argument remains the same: people with autism fail at empathy. Adults with autism disagree, but they do so within the terms already set. They say they experience empathy but arrive at it and express it in ways that are difficult for neurotypicals to recognize.[23] This dissent is significant, and the scientific claims about autism and empathy have obvious limitations. It remains true, however, that autism can mean, in practical terms, that an individual is less tightly bound into the network of relationships that sustain most of us.

This is not the place to enter into a complex discussion of the human rights of people with disabilities and why people with autism deserve support and respect as full, rights-bearing humans and citizens.[24] It is clear that many parents have little trouble committing themselves to the well-being of their child and seeing their child as a complete person, even if their child does not reciprocate their caring in familiar ways. The question that is relevant to this book is whether researching cures for autism or choosing an intervention with the expectation that it can treat or cure autism—and by doing so, help people with autism participate more fully in the give and take of human relationships—can be an ethical choice. I demonstrate that people who provide services for or do research on or spend their time caring for children and adults with autism make ethical decisions about treatment. This is not a claim about the efficacy of particular treatments or the rightness of specific choices. What I mean is that they weigh their decisions in terms that are familiar to students of ethical philosophy. Some of those decisions are life-changing in the sense that they entail therapies that can alter or eliminate the symptoms of autism. I will argue that these actions, whenever observers do describe them as effective and beneficial, begin and end with close, attentive relationships.[25]

These types of ethical thinking are important beyond the specific question of autism treatments. Alasdair MacIntyre has argued that disability and dependence characterize our lives; and, to the same extent that our ability to reason depends on our intelligence, our humanity is characterized by inevitable periods of profound dependence on the care of others.[26] Nevertheless, many philosophers have begun their descriptions of social relations by assuming that humans are autonomous, independent agents. We need to think harder about our obligations to those with disabilities, including those who are entirely dependent or unable to speak for themselves. The reality of dependence without the prospect of eventual autonomy has an additional implication. Inevitably some members of society will be charged with making good decisions about the care of dependent people.

This book argues that parents think about these decisions in ethical terms, and that their love for their children is something that they cite as central to their ability to choose wisely. The two, love and ethics, may be related. To care well, Kittay argues, caregivers must not only go through the motions of care, but they must also care about the person who depends on them, because without it "the open responsiveness to another that is so essential to understanding what another requires is not possible." In order to do a good job with the rational, arduous, daily labor of caring, an "affective bond" is necessary.[27]

Think of the decision to choose residential care for a child for the long-term benefit of both child and family. In the short term, the decision is utterly wrenching for both. Or the decision that a parent makes to begin a regimen of behavioral therapy, against a child's immediate wishes, because the child may flourish as a result of the temporarily unpleasant drills and repetitions. Children with cognitive disabilities are especially vulnerable to wrong decisions about their care and depend on the caring of others. The problem is that people rarely talk about these decisions in public. Such parents have few guidelines. In the United States, where pregnancy and motherhood represent "a private dimension of public life," in Rayna Rapp's phrase, parents must act as "moral pioneers" in their decisions about the justifiable limits of parental obligations.[28] Put bluntly, parents are utterly on their own.

What ensures a coincidence of interests between the child and his or her caregiver? Our ability to reflect on our actions, values, and beliefs is necessarily tempered and guided by our ability to love. The philosopher Harry Frankfurt calls love an act of "volitional necessity." It is something we experience if not involuntarily than at least unavoidably. It is also a choice, a relation that is entered into willingly, not instinctively or unconsciously. Humans may have a unique and near-compulsive capacity to reflect on their actions, values, and beliefs, but constant reflection would be paralyzing without an equal capacity to love. Reflexive thought and reason matter crucially to functioning in the world, but if we are to survive and "get it right," that is, live a meaningful life, we need to care deeply about particular things in order to make choices about our goals and actions.[29] Reason has no practical application without love, and reason has no fit with lived experience without the winnowing power and narrowed focus that love confers.

Because of the close connection between reason and love, "the ultimate source of practical normative authority lies not in reason but in the will," meaning our choices about what or whom we will care about most deeply.[30] The psychologist Erich Fromm made the same point fifty years ago when he described the art of loving as a practice that involves technical demands of "discipline, concentration, and patience." For Fromm, love required "rational faith," that is, a future-oriented focus on the object of love, not only as it is, but as it might become given the opportunity to flourish. This nurturing attitude could describe the focus and passion required for fostering scientific research as well as child development.[31] An orientation toward the future is central to the care of children with disabilities. It is why parents may accept the calculated risk of choosing a treatment plan that places more demands on their child but offers the prospect that he or she will have access to more experiences as they grow older.

Frankfurt's description of a necessary alliance between reason and love may not apply to everyone, but it fits many parents of children with disabilities. Consider those engaged in the type of everyday moral philosophy that Rayna Rapp suggests is fostered by their unique position. Although Rapp discusses prenatal testing in particular, parents typically continue to wrestle with difficult questions of dignity, respect, and rights long after making the decision to carry a pregnancy to term. Parents decide what is most important in their child's life. Where a child does not ask for a greater range of experiences but seems content with a sharply circumscribed set of activities, what ethical imperative allows parents to demand more of the child? Eva Kittay and others suggest that imagining independence as the exclusive goal can be both damaging and unattainable for many. However, parents are obliged to increase their children's "capacities to experience joy," which can best be done by broadening their range of possible experiences—for instance, by pushing a child who does not process visual information well to learn to watch and enjoy movies, because learning how will eventually broaden that capacity.[32] It is hard to disagree.

I draw on these philosophical concepts in order to more accurately represent the people that I care about, the families and children who are the central concern of this book. Many children with autism have language delays. Others are nonverbal. Even those considered "high-functioning" or mildly affected may have difficulty serving as advocates for their own cause. They have more effective representatives among the hundreds of thousands of parents, practitioners, and researchers devoted to autism.[33] Of necessity, much of my story centers on actors, technologies, and knowledge systems that affect these children. The children themselves play a limited role in the debates that swirl around them.

Adults with autism are a different story. These often highly effective self-advocates matter to arguments about the appropriate and ethical treatment of children with autism, and I agree that they are better equipped than others are, myself included, to represent their experience. Self-advocates have enjoyed greater visibility and a bigger voice within parent organizations in recent years. Organizations such as Autism Network International, the Global and Regional Asperger Syndrome Partnership, and the Autistic Self-Advocacy Network, founded both by and for autistic people, are an important presence within the world of autism advocacy. Children, adults in institutions, parents who feel that the state and the medical industry disregard their complaints, and researchers excluded from mainstream biomedical research are all silenced in one form or another.[34] The burden for all of us who do have an audience is to act as adequate witnesses for those who are not speaking and to avoid the temptation to assume that their silence is equivalent to agreement or assent.

As should be clear, I am centrally concerned with how parents understand their children in biomedical and affective terms, and what they do with that understanding. I am interested in how the different identities of parents and professionals work in the scientific field, especially when it comes to making claims about effective treatments. Much of the time, the social mechanisms through which scientists maintain their cultural authority—desire for credit from their peers, willingness to share and dispassionately critique each other's results, and a collective belief in the project of increasing knowledge about the natural world—help produce reliable information. However, struggles for authority in autism research have not enabled practitioners to progress steadily toward increasing independence from external interests.[35] The central role of parents in the history of autism research helps illustrate how investments and commitments from outside have shaped the sphere of scientific research.

Autism in History

Like other disorders, autism has become a site for evocations of the stresses, tensions, and catastrophes of modernity. Professionals have described autism as a symptom of postindustrial and suburban modernity, and a range of techniques and specializations have developed to define and serve the population. The literature on autism brims over with metaphorical as well as technical uses of the idea of autistic isolation, and autism has become, in popular culture, a generic synonym for emotional isolation and conceptual solipsism.[36]

Autism has proven almost infinitely mutable. For a mother struggling to implement a behavioral therapy program in the 1960s without the support of her skeptical, sometimes hostile husband, and plagued by fears that she caused her son's illness through unconscious rejection, the disorder is a behavioral anomaly that can be cured through hard work. If the head of an autism genetics project were to read that mother's memoir, however, he or she might pay more attention to the husband's aloof personality and difficulty articulating his emotional states. This reader might also pick up on the mother's chain smoking and lupus as indicators of compulsive behavior and tendencies toward autoimmunity, possible familial risk factors.[37] For others, autism has been a metaphor. Bruno Bettelheim's famous account of "Joey: A 'Mechanical Boy'" detailed how a patient's fantasy of himself as a machine was so effective that "not only did he himself believe that he was a machine, but more remarkably, he created this impression in others." Joey's case was a parable of "emotional development in a mechanized society," ripe for psychoanalytic dissection.[38] It looks different to a contemporary reader. Joey's obsessions and adherence to ritual, his idiosyncratic use of language, and his alarm at human contact characterize almost perfectly a person with Asperger syndrome, another disorder on the autism spectrum.

Some contemporary autism researchers speak of "secular trends" in autism, noting that the emphasis on early intervention has changed the natural history of the disorder itself.[39] Like children with Down syndrome, many of whom have blossomed under the combined influence of improved medical management and heightened expectations of their intellectual capacities, children with autism today don't "look" like the children that these researchers remember from the early years of their work. Anecdotally, they are less like Leo Kanner's original descriptions of isolated children consumed by repetitive behaviors. They struggle more with communication impairments, social reciprocity, and according to some doctors, systemic illnesses.

The shifts in the symptoms that constitute autism tell us much about how different professional and social communities understood psychology, neurodevelopment, and disability during the second half of the twentieth century. They tell us even more about the practical aspects of medical treatment and the ways that physical acts and interpersonal relationships have contributed to knowledge of bodies, development, and relationships. Parents' and caregivers' accounts can provide valuable insights into informal aspects of care in the history of intellectual and developmental disabilities. That history has often been written from the perspective of professionals and institutions, with a focus on the way that diagnostic labels have been used to control populations, rather than on how disabilities have been experienced by individuals and families.[40]

The history of the autism diagnosis is also an inseparable part of a larger story about biomedicine. Autism may have begun as a category in child psychology, but it is an increasingly *biomedical* diagnosis. Biomedicine itself is more than a static system of knowledge. It is also a powerful way of perceiving and altering the world. When I use the term I mean the particular complex of social and technical practices that emerged after World War II at the intersection of molecular biology, genetics, immunology, and clinical applications derived from this laboratory-based knowledge.[41] This research in universities and corporations fostered the development of new medical technologies, including pharmaceutical research in particular. It also provided the context for doctors' increasing focus on diagnostic standardization as the first step toward characterizing a disease in terms of its underlying biological causes. Standard diagnoses became, in turn, a key way that managed-care organizations determined insurance coverage and reimbursement schedules. These trends in research, health coverage, and product development encouraged clinical and laboratory researchers to develop a mania for "specificity," the idea of a perfect correspondence between pathological mechanisms, diagnostic categories, and disease-specific treatments.[42]

Research on autism spectrum disorders took shape within a late-twentieth-century scientific culture shaped by the cold war, dreams of precise control over life processes, and the dominance of biological models in psychiatry.[43] All of these intellectual trends shaped the scientific culture of which autism research is a part, lending models from computing, cybernetics, defense systems, and behavioral research to investigators' theoretical frameworks. The successes of the American pharmaceutical industry have encouraged popular acceptance of an idea of neurochemical imbalances as the main cause of mental illnesses. Brain imaging techniques and the wide circulation of computer-enhanced images of diseased and typical brains have reinforced public belief in mental illness as something firmly lodged in brain structure and function, rather than as having its source in early childhood experiences or interpersonal relations.[44] One challenge of understanding patient advocacy groups involves placing them within a broader history of American biomedical knowledge. Likewise, it is important to understand parent advocates in terms of the illness-based groups that preceded them in areas like HIV/AIDS treatment activism.[45]

The American culture of scientific parenting plays a role in autism's history as well. Parenting in the twentieth-century United States was influenced by a fascination with psychoanalysis and by ideologies of childhood and child development that emphasized both autonomy and fragility.[46] Mothers did not always submit willingly to the intrusion of medical experts into the domestic sphere, but the pronouncements of medical authorities nonetheless shaped American childrearing practices.[47] Likewise, mothers themselves helped create a culture of competitive parenting that incorporated expert ideas about child development and parental obligations.[48] The experience of autism in the twentieth and early twenty-first centuries is difficult if not impossible to disentangle from ideas about the nature of a "good childhood" and beliefs about normal patterns of socialization, development, and relationships.[49] That said, families of different social and economic classes have not always been subject to the same expert recommendations. There is no single history of American childhood.

Biosociality and Contested Illnesses

Autism is one of a number of contemporary contested illnesses, including Gulf War syndrome, multiple chemical sensitivity (MCS), chronic Lyme disease, and breast cancer. We find similarities in explanations for all of them, from changing human environments and toxic burdens to individual vulnerabilities. Patients have similar difficulties finding professionals who will accept the reality of their symptoms when they don't correspond to generally recognized disease entities.[50] All reflect contemporary trends toward patient networking via new communication technologies, even if in the case of autism such networks predated the Internet. They are also all "embodied health movements" in the sense that disagreements focus on the reality and nature of physical suffering. Treatment strategies often involve tinkering and experimentation, and knowledge about the cause and cure of the disorders is built up in close relationships between doctors and patients, making that knowledge particularly difficult to test or standardize.[51]

Battles over the identity of biomedical groups are one type of classification struggle.[52] These disputes emerge not only from differences in access to material or symbolic capital but also from different ways of using empirical evidence and affective knowledge. The profusion of interest groups surrounding autism research includes autistic self-advocates who see the search for a cure as devaluing their own unique abilities. Psychologists use autism as a platform for constructing theories of cognition and gender. There are parent advocates who are committed to a theory of vaccine-triggered autism, and other parents equally convinced that autism is a genetic disease. Representatives of all these groups push for their positions as much through politics as through mustering empirical evidence. They counter the evidence of their opponents by raising questions about conflicts of interest, compromised objectivity, and suspect funding sources. When what is at stake is the question of who has the authority to act in the name of vulnerable populations, research methods can become as contentious as the findings themselves.

It would be naïve to suggest that access to resources and political power play no role in parents' pursuit of innovative treatments or their founding of advocacy groups. Researchers have long observed that autism is more frequently diagnosed among children of wealthier and more educated parents, although they have disagreed about whether this points to better access to health care or a genuinely higher incidence. Family experiences of autism in different cultural and socioeconomic contexts deserve more study, especially as those experiences are shaped by variable diagnostic standards and different diagnostic expectations among parents.[53] Nevertheless, if middle-class parents may be more likely than those in lower income brackets to trawl Medline, the National Library of Medicine's bibliographic database, in search of promising leads and confront their doctors for access to experimental treatments, skepticism about the prognoses and therapies offered by medical experts crosses class boundaries.[54] Parents' capacity to choose different treatment possibilities within a biomedical framework may be limited by their access to scientific information and professional guidance. However, the choice to acquire these capacities is less an indicator of social class than it is a form of participation in the biomedical community of parents of children with autism. It is difficult if not impossible to reduce disputes among parents over how to treat children with autism to simple differences in their access to economic resources.

Contested illnesses are especially useful for exploring the ways people mobilize around illness categories. Any illness category can destabilize when debates emerge about when and how to intervene and with what tools, or on the possibility and desirability of preventative measures. Medical diagnoses share a second characteristic, however, to which I have tried to remain attentive. Scholars have long recognized processes of "closure" regarding scientific facts about medical conditions.[55] Stability in biomedical facts is achieved at a cost, so that what seems to be a triumph of understanding in the present may in the future turn out to have led to the abandonment of otherwise fruitful approaches. Even the supposedly irrefutable evidence of a medical cure can look quite dubious in retrospect. Throughout this book I am concerned with theoretical and therapeutic stability as well as change in biomedicine, and the extent to which both theory and practice are necessary for a community to believe that a particular intervention is effective.

Scholars in the anthropology of science and medicine have observed the tendency of people to form social groups based on illness. Their work sometimes implies that it is the disorder itself that leads groups to form or that the biological similarities among members of an illness category are what bring them together. My work on autism leads me to question the spontaneity implied by terms like "biosociality."[56] Disorders like autism do not act as agents that construct the social or biological identities associated with them. Designers of research programs and clinical trials, on the one hand, and organizers of advocacy groups, on the other, must all work hard to construct illness-based identities. Communities form around the diagnostic as much as the biological reality of the medical condition that comes to define them.[57]

Genetic research in autism has developed alongside increasing knowledge about other disabilities with genetic components and the formation of patient groups around those diagnoses. Autism's ambiguous status as a genetic disorder and the immense heterogeneity contained under the diagnostic label make it different from these disorders and related forms of "genetic citizenship."[58] Ways of relating based on the idea of genetic kinship have certainly influenced autism advocacy. However, the purposefully experimental approach adopted by many parents suggests that they resist the "pastoral" care that medical and genetic authorities offer those with well-defined genetic conditions.[59] Parents' sense that their obligations to their children extend beyond nurturance to systematic monitoring and medical interventions is nevertheless in keeping with accounts of ethical responsibilities engendered by new genetic technologies and individualized medicine.

By virtue of its status as both a developmental and, mistakenly, a childhood disorder, autism can teach us about the political economy of disability in the contemporary United States. Medical and popular understandings of development both reflect and promote invisibilities in care and lapses in services. The definition of autism as a disorder of childhood has had tragic consequences for families of adults with disabilities who have fallen outside the purview of state-sponsored educational or therapeutic programs. Diagnostic requirements under disabilities legislation have influenced autism advocacy and the framing of autism as a developmental disorder.[60] We can go beyond an understanding of biosociality as the motivating force for forming patient organizations and move toward understanding the political and economic context that makes it necessary to organize around illnesses and biomedical facts in the first place. Biosociality might best be thought of as one kind of politics that interest groups use, rather than as a fundamentally new form of social organization.

Parent advocates in autism research have argued for an authority grounded in their particular perspective and degree of investment. One source of their beliefs is the economics of contemporary U.S. health care. Behavioral therapies and other interventions not covered by insurance or supplied by school districts must be administered in the home by parent experts or by assistants that they have trained. The unpaid, home-based labor of parents that is required by our health care system also contributes to parents' legitimacy as experts about their children. These same parents argue that producing better biomedical knowledge in a world full of visible and invisible risks requires us to learn more about the commitments and passions involved in producing knowledge about bodies. The goal is not some kind of more dispassionate knowledge but a better understanding of passion's importance to producing reliable knowledge about individuals as well as populations.

Affective investments can bolster claims of commitment and entitlement and at the same time weaken claims of objectivity and knowledge. Parent activist groups find the scientific work that they support marginalized because of their nonobjective, nonneutral position. Their work nonetheless suggests that partiality and objectivity are techniques that are not always in conflict. Rather, the networked interactions of parents constitute one dispersed laboratory in which a type of situated knowledge is produced.[61]

Methods, Questions, Interactions

Understanding Autism engages with both texts and communities. I pay attention both to the factual explanations that participants offer for their actions and the embedded meanings that they attach to practices. I treat these practices, whether contemporary or decades old, as taking place within a particular culture of parenting and biomedical knowledge, so even when I work with texts, I treat them as artifacts that provide insight into a particular culture.

Although I spent time with a wide range of professionals, I focused on the role of parent advocates in autism research. These extraordinary individuals act as proxies and representatives for their children. They work to mobilize networks for information sharing and lobbying, and they serve as citizen-scientists arguing for changes in the criteria required for credible scientific research. They do so even while devoting the vast share of their energy and resources to the daily work of caring for their own children. Parents who work as activists do not represent all parents of all children diagnosed with a spectrum of disorders that affect as many as one in every 110 children in America, but many more act as advocates, if only for their own children.[62] Taken together, activists' statements represent a broad range of ways of thinking about autism. Although not all parents have extra resources or time to spend on advocacy, those who do can tell us about the ways that parenting in contemporary America involves an investment of love together with other more scarce resources.

I carried out research for this book in many different places.[63] Over the course of five years, I spent time with designers of diagnostic and assessment tools, screeners who employ these tools, primary care practitioners with diverse orientations and beliefs about autism etiology and treatment, and members of an interdisciplinary team designing and implementing a Centers for Disease Control–funded epidemiological project to establish valid prevalence and incidence rates. I attended conferences on medical interventions for autism. I participated in intensive workshops on these interventions, and I visited practitioners who use these techniques at their homes and offices.

I interviewed linguistic psychologists, geneticists, and neuroscientists at their laboratories and clinics in the United States and United Kingdom and attended talks and conferences in the fields of autism research and neuroscience. I spent time at integrated treatment and research centers. I observed National Institutes of Health meetings on funding and priorities for autism research and on coordinating research programs. I also attended Institute of Medicine hearings on the connection between vaccines and autism, conferences devoted to biomedical treatments for autism, and neuroscience meetings where autism was only one topic on the agenda. I subscribed to listservs for parents and for practitioners who treat autism spectrum disorders. I visited schools for children with autism, biotechnology corporations specializing in treatments for autism spectrum disorders, laboratories with specialized tests for food sensitivities and other conditions associated with autism, and the offices of a gene bank. I spent time at a retreat for adults and children with autism diagnoses, and joined in a fundraising walk for a major autism organization. I wrote articles, corresponded, commiserated, and joked with any number of astonishing, resilient, and utterly brilliant parents, practitioners, scientists, and people with autism.

Autism has a history as both a diagnostic and clinical entity. Some of that history is told here for the first time. I worked in special collections in Chicago and New Haven. I spent a week in the then-uncatalogued Bruno Bettelheim papers and spoke with Jacquelyn Sanders, Bettelheim's successor as director of the Orthogenic School. I studied Amy Lettick's correspondence and followed up by interviewing her and Bernard Rimland. I read memoirs and publications devoted to autism and developmental disorders dating from the first years of autism research through the present.

"Studying up," or "studying at home," by concentrating on highly educated participants in knowledge production who are frequently aware of the limitations in their own work, entails a unique set of hurdles.[64] Scientists are obviously not a "vulnerable population." They spent some time and energy trying to shape my account. Parents are like scientists in this regard. I enjoyed it. I also realized early on that it would not be possible to maintain the position of detached observer. My temperament played a part, but so did my growing understanding of the process of research. Resistance seemed out of keeping with the work, especially when I saw my collaborators and subjects producing good knowledge in the midst of and through their own affective commitments.

Love Stories

I was trying not to watch and I couldn't help watching, the way it always is with pain. I thought that I could learn about diagnostic screening for autism spectrum disorders by sitting in on sessions in a university clinic. Although diagnostic screeners lack the authority to provide an official diagnosis, the doctor across the hallway was in a position to do so, and clearly had. I remember a mother weeping and I think that the father took their daughter, who had just been diagnosed as "on the spectrum," for a walk down the hallway outside the doctor's office. Their pain was palpable. Even though they had been living with their daughter's disabilities, a diagnosis can change everything.

I was standing in the exhibit hall of a meeting for a group promoting biomedical approaches to treatment for autism spectrum disorders. Even though I had been lurking on a listserv connected with this group, and even though I had been starting to hear about these interventions, I was nervous and found myself unprepared for the experience. Parents wore photographs of their children tucked under the plastic covers of their conference badges. I listened in on one lecture on the health benefits of omega-3 fatty acids marketed by the speaker, another that directed listeners to recipes for gluten-free/casein free chicken nuggets, and another on the myriad hazards of vaccination. It didn't matter that I had immersed myself in the scientific literature on autism. Like many of the "first time" or "newly diagnosed" parents there, I didn't know what to believe. Someone asked me if I had an affected kid, maybe because I was standing in front of a table of supplements, fingering the packets of samples, looking lost, or maybe just because I was there.

We drove a couple of hours through the Florida marshes to visit the offices of a medical practice that specialized in treating kids with autism spectrum disorders, including the son of one of the two owners. The shelves were lined with nutritional supplements bearing a biblical allusion for a brand name. One of the doctors invited us to watch while he demonstrated a quantitative EEG technique on a boy with severe autism. The boy's parents and a visiting politician stood nearby. The child watched videos of animated vegetables narrating bible stories while my colleague and I discussed disease definitions with the doctor and environmental health with the wor-

ried father, who had a degree in toxicology and wondered about the substances that might have affected his son's development.

More than a year later, I watched the same politician give a speech at an Institute of Medicine meeting on vaccines and autism. The published guest list included lawyers, congressional aides, pharmaceutical sales representatives, medical doctors, researchers, administrators from the Centers for Disease Control, antivaccination advocates, and a number of people who listed their institutional affiliation simply as "parent" or "mom" or "mother of a five-year-old autistic child." During the brief public comment period at the end, one mom stood up at the back of the auditorium and spoke to the committee members while her friends held up a poster of the heavy metals excreted from her son's tissues during chelation, a process for binding and removing metals from the body. A father stood up. He was long-limbed and looked like a person who was used to laughing easily. During his allotted time of two minutes he said, "You have friends; you have fallen in love. I want my son to have friends, to fall in love." He had waited through the entire meeting to say this.

These descriptions are from notes I made while researching this book. I offer them here as a way of explaining how love functions in this book not only as an object of analysis for my subjects and a description of practices that are invisible in biomedical research, but also as a description of my position as an observer. I try to be honest about my affection for and caring about my subjects, my emotional responses to the stories that they shared with me, and my own identity as an imperfect and invested observer of the human interactions that make up autism research.

The chapters that follow are loosely chronological accounts. They are love stories, although some of them contain elements of tragedy. They are about the late, beloved psychologist and parent advocate Bernard Rimland, who diagnosed his son's autism using an old college textbook; anthropologists visiting the homes of "disturbed" children to observe the interactions between parents; mothers forming lasting friendships on the strength of exchanged letters and shared grief; and the hundreds of newly diagnosed "little professors" with Asperger syndrome in Silicon Valley. Some books about autism use the conventions of genre fiction. Having autism is like a detective story, where the task is to understand an impenetrable maze of social norms, or like science fiction, where people inhabit other worlds.[65] Some researchers describe autism as a disorder of narrative. Therapeutic techniques like Carol Gray's "social stories" teach people with autism to craft accounts of human relationships.[66] I use stories to call attention to the fact that most explanations draw on the conventions of narrative in order to shore up the connections between disparate observations.[67]

Although I have organized the next eight chapters around key political, practical, and epistemological battles, it is important to remember that lines were not always so sharply drawn. Parents of children diagnosed with autism, from at least the 1960s through the present, explored treatments ranging from holding therapy and psychoanalysis through operant conditioning, megavitamin therapies, and heavy metal detoxification. Membership in social and research networks overlapped. Eric Schopler, who founded the TEACCH program in North Carolina, joined other prominent researchers to work alongside parents in founding the National Society for Autistic Children (now the Autism Society). In the 1960s, the psychologist Bernard Rimland collated the scattered evidence for the non-psychogenic and possibly genetic origins of autism, but he was as active in studying behavioral treatments for autism as he was in promoting megavitamin therapy. Uta Frith, Lorna Wing, Edward Ritvo, and Michael Rutter pioneered autism research in England. Rosalind Oppenheim, a mother in Illinois, read all of them as she developed educational programs.

Just as it is wrong to see affiliations or research commitments as exclusive or fixed, it is wrong to imagine that understandings of autism have evolved in a linear fashion, from psychogenic to neurological to genetic models. It is wrong not only because Bruno Bettelheim was able to review both Ivar Lovaas and Bernard Rimland in *The Empty Fortress*. Parents struggling with autism diagnoses in the 1970s and 1980s read Bettelheim and heard their pediatricians speak in psychogenic terms, but they implemented behavioral programs anyway. While it may be appealing to represent autism research as a succession of theories, it is more accurate to consider it as a series of temporary configurations made unstable and more theoretically diverse by the variety of disciplines involved, the centrality of parental participation in research, and changes in the population that the term "autism" represented. As I show, the continuities that have existed have been at the practical level, in terms of courses of action, modes of relating to children with autism, and in the language that has been used to describe autism and autism treatment. This language has continually incorporated ideas about love and its role in human development. The shared language of love is the key to understanding continuities among practices—all require caring labor.

Each chapter in this book illustrates an intersection between structured, formal knowledge and daily life, and in doing so highlights the way that emotional commitments allow biomedical knowledge to become part of caring labor, of telling stories and of putting lives together. Each deals with the practical problems that people encounter when they try to transfer expert knowledge and techniques—whether psychotherapeutic milieu therapy, behavioral therapies, genetics, biomedical interventions, or immunizations—into the messy and indeterminate realm of everyday life. In almost all of these instances, the participants have discovered that their affective commitments—their love—played a crucial part in the efficacy of their techniques or comprised an important element in their beliefs. Love made their techniques make sense, but it was also what made them difficult to explain, transfer, or justify.

This book is divided into two parts. Part One covers the history of theories and treatment practices. Part Two brings us to the present. In chapter 1, I track the evolution of the concept of autism from its first characterization as a rare emotional disturbance in 1943 to its present status as a potential epidemic. The point is that autism, as a diagnostic and clinical entity, has never *not* been a subject of debate with respect to its parameters, its utility as a distinct diagnostic category, and its relationship to an underlying population characterized by a distinct biological identity.

In chapter 2, I describe what happened when the child psychologist Bruno Bettelheim, director of the Orthogenic School at the University of Chicago, designed a research program for training counselors based on the idea that autism represented a form of halted ego development. I analyze the particular social system in which counselors at the School experienced their treatment efforts as worthwhile and effective.

Chapter 3 considers parents emerging from the experience of wide-ranging psychogenic theorizing about autism during the 1950s and 1960s, of which Bruno Bettelheim's work was but one, well-known example. Parental efforts to help their children by training themselves in treatment practices became part of the formal methods of behavioral therapies as described by experts in the field. In both the case of the Orthogenic School's milieu therapy and parental work in behavioral therapies, the affective involvement of "semiprofessionals" was key to what was experienced as the success of the interventions.

In a brief interlude, I describe how advocacy for disability rights has influenced parents' understandings of their children's needs and how parents have justified their desire for treatments in ethical and experiential terms.

I begin the second part of the book in chapter 4, where I tell the story of two parent groups and their efforts to promote genetic research on autism. Parents have argued with self-advocates about the status of kinship as entailed by genetic relationships and the meaning of genetic research.

Chapter 5 turns to the longstanding practice of biomedical interventions. These treatments rely on intensive observation and commitment. My analysis emphasizes how parents describe their ways of knowing about their child's distinct physical symptoms and metabolic needs as a particular form of knowledge.

In chapter 6 I address the contested issue of the relationship between childhood vaccines and autism. As parents make claims about the environmental causes of autism, I consider their explanations about the onset of their children's symptoms and the ideological importance of intervening in processes of injury rather than disease. In my conclusion, I briefly discuss some consequences of this work for other research on advocacy groups before returning to the general question of love's relationship to responsibility and to biomedical knowledge.

Autism research is a volatile field, not only because of the high political stakes involved or the ubiquity of love and related passions, but because of the often unexpected ways that knowledge and focused interests can come together to make accepted facts about the world change quite abruptly.

I am attending a meeting of a NIH committee devoted to coordinating autism research across the different member institutes. The members of the committee are drawn from a number of government agencies, member institutes, and parent organizations. A presenter from a major autism organization unveils a new advertising campaign designed to achieve the same level of prominence as a series of public service announcements from the 1980s that we all still remember. The new ad is meant to change minds, and its message is: the odds of getting autism are far higher than most parents realize. It could easily be your child, and all parents should be aware of the warning signs. A later presentation is devoted to diagnosing autism at ever-younger ages—researchers think that they can perceive the risk of autism in a six-month-old. A parent advocate is standing next to me at the break, and I mention to him that, if the number of children with autism has already dramatically increased, a campaign to increase diagnoses will be sure to strain overburdened educational and support systems. He shakes his head: "They have no idea what they are bringing on."

Before I can begin to answer how a parent organization—or anyone else—changes the life of child and a family by encouraging parents to ask about typical development or doctors to recognize and diagnose a case of autism, I have to explain how autism became a condition that could be diagnosed. Psychiatrists and parent advocates worked over many decades to establish the autism diagnosis. Despite their continuing efforts to craft an objective and stable category, the characteristics of autism have shifted over time, and diagnosticians have had to combine intimate knowledge with standard protocols to arrive at reliable diagnoses. It is this history that I turn to in the next chapter.

One

Research Programs, "Autistic Disturbances,"
and Human Difference

Historians of medicine like to make the point that explanations for disease reflect the historical moments in which those explanations were produced. They incorporate not only clinical observations but also notions of the "good life" or of the "typical person," and anxieties about the pressures and stresses to which human bodies and minds are subject.[1] Diagnostic categories are mutable things. They make groups of subjects visible and distinct by describing them, but they then set them free to carry on their business, to resist, reshape, and reform that definition through their own actions. In other words, disorders constitute a modern process for creating types of humans, or what Ian Hacking calls "making up people."[2]

Disorders are useful ways for doctors to think about medical categories, but just what symptoms—or type of person—a disorder refers to may change a great deal over time, whether through bureaucratic fiat or through the activism of groups who adopt or reject a medical definition. In this respect, autism is like many other disorders. Practitioners may maintain that through the course of their long careers they have gained the ability to recognize autism on sight as, one expert suggested, one might learn by studying a range of examples to recognize the distinctive style of a particular artist.[3] Still, much about the diagnostic criteria, practices of identification, modes of treatment, and daily experience of autism has changed, and changed radically.

Autism has commanded increasing international attention since the early 2000s, to judge from the press coverage, books, weblogs, and specialized research publications. The increase parallels the growth in federal funding authorizations for autism-related research in the United States.

The Children's Health Act of 2000 called for the coordination of autism research efforts across the National Institutes of Health and authorized unprecedented federal support for investigations in the area. These provisions increased under the 2006 Combating Autism Act. This fascination and concern with autism is by no means unprecedented. *Time* magazine profiled Leo Kanner, who first wrote about autism, in 1960.[4] *Life* magazine reported on O. Ivar Lovaas's work with autistic children in 1965. And Bruno Bettelheim's 1967 *The Empty Fortress* met with both critical acclaim and immense popular interest. These are works that I will return to in later chapters.

By most standards autism is a new disorder. It is startlingly recent in origin compared to familiar conditions like tuberculosis or kidney failure, but it is even recent compared to bipolar disorder or schizophrenia, which originate in descriptions dating from the mid to late nineteenth century. There are some historical descriptions of "feral children" that are likely candidates for retrospective autism diagnoses. Nineteenth-century medical records also depict children with symptoms that might fit present-day criteria. Yet the authors of those descriptions did not believe that they had identified a unique set of pathological symptoms or that they were pioneering the diagnosis of a new disorder.[5] They made no difference to medical practice. They certainly didn't cause parents to look at their remote or late-talking child and wonder whether they ought to bring him or her in for an evaluation.

Autism is also a very *modern* disorder, with all of the implications of that term. It is characterized by expert knowledge. It is subject to systems of measurement and quantification. It became visible through attention to language and communication failures, and it has been framed in terms of numerous overlapping systems: the family, sensory feedback loops, brain damage, biochemistry, and metabolism. Because the symptoms of autism could seem so obviously the result of atypical development and yet simultaneously so amenable to explanations that assumed an environmental cause, it came to share shelf space with other childhood disorders of uncertain etiology like attention deficit hyperactivity disorder or even severe childhood allergies.

In order to represent the emergence of autism as both a diagnostic category and a term applied to specific sets of people, it is necessary to explore several issues. The first is the development of standard descriptions of autism and their relationship to different theories of causation. The second is the application of these criteria to the practice of epidemiological surveys. I look at the effects that changes in criteria have had on findings about autism rates. The third is the use of published screening and diagnostic instruments.

The neutral tone of this list belies the significant emotional consequences of each of the practices. Theories about the cause of autism have been sources of wrenching pain for parents, just as authoritative and often dire descriptions of autistic limitations have confused and frustrated the people to whom they have been applied. The possibility that the rising reported incidence of autism represents an epidemic has been the subject of fervent editorials, irate hallway confrontations at otherwise sedate conferences, and several full-length books. Meanwhile, the question of early diagnosis and the potentials and dangers that this represents is a source of real concern to many professionals and parents.

Much of the early research on autism originated in the disciplines of child psychiatry and abnormal psychology. Researchers often consciously or unconsciously incorporated the elements of theories that were popular in their discipline at the time into their descriptions of autism. Later, new tools for studying the brain came to be seen as potential keys to autism. Experts were also concerned with identifying research populations and constructing broad-based cognitive theories, using their study of atypical development as a window onto typical development.

Real populations are messy and difficult to manage, epistemologically and institutionally. A diagnosis describes some shared characteristics, but it is mute on the matter of individual difference. The children that were most useful to researchers were "pure types," those who expressed the social, behavioral and communicative deficits in autism without the complication of comorbid medical or genetic conditions or impairments so severe as to render testing impractical or impossible. The difficulty, as with many research populations, is that such pure types did not always reflect the needs of clinicians and parents—who must treat children of all types—or the natural history of the disorder in human populations.[6] By framing autism as a behavioral syndrome, researchers have elaborated on the nature of many of the deficits but few of the underlying causes. They have produced even fewer insights into intermediary mechanisms, and less still into the tasks of managing daily life.

A few elements in the history of autism distinguish it from other psychiatric or neurological disorders that have been affected by the same overall trends in theory or diagnosis. First, autism has often been construed as a disorder of love. Researchers spoke of the absence of "affective contact" in children, others of the lack of bonding in parents. Second, parents have never been far from expert discussions about autism treatment and autism research. They have been incorporated into theories of etiology and built into research programs as well as the daily practices of treatment. Third, the history of autism has been resolutely experimental. Although some published histories tend toward the view that autism research progressed over time toward more empirical and experimentally based work, both autism researchers and the parents who consumed, modified, and translated the researchers' work for their own purposes have seen themselves as experimentalists from the beginning. As the ethologist Niko Tinbergen and his wife Elisabeth put it, in the course of daily life, "'experiments by nature' happen all the time to autistic children. Parents, visitors, strangers met in the street, and last but not least doctors perform them, but usually without being aware of it."[7]

Describing Autism

Autism has been treated alternately as a psychological, neurological, behavioral, or genetic disorder, often paralleling trends in medical research and popular interest. Leo Kanner, a pioneer in the field of child psychiatry who headed the Behavior Clinic for Children at Johns Hopkins University in Baltimore, introduced the diagnostic category of autism to the world of medicine in his 1943 case series of eleven children, published in the second issue of the journal *Nervous Child*. During the next two decades, while the number of children receiving the diagnosis was still quite small, child psychologists and psychiatrists recognized the need to standardize use of the term.

It is hard to fault Kanner's descriptions, which were models of careful observation, but the category and the range of interpretations that "autism" could encompass quickly slipped beyond his control. As a disorder that seemed to straddle the divide between the psychological and the neurological, between affect and brain chemistry, autism became a subject about which biologically oriented psychiatrists and their more psychoanalytically inclined colleagues struggled to find common ground. Kanner should not have been surprised. The confusion began with his original descriptions of children who seemed to represent "pure-culture examples of *inborn autistic disturbances of affective contact*," a psychological problem that nonetheless seemed to have its origins in disordered biology.[8]

Leo Kanner was in a good position to discover a new disorder. He was born in the Ukraine and immigrated to the United States from Germany in 1924 after receiving his medical degree and doctorate. Although he had avoided the depredations of Nazi Germany, he had a keen sense of the injustice of conventional approaches to treating people with intellectual disabilities, and he became an advocate for their rights. Kanner argued that research on mental deficiency ought to be placed firmly within the concerns of child psychiatry, education, and guidance, as an issue central to the study of all human development, and not "merely an appendix."[9] As the author of a definitive textbook in the field, Kanner had virtually invented the specialty of child psychiatry. The Behavior Clinic for Children that he was tapped to head in 1931 became a model of its kind. As the director of a teaching clinic that was part of a department of pediatrics, Kanner developed a style of instruction based on case consultations with interns. This meant that the most difficult and complex cases were usually referred to him or to a close colleague, leaving Kanner with a wealth of examples to draw on in his writing.[10]

In the introduction to the issue of *Nervous Child* that featured his article, Kanner distinguished between studying inborn inabilities to form affective contact and studying intelligence. " 'Mind' has much too often been identified with 'intelligence.' "[11] Kanner and his colleagues were interested instead in the formation of emotional relations and in the idea that some children might have difficulties in this area in much the same way that some children had physical or mental impairments.

Kanner opened his article with an epigraph by child psychologist Rose Zeligs that suggested at least one source of his fascination with these children:

> To understand and measure emotional qualities is very difficult. Psychologists and educators have been struggling with that problem for years but we are still unable to measure emotional and personality traits with the exactness with which we can measure intelligence.[12]

His ambitions stretched beyond defining a specific disease entity, "autism," a term he borrowed from Swiss psychologist Eugen Bleuler, who had used it back in 1910 to describe symptoms of schizophrenia.[13] Kanner hoped to point the way to a subfield dealing with a range of emotional deficiencies. Nonetheless, the article did not suggest precise mechanisms through which children might become affectively impaired, but merely described eleven cases in exacting detail.

The publication straddled two perspectives on children exhibiting deviant or perplexing behavior. Nervous conditions, or those syndromes that seemed to stem from aberrant mental processes, had once been the province of private neurologists. Children who were "feebleminded" were generally treated with the assumption that their condition was permanent and lifelong, and not on the whole caused by psychodynamic processes.[14] By 1943, both categories were becoming the province of psychiatrists. Psychiatrists had struggled for status within the medical profession and had often found themselves stuck in bureaucratic positions within asylums rather than winning prestigious research appointments. As they began to adopt methods that combined the techniques of psychoanalysis with clinical medicine, they became newly confident of their security within the institutional structure of hospitals and clinics.[15]

Perhaps because Kanner largely abstained from presenting any explicit theory about the causes of autism in his careful description, scientists and advocates have found in it support for a range of positions in the debates that emerged since the publication of his work. They have interpreted it as a condemnation of unresponsive parenting, as a prescient identification of genetic or hereditary aspects of autism, as a careful documentation of the many medical conditions that can occur alongside autism, and as a chronicle of symptomatic and diagnostic unity in the context of clinical heterogeneity.

Kanner himself leaned toward an organic interpretation of autism. He thought that it was caused by an innate, structural difference in the brains of the children, but his writing left the possibility open for multiple interpretations. Starting in 1938 a set of children had arrived at the clinic at Johns Hopkins with symptoms that stood out "so markedly and uniquely from anything reported so far" that each case deserved an independent discussion. Instead, he offered a "condensed" description of the history and behavior of the eight boys and three girls. His presentation of these eleven cases as a group worked to establish them as a meaningful set that might be tracked over time to better establish the existence of this new diagnostic entity.[16] As a colleague of his would later write, Kanner's "genius" was to identify a set of stable traits in the midst of such vast individual variation. Later generations of psychiatrists would modify these criteria with consequences for the number of children diagnosed and for theories of the causes of the disorder, but they would maintain that it was Kanner himself who had "recognized the essential core of the disorder."[17]

The children who had arrived at the clinic were a remarkable group. None appeared to have any intellectual disability, although one, Virginia, had been "dumped" in a state school for the feebleminded where she stood out as unlike any of the other children. Donald, the first case, had exceptional memorization skills, but rarely used language to communicate, instead repeating nonsense phrases like " 'Chrysanthemum'; 'Dahlia, dahlia, dahlia'; 'Business;' 'Trumpet Vine'; 'The right one is on, the left one is off';

'Through the dark clouds shining.'" He seemed unintere‹ around him and didn't desire affection. He had troubl‹ like "you" or "I," so that when he wanted a bath, he wo want a bath?" repeating the phrase that his mother woul He hummed to himself and flicked his fingers in the ai by spinning objects, and liked to line up beads and bloc color. He hated deviations from routine and demanded ʌʜᴀ‹ ʜɪs ᴍᴏᴛʜᴇʀ adhere to certain "rituals," repeating a precise verbal exchange with him, for instance, at every mealtime. Nevertheless, in the three years following Donald's initial visit, he gradually became more oriented to his surroundings and his mother expressed surprise at how well he was doing when she visited his classroom at school.[18]

The other children in Kanner's case series behaved in similar ways. Frederick was terrified of egg beaters and vacuum cleaners, and he repeated questions that were put to him rather than answering them directly, a symptom called echolalia. While it was hard to get him to cooperate on intelligence tests, he performed well on tasks that required recognizing and manipulating geometric shapes. Richard, who seemed physically healthy on the whole, was drawn to light switches and didn't seem to speak at all until, at four years old, he said "good night" to his foster mother. Elaine "independently went her own way" at nursery school, "not doing what the others did." For instance, she "drank the water and ate the plant when they were being taught to handle flowers." When she was placed in a residential school, she learned the names, eye colors, and other features of all of the children, but "never entered into any relationship with them."[19]

Although many of the similarities among the cases emerged through his simple reiteration of details, Kanner waited until the end of his paper to discuss the similarities among the cases in depth. The central feature of these children, Kanner believed, was their "*inability to relate themselves in the ordinary way to people and situations from the beginning of life.*" Their "autistic aloneness" appeared to have been present from birth—the children had not so much withdrawn as failed to establish relationships in the first place. Kanner emphasized that all of the children seemed to come from "highly intelligent families" in which both parents were often exceedingly accomplished.[20]

Kanner limited his interpretation of the cases, restricting his discussion of causation to only a few comments, a choice that probably contributed to the durability of his article.[21] Although he took care to record the phrases that the children chose to repeat, unlike many of the psychologists who followed him, he did not try to ascertain a hidden meaning in

...ies like Donald's "Dahlia, dahlia, dahlia." He believed that many of the children's behaviors could be explained in terms of their profound resistance to intrusions upon their isolation, and that this was the source of the feeding difficulties that so many of them had. Food represented only the earliest and most persistent intrusion upon their solitude. Inanimate objects, in contrast, did not threaten their seclusion, and the children related to them easily and comfortably. Kanner also emphasized that there was a "great deal of obsessiveness in the family background," some of which had actually aided his research because the parents were able to provide detailed accounts of their children's development and skills.

"One other fact," Kanner wrote, "stands out prominently. In the whole group, there are very few really warmhearted fathers and mothers.... Even some of the happiest marriages are rather cold and formal affairs. Three of the marriages were dismal failures. The question arises whether or to what extent this fact has contributed to the condition of the children," although it was hard to believe that it was caused entirely by the parents since the children seemed different "from the beginning of life."[22] For this reason, Kanner concluded that the disorder was innate and inborn, not acquired.

In the present, autism is generally described as a lifelong disorder that is treatable but not curable. Few clinicians talk about cases of autism resolving over time, and the American Psychiatric Association's *Diagnostic and Statistical Manual of Mental Disorders* (*DSM*) has not included a classification for a "residual state" of autism since 1987. In contrast, Kanner argued that the condition of the children he had observed seemed to improve as they developed. If the children's "basic desire for aloneness and sameness has remained essentially unchanged," follow-up visits and reports of the children showed that they had also gradually learned to recognize and tolerate some people, to vary their routines, and to use language to communicate and express ideas. Their tendency to panic and obsess seemed less severe, and if they never really learned to play with a group, they at least seemed comfortable "on the periphery *alongside* the group," enough so that their parents felt that real progress had been made.[23]

Kanner's article is routinely cited as the first description of classic autism, sometimes called "Kanner autism." His account of a child who created his own vocabulary for items and insisted that they be referred to in these terms alone, of another obsessed with spinning objects or parts of objects, and of another who reversed pronouns are recognizable to anyone who has worked with children with autism. The article gives the impression of sketching out a previously unrecognized and invisible natural kind, identified and set out so skillfully that it would henceforth be difficult to ignore. After Kanner, autism became visible. Yet the similarity between Kanner's cases and cases of autism in later places and times may be specious because of investigators' reliance on particular diagnostic criteria for classic autism. This apparent similarity has led generations of theorists to propose global theories of autism that downplay the possibility of variation within the diagnosis.

When Kanner published his findings, Hans Asperger, a doctor working at the University Children's Hospital in Vienna, was carrying out a strikingly similar analysis of another set of children, also borrowing Bleuler's term to describe them.[24] Asperger's case series resembled Kanner's, with some important exceptions. Like Kanner, Asperger found his cases because they were referred to a psychiatric clinic where he worked. He also believed that the syndrome was characterized above all by isolation and self-sufficiency, and like Kanner, Asperger noted the children's unusual and idiosyncratic use of language. Asperger did not describe the syndrome as a disability but rather as an "abnormal personality structure," and took pains to emphasize the talents and potential of the children that he described in his 1944 article on the subject.[25]

Even though Asperger described the syndrome in terms of personality, he suggested that it was biological in origin and might even be heritable. He saw qualities in the parents similar to those of their offspring, noting for instance that one mother who "seemed strange and rather a loner" took care to point out the ways that she and her son were alike.[26] He thought that these children could grow to be successful in professional life despite their social oddities, and that they showed no evidence of cognitive disability. Rather, they demonstrated potential for great creativity and originality in their thought processes, "as if they had compensatory abilities to counter-balance their deficiencies," such as their ability to focus narrowly on topics of special interest.[27] Most important, Asperger's cases did not evince the same difficulties with language that Kanner had found. While their language at times did not seem to be used to communicate, they could speak well, a few with the vocabulary and pedantic qualities of academics. Many of the children in Asperger's clinic were obsessed with topics of special interest to them and could discuss them at length, often past the point of exhaustion on the part of the listener.

Whereas Asperger believed that "autistic psychopathy" was not only organic, but also quite possibly heritable, Kanner left the matter of etiology more open to interpretation. The ambiguities in his early writings make it easy to see how readers interpreted his characterizations of parents as explicit claims about pathology and causation:

I have dwelt at some length on the personalities, attitudes, and behavior of the parents because they seem to throw considerable light on the dynamics of the children's psychopathologic condition. Most of the patients were exposed from the beginning to parental coldness, obsessiveness, and a mechanical type of attention to material needs only. They were the objects of observation and experiment conducted with an eye on fractional performance rather than with genuine warmth and enjoyment. They were kept neatly in refrigerators which did not defrost. Their withdrawal seems to be an act of turning away from such a situation to seek comfort in solitude.[28]

Elsewhere, Kanner explicitly rejected the idea that autism was a heritable disorder. In 1954 he wrote that, while it was tempting to "think of a familial trend toward detached, obsessive, mechanical living," still, "it should not be forgotten that the emotional refrigeration which the children experience from such parents cannot but be a highly pathogenic element in the patients' early personality development, superimposed powerfully on whatever predisposition had come from inheritance." Two years later he argued that "the emotional frigidity in the typical autistic family suggests a dynamic experiential factor in the genesis of the disorder in the child."[29] From Kanner's early characterizations, the authors of popular articles drew the term "refrigerator mothers," a term that, in all its potent suggestiveness, persisted in the popular imagination long after researchers, Kanner included, had abandoned the hypothesis.

By the 1960s, both new research on autism and the growing consensus of practitioners who used behavioral therapies suggested that autism was neurological in origin. Nevertheless, popular discourse and practitioners in medical fields outside of psychiatry continued to emphasize the psychogenic theory, associated most in the public mind with Bruno Bettelheim and his 1967 best-selling *The Empty Fortress: Infantile Autism and the Birth of the Self.* Kanner himself became aware of the considerable suffering that the psychogenic theory had caused. Ruth Christ Sullivan, the first elected president of the National Society for Autistic Children, recalled that Kanner delighted the assembled parents at their meeting in 1969, declaring that "I hereby acquit you people as parents" while dismissing Bettelheim and his "empty book."[30] In later years, he distanced himself from theories of psychogenic causation, both in public speeches and in print. In a 1971 follow-up essay on his first eleven cases, Kanner noted his original claim that autism seemed to be organic in nature, "*innate*" and "*inborn.*" "Some people," he wrote, "seem to have completely overlooked this statement, however, as well as the passages leading up to it and have referred to the author erroneously as an advocate of postnatal 'psychogenicity.' "[31]

At the time, the question of causation interested parents and had potential relevance for treatment, but it did not seem urgent given the rarity of the condition. During the period from the 1940s through the 1970s, autism remained an uncommon diagnosis. Kanner's diagnostic criteria, described in collaboration with Leon Eisenberg in 1956, delineated the syndrome narrowly. A diagnosis required extremely aloof behavior, repetitive and circumscribed activities, and near-typical intelligence.[32] This appeared to describe a very small set of children. Researchers had made few efforts to ascertain either the prevalence (the number of cases in a given population at a particular time) or incidence (the number of new cases) of autism. Diagnostic practices were far from standardized. Doctors tended to rely on prior experience, if any, of children with autism and their knowledge of Kanner's descriptions.

Nevertheless, by 1971, there was sufficient interest in autism among psychologists and other specialists in development that Leo Kanner could found the *Journal of Autism and Childhood Schizophrenia* to promote collaboration across the disciplines of child psychiatry, psychology, psychometrics, and neurology. The original editorial staff and editorial board included the leading names in autism research and child psychiatry: Leon Eisenberg, Carl Fenichel, Michael Rutter, Lauretta Bender, Stella Chess, Bernard Rimland, Edward Ritvo, D. Arn Van Krevelen, and Eric Schopler, who would eventually succeed Kanner as editor. The board included psychiatrists, psychologists, and psychoanalysts, and the articles that they included in the journal reflected their often sharply divergent approaches to the disorder.

In his early writing, Kanner had left open the question of the relationship between infantile autism and childhood schizophrenia, and the name of the new journal reflected that diagnostic flexibility. In 1949, he had explained that autism was the "earliest possible manifestation of childhood schizophrenia" and doubted that it would ever be "separated from the schizophrenias." Indeed, autism offered proof that "schizophrenic withdrawal can and does begin as early as in the diaper stage."[33] Although some authors thought that childhood schizophrenia was a distinct entity, characterized by psychotic and possibly delusional behavior, most followed Kanner's lead and used the terms "childhood schizophrenia" and "autism" interchangeably. Through the 1960s, infantile autism was seen as a promising model for adult schizophrenia, because of the "briefer environmental history" of the psychosis present in autistic children.[34] In other words, if both types of schizophrenia were caused by exposure to pathogenic family environments, childhood schizophrenia was less difficult to study because of the relatively shorter experience of children compared to their adult counterparts. For the next decade, articles in the *Journal of Autism and Childhood Schizophrenia* referred to "psychosis," "childhood schizophrenia," and "infantile autism" virtually interchangeably, although choices did occasionally reflect commitments to psychodynamic or neurological explanations.

By the time he founded the journal, however, Kanner had abandoned the idea that infantile autism was related to adult forms of schizophrenia. Unfortunately, the fact that infantile autism was not a form of psychosis "had not quite percolated" to the editors of the *DSM,* then in its second edition. As a result, the diagnosis of "schizophrenia, childhood type" remained "the only available legitimate port of entry" for children with autistic symptoms. The 1968 *DSM*-II described "schizophrenia, childhood type" as a condition that "may be manifested by autistic, atypical, or withdrawn behavior; failure to develop identity separate from the mother's; and general unevenness, gross immaturity, and inadequacy in development." The entry specified that "these developmental defects may result in mental retardation, which should also be diagnosed."[35] During the 1960s and 1970s, psychiatrists and other clinicians not working specifically on autism were more likely to use a diagnosis of childhood schizophrenia or mental retardation "with autistic features" than a diagnosis of autism.

The situation was different by the end of the 1970s. Eric Schopler, now editor of the renamed *Journal of Autism and Developmental Disorders*, explained the change to readers in 1979. The new name responded to a revised understanding of the distinction between autism and schizophrenia and the growing recognition that autism was a developmental disorder that affected individuals throughout their lives.[36] The articles published in the journal's first eight years had reflected the fertility of the field, but also the confusion that inevitability resulted from overlapping and sometimes conflicting diagnostic frameworks and treatment modalities. The editors also nodded to the growing recognition that the category of autism consisted of different subtypes, including groups with mental retardation, a family history of language disorders, problems with motor control, or genetic diseases regularly associated with autism such as Lesch-Nyhan syndrome, each of which might have different educational and treatment needs. The shift in focus for the journal also reflected trends in psychiatry more generally. By the mid-1960s, armed with newly available psychopharmaceuticals, many psychiatrists had begun to see most behavioral anomalies as neurological or neurochemical in origin, even in advance of any concrete evidence that this was the case.

Theories and Mechanisms

When the inaugural issue of the *Journal of Autism and Childhood Schizophrenia* was published in 1971, most researchers had concluded that environmental influences in general, and the personalities of parents in particular, were not the primary cause of autism. When psychologists studied parents to identify the sources of psychogenic influences, they instead found that the parents of autistic children were not particularly different from the parents of other children with developmental problems. "Such parental abnormalities as do occur are at least as likely to result from pathology in the child as the other way around."[37] Surveying the state of research in 1996, Michael Rutter observed that "old controversies over the supposed relationship between autism and schizophrenia, and over its postulated psychogenic causation, have disappeared as the evidence has made it clear that autism is a neurodevelopmental disorder, involving basic cognitive deficits, with genetic factors strongly predominant in etiology."[38]

While explanations of this kind might have seemed adequate to researchers within the field, the accumulation of evidence alone was not sufficient to change professional thinking about the causes of autism. I discuss the relationship between theories of causation and treatment practices at length in later chapters. Here I briefly survey major theories about autism's cause and their connections to more general trends in psychological, genetic, and neurological research.[39]

Bruno Bettelheim was only the best known among researchers who located the cause of autism in the family environment. Specialists insisted that they did not "blame" parents for pathogenic attitudes toward their children. Their feelings were, after all, products of unconscious motivations, physical illnesses, or their own flawed upbringing. They were simply acknowledging the parental component in the causation of autism.[40] For many parents, that distinction was hard to perceive, if not entirely meaningless.

Three years before Bruno Bettelheim published *The Empty Fortress*, Bernard Rimland had already amassed a book-length summary of evidence against the psychogenic theory and in support of a definition of autism as a neurological disorder. He tentatively hypothesized that the disorder originated in the reticular formation, a region of the cerebellum associated with attention and wakefulness.[41] Leo Kanner wrote a complimentary introduction to Rimland's *Infantile Autism*, criticizing his profession's use of autism as a "pseudodiagnostic wastebasket for a variety of unrelated conditions" and praising Rimland's willingness to suggest a theory of biological causation that "lends itself to respectfully sober scrutiny."[42]

Rimland did not so much produce new data on autism as analyze and synthesize existing data in such a way that it became difficult to deny autism's biological, as opposed to psychological, causes. He observed that psychotherapy rarely helped children with autistic symptoms, and he reinterpreted psychoanalysts' observations about the parents of autistic children. "Since many of these practitioners are deeply committed to the psychogenic point of view," he wrote, "they tend to see the parents as highly pernicious. As a consequence, the use of terms like 'compulsive,' 'narcissistic,' 'rigid,' etc., in their reports is not unexpected."[43] Returning to these descriptions, much could be explained by parents' uncomfortable interactions with psychologists—it was hard to appear relaxed and socially comfortable when you were dealing with a professional who thought that you had irreparably damaged your own child. However, Rimland wanted to hold on to the claim that the parents of autistic children had unusual personalities. When you dropped the assumption that parents were pathogenic, the features that stood out were their objectivity, their unemotionality, and their goal-directedness, cognitive (as opposed to affective) attributes that could in many cases be viewed as assets.[44] These same traits seemed to be expressed in extreme versions in their offspring, as though a genetic predisposition to a particular cognitive style had somehow been amplified.

The tension between primarily psychodynamic theories and those proposing an underlying biological cause continued for decades. Years after Rimland published *Infantile Autism*, psychiatrists like Margaret Mahler still explained autism as a disorder of ego development and differentiation, albeit one that arose early in infancy, and possibly as a result of a child's disposition rather than its mother's. She considered autism a variety of psychosis resulting from a child's failure to relate normally to its mother early in development. Unable to use their mothers as formative reference points for the idea of self and other, children with infantile autism retreated from human relations altogether.[45] In England, Frances Tustin developed similar ideas about autism, locating the origin of the syndrome in an abnormal closeness between mother and child following the child's birth that led to trauma and withdrawal as a child became aware of its separate existence.[46]

Researchers at major autism treatment centers continued to employ psychodynamic explanations for autistic behaviors through the 1980s.[47]

In experimental settings, behaviorists like Ivar Lovaas, Laura Schreibman, and Robert Koegel were developing theories that interpreted autistic behavior patterns in terms of "stimulus overselectivity." They based their ideas on the observation that children with autism often seemed to favor one sensory modality, for instance, vision or hearing, over others. In cases where they were presented with a number of stimuli in one modality, multiple sounds, for instance, they tended to "overselect" one to the exclusion of others, despite the fact that they did not seem to have a hearing impairment. These patterns seemed to explain the difficulty that children with autism had comprehending speech and their "unresponsivity" in general, especially when they were distracted by another source of information. The finding had obvious implications for how educational programs were designed and appeared to extend to problems that autistic children had with social learning.[48]

Ivar Lovaas believed that the causes of autism did not matter to treating the disorder. Children with autism did not experience social stimuli as rewarding and so failed to seek them or respond to them. It mattered little why their response was absent for the purposes of teaching them how to respond appropriately.[49] Nevertheless, many other researchers remained interested in autism as a potential key to other developmental and communication disorders and in terms of its own biological and behavioral features. Although in the early 1970s genetics had not seemed like a promising avenue—research was at yet "disappointingly limited and inconclusive"—some researchers had taken a cue from Rimland's observations about autism's likely neurological and genetic underpinnings.[50] For instance, Michael Rutter and Susan Folstein moved beyond suggestive but isolated case reports of autism in twins to look at large numbers of twin pairs.[51] They found a significant degree of concordance between identical twins, meaning that both twins had autism. This suggested that autism had a genetic component, although the higher rates in twins could also have been caused by birth complications that affected both children. Lacking more powerful techniques for genetic research, studies were fairly limited, enough so that a definitive review of the field was titled "The Genetics, If Any, of Infantile Autism and Childhood Schizophrenia." The authors came down firmly against genetic involvement, arguing that the weight of evidence suggested that the syndromes were "biological but not genetic."[52]

As consensus grew that autism had to arise from some fundamental cognitive difference, researchers turned to comparing autistic and typical brains. Advances in computing and radiography yielded new techniques, including computed tomography in the 1970s and magnetic resonance imaging in the 1980s. These new tools allowed researchers to look with increasing clarity at the brains of people with autism for evidence of structural abnormalities.[53] Early research seemed to confirm the suspicion that most autistic children were "brain damaged," a catchall term that could refer to any number of conditions that affected brain structure and function. They appeared to have abnormalities in brain structure, although the range of abnormalities that the researchers found gave no clear indication that any difference was consistently associated with autism.[54]

In 1985, two major articles from very different disciplines suggested new ways of thinking about the relationship between brain and behavior in autism. A team at Harvard took tissue from the brain of a young man with autism who had died and compared it with tissue from a developmentally typical brain. They found numerous microscopic differences between the two brains. In the autistic man's brain, the neuronal cells in portions of the brain associated with the limbic system were smaller and more densely packed, and there seemed to be less of the Purkinje cells, which form a layer of the cerebellum. It seemed that they had died off or never formed in the first place. The researchers saw no evidence of damage in the region and concluded that the changes had occurred during development.[55] Their research, and findings by another team that pointed to abnormal enlargement of parts of the cerebellum in autism provided justification for further research on structural variation in autistic brains. For a time it appeared that the cerebellum might play a central role in the genesis of autistic behaviors.[56]

Meanwhile, a team of social psychologists proposed that individuals with autism lacked a "theory of mind," a concept that had been developed years earlier to describe the ability to infer mental states in others. Children with autism were largely unable to pass a simple test for theory of mind in a laboratory setting, unlike the groups of typically developing children and children with Down syndrome that the researchers used as a comparison. The resulting article, "Does the Autistic Child Have a 'Theory of Mind'?" remains one of the most-cited articles in the autism research literature even decades later.[57]

Theory of mind seemed poised to replace communication as the primary deficit in autism. Researchers wondered whether difficulty with "mindreading" might exist alongside a problem with executive function, the ability to plan and carry out goal-directed actions. Others proposed that the disorder resulted from weak central coherence, that is, the ability to organize and synthesize information.[58] They argued that these dysfunctions could cause difficulties in understanding and participating in social interactions and might also lead to the other behavioral characteristics typical of autism. These differences in cognition might help explain the otherwise confusing observation that children with autism outperformed typical children on certain tests, for instance those that required them to recognize or construct patterns. Most important, cognitive and social psychologists joined those whose research focused on brain structures in their conviction that all of the symptoms of autism, including those that affected emotional understanding, resulted from brain damage or "brain abnormalities" that might be genetically determined.[59]

Others struggled to explain the gender gap in autism diagnoses, another feature that might elucidate biological mechanisms of the disorder. Kanner and Asperger both described more male than female patients—Kanner and Eisenberg reported a ratio of four boys to every girl in their clinic, and that estimate has remained fairly stable in the decades since.[60] Female patients seemed more likely to have severe autism alongside mental retardation, and Asperger syndrome appeared more common in males. How much of this difference had to do with self-referral, diagnostic biases, and a tendency for autism to manifest differently in girls remained unclear.[61] Psychiatrists, despite their determined focus on failures of mothering as a causal factor, seemed disinclined to regard the disparity in cases as anything other than evidence of underlying biological causes. Those biological causes, however, were described in terms that expressed researchers' beliefs about gender differences.[62] Contemporary clinicians have only gradually moved to consider how girls' upbringings may result in milder social disabilities and lower rates of diagnosis. Although boys with autism may have more difficulty early on, adolescent girls experience a distinctive agony when they are unable to keep up with their peers socially.[63]

Asperger considered the overrepresentation of male cases important, suggesting that the syndrome reflected a "sex-linked or at least sex-limited mode of inheritance." He claimed that he had seen no female patients with the full syndrome, and those that did fit the pattern seemed to have developed the disorder as a result of illness. However, he did note that he had "seen several mothers of autistic children whose behavior had decidedly autistic features."[64] Taking his cue from Asperger, Simon Baron-Cohen wrote extensively on autism as the "extreme male brain." He observed that all individuals have a spectrum of abilities in the domains of empathizing and systemizing. Those characteristics that cause social impairments in people with autism and Asperger syndrome diagnoses, meaning a high degree of systemizing ability and poor empathizing skills, Baron-Cohen saw in milder form in most males, although he pointed out that some women also have "male brains."[65]

If in 1971 a genetic etiology for autism had seemed unlikely, researchers came to markedly different conclusions by the 1980s. Higher rates of diagnosis had revealed that siblings of children with autism had at least a 3- to 4-percent risk of having autism themselves, and researchers were paying more attention to the association of a number of genetic disorders, for instance tuberous sclerosis, with autism.[66] By the mid-1990s, most experts agreed that autism was a highly heritable neurological disorder with a genetic basis. This certainty had its source in Rimland's carefully argued case for research into the genetics of autism, but Rimland's research had been followed by a slowly accumulating set of studies that appeared to provide solid evidence for genetic causation.

Researchers also began to consider the possibility that autism might comprise multiple, distinct genetic disorders that corresponded to different symptomatic subgroups or "endophenotypes." Wing and Gould's introduction of the concept of an "autism spectrum" in their epidemiological research of the late 1960s had anticipated the idea. These groups might display severe symptoms or milder ones, associated with the increasingly recognized categories of Asperger syndrome and pervasive developmental disorder not otherwise specified (PDD-NOS). Groups might also manifest different combinations of the standard deficits. Geneticists began talking about a "broader autism spectrum" or "broader phenotype" for the purpose of genetic studies, in order to take into account autistic traits in close relatives of people with autism.[67]

Epidemiologists and diagnosticians also came to recognize a subcategory of children with "regressive autism," who developed typically, or at least with fewer symptoms, for the first few years of life, and then lost skills.[68] Not only had researchers placed less emphasis on the pattern of onset, in some cases they dismissed the reports of parents who described their children as having regressed.[69] Yet the idea that autism could develop after a period of apparently normal development was not new. As early as the 1950s, Kanner and Eisenberg noted cases of regression, confirmed by other researchers.[70] By the 1970s, many recognized multiple possible patterns of onset for the disorder, which might each be connected to different modes of causation.[71] Parents drew attention to a feature of autism that investigators had noted but not emphasized. They also provided the evidence, via home movies, of children who regressed after their first birthdays.[72]

As parents began to think about autism as a medical condition, they returned to Kanner's original case series. Almost all of the children Kanner described had feeding problems of some sort, including constant vomiting during the first year of life, an inability to tolerate breastfeeding, and disinterest in or refusal of food; one child needed to be fed through a tube for her entire first year.[73] Although Kanner had interpreted these difficulties with food in terms of the children's autistic psychology, parents now saw them as evidence of possible digestive difficulties, allergies, or immune dysfunction. The child whose mother had described him as developing normally for his first year and then having gradually "gone backward mentally" had suffered diarrhea and fever following his smallpox vaccination at twelve months. Another seemed to have regressed after a fever. One child suffered from recurring colds and ear infections, while another seemed to never get sick at all—both possible signs of immune problems.[74] Finally, parents who were concerned about vaccines as a possible causative agent in autism returned to another of Kanner's observations. The parents of the first cases were all educated and middle class, which could indicate that these parents were more likely not only to have identified developmental problems in their children, but also to have had them vaccinated completely and on schedule.

Counting Autistic Children: Categories, Refinements, and Standards

Early estimates of autism prevalence put the figure at approximately 4 children with autism in 10,000, and possibly lower.[75] Experts considered autism interesting but not a matter of urgency. Starting in the late 1990s, however, rates of autism began increasing dramatically. Depending on the study, epidemiologists began reporting rates as high as 1 in 175, 1 in 150, or even 1 in 86 children with an autism spectrum disorder broadly defined, and from 1 in 500 to 1 in 257 children with the narrower diagnosis of autistic disorder.[76] This increase in rates occurred in all of the countries that had been recording cases, including the United States, Sweden, and England, although the precise level of increase appeared to vary. Although rates of other childhood disorders had also increased during this time period, the increase in autism incited far more public and professional concern and interest.[77]

The majority of epidemiologists working on autism, including those who have been central in measuring the increase, believe that the rise is a result of broadened diagnostic criteria, more thorough identification of cases in epidemiological research ("ascertainment" in the literature), and better detection because of improved public and professional awareness.[78] Others have argued that introducing autism as a category in special education records in the United States and the social stigma of mental retardation led parents to push for autism diagnoses and doctors to accede to parents' wishes, encouraging the false perception of a real increase in autism as one diagnosis was substituted for another.[79] They are joined in these arguments by a number of specialists in psychiatry, psychology, and genetics, and also by self-advocates with autism diagnoses.[80]

In 1966, Victor Lotter conducted the first epidemiological survey of autism prevalence in a large population in the English county of Middlesex. Lotter used a combination of criteria that "aimed to clarify the behavioral descriptions and avoid interpretations of behaviors." He found a prevalence rate of 4.5 "autistic" children in 10,000, and noted that when he applied behavioral criteria evenly, without following Kanner's practice of excluding children with intellectual impairments, he found a large proportion of children with autistic symptoms alongside evidence of developmental delay and "brain abnormalities," perhaps warranting a separate category for prognostic purposes.[81]

Starting in the 1970s, Lorna Wing began an epidemiological study in the London borough of Camberwell with her colleague Judith Gould. They restricted their subject population to children under the age of fifteen "who were known to the local health, education, or social services for reasons of physical or mental handicap or behavior disturbance." They then conducted their own assessments of the children. Like Lotter, Wing and Gould concluded that the "boundaries [were] not as rigid" as Kanner had thought. Autism seemed to occur along a "spectrum" of severity, perhaps encompassing many different conditions. And, contrary to Kanner's beliefs and those of many researchers at the time, there was no "bias" toward the middle class in autism cases. The two authors called for a revised definition in terms of a "triad" of deficits in social communication, social ability, and social imagination, accompanied by a restricted pattern of activities.[82]

The work of Lotter, Wing, and Gould transformed psychologists' images of the autistic child. The children's intellectual skills and behaviors varied widely. They came from a diversity of class backgrounds. Even their symptoms varied, from "aloof" children who seemed genuinely uninterested in social contact and often had considerable cognitive delays, to "active but odd" ones who desired connections but seemed unable to decipher the unwritten rules of social interactions. Wing and Gould began to question the "usefulness of regarding childhood autism as a specific condition," although the long-term effect of their work led researchers not to question the integrity of the diagnosis, but to broaden its parameters.[83] Their findings also suggested that, contrary to Kanner's assertion that autistic children seemed to be of normal or above-average intelligence, autistic symptoms often occurred alongside significant cognitive impairment. By the 1990s, the conventional wisdom was that the majority of children with autism had some degree of intellectual disability, although the claim was based on intelligence tests that provided few accommodations for autistic children's social and communicative differences.[84]

As experts turned to studying autism as a subject in its own right as opposed to a model for understanding other disorders, they recognized the need for more accurate and consistent diagnoses. During the 1940s and 1950s, doctors had diagnosed autism largely through their own clinical experience. Kanner did not produce formal criteria until 1956, when he and Leon Eisenberg identified two factors as central to the category: "extreme self-isolation" and "the obsessive insistence on the preservation of sameness."[85] Nearly two decades later, in 1978, Michael Rutter brought the centrality of language impairments in Kanner's original observations and in his own experience to bear on the matter of diagnosis. He argued for the inclusion of language and communication as a third diagnostic factor.[86] These were essentially the criteria included in the 1980 *DSM*-III, the first time that autism was included by name in the *DSM*.[87]

The choice to include language use as a symptom altered the way that clinicians thought about autism. By removing the disturbed, absent, or idiosyncratic language associated with autism from the realm of meaningful behavior, symptoms such as pronominal reversal (e.g., substituting "you" for "I") lost their value as meaning-laden statements, where psychologists had previously devoted significant efforts to their close study and analysis. For child psychologists who followed Kanner, speech provided important clues to emotional disturbances. For later researchers, lack of speech signaled developmental delays or sensory processing problems, and for neurologically inclined researchers, it indicated the presence of localizable brain dysfunction. It would take nearly three decades for the speech and writing of children and adults with autism to be analyzed closely for particular meanings tied to individual experience, and this time this attention would come from parents as much as from brain researchers.[88]

While professionals worked to refine the category of autism for diagnostic purposes, parent advocates sought to alter its definition for political ends. In 1975, the National Society for Autistic Children (NSAC, later the Autism Society of America,) lobbied to include autism as one of the developmental disabilities covered under the Education for All Handicapped Act. They succeeded. The bill, later revised and renamed the Individuals with Disabilities Education Act, entitled children with autism and other developmental disabilities to a "free, appropriate, public education."[89] The NSAC also demanded autism's inclusion in the Developmental Disabilities Act, a bill authorizing services and support. The group's effective lobbying for a "noncategorical definition" of developmental disabilities rather than simply a list of eligible conditions ultimately won them the admiration of other parent groups and helped NSAC establish a presence in Washington.[90] In 1981, members of the society helped convince the U.S. Department of Education to take autism out of the category of "severe emotional disturbance," a characterization that had only served to reinforce professional biases against the parents of children with autism.[91]

Lorna Wing, the psychiatrist whose epidemiological work was so instrumental in pushing researchers to recognize a spectrum of autistic conditions, also helped bring Asperger syndrome to the English-speaking world. In the early 1970s, Wing, who was also raising a daughter with autism, came across a paper by D. Arn Van Krevelen in the first issue of the *Journal of Autism and Childhood Schizophrenia*. Van Krevelen argued that those psychiatrists who knew of Asperger's work assumed incorrectly that he and Kanner had described the same population. In fact, Asperger had defined a syndrome distinct from Kanner's early infantile autism. Asperger's work had been largely neglected in the English-language literature, although Japanese and European researchers had been aware of it for decades.[92] His descriptions fit the patients in the psychiatric ward where Wing was practicing at the time. The diagnosis made sense for those patients unable to comprehend social cues, some of whom had been misdiagnosed as having schizophrenia. In 1991, Uta Frith published a full translation of Asperger's paper, which began the process of establishing Asperger syndrome as a diagnostic category for clinicians in the United States and United Kingdom and a new research area for those interested in the autism spectrum and the role of social learning in typical development.[93]

Asperger had not read Kanner's work when he wrote his case series in 1944, but he had read it by the late 1970s, when he and Lorna Wing met and discussed the relationship between the two syndromes. They "cordially agreed to differ." Asperger believed that he had described a distinct syndrome, while Wing thought that Asperger syndrome represented the high-functioning end of the autism spectrum.[94] The "agreement," needless to say, did not end the debate in the research community at large, and to this day diagnostic practices for Asperger syndrome remain frustratingly inconsistent. Asperger thought that the children he observed seemed to "delight in malice" and in making their parents and teachers suffer, a characteristic that is quite absent from contemporary descriptions of the disorder.[95] Lorna Wing, in contrast, would describe people who "give the impression of fragile vulnerability and a pathetic childishness, which some find infinitely touching and others merely exasperating."[96] In the present, even among those who agree about the validity of the diagnosis, some clinicians decide what label is appropriate based on when a child began speaking, others on a child's current level of language skills, or on their social abilities, their intelligence, or their personality.[97]

The failure to identify reliable biomarkers, consistently recognizable biological indicators, for the disorder has reinforced a behavioral definition of autism. The behavioral slant fit well with the premises of the post-1980 versions of the American Psychiatric Association's *DSM,* which sacrificed causal hypotheses about disorders' origins in favor of diagnostic reliability.[98] The editors of the 1980 *DSM*-III used field trials to establish the accuracy and precision of their categories, and they dispensed with psychoanalytic diagnoses like neurosis. Psychiatrists working independently needed to agree on a diagnosis based on the *DSM* criteria, ensuring that a single patient could reasonably expect to receive the same diagnosis at different places and times. These changes accompanied the first mention of "infantile autism" in the *DSM,* under the *DSM*-III category of "pervasive developmental disorders."[99] Since then, shifts in the criteria for autism in the *DSM* have subtly impacted the contours of the autism category and the features of admissible cases.

The *DSM*-III criteria for autism were fairly stringent. They were oriented toward identifying severe cases in young children. The *DSM*-III-R (1987) had a broader scope. "Infantile autism" became "autistic disorder," "in tacit recognition of the fact that most autistic individuals continue to exhibit the disorder after early childhood and in recognition of the need for a more developmental orientation to the diagnosis."[100] The revised edition both standardized and broadened the set of impairments required for diagnosis.[101] The editors hoped to ensure that "the entire spectrum of dysfunction," including a range of cognitive abilities, would be represented by the category. In practice, the changes may have encouraged psychiatrists to diagnose more children with autism spectrum disorders.[102]

The editors of the *DSM*-IV (1994) tightened the criteria somewhat by reintroducing the *DSM*-III's requirement for early onset in autistic disorder. They also included additional categories, including "childhood disintegrative disorder" (previously called Heller's syndrome), a rare disorder characterized by at least two years of typical development followed by a rapid and severe loss of skills; "Rett syndrome," a genetic disorder affecting primarily girls; and "Asperger's disorder" under the broad category of "pervasive developmental disorders."[103] Although practitioners thought that the Asperger's disorder category was too close to autism to have any utility, in practice Asperger syndrome became an increasingly common diagnosis.[104]

The *DSM-5* will be published in 2012. The authors plan to replace the *DSM*-IV category of "autistic disorder" with a broad new category of "autism spectrum disorders," encompassing all subtypes of pervasive developmental disorders. They explain that the change is a response to the ambiguity surrounding distinctions among different subcategories like Asperger's disorder and pervasive developmental disorder not otherwise specified (PDD-NOS). The new category makes room for the range of strengths and weaknesses that any individual may possess.[105] The proposal was met with dismay by some psychologists, who argue that Asperger syndrome has not been studied for long enough to confirm or discount its existence as a separate entity, and geneticists, who think that a single category incorrectly downplays the biological heterogeneity of the syndrome.[106] Self-advocates are concerned that association with people with more significant impairments will undermine their demands for self-determination and respect. They value the way that Asperger syndrome works to succinctly explain their differences.[107]

The successive editions of the *DSM* established autism as a behaviorally defined disorder, one that experts understood to be biologically based, but for which they had yet to locate convincing biological explanations. As a result, diagnosis came to rely exclusively on the ability of practitioners to recognize the symptoms of autism and distinguish them from other developmental disorders. Despite the clarifications of the *DSM*-IV, the extent to which administrative records have included PDD-NOS and Asperger syndrome cases as "autism" remains unclear, making the job of epidemiologists tasked with retrospectively determining autism prevalence that much more difficult. Although epidemiologists generally accept Wing and Gould's finding that autism is not significantly more common in wealthier families, more affluent parents are likelier to have their children evaluated and diagnosed. This means that children in lower-income families remain underdiagnosed and underreported, and that autism rates will continue to rise as these cases are identified.[108]

As I noted, most epidemiologists believe that changes in formal diagnostic parameters coupled with increased awareness on the part of pediatricians and the general public fully account for the increases in autism rates seen since the 1990s. Lorna Wing still has the computer dataset of the original Camberwell study. She periodically reanalyzes the data as formal criteria change. By applying the current diagnostic criteria from the *International Statistical Classification of Diseases and Related Health Problems,* 10th edition (*ICD*-10), the World Health Organization's guide, and *DSM*-IV, she found a prevalence rate three or four times higher than her original rate. That is, the result suggested that with each successive modification of criteria, epidemiologists coded more children with autism in their studies.[109]

For others, although these factors may explain the phenomenon in part, a real increase cannot be ruled out because it is impossible to establish a reliable and comparable data set of past cases. As one epidemiologist concluded in 2006, "given the behavioral basis of the autism diagnosis, the lack of knowledge about autism's underlying etiology, and the limitations of retrospective analyses, we are not likely to develop a conclusive body of evidence to either fully support or fully refute the notion that there has been some real increase in autism risk over the past two decades."[110]

In contrast to the more reserved statements of epidemiologists and psychological professionals, parents have become forceful advocates of the idea that increases in autism rates represent an epidemic. Doing so has gained them political recognition and social capital. It has also functioned as a shorthand way to demand that scientists and the public acknowledge that their children's autism is not a matter of chance and heredity, but is a preventable and treatable environmental illness demanding accommodation, remediation, and political attention. They have worked hard to raise public awareness about autism rates, but they have spoken up in professional circles as well, publishing articles refuting the idea that changes in criteria or the substitution of diagnoses of mental retardation for autism were sufficient to account for the increase.[111] In at least one case parents challenged the authors of an article published in the *Journal of Autism and Developmental Disorders* effectively enough that the authors conceded their mistaken interpretation of their own data.[112]

Parents connect their arguments about an increase to claims about causation, but the diagnostic category itself says nothing about the cause of autism. While many contemporary psychiatrists presume that all disorders of the mind have their origins in the brain, from the *DSM*-III onward the editors took no position on the matter of etiology. Nevertheless, psychopharmaceuticals need to be targeted to specific diagnoses in order to be medically valid, and the *DSM* provides the clear boundaries between conditions that psychiatrists need, even if such boundaries ignore the blurry distinctions among real populations.[113]

The practices of autism diagnosis reflect these assumptions about specificity. They also tend to reinforce the view of researchers who think autism is a single disease entity that will eventually resolve into a condition with a specific treatment. Such an outcome would be more manageable than finding that autism represents a cluster of syndromes, multiple "autisms" that share behavioral but not necessarily biological features, a concept supported by the claims of many parents that their children suffer from a range of medical conditions associated with their autism.[114] Even this view of multiple autisms may be too simple. There is good evidence that not all children diagnosed with autism have all of the same features in the three categories of impairment, and closer segmentation could reveal multiple behavioral syndromes.[115]

Although explanations that focus on the way epidemiologists work or bureaucratic institutions maintain records may be compelling, they do not necessarily explain changes in diagnostic practice more broadly. Clinical settings matter more than research settings to understanding the history of autism diagnoses. We need to explain psychiatrists' increasing tendency over the past two decades to describe noncommunicative children with severe behavioral problems as having autism, and we need to explain their choice to see the development, educability, and social relationships of these children in terms of a standard set of cognitive impairments associated with that disorder.

Testing Instruments: Diagnosis as Practice and Product

Diagnostic codes in the *DSM* both standardize therapeutic practices and determine insurance coverage and educational accommodation, matters of central importance for children with neuropsychiatric disorders. A majority of children still receive an autism diagnosis from their pediatricians or developmental specialists who use the criteria set out in the *DSM* as a general guide without employing a published diagnostic instrument. Conventions are different in research settings where, to ensure a consistent population, investigators use assessment tools. The Autism Diagnostic Interview (ADI) and the Autism Diagnostic Observation Schedule (ADOS), the current gold standard for autism diagnoses, were designed using the *DSM*-IV criteria. For clinical and basic research studies and for epidemiological studies, the most reliable diagnoses are those generated by these proprietary instruments.[116] The instruments have been increasingly used in clinical settings as well.[117]

An international team headed by Catherine Lord and Michael Rutter designed the two instruments and released them in 1989.[118] Both investigators had worked on autism for decades. They had designed the ADOS and ADI to conform to the *DSM*-IV and *ICD*-10 criteria for autism, but built in a degree of rigor that would not be found in a clinical diagnosis based on observation and simple knowledge of the criteria. The objective was to guarantee that a population of subjects would be consistent across different study sites or even different studies, and to ensure that findings could in theory be generalized to people with autism as a group.

The two instruments differ in key respects and were meant to complement each other. Lord and Rutter's team designed the ADI to be administered to a child's primary caregiver. It consists of an extensive list of questions, and knowledgeable parents often arrive at an appointment for the ADI with pages of notes and recollections. In contrast, the ADOS is a carefully structured, timed test that is optimized toward children and adults on what practitioners call the higher-functioning end of the autism spectrum. It is best used for distinguishing among pervasive developmental disorders, or for diagnosing autism in a person with significant language skills and the ability to navigate certain social situations. The test is organized as a series of "pushes" or challenges, which are intended to provoke a range of responses or examples of skills on the part of the subject. The screener must rate these responses on a scale of one to three in terms of the degree to which the person being screened exhibits features of autism.

The screener's skills in administering and scoring both instruments matter a great deal. Both instruments also depend on the direct knowledge that comes from interacting with an individual. In the ADI, the interviewer needs to learn to use questions as prompts to elicit very precise descriptions of behaviors from caregivers. The key is to obtain the type of specific and textured details that come from living with someone and being attentive to their needs. For the ADOS, interaction is such a key component that the designers of the instrument discovered the test did not work unless the examiners performed the "pushes" themselves, making requests of the children and playing with them. If they stayed in the room and observed another investigator performing the test, their scores were not as accurate.[119]

The ADOS, which yields the most reliable diagnoses of autism, requires an elaborate system of checks to ensure interrater and test-retest reliability. It involves almost no active recollection on the part of the parents, although their presence and occasional participation is necessary for the exam, especially when it is administered to severely affected children. In order to become certified to use the ADOS, screeners must complete an intensive three-day program, which they begin at home by watching videotapes of sample exams. To ensure that workers use the instrument in the same way at each site that adopts the test, videotapes of children receiving an ADOS screening are sent to outside raters to code. Their diagnoses are matched against those of the technician who administered the test. These outside raters are either the designers of the test or trained by them, creating a technique in which perception and interaction with subjects are as consistent as possible.[120] Although some screeners are skeptical that the built-in degree of oversight is actually reached in practice, it may be more important that screeners understand that their reliability depends on adhering to the routines that they have learned. Their confidence in their diagnoses comes from faith in the instrument and their sense that an experienced screener or diagnostician can recognize a case of autism immediately, even though the diagnostic schedule is necessary to maintain the level of reliability that research requires.

Although psychological testing was once primarily a domain of male professionals, many trained screeners are young women. Screening may be a low-status occupation, but it is hardly trivial work. Like the intensive behavioral therapies used to treat children with autism, testing requires not only extensive training but also the ability to adapt to a widely variable population. It also requires what might be called emotional labor. A typical ADOS screen requires the person performing the assessment to engage empathically by trying to share pleasure and conversation with the subject. Testers must laugh, tickle, make faces, applaud, and occasionally console a distraught subject. The fine labor of diagnosis has become a type of work that demands exquisite skill, and one in which the rewards of questioning the design of the instruments are relatively low.

I observed a number of ADOS screenings at a children's hospital. The tester recognized the difficulty in determining how an individual performs in a familiar daily environment via a single screening session. She was potentially under evaluation as well, because her judgments could be measured against their fit with or deviation from those of external reviewers. She had learned to train her observations and interpretations in line with the requirements of the test. It was a matter of job performance and also of pleasure. The ability to distill forty-five minutes of close observation into a diagnosis has its rewards, even if revealing the diagnosis might cause pain. Parents, however, did not see the tester as the diagnostician. Although she coded the test and thus knew the outcome, the parents instead believed that a doctor would arrive at a conclusion at a later date, and the examiner said nothing to contradict their assumption.

Although most clinicians and epidemiologists use the ADI-R (a revised version of the ADI) and ADOS to screen study candidates, these two instruments are only a few of the available tests that might be administered to a child with autism as specialists evaluate him or her.[121] Psychologists might administer a standard IQ test in order to assess cognitive abilities, although many experts acknowledge that IQ testing may not accurately measure the cognitive abilities of people with autism. The Weschler Adult Intelligence Scale, for example, assumes a certain level of attention and that the subject is willing to attempt the test. Adaptive behavior scales like the Vineland look at an individual's ability to carry out skills involved in daily life like answering the telephone or getting dressed, as well as the ability to communicate and interact on a basic level. A whole series of specialized neuropsychiatric tests might be used to measure specific abilities. Other tests are optimized for different purposes, like the Gilliam Autism Rating Scale (also based on the *DSM*-IV), and the Childhood Autism Rating Scale, both of which take far less time to administer than the ADOS or ADI, or the Checklist for Autism in Toddlers (CHAT) developed by Simon Baron-Cohen and colleagues, which helps clinicians and researchers identify potential cases of autism before children are old enough to receive an official diagnosis.

Diagnostic Consequences

Although diagnostic instruments are designed simply to identify individuals who would also be recognized by an experienced pediatrician familiar with autism, tools like the ADI and the ADOS inevitably incorporate assumptions about the nature of the disorder, if only by virtue of what they are not designed to assess. Despite the precision with which researchers can characterize cognitive and developmental abnormalities, very few techniques exist for measuring the outcome of treatments for autism because autism is understood to be a relatively static and lifelong disorder, with symptoms that are stable over time. In some cases, tests like the Childhood Autism Rating Scale developed by Eric Schopler are revised to enable raters to measure treatment outcomes. In theory, children can be retested using an instrument like the ADOS to see if they continue to qualify for an autism diagnosis. Some specialists argue that true outcome measures need to be developed in order to measure improvement as a direct result of different therapeutic interventions. Many parents, caregivers, and professionals believe that symptoms, behaviors, and abilities can change dramatically, either as a result of intensive therapeutic measures or as the result of development and maturation.[122]

Screening instruments also have a popular life beyond their utility for experts. Simon Baron-Cohen, who heads the Cambridge University Autism Research Centre, has developed a questionnaire used to identify milder forms of neurological variation that would not qualify for a diagnosis of autism or Asperger syndrome. The Autism Questionnaire, or AQ, is available on the Internet and appears in excerpted form in mass market magazine articles.[123] Although it is not presented as a diagnostic instrument, the design of the AQ encourages self-diagnosis and suggests that anyone can be located somewhere in a spectrum of neurological types. As Baron-Cohen and his colleagues wrote, "The AQ is thus a valuable instrument for rapidly quantifying where any given individual is situated on the continuum from autism to normality."[124]

Sociologists of medicine have pointed out the possibility that diagnostic categories, made stable and rendered consistent and standard by tests, can serve to reinforce the appearance of disease entities as simple facts about nature. The effect is to hide the underlying truth that the categories themselves have been shaped by social and political considerations, and in some cases the needs of researchers, rather than the best interests of patients.[125] By introducing an apparently objective scale, diagnostic instruments can erase many of the subjective elements of diagnostic practices and the theories of illness and disability that inform them. One question is what symptoms are required for a diagnosis—for instance, communication deficits versus feeding problems or sensory disturbances. Another is what constitutes a symptom versus a benign difference—for instance, a failure to express interest in social interaction. In other cases, diagnostic instruments are incorporated into educational or health care bureaucracies such that screeners are rewarded for producing the kind of consistent and clear-cut diagnoses that conform to the requirements of record-keeping, but are less able to highlight important individual variations that are relevant to an individual's needs or prognosis.

As an experienced test designer explained to me, neuropsychological tests have a tendency to "reify the diagnoses" that they seek to measure, taking a constellation of characteristics and making it seem as though they support a more general claim about what causes and constitutes a cognitive disorder. The same is true of many screening instruments. It is difficult to design an instrument that measures cognitive abilities without building in a theory about the source of deficits or their relationship to one another. The result is that diagnostic tests contribute to the as-yet-unproven assumption that "autism" is a uniform disorder, with a consistent presentation of symptoms and a single cause. They also, intentionally or not, lead to a diagnosis that many parents experience as a final pronouncement that suggests no logical or necessary next step, and in which their own input and questions are often effectively silenced.[126]

This impression that a diagnosis of autism is both static and justified by a structural difference in the brain has both therapeutic and theoretical implications. In terms of brain research, the belief encourages specialists in the field to design research programs that assume that the symptoms of autism are caused by specific, focal deficits rather than dysfunctions in, say, the relationships among different cognitive domains or pervasive factors like inflammation that affect the brain as a whole. Although exams like the ADI or ADOS do not presume any particular cause for autistic behaviors, they can also encourage researchers to think of the behaviors that they test for as the basis for autism, the central facts of the disorder, rather than the results of more fundamental neurological processes. Autism acquires an identity as a set of "core deficits," rather than a syndrome that happens to be identifiable by those deficits but is not identical to them. As we have seen, researchers have spent a great deal of time working to precisely characterize the central deficits in autism. In most cases, they have been conceptualized in very similar terms to Kanner's original descriptions of disturbed social affect, repetitive behavior, and resistance to change; or the "triad" of deficits in social communication, social ability, and social imagination, accompanied by a restricted pattern of activities, that Lorna Wing and Judith Gould abstracted from their own observations during the 1960s and 1970s; or the impairments in social interaction and communication and the "stereotyped patterns of behavior" of the *DSM*-IV and *ICD*-10.

Theories that explain autism in terms of poor executive function, weak central coherence, or problems with attention all describe the syndrome in terms of properties that are more basic to cognitive function than complex activities like communication, behavior, and sociability. Researchers, however, have only recently begun to connect these processing dysfunctions to actual changes in brain structure, changes that may be distributed rather than localized.[127] It is much easier to think about the connection between modular theories of brain function—those that assume that particular areas of the brain are designated from birth for particular functions—and brain structure. It makes intuitive sense, given the symptoms of many brain injuries, which when they occur in adults are known to impair specific brain functions. Think of the way that a stroke can cause paralysis or language loss, depending on where it occurs. This is one of the reasons that many researchers working on brains and autism continue to look for localized lesions, using ever more powerful imaging techniques to try to identify sites of structural difference in autism, just as they have been doing since the late 1960s. The problem is that although such approaches provide compelling theories about how and why autism occurs, they may not be the best way to discover what is actually occurring in autistic brains.

I have provided this discussion of the history of the autism diagnosis and contemporary diagnostic techniques for two reasons. The first is to explain how researchers have described autism and how their assessments of the key features of that syndrome have changed over time. In many instances, those changes have reflected researchers' interests in new technologies, such as CT scans, or in growing areas of research, like genetics. It was not always the case that new evidence or a conclusive refutation of some earlier theory determined a new course of investigation. In these respects, the history of the autism diagnosis resembles many other modern psychiatric and developmental disorders. Autism has been constituted as a neurological and genetic disorder and this belief is supported by a broad consensus among the research community, but the precise mechanisms of causation remain obscure. This history of diagnostic parameters and investigative techniques serves as introduction and background to the story that I tell in the next chapters about how knowledge about autism has been produced.

The second reason is to clarify that, while autism is a disorder of social relationships, diagnoses cannot take place without the fact of intense, even intimate human interaction. A diagnosis depends on skillful observation and close interaction with a patient. Test designers have understood this, crafting instruments like the ADI that make use of parents' and caregivers' intimate knowledge of children with autism. In the case of the ADOS, they designed an instrument that creates an environment that simulates and condenses a long series of social interactions. Treating the disorder requires the same close contact.

The rest of this book traces the knowledge that grows out of intense involvement with children with autism. Symptoms are closely observed, recorded, and interpreted, but those symptoms tell the men and women in this story not what children with autism "are," or "have," but how to engage them, what they need, and how best to approach, understand, and respond to them.

Love Is Not Enough: Bruno Bettelheim, Infantile Autism, and Psychoanalytic Childhoods

Bruno Bettelheim once rivaled Montessori, Piaget, and Anna Freud in popularity and influence in the fields of child psychology and development. He is probably best known among the general public for his 1975 study of fairy tales, *The Uses of Enchantment*. Eight years earlier, he had written an enormously influential book on treating autistic children, *The Empty Fortress: Infantile Autism and the Birth of the Self*. Although both books captivated the public at the time of their publication and for years afterward, many readers have since focused on flaws in these works and Bettelheim's questionable research methods. After Bettelheim's suicide in 1990 at the age of eighty-six, his reputation plummeted. He was accused of substantially plagiarizing his groundbreaking work on fairy tales. Observers claimed that he had beaten and verbally abused both children and staff during his thirty-year tenure as director of the Sonia Shankman Orthogenic School at the University of Chicago. He had knowingly contributed to the cruel and damaging portrayal of the mothers of children with autism as "refrigerator mothers."[1] Most damning of all, he had refused to alter his position even as evidence accumulated against the psychogenic theory of autism. This was indeed a sharp decline in status for "a hero of our time," the man who was daring and compassionate enough to work with children whom others considered "hopeless and worthless."[2]

These controversies ought not to confuse us about the weight Bettelheim's books, magazine articles, reviews, and public presence carried in the 1950s and 1960s. Bettelheim popularized psychotherapy in a postwar America hungry for the vision of humanity offered by psychoanalysis, with its humanistic emphasis on what Freud had called "a cure through love."[3]

The country's fascination with psychoanalysis could itself be called a "romance."[4] Countless magazine articles referenced psychoanalytic terms. Popular books on psychotherapy and psychoanalysis enjoyed high sales. Film plots featured virtuoso performances of therapeutic interpretation and cures. Psychoanalytic training was a standard part of medical education, while psychologists enjoyed growing influence in public policy.[5]

Postwar Americans, especially those in the middle class, imagined that the science and art of psychoanalysis could be applied to children to manage their development into healthy and well-adjusted adults.[6] Psychoanalysts and popular promoters of psychoanalytic theories responded to their interest, adding to an already substantial collection of childrearing advice and parenting manuals.[7] Nor was psychoanalysis the only movement to argue for the influence of mothers' actions on the early development of children and to offer conflicting statements about good mothering either as an innate or acquired skill. "Parenting," understood as a technical practice best carried out with input from experts, became part of the American vernacular as both pediatricians and advertisers urged mothers to seek guidance on childrearing.[8]

As early as the 1940s, experts themselves cautioned against an excess of expert authority in childrearing. In 1941, Leo Kanner wrote the short handbook *In Defense of Mothers*, and in 1945 Simon & Schuster published *Dr. Spock's Baby and Child Care*, the best seller that reassured rattled mothers that "you know more than you think you do."[9] Spock's matter-of-fact advice, unfortunately, provided few suggestions for parents struggling with the work of raising children with developmental disabilities. Nevertheless, postwar theories of childrearing affected how parents treated children with disabilities as well as their siblings. Dr. Spock's *Baby and Child Care* shared shelf space with Bettelheim's *Love Is Not Enough* in the homes of families of both disabled and typically developing children.

The story of Bettelheim's involvement with autism illustrates the ambivalent and sometimes tragic qualities of the affective, institutional, and professional commitments that drive research and therapeutic programs. Psychoanalytic approaches to autism were not a developmental stage through which treatment strategies had to progress before more effective approaches could be found, but neither were they an accident or aberration. They have existed alongside behavioral and medical approaches, sharing vocabularies, methodologies, and, often, ideological commitments with them. Understanding why participants believed that they worked, and how they worked, can do much to illuminate the ways that attention, affective commitments, and techniques work together to create a cohesive belief system and sense of efficacy.

Autism functioned as a focal point for ideas about motherhood, childhood, and development in twentieth-century America. Bettelheim's writings on the Orthogenic School and on autism served as meditations on human experience and existential dilemmas, as "a passionate description of *deliverance*, as it may be achieved for one child and denied to another," as much or more than as accounts of clinical treatment.[10] They became part of a national conversation about "natural" forms of love, caring, and bonding. Understanding the appeal of this work inevitably involves writing a kind of psychohistory, not only of Bettelheim, but also of a profession that drew on psychoanalytic theory in treating autism, and of the parents who accepted a vision of childhood as a vulnerable experience best managed by experts. Although the Orthogenic School was a unique institution, Bettelheim's desire to use ideas from psychoanalysis to understand and treat autism was not unusual. He was one of a significant number of psychologists and psychiatrists who shared the ambition to decode autistic language and interpret children's symptoms as effects of their family environments.

Bettelheim's great literary and personal appeal reflected the culture of cold war America, as well as mid-century beliefs about childhood and about the forms of emotional labor called parenting and therapy. As such, his work is very much part of the history of autism as one of love and labor. Both were present in the work of Bettelheim's Orthogenic School counselors, and both were the focus of discussion when Bettelheim attributed failures to the mothers of autistic children. Counselors provided the kind of receptive and responsive interactions that Bettelheim imagined mothers had failed at. Bettelheim has also been remarkably hard to escape. The view of autistic children and their families that he popularized has remained both a reference and a foil for generations of parents. His claims resonate in contemporary psychological literature and in the corridor-talk of practitioners and policymakers.

Bettelheim and the Orthogenic School

The Sonia Shankman Orthogenic School, Bettelheim's main institutional home at the University of Chicago, was founded in 1915 as a school for cognitively disabled children. The university purchased it in 1931, converting it to a laboratory school for studying human development in collaboration with the Department of Education. They renamed the school, choosing a term meant to evoke the idea of straight growth.[11] By 1944, the school was foundering as the acting director struggled to transform a custodial institution into a residential treatment program for emotionally disturbed children and youth. Bettelheim had been working part time for the University of Chicago, and he was effectively forced into the director's position after agreeing to evaluate the school and suggest improvements. He initially considered it beyond repair.[12]

When Bettelheim took over, he was just beginning to achieve prominence with the 1943 publication of "Individual and Mass Behavior in Extreme Situations," an account of the psychological effects of concentration camps. The text drew on Bettelheim's personal experience as a prisoner in Dachau and Buchenwald, where he was held for about a year during 1938–1939.[13] The article took on "instant authority" as one of the first analyses of what had happened inside the concentration camps.[14] Bettelheim had no background in child psychology and no formal training in psychoanalysis. He had attended the University of Vienna where he received a doctorate in Philosophy and Aesthetics. After escaping to the United States, he held a variety of jobs, which included designing art appreciation tests for schoolchildren and teaching part time at a women's college. Although he did not seek out the director position at the Orthogenic School, it represented a great improvement in terms of job security and the route to the academic prominence that Bettelheim sought.

Bettelheim traced his interest in helping troubled children, and those with autism in particular, to his experience with an American child who came to stay with him and his first wife in Vienna. The child psychologist Anna Freud had determined that the child's only hope was a "psychoanalytically organized environment." Whether Bettelheim, at the time working in his father's lumber business, could have provided that has been a matter of debate. Years later, Bettelheim explained how "the severe pathology of [the child's] case permitted observing a phenomenon also seen in normal behavior but as if it were under microscopic enlargement, or thrown into bold relief by a bright light." He "carefully respected her wish to be left alone, while still trying to take careful, loving care of her, before she moderated her total isolation and permitted occasional approaches, although she did not respond to these in any discernable way." After a year and a half of gentle child's games that helped her accept and acknowledge other people, she spoke her first sentence in perfect English. Bettelheim concluded that her condition, which he believed to be autism, resulted from her fatherless upbringing and rejection by her mother.[15] He hoped to continue to work with her when he arrived in the United States. The opportunity fell through, but his experience with the child intrigued him and his sense of the importance of the attention that he and his wife had provided gave him confidence in pursuing a career treating emotionally disturbed children.

The contrast between Bettelheim's unorthodox training and the significant public authority he later enjoyed as a child psychologist led later writers to question his credentials. After his death, some suggested that he allowed potential employers to understand that he had earned a degree in psychology. He had also never undergone a full psychoanalysis. The credentialing of psychoanalysts by local psychoanalytic societies in the 1950s required a training analysis, although it was not a requirement for practice as a clinical psychologist, a title that more closely fit Bettelheim's work. Nevertheless, counselors who worked with Bettelheim recollect that it was "common knowledge" among them that Bettelheim's degree was not in psychology.[16] He eventually became a "non-therapist member" of the Chicago Psychoanalytic Society, a position that reflected his lack of formal training and perhaps also the ambiguous position of child psychology at the time.[17] Bettelheim may have intentionally misled various publics about other aspects of his past, including his connections to Freud and the nature of his internment in concentration camps. However, biographers also note that Bettelheim's generation might have regarded this type of untruth as an exigency. Among millions of displaced persons, each felt the need to make themselves as desirable to employers in the States as possible.

Bettelheim instituted sweeping changes at the Orthogenic School. He demanded an increased level of training for, and dedication from, the school's counseling staff and a larger budget from the University of Chicago.[18] He remade the school into a physically welcoming space in which the entire staff focused on the recovery of the students. At the same time, he sought alternative placement for all of the children there who he believed had neurological impairments. He wanted the school population to comprise only "emotionally disturbed" children whom he and the counselors might reasonably expect to help using the methods at hand.[19]

Through his accounts of work at the school, Bettelheim also became a public intellectual. Positioned as both scientist and observer of the traumatic events of the present, he appeared uniquely suited to speak to the trials facing children and parents in a culture that he approached as both an admiring outsider and engaged participant. Bettelheim published as much or more in popular venues than in professional journals, sometimes borrowing liberally and without attribution from more academic sources.[20] He wrote about the changing role of women in the home and workplace, the student antiwar movement, educational problems for normal children, and childrearing. He returned to the themes of autonomy and of children's self-authorship achieved through infantile desires for gratification and, later, their self-conscious assertion of their needs and identities. Magazine profiles reflected Bettelheim's own self-fashioning. They frequently opened with a physical description and included a photo. His bald head, prominent ears, and the heavy frames of his glasses became immediately recognizable.

Bettelheim linked his claims regarding the malleability of the human psyche to his observations of behavior during wartime, particularly that of his fellow inmates in the labor camp. As a survivor, Bettelheim enjoyed a unique, almost anthropological authority. As a witness, he could speak to the motivations underlying fascism and authoritarianism, and as therapist, he could claim a theory that transmuted the negative power of the camps into a positive therapeutic insight, just as Ivar Lovaas recalled that witnessing fascism made him realize how malleable the human psyche might be.[21] Bettelheim claimed that, in contrast to other prisoners, he had been able to avoid "a disintegration of his personality" and pathological identification with prison guards by maintaining a scientific attitude of detached observation.[22] Bettelheim's claims about the therapeutic possibilities of a "total environment" and the importance of autonomy to the growth and preservation of a sense of self resonated with a contemporary movement toward milieu therapy as well as with public interest in moral autonomy and the social environment's role in shaping subjective experience.

The Empty Fortress Enchants America

Most accounts of the Orthogenic School at the University of Chicago, whether by former students, staff members, or participants in the larger world of twentieth-century psychotherapy and psychology, reflect long-standing loyalties and commitments. As with many therapeutic practices in the history of mental illness, it is hard if not impossible to speak in absolute terms about the effectiveness of the therapeutic activities that took place within the walls of the school, judged against other treatments at other times.[23] In the case of the Orthogenic School, as in other cases that I describe, the institutional location and the interactions between practitioners and subjects mattered, as did the forms of social learning and tacit knowledge used to reproduce particular interventions. Therapies changed both patients and practitioners, as each became increasingly committed to the therapeutic program, a mutual influence that has parallels in other biomedical treatments.[24] Unlike the majority of modern diagnostic and treatment strategies, which derive much of their authority from the appearance of what Charles Rosenberg has called therapeutic "specificity," psychotherapy as practiced by Bettelheim never placed much weight on diagnostic accuracy or on treatments tailored to a diagnostic group. The salient categories were the universal human psyche and the individual sufferer.[25]

When it appeared in 1967, *The Empty Fortress: Infantile Autism and the Birth of the Self* became a best seller, featured in major national newspapers and magazines, from the *New York Times* and the *Saturday Evening Post* to the *New Yorker* and *The New York Review of Books*. Reviewers greeted it as a philosophical rather than a technical work, a meditation on the drama of childhood and the triumphant "search for self" that Bettelheim claimed to both facilitate and chronicle. Few readers cared about or took the time to evaluate Bettelheim's accounts of his specific methods for treating autism or his rates of success. A reviewer in the *New York Times* invoked Bettelheim's account of a year spent in German concentration camps, proclaiming that "it is evidence that the informed heart is possible and that the alienations in our age—whether they are the planned dehumanization of the concentration camps or the unintentional dehumanization of modern mass society or the still largely mysterious dehumanization of individual psychosis—need not be accepted as the permanent condition of man."[26] Other reviewers wrote of Bettelheim's compassion and generosity, of the mothers "who believe in him" and seek his advice, and of Bettelheim's "real love, warmth, understanding, and years of infinite patience and hope."[27]

With the encouragement of his publisher, Bettelheim chose to write *The Empty Fortress* for a broad audience, avoiding jargon and technical terminology. He wrote with a comfortable and resoundingly self-confident style, an approach that he also brought to his public appearances and magazine columns.[28] His intended audience was not looking to investigate treatment options for their own children or patients, but instead wanted to comprehend their anxieties about their own, typically developing children and the "problem of parental preoccupation and indifference" as a uniquely modern risk to child development.[29] For such readers, autism represented not a practical concern but a metaphor for American anxieties about childrearing, the changing roles of women, and the formative power of love.[30] Bettelheim seemed to offer a series of salvation stories, a promise of help for the previously untreatable.

Not all parents of autistic children who read the book agreed. Amy Lettick, the founder of Benhaven, a residential program for developmentally disabled children and adults, asked the director of the Nassau Center for Emotionally Disturbed Children whether she had read the book yet.

> Fascinating. I think this book alone is enough to have him committed. He has marvelous descriptions of autistic behavior, but the reasoning he ascribes to it is unbelievable. Wait till you read how 12 year old Joey cured himself by giving birth to himself out of a chicken egg. Mira Rothenberg [another promoter of psychotherapeutic techniques] should have rushed out to Chicago with her incubator![31]

Another mother, Judy Barron, recalled that she and her husband "fumed" when they read the book and wondered how anyone could believe Bettleheim, then were astonished to discover that "almost everyone did."[32]

Like Lettick and other parents, reviewers in clinical journals noted the failure of the book to offer pragmatic advice or specific treatments. They also questioned Bettelheim's tendency to interpret any behavior through the lens of psychoanalysis, often in the absence of detailed clinical descriptions of the behavior in question. One frustrated reader complained that Bettelheim's complex interpretation of the unwillingness of children with autism to be treated by dentists failed to mention—or perhaps to recognize—that such problems were common with other "non-verbal subnormal children." Similarly, Bettelheim's theory that the actions of mothers were perceived by their autistic child as a "threat to his very existence" failed to explain why some mistreated children developed autism and some developed normally. Others simply wished that he had addressed the neurological aspects of the disorder.[33]

By 1967, the psychiatric community had in fact abandoned many of the ideas about autism upon which Bettelheim based his treatments, as Jacquelyn Sanders, a counselor who later became director of the school, has noted.[34] Most had concluded that there was "little evidence that psychotherapeutic treatment of a child influenced prognosis."[35] Nevertheless, Bettelheim presented *The Empty Fortress* as the culmination of work funded by a 1956 Ford Foundation grant. He divided the book into sections devoted to theory, case studies, and an extensive review of the published literature on autism. He situated autism as a theoretical problem within developmental psychology, contrasting typical human development and ego differentiation with the failures of ego formation in the three cases that he described.

To the contemporary reader of his work, Bettelheim's relentless psychoanalytic interpretation of behavioral and physiological symptoms can be perplexing. He described "twiddling," pronominal reversal, rocking, dietary restrictions, obsessions with order and with organizing time, sensory abnormalities, and head-banging, all symptoms familiar to contemporary diagnosticians and parents.[36] However, he believed that through the "process of personality integration" at the School, "psychosomatic manifestations of long standing—such as allergies, neuro-dermatitis, ocular-motor disturbances, mucous colitis and other disorders of the digestive tract—also disappeared spontaneously."[37] The physical symptoms were merely epiphenomena, incidental to autism's root cause. Readers encountering the text at the time of its publication, like Peter Gay, a biographer of Freud, admired these curative feats without questioning them.

> Obviously (Bettelheim is enough of a Freudian to be convinced of this) all aspects of autistic behavior are meaningful; all of it—the twiddling, the peculiar modes of defecating, the silent rocking, the refusal to eat—is a kind of language, even if it is directed at no one. But since symptoms vary so enormously, and since the therapist has no way of checking his hunches with the patient, as he does in psychoanalysis, the interpretation of the "language" autistic children have available to them demands the utmost concentration, intelligence, empathy, and persistence.[38]

Despite his readiness to rely on psychoanalytic interpretations of autistic behavior, Bettelheim had read widely not only in the psychoanalytic literature but in child development. His characterizations of autism drew on theories of development as an interactive process in which parents were central. He began with Sigmund Freud. But Bettelheim also turned to John Dewey's work on education and to the psychoanalysts Erik Erikson, August Aichhorn, and Anna Freud.[39] For accounts of abnormal ego development, he relied on René Spitz's studies of institutionalized children who showed emotional withdrawal. Spitz had concluded that even typical children regressed when they were deprived of their emotional connection to a "love object, such as the mother" but recovered when their mother or a "substitute love object" was returned to them.[40] Perhaps most important, he drew inspiration from Leo Kanner's arresting image of children "kept neatly in refrigerators which did not defrost," and parents who attended them with the "mechanized service of the kind which is rendered by an overconscientious gasoline station attendant."[41]

Harry Harlow's experiments on infant monkeys served as an important source for the devastating effects of deprivation, establishing for both scientific colleagues and the readers of *Life* magazine the idea of "natural" childrearing as characterized by an abundant supply of maternal warmth. Harlow's ability to simulate innate disorders of affect through sensory deprivation seemed to support Bettelheim's psychoanalytic theories. By isolating young rhesus monkeys in a stainless-steel chamber, Harlow and his colleague Stephen Suomi believed that they had produced something akin to the "well of despair" described by humans suffering from depression.[42] Harlow noted the "striking" similarities of the monkeys to autistic children, referring to the "coldness, ambivalence, double binding messages and lack of physical contact" that caused some children to develop "infantile autism, other forms of childhood psychosis, or severe behavioral disorders."[43] Harlow's chilling images of baby monkeys clinging desperately to wire "mothers" looked to popular audiences like icons of childhood instinct. For Bettelheim, the failures of these monkeys to develop normally demonstrated the necessity of what he elsewhere called "dialectics of hope" between mothers and children.[44]

People typically misremember Bettelheim in *The Empty Fortress* as having compared mothers of children with autism to concentration camp guards. Although Bettelheim's descriptions of the mothers were hardly generous, he had first reached for the concentration camp in explaining the milieu therapy used at the Orthogenic School. He argued that personality change could be effected through the institution of a total environment, a claim based on observations of his fellow inmates in a labor camp.[45] A decade before publication of *The Empty Fortress* he had concluded that the stunted ego development of a child with autism resulted from the child's unconscious sense of a deep ambivalence on the part of the mother. Children responded with terror to their mothers' mixed feelings. Unlike real prisoners, Bettelheim stressed, infants lacked the capacity to make rational judgments and merely had to believe that their lives were in danger. Perhaps, Bettelheim conceded, the mother's rejection was itself a response to a child who had failed to bond with her. "All children are born with differential sensitivities and react differently to their environment. . . . In the realm of interaction, it really matters little who makes the first move, who begins the interaction, or even the nature of the action. What counts is whether the action is interpreted correctly and meets an appropriate response," a complex choreography in which a single misstep in breastfeeding an especially sensitive child might precipitate a cascade of developmental maladies.[46]

Following the case studies, Bettelheim provided two literature reviews, explaining that they were not "systematic" but replicated his own reading into the "nature of the disturbance" in the children that he had treated. The first section, "Etiology and Treatment," began with Leo Kanner's 1943 monograph and proceeded to Bernard Rimland's *Infantile Autism*, published in 1964, just a few years prior to Bettelheim's book. Rimland wrote *Infantile Autism* primarily to refute the psychogenic theory of autism, and Bettelheim dismissed it as an argument without merit. Rimland's careful compilation of evidence mattered little because "even if a specific neurological dysfunction should some day be found to correlate highly with the syndrome of infantile autism, it would still be compatible with the psychogenic hypothesis.[47]

Bettelheim did not entirely dismiss the possibility of organic correlates for autistic behaviors. "While I do not accept the hypothesis that autism is due to an original organic defect, I do not feel I can rule out its later appearance. On the contrary, I tend to believe that far from being organic in origin, infantile autism, when persisting too long, can have irreversible effects."[48] It was through psychotherapy, however, that he hoped to offer treatment, and a psychogenic theory implied malleability and the potential for healing.[49] Writing at Bettelheim's death in 1990, a former counselor at the school explained that "Bettelheim's view was that until mental health professionals came up with a specific neurological disorder that was responsive to medication, psychotherapists had little choice but to continue with treatment efforts."[50] This confidence in the prospect of curing the disorder through psychiatric treatment faced relentless opposition from Rimland and other advocates of research into organic factors. So did his dismissal of the behavioral treatment methods developed by Ivar Lovaas, which Bettelheim said reduced autistic children "to the level of Pavlovian dogs" or made them into "more pliable robots" with new symptomatic behaviors.[51]

In practice, Bettelheim's commitment to a psychogenic framework appeared neither understanding nor humanistic. Richard Pollak, one of Bettelheim's most critical biographers, recounts a meeting in which Bettelheim, years after the deaths of Pollak's autistic brother and his mother, maintained that the brother had committed suicide in response to his mother's hatred. " 'What *is it* about these Jewish mothers, Mr. Pollak?' he asked. I was stunned by this casual anti-semitism, coming as it did from a Jew who had suffered in the camps, and by the ferocity of his antagonism two decades after Stephen's death."[52] His brother had fallen from a hayloft. The accident filled Pollak with guilt and drove him to exonerate both his mother and his brother. Bettelheim never stopped insisting that children with autism suffered from a deficit of affective contact on the part of their mothers. He did not see this as a conscious or blameworthy act on the part of parents: "They did as they did because they could not help themselves to do otherwise. They suffer more than enough in having such a child. To make them guilty will only add to the misery of all and help none."[53]

The Empty Fortress represented both a synthesis of Bettelheim's experience with autism at the Orthogenic School and one work in a corpus that Bettelheim clearly regarded as interconnected. Throughout the text, he referred to his books on the structure of the Orthogenic School, *Truants from Life* (1955) and *Love Is Not Enough* (1950), to explain the creation of the therapeutic milieu. Likewise, he referenced his work on authoritarian aspects of contemporary society in *The Informed Heart* (1960) and his research on childrearing and personality development on the kibbutz (published later as *Children of the Dream*, 1969). The work that led to *The Empty Fortress* used treating children with autism as a way to understand the course of typical human development. Bettelheim alluded to this objective in his interim reports for the Ford Foundation, writing that their hope was to "arrive at a much better understanding not only of the nature of this disorder and its appropriate therapy, but also of certain, so far poorly understood, aspects of early personality development," and later that "clarification of some still very baffling problems of the earliest ego development forms the core of the research."[54] For Bettelheim, claims about children with autism were intimately connected to claims about the efficacy of his school and the theories behind it.

Bettelheim built *The Empty Fortress* around four lengthy case studies. The best-known chapter dealt with "Joey: A 'Mechanical Boy,'" an account that he had published earlier in *Scientific American*. Joey's symptoms lent themselves to easy interpretation. "Machine-like" in his movements and speech, Joey drew engines and described himself as a mechanical person. Bettelheim offered the case as proof of his success in treating autistic children. Joey's emergence into the human world was an allegory for "emotional development in a machine age."[55] Contemporary writers have suggested that the metaphorical richness of Joey's conversations about power sources, emissions, and the like, let alone his art, reflected the kind of symbolic reasoning that children with autism are now seen as lacking, but he also tended to reverse his pronouns, insist on routine, had difficulties with eating, and lacked a useful emotional vocabulary. These are all characteristics of what psychiatrists would now call high-functioning autism or Asperger syndrome.

Bettelheim and the counselors realized that Joey wanted badly to be "reborn," and that doing so would require him to progress through an infant's developmental stages.[56] They helped Joey come to terms with his early and strict toilet training by encouraging him to defecate in a wastebasket and later to "eliminate freely wherever he happened to be," and were rewarded by Joey's increasing willingness to picture himself as an integrated human being and not a machine.[57] His emerging ego and personality development culminated in an interview with Bettelheim at the time of his graduation from high school three years later. The interview itself demonstrated a certain psychoanalytic subjectivity. Prompted by Betttelheim, Joey spoke about his fear of expressing his emotions and about the importance to him of his intimate connections with the staff. He recalled in particular that counselors had held him like a child and fed him in the School's dining room. It is hard to tell whether Joey had only mastered Bettelheim's vocabulary and view of the self or if Bettelheim and the counselors had indeed cured him. Within the terms of the Orthogenic School's milieu therapy, it was difficult to tell the two transformations apart.[58] Joey's paintings are preserved in the Bettelheim archives, and in picking up and examining each cracked and fragile page, I did indeed gain a palpable sense of one boy's transformation.[59]

In a second case, "Laurie," Bettelheim elaborated his theory of the origins of autism.

> Throughout this book I state my belief that the precipitating factor in infantile autism is the parent's wish that his child should not exist. While the same wish may not cause the same disturbance in other children, and while at some future time we may learn that some organic factor is a precondition of autism, the fact is that almost all organic conditions that have so far been linked to this disease are also present in nonautistic children.[60]

In the case of children who had already developed autism, their apparent lack of interest made their parents further ambivalent, which would then make the child turn away entirely.[61] Bettelheim understood autism as a kind of feedback between infant withdrawal and inadequate parental response precipitated by factors that could only become legible through psychotherapeutic intervention. Mothering became the careful management of libidinal impulses and drives, because their expression could exact real harm on the developing child. The mere thought of rejection became a harmful act. Hence, mothers needed to be constant interpreters of their children's struggles, for autonomy on the one hand and for affirmation on the other. Failures at reading became failures at love.

The Romance of Bettelheim: Motherhood, Ambivalence,
and Psychological Expertise

If Bettelheim exercised a particular appeal among the public, he was not
the only psychologist to do so at a time when the profession sought public
influence by "giving psychology away."[62] Freud traveled to the United States
for the first and only time in 1909, and in the intervening decades Freudian psychology was modified and adapted to the needs and tastes of the
American population. Americans were more interested in ego psychology
and in applying psychoanalytic theory to problems of human management
and child and adult development than in the unconscious. Interest groups
and activists adapted Freudian theories to provide support for a variety of
issues, from autonomy and self-determination to women's liberation and
social equality. During the 1950s, American psychologists wedded Freudian theory to behaviorism, drive theory to theories of conditioning. Individual experiences of psychotherapy, likewise, took place within an American—and frequently middle-class—milieu, where people were concerned
with the trajectories of their careers and questions of social performance.[63]

Just as psychologists sought to become purveyors of expert advice during the 1950s, they also worked to expand their clinical influence to reach
not only the emotionally disturbed, but also healthy "normally neurotic"
individuals seeking help for a variety of problems in their daily lives.[64] The
treatment of war neuroses and preventative measures aimed at keeping
troops psychologically healthy had provided a means for psychological
professionals to argue for their specialized skills during the war.[65] Afterward, the reintegration of soldiers into American society was framed as a
problem in "readjustment." The GI Bill was a means for providing the tools
for this reintegration into American society and for filling the ranks of the
mental health professions through specialized training.[66]

While soldiers enrolled in campus courses in psychology, their spouses
looked to incorporate psychological expertise into their own work as
mothers and wives. To meet this demand, Bettelheim ran a series of
"Mothers Meetings" in the Hyde Park area near the Orthogenic School
and University of Chicago. They were transcribed and edited as *Dialogues
with Mothers*.[67] The transcripts show concerned mothers and some fathers
eager to inspect their interactions with their children. The mothers themselves seemed comfortable employing a psychoanalytic perspective in their
childrearing, transforming their concerns about normality into questions
about strategies for developing healthy children. The interpretive framework of psychoanalysis could be applied as easily to typical children as to

highly disturbed ones. Bettelheim's dialogues, which some critics called "diatribes," encouraged mothers to examine their part in problematic interactions with their children in order to determine their contributions to their children's difficult behaviors. No action on the part of a child was carried out in emotional isolation from his or her family, but mothers were also to understand their children's actions as autonomous expressions of desire and frustration. Love was an intuitive technique, but one that could be honed, tested, and critiqued. Love was innate but it could be improved and refined, carried out reflexively, and on occasion, skewed or corrupted.

Bettelheim argued against the belief that there existed a single, correct method of parenting guaranteed to produce desirable results. As the title of his book on childrearing stressed, borrowing a phrase from the child development expert D. W. Winnicott, one need not be perfect, but merely "good enough." "Whatever we do with and for our children ought to flow from our understanding of and our feelings for the particular situation and the relation we wish to exist between us and our child."[68] He addressed his frequent columns in women's magazines to a psychoanalytically literate readership, one accustomed to understanding individual development as a series of moral achievements by parents, children, and the wider culture. In the predictable daily battles over appropriate clothing, learning to read, and toilet training, life history and desire mattered more than biological or cognitive limitations. Bettelheim wrote for two separate groups, one, "intelligent and highly motivated mothers of more or less normal youngsters," and the other, counselors such as the staff of the Orthogenic School. Both groups might benefit from insights into the "ever-changing situations in which they find themselves as the adult raises a child and as the child reacts to being raised."[69] The parents of children suffering from "severe psychological impairments" were a different case. Bettelheim never imagined them as an audience. Treating their children was the domain of the properly trained.

If Bettelheim placed high demands on mothers, his positions reflected broader trends in 1950s psychoanalysis and public discourse.[70] Ideals of "scientific motherhood" increasingly clashed with the many other demands on women in the postwar era.[71] Philip Wylie's "momism" was one extreme portrayal of mothers as a suffocating menace to the autonomy of their sons, but milder versions of such theories proliferated. Nevertheless, women embraced psychoanalysis, although during the late 1960s they would begin to offer their own critiques of psychoanalysts' and psychiatrists' contributions to inequality between the sexes.[72] A public culture of psychoanalytic discourse gained ground even as so-called "traditional" roles strained under the weight of women's entry into the workforce and the professions.

The 1950s also witnessed an explosion in referrals for parents—mainly mothers—of children diagnosed with autism. Bettelheim was far from the only expert insisting that those who treated autistic children should realize "that the child's behavior no matter how bizarre or seemingly isolated has meaning." For instance, a 1957 article in the *American Journal of Orthopsychiatry* advocated simultaneously treating both parents and children. As the authors, staff members at a Massachusetts treatment center, explained, "the core anxiety of the parents and their schizophrenic child is fear of annihilation," which mothers managed by rigidly separating the roles of "mother, housewife, working woman," leading to their refusal to acknowledge their child's identity as a separate person.[73]

Parents submitted to psychoanalytic treatment because their doctors told them that the best way to improve the welfare of their child was to be treated themselves.[74] One mother recalled how

> they never were interested in really seeing the child, but they had my husband and I come in forever—really doing the trick on us. We both thought we loved each other before we went there, and after that things have never been the same—even though it was fifteen years ago . . . but I never accepted Bettelheim. No. Nobody ever loved anything or anybody like I love this kid. I would gladly, at a moment's notice, give my life for the slightest improvement in him—I mean that. I'm doing it every day.[75]

Another, writing in 1992, described an encounter with a psychotherapist at a residential school.

> "How did you feel when you discovered you were pregnant?" he asked. "Did you want this child?"
> I felt the heat of rage rising to my head. "Yes. I did want Sean. *I still do.*" I stared at him. His eyes shifted, and he smiled slightly at something just to the left of my ear.
> "Ah, sometimes we think we want something we really don't want at all. Sometimes, you see, we are afraid of the truth."[76]

Bettelheim's Ford Foundation grant funded the anthropologist Jules Henry's research on the home environments of children with autism. Henry brought a "social-anthropological" perspective to studying the role of culture and family in the disorder.[77] The ensuing book-length report demonstrated his commitment to Bettelheim's approach. Each chapter described a pathogenic family environment, in which the ambivalence of parents generated emotional disturbances in their offspring. Henry had come to the conclusion that "we are not loving our children right."[78]

What is most striking is the complete absence of the children from Henry's account. Henry knew the children but seldom observed them interacting with their parents. He crafted explanations based on family dynamics through what one reviewer described admiringly as the work of an "intuitive psychologist."[79] As he entered their homes to observe the families, the mothers underwent psychoanalysis. At the end of the first year of the study, Bettelheim reported:

> According to our findings their most characteristic attitude is either one of "towering rage" against everyone in their family, or "humiliation run rampant," directed most of all against the child who becomes autistic. Unable to act in accordance with this rage because of guilt, they try to protect the child by emotionally totally removing themselves from him, often using empty but rigidly enforced schedules as a device to protect the child from their anger. Matters are compounded by the fact that the fathers seem to show uniformly an implacable paranoid distance from their wives.[80]

In the second year of the study, Bettelheim expanded its scope to include parents of schizophrenic children who were not in the school. By comparing them to the parents of children living at the school Bettelheim hoped to answer the question of "whether it is the nature and degree of the disturbance of the child that makes placement in a treatment institution necessary, or whether the psychology of the parents is decisive for whether or not a schizophrenic child can be treated ambulatory or requires hospitalization."[81]

While some parents resisted psychoanalytic interpretations of autism, others accepted responsibility for their child's problems—after all, if they had consciously or unconsciously caused the disorder, they might also possess the key to a cure.[82] Jules Henry wrote with some admiration of one mother's knowledge of current psychoanalytic theory.

> Mrs. Wilson—who never studied psychology and who never attended college—has such fine insight into the causes of primary infantile autism that I sometimes think I may have gotten my own theory of it from her. Her description of Donald's isolation—of his general "stimulus impoverishment"—also describes my view of the cause of this disease perfectly. And because she believes it, because she blames herself, guilt is a devil riding on her back; she gets very

little sleep, even with the aid of pills. She blames herself for leaving Donald alone, for following the directions of the pediatrician and for leaving him for two days with the sitter. Meanwhile her husband brushes all her explanations aside, as he does his own guilt. He is calm; she is almost beside herself.[83]

Henry's work enjoyed considerable influence both in his profession and in the culture at large. A reviewer in *Time* magazine zeroed in on his portrayal of families who, although they seemed "quite average," were in fact seething below the surface with poorly expressed anger. To an acute observer like Henry they offered prime examples of "shamming" performances of false emotions and love promised but ultimately withheld.[84] Henry himself emerged as "a brilliant, sensitive student of human behavior," a "prophet and scientist" who saw the human sciences as instruments of social reform.[85]

The efforts of mothers to convince professionals that their autistic children were truly—consciously and unconsciously—"wanted children" were never sufficient, as long as experts felt confident of their theories. Within the confines of the Orthogenic School, however, the origins of disability were less a concern than the needs of the individual child and the training of the therapists who worked with them.

The Therapeutic Milieu: Treating Children and Training Counselors

Bettelheim explained his approach to treating autistic children as an outcome of his life experiences, including observations of "total environments" and what he learned about human behavior in the face of powerlessness and fear. He believed that an environment that encompassed all aspects of life could produce psychological change, working as a "concentration camp in reverse," where the children were free to wander outside, but outsiders were barred from entering.[86]

> A total therapeutic setting implies a separation of the child from his family and protection against those influences coming from the outside which led to that mortal anxiety which caused the child to withdraw to the autistic position. It also demands careful study of his behavior in order to understand the hidden motives which cause it and a therapy based on this understanding.[87]

Bettelheim borrowed the idea of the therapeutic milieu together with the prescription that children should be removed from the home environment from the Austrian psychoanalyst August Aichhorn, a source that he acknowledged.[88] Bettelheim was among the first in the United States to employ a treatment milieu with emotionally disturbed children, but by the 1950s others were trying the method in a variety of settings, and with a range of disorders from schizophrenia to "mental deficiency." Psychologists in the 1950s and 1960s understood themselves as members of a profession that acted on the basis of an established body of theories and methods. Milieu therapy was one reputable, if experimental, practice that received serious attention, although the number of centers declined in later decades, partly owing to the monumental devotion required of the staff.[89]

The approach deviated significantly from the methods previously used at the Orthogenic School. Bettelheim described the school's framework for treating students and training staff in a series of articles that he coauthored with Emmy Sylvester, a consulting child psychiatrist, near the time of his appointment. Bettelheim emphasized psychoanalytic theory, but largely ignored traditional psychoanalytic technique. Instead of maintaining the school as a custodial institution, he turned it into a therapeutic and experimental environment, a place where the practice of milieu therapy could be refined but also a place where systematic insights into the children's emotional development might be obtained. Counselors worked both in child care and as research assistants. Bettelheim referred to them as "participant observers," simultaneously his protégés, research assistants, technicians, and instruments of observation.[90] Although students at the Orthogenic School had been research subjects before Bettelheim's arrival, those studies had not focused on specific diagnoses.[91] As his work at the school progressed, Bettelheim saw the opportunity for a research program built around the unique constellation of symptoms associated with one particular syndrome, autism.

In retrospect, Bettelheim's claims to have successfully treated a number of autistic children seem questionable if not willfully false. However, as Jacquelyn Sanders has suggested, autism "in the field at large" at the time was not so different from autism at the Orthogenic School, either in terms of clinical understanding or treatment practices.[92] It was Bettelheim's refusal to alter his position over time that eventually relegated him and his approach to the margins of the profession. Sanders argues that it is important to understand the context in which Bettelheim and his staff attempted to treat children with autism and other emotional disturbances. These interventions, directed at children who to readers today clearly suffered from neurological disorders, were carried out with the utmost seriousness and sincerity. Most significantly, in their work as both trained counselors and surrogate parents, the staff of the Orthogenic School did not emphasize Bettelheim's framework of mortal fear and maternal ambivalence. Caught up in the daily effort of caring for and working to understand autistic children, their labor drew on their empathy and identification with the children.

Bettelheim's practices at the school came under attack after his suicide, when counselors came forward to condemn his violent disciplinary techniques.[93] Former counselors at the Orthogenic School, troubled by the degree of vitriol directed at Bettelheim and by implication their own work, have situated their mentor's beliefs and their own in the context of the therapeutic milieu, their training as counselors, and the specific program Bettelheim committed to under the terms of his Ford Foundation grant. Jacquelyn Sanders was a "counselor and assistant" for fourteen years, during which time she received a doctorate in psychology. She succeeded Bettelheim as director of the school.

> In November of 1952 I began my first intensive engagement with an autistic child. My first memory is of his back as he leaned over the drinking fountain and Joanne, a senior counselor, spoke gently to him while I watched with admiring fascination, both the counselor and the child. At that time what autism meant to me was simply the extreme of my own deeply introspective tendencies, coupled with a refusal to engage in communication. I was convinced that guided by my empathic understanding I would overcome that refusal. I was one of a group of unrealistic but devoted optimists.[94]

Most exciting of all, "the least trained—the counselors (i.e., childcare workers)—were viewed as being pivotal in the success of this wonderful enterprise. It was thrilling to be a part of it." The end of the experiment was heartbreaking.[95] After years of intensive therapy children that she had worked with closely were transferred to custodial institutions. Her observations suggest that Bettelheim did not persist in his beliefs merely out of stubbornness. For the school staff, the approach to autism was part and parcel of a worldview that gave profound meaning to their hours of work and guided decisions from the choice of art on the school walls to the arrangement of seats in the dining room.

Bettelheim drew on the cases of the school's autistic children in his writing on the school, but what he and the counselors meant by "autism" is complicated, as Sanders's recollection suggests. As we saw in chapter 1, many clinicians used the terms "childhood schizophrenia," and, as in the case of

Joey, "autistic tendencies," almost interchangeably until at least the late 1970s, much to the consternation of professionals concerned with psychiatric nosology. Karen Zelan, a counselor who worked with many of the children, maintained that Betteleheim's criteria fit Kanner's 1943 definition of autism, including children who were "symptomatic" but not mentally retarded.[96]

However, Bettelheim and his staff treated autism as a symptom rather than a biological category. The school depended on the ability of the counselors to "put themselves in the position of the children" meaning that the symbolic worlds of the children could be comprehended and that they mattered to treatment. For example, Bettelheim praised Karen Zelan for adapting her footsteps to those of "Marcia," an autistic girl who feared crossing the street.[97] Similarly, the staff knew not to disturb Joey's elaborate system of motors and wires. Bettelheim explained the children's language problems as the outcomes of emotional blockages. This attention to the symbolic meanings of actions made heavy demands on the patience of therapists who had to attend to every nuance of a child's behavior. Ultimately, the counselors' practices and the quality of their interactions mattered more than theories about disease mechanisms, with the exception of the foundational assumptions that behaviors had meaning and that healing required a process of interaction between counselors and children.

Autistic children cultivated what Bettelheim identified as "passionate indifference." They only appeared unconcerned with their surroundings and relationships, where in fact they cared so deeply that they feared expressing it. Likewise, Bettelheim urged his counselors to develop an equivalent attitude of committed detachment, which would permit them to withstand physical assaults from the children while maintaining an absolute devotion to the project of curing them. Bettelheim believed that the counselors would do so in part because of "all the narcissistic and interpersonal rewards" they received from their central role in the children's treatment.[98] Bettelheim and Emmy Sylvester encouraged counselors to see themselves as the primary therapists for the children, the "crucial ones" who "got all the credit for whatever happened to the kids."[99] Many former counselors testified to their participation in the life of the school as a learning experience of the utmost value. A shared psychoanalytic perspective, evident in their interpretation of cases at the time as much as in their recollections decades later, shaped the collective ethos. Bettelheim saw these two components—total devotion on the part of the counselors and a "consistent therapeutic philosophy"—as critical to the creation of the school's unique milieu.[100]

In Bettelheim's reports to the Ford Foundation, he presented autism as a means to understand typical development. All twelve of the original children in the study—Bettelheim referred to having observed "over forty" children overall—were given a clinical diagnosis of "childhood schizophrenia, autistic type," and Bettelheim and his staff observed them closely, sometimes filming them. Because Bettelheim believed that autism represented an instance of development halted early in life, a successful cure would allow children to resume a normal course of progress. The counselors spent their days recording the steps the children took toward health, and in doing so observed a process that was normally hidden or at least unobserved, because changes happened quickly in typical children, and at a much younger age.[101] If Bettelheim could understand the halted developmental pathway in autism he would be capable of inferring from this to the progress of typical personality and ego development.[102] According to the models of psychological development current at the time, personality and ego development proceeded in much the same fashion as physiological development, along a predefined course. Deviations from this course, whether as a result of heredity, faulty parenting, or injury, inevitably led to harmful outcomes.

The five-year Ford Foundation grant of $342,500 (about $2,685,000 in 2008, a significant sum for the school) awarded in 1956–1962, involved several components. Bettelheim and his team would study "formation of personality in autistic children" and the "family background" of the children. "But," noted an interim progress report, "the most important study will simply seek to learn what it is that this school does that works, so that its success in dealing with a tragic problem may be duplicated more readily elsewhere."[103] In other words, Ford had funded a study not of autism but of treatment methods. Bettelheim thus may have felt pressured to present positive results to the grant committee in his yearly reports and in his research culminating in *The Empty Fortress* in 1967.[104]

The total environment of the school—the commitment and emotional labor required of the counselors, the emphasis on the ability of the environment to alter both students and teachers alike, and the holistic focus on daily life as an avenue to healing—all made the school a special type of social and therapeutic technology. Turning the school into an environment that seemed more like a home than a hospital represented a fundamental change in treatment strategy. Bettelheim and his colleagues also took seriously the idea that "the primary agents of treatment were the people who were with the children in their daily activities—the counselors who were with the children during all of their waking out of class hours, and the teachers."[105] Psychiatrists served as consultants, but played a supportive rather than central role at the school.[106] In addition, Bettelheim brought his charismatic personality and his desire to make meaningful contributions to studies of treatment methods, although he insisted that research not overshadow the goal of individualized treatment.

There is little doubt that the Orthogenic School was a unique environment. Some former students have written warmly of their experiences. Bettelheim explained that for a student "to live in an institutional setting which protects him against the vagaries of life, and in which contrary to his past experiences, those people important to him are characterized by a deep commitment to his physical and emotional needs—this in a slow process should heal his diseased mind."[107] The physical space of the school reflected Bettelheim's vision. Visitors remarked on the beauty of the grounds and the welcoming interior, comfortable furniture, and fine china used to serve meals. Bettelheim believed that the surroundings encouraged the children to treat their environment with care. At the same time, they might feel respected in a way that many did not in their lives outside the school. Bettelheim worked to create "a setting whose smallest detail was inspired by the recognition [of] psychoanalysis that implicit meanings must be made explicit in terms of their significance for the lives of children." Staff at the school recalled that they "sort of fell in love with the place."[108]

The therapeutic milieu produced a strange kind of asylum, a fact not lost on observers. The Orthogenic School had roots in the design of Victorian-era mental institutions that equated a calming built environment with mental order, but Bettelheim introduced some crucial modifications and revisions.[109] The children could leave the grounds at any time, but visitors needed permission to enter. The institution protected those living there from real and imagined threats outside the gates, even as the staff encouraged independence. Bettelheim's school had none of the oppressive restraints common to other institutions. Classrooms were bright and cheerful spaces, and students could keep toys and other belongings with them in the dormitories.[110]

Bettelheim stood unquestioned at its center, exerting what all accounts agree was an awesome force in his overlapping roles as parent figure, interpreter, disciplinarian, instructor, and architect, a "cross between a janitor . . . and a policeman," he said.[111] As a former counselor reported,

> Bettelheim functioned as a sort of superego. He expected every child to work hard to solve its problems. He oversaw the institution as a whole, for example, by making rounds every evening as the children were put to bed and by conducting daily staff meetings where he not only searched a child's behavior for meaning but also brilliantly instructed the child's "central persons."[112]

This absolute authority may explain the extreme reactions to Bettelheim on the part of staff members. As I noted, they tended either to treat him with great loyalty, crediting him with aiding in the formation of their present selves, or to reject him entirely.[113]

The counselors were frequently young, unmarried, and female, adept at the work of emotional involvement and attentiveness. Child care was considered "a woman's job."[114] They often had little prior experience in the psychoanalytic or psychiatric professions. Some, like Jacquelyn Sanders, went on to obtain clinical degrees. Others married and moved on. Still others spent their entire careers at the school. At a facility that was as much an educational environment for the teachers as it was a therapeutic environment for the students, some had difficulty identifying the boundary between training and therapy.

Each staffer underwent daily debriefings with "Dr. B," and given Bettelheim's propensity to regard any conflicts arising between students and counselors as a dyadic process involving contributions from both parties, the distinction between debriefing and psychoanalysis may have been a thin one. Bettelheim encouraged his staff members to see how their own emotional lives affected interactions with the students. As the "ego supports" for children whose ego functioning had "lapsed," they were literally incorporated into the emotional and psychological structure of the school.[115] Bettelheim suggested that transference, that is, the projection of unresolved issues in a counselor's unconscious life onto Bettelheim, began inevitably from the moment of the initial employment interview.

Bettelheim wanted teachers to review their interactions with children in terms of their own anxieties and fears. In some cases, he used psychological tests to evaluate them as their work progressed.[116] Counselors were taught that in the course of their work they might undergo countertransference, acting out their own unresolved emotional issues with the students. They learned to assume that a student's misbehavior might be a response to his or her counselor's own disordered behavior. Many remember feats of interpretive virtuosity on the part of Bettelheim, in which he helped staff members realize that a student's aggressive action resulted from their own failures to act in accordance with the child's needs. Bettelheim relentlessly criticized his teachers and they in turn measured his confidence in their performance by the harshness of his critiques.

If the work of the counselors resembled the routine of an introspective and responsive parent, it brought with it the same hazards that Bettelheim often ascribed to parental love. *The Empty Fortress* recounts Laurie's "collapse" and "total withdrawal from the world," precipitated by a counselor's ambivalence. The counselor's "bondage to her own needs and desires" led her to "misread" Laurie's intentions.[117] Bettelheim purposely chose counselors who had not undergone analysis themselves because he believed that their unresolved conflicts with their parents enabled them to identify with the students in ways that ultimately helped both to learn and mature. He explained the surprise of one counselor, "Jane," to a student's relief after being disciplined. Jane had been overly permissive in the past because she empathized with the girl's feelings of anger toward her mother.[118] Jane gained confidence as a therapist, but only by coming to terms with the unfinished business of her own childhood.

Jules Henry, the anthropologist who observed the staff as part of his research on "ideo-emotional" factors in institutional membership, and whom Jacquelyn Sanders remembered from her early years at the school, saw the social structure of the Orthogenic School as a welcome antidote to the detachment of staff members in the "contemporary psychiatric hospital."[119] The milieu model was a remedy for the disinterest and detachment chronicled by observers of state institutions of the period, one of many shortcomings that seemed to justify their wholesale closure in the following decade.[120] Ten years after Henry's visit, another group comparing the effectiveness of state institutions against therapeutic milieus came to a similar conclusion. Compared to custodial care, the intimate setting of a "psychoanalytically-oriented day-care unit which emphasizes the emotional relationship between staff and children" offered a far better opportunity for behavioral improvements. It did not appear to matter that many of the program's theoretical premises fit autistic children poorly if at all.[121]

Henry concluded that success at an institution like the Orthogenic School required absolute emotional and personal commitment to the therapeutic project. He argued that the intense involvement of the counselors in the lives of their patients was the only thing that could explain their long tenures at a school that paid them little, yet made relentless emotional and psychological demands.

> Another consequence of the deep mutual involvement of counselor and child is that most of the counselor's energies go into the children. The following question must now be answered: Given the exacting nature of the counselor's task, from where does she derive the necessary strength and incentive to carry on?[122]

Counselors found rewards in the form of their own growing autonomy through the process of "self-seeking" as they worked with the children. The school formed a system in which children, director, and counselors all played critical and interrelated roles. "In the School the children are in the center of the therapeutic and *emotional* interest; for the successful counselor the child remains the focus of her emotional life for a long time."[123]

Jacquelyn Sanders described the functioning of the educational aspects of the school under her guidance in terms that reflected Bettelheim's own accounts. In the introduction to her book, evocatively titled *A Greenhouse for the Mind,* Sanders recalled that "we created a world for them based on our understanding of the theory of psychoanalytic ego psychology, on anything else that any of us might know, and on the dictates of our hearts."[124] For Sanders, techniques emerged intuitively, based on evolving self-understanding and close observations of the counselor's own interactions with troubled children. The children established strong connections with individual workers, with whom the long-term therapeutic relationship progressed day and night. If these relationships were understood both by workers and students in psychoanalytic terms, it was still the relationship that held meaning and resided at the center of the school's practices.

The Politics of Treatability

Bettelheim made autism stand for childhood disorders in general—as the model through which the therapeutic milieu would be tested—and, through his interpretations, for modern forms of psychopathology. Thus, any concessions to arguments about the neurological basis of autism potentially undermined his entire research program. His commitments were not only to his theory of autism, but to a psychoanalytic perspective on development and survival. If autism was organic, it was also fixed and inalterable, a failure of neurons and not attachment. For Bettelheim, there really was no choice. Even though he allowed that vulnerabilities might predispose one child and not another to develop autism, his successes in treating the disorder proved the correctness of a psychogenic interpretation. "It is only when, after years of frustrated attempts, these children begin slowly to respond to treatment efforts based on psychoanalytically oriented hypotheses on the nature of the disturbance, that the psychogenic explanation becomes more and more convincing."[125]

Bettelheim nonetheless found others much less convinced than he was by his account of autism. Bernard Rimland was one. Following the 1964 publication of *Infantile Autism*, Rimland emerged as a major figure in his own right, who, unlike Bettelheim, defined himself by the heterogeneity of his theories and practical commitments rather than by his adherence to a single approach.[126] Bettelheim seemed relatively unconcerned with how his theories were applied within the psychoanalytic community or by general practitioners in their interactions with parents of autistic children. As a parent himself, Rimland knew how parents' encounters with medical authorities who saw in their hunger for information only further evidence of their "cold intellectuality" deprived them of the confidence they needed to help their children.[127]

The two engaged in an uncomfortable correspondence between 1965 and 1966 in which they debated how best to treat autism. For Rimland, the stakes were high. Psychotherapeutic approaches competed with behavioral treatments and biomedical research for scarce resources and professional attention. In a lecture that he presented to chapters of the National Society for Autistic Children between 1967 and 1970, Rimland rehearsed the conclusions of a number of experts that parents were not the cause of learning and behavioral disorders, and that psychotherapy had failed to help children with autism.

> The psychogenic theory has cast blame on the parents, and thus immobilized the child's strongest ally in what should be his struggle to recover. It has caused stagnation in research—which biochemist wants to analyze a "fractured oedipus complex?" It has caused educators to shrug their shoulders and leave the problem in the hands of the psychiatrists, psychologists and social workers. It has cost families untold fortunes in money, time, convenience and human dignity. And, worst of all, it has cost far too many children their lives. Such children are not medically dead—just psychologically dead, existing like human vegetables in institution after institution.[128]

Bettelheim and Rimland's correspondence began before Bettelheim published *The Empty Fortress*. Rimland sent Bettelheim a version of his "Diagnostic Check List for Behavior Disturbed Children," a device initially designed to refine diagnoses, but which Rimland hoped would eventually guide treatment based on a child's unique symptom profile.[129] It signified Rimland's conviction that an "impersonal checklist" was an instrument equivalent in worth to a "personal clinical impression," the authority that Bettlheim relied on for his own diagnoses. [130] He asked Bettelheim to help him obtain blood samples from autistic children. Bettelheim refused. "I regret to inform you that I am very critical of the approach that you are using to study infantile autism. In my opinion your book contains gross errors and misstatements. I therefore shall give you no help in a study of autistic children which I consider ill-conceived and based on erroneous and biased judgments."[131] In response to another letter, he told Rimland that "since you seem committed to the convictions that infantile autism is an inborn disease and incurable, no matter what the contrary evidence may be, I see little point in discussing treatment results. Suffice it to say that better than eighty-five percent of our former students have made an adequate adjustment to life, including some who are your and my colleagues as Ph.D.'s in psychology."[132] Despite the fact that Rimland was indeed quite interested in treating autism, Bettelheim found it impossible to believe that he could be genuinely committed to identifying treatment strategies given his view that autism was a neurological disorder.

After publishing *Infantile Autism* in 1964, Rimland began working on a follow-up volume on treatments, and he wrote to Bettelheim in 1966 with another request: "I propose that we set the precedent—pretty nearly unheard of in polemics—of granting each other a small section of response room [at] the end of each of our forthcoming books."[133] Bettelheim's angry response stood in marked contrast to his customary cordial style with parents and former patients. "The idea that after you have written a book, I should write something within its covers to detract from it is repellent to me. You see, feelings are unimportant to you, and to me they are the most important thing in dealing with human beings. But the most important reason is that I abhor arguments. I firmly believe that scientific progress is best made by each man stating his opinions and allowing the present and future generations to decide on their merits."[134]

His position was unchanged in the late 1970s when he co-taught a graduate seminar at Stanford. In one exchange, Bettelheim responded to a question asked by "Dan Berenson," a child psychiatrist working with autistic children, modeled on the child psychologist Bryna Siegel.[135] Siegel was planning a study of symptomatically similar autistic children with the hope of identifying an underlying biochemical marker. Bettelheim criticized this approach because it required an experimental protocol that, he suggested, treated the children merely as a means of fulfilling the researchers' agenda. The discovery of a "molecular oddity" would legitimize the tendency to view these children as "alien." If this happened, their actions could be seen as unsusceptible to sympathetic and individualized interpretation. Declaring these children biologically abnormal would be an unforgivable demonstration of the "laziness of the heart." "Isn't that laziness what prevents people from having empathy with these children's terrible suffering?"[136]

Eric Schopler, a clinical psychologist who went on to found Division TEACCH, the first statewide autism treatment program in the United States, said Bettelheim similarly "rebuffed" and "ridiculed" him when he asked for help with his doctoral research on neurological factors in autism.[137] After visiting the Orthogenic School, Schopler concluded that Bettelheim had "scapegoated" parents to make up for a lack of empirical research about the condition.[138] By 1974, as editor of the *Journal of Autism and Childhood Schizophrenia*, Schopler's editorial policies effectively downplayed psychogenic theories of autism by emphasizing "objective experimental studies" and "objective clinical data," and by directly soliciting parents' insights and responses to research.[139]

Why Bettelheim so adamantly refused to alter his position with respect to autism is a difficult question to answer. He oversaw an apparently productive research program in autism at a moment when psychology was struggling to create an identity for itself as a scientific profession with proven outcomes.[140] He had invested considerable time and money to build a staff trained in and committed to his treatment method. The Orthogenic School and its students was a rich resource that the prolific writer continued to exploit. Not least, his methods appeared to do some good, both for the students and for Bettelheim and the staff. This efficacy matters a great deal to understanding Bettelheim within his own milieu. It is not necessary to dismiss the pain that Bettelheim's theories caused parents to recognize that if he ruled harshly, his realm was still very small, and others bear responsibility for the broader application of psychogenic theories.

Other Psychotherapies, Other Autisms

By the 1970s claims about the efficacy of any therapy had to contend with the assumption that damage to brains in autism was congenital. Even before autism was reclassified in the educational system from an emotional to a developmental disorder, parents had come to understand their children's disabilities as outcomes of brain function rather than psychology. The transition from a psychoanalytic interpretation of the disorder to neurological and genetic accounts of etiology represented a new way of relating to these children and thinking about interventions on their behalf. The gradual decline of psychoanalytic thought in American culture makes it difficult to imagine a context in which inquiring and observant adults believed in milieu therapy as an effective treatment or believed that parents of autistic children needed psychotherapeutic treatment themselves. That a child need only eat from a counselor's hand or that a counselor need only listen sympathetically to a child's private language to effect positive change nevertheless made sense within the context of Bettelheim's school.

Our desire to avoid similar mistakes is one reason that it is important to understand Bettelheim's work, but there are other reasons why it is crucial to look at the role of Bettelheim, the popular appeal of his work, and the social organization of the Orthogenic School. Bettelheim epitomized the psychological perspective on autism during the first two decades that the diagnosis existed. This perspective encouraged an attitude toward the mothers of children with autism that exists even now and that informs the contemporary activities of parent advocacy groups. Unlike parents of children with other disorders more clearly marked as genetic or due to pre- or neonatal injury, such as cerebral palsy, parents of children with autism dealt with stigma through the 1950s, 1960s, and much of the 1970s. That stigma continues to exist albeit with subtle variations. Today professionals may suggest that parents manifest mild symptoms of autism themselves, and that their seeking after cures is a kind of "perseveration." Other experts continue to see parents as unresponsive, if only as a result of their child's own detachment. These writers understand rage, distress, and energetic self-education as defenses against the obvious fact of a child's disability, symptoms rather than reasonable responses.

The ideas that underpinned Bettelheim's experiment in Chicago and that helped to legitimize his work, including attachment theory, maternal deprivation, milieu therapy, and the role of parent–child interaction in cognitive development, all existed prior to Bettelheim's influential run as an authority on autism. They persisted long after his reputation in that field declined. That complex legacy has cast a long shadow over the tradition of psychoanalytic work with autism in the United States. Its proponents have understood their theories about the social or familial environment as a cause of mental illness to be a progressive alternative to those that emphasized an individual's temperament or heredity. In contrast, their theories seemed to offer the possibility of successful treatment through interventions in the family or educational environment, drawing scrutiny away from the individual patient's deviance. Symptoms might represent a logical response to a pathogenic situation.

The specter of Bettelheim may haunt autism research and advocacy, but psychoanalytic approaches to treating autism were never his project alone. Bettelheim's worldview was one among many examples of postwar attitudes toward childrearing, including an intense focus on development of selfhood and the growth of autonomy, and critiques of behaviorism's focus on innate tendencies and patterned responses. Many others shared a psychoanalytic perspective on mental disorders, of which autism was understood to represent a classic case. The child psychologists Mira Rothenberg and Virginia

Axline, like Bettelheim, located the source of autism in early experiences that made children either literally or metaphorically fear for their lives. Both published books that were warmly received by professional colleagues and popular audiences and remained in print for decades.[141] Contemporary psychiatric approaches to autism still seek to interpret symptoms as meaningful communicative behavior and to unpack the effect of parent–child bonding. In other countries, psychoanalytic approaches to autism remain standard and institutionalized, into the present, even when psychiatrists have adopted a biological interpretation of autism's causes.[142] Bettelheim's protégé, Karen Zelan, uses many of his methods in her own therapeutic work, abandoning only his insistence on a purely psychogenic explanation for autism.[143]

For Bettelheim, the counselors at the Orthogenic School, and his many readers, love took work and, even then, it was often "not enough" unless combined with interpretive acumen and clear-eyed introspection. Bettelheim did not question that parents loved their autistic children. He merely, devastatingly, maintained that they loved them incorrectly. Counselors at the school, in contrast, might not even have described their relationships with the students in terms of love, but they almost certainly would have identified the detailed, empathic responsiveness of their interactions with the students as key to any successes they witnessed. Jacquelyn Sanders pointed to underlying similarities between different approaches when she recalled films of a treatment based on operant conditioning, where "the therapist practicing a conditioning protocol would treat the youngster in very much the same way as we would at the Orthogenic School in terms of respect and empathic sensitivity, but . . . would report only on the conditioning techniques," suggesting a difference of emphasis and perspective more than of practice.[144] Indeed, while the Orthogenic School continues to provide individualized psychotherapy, small classroom environments, and resident counselors, it has now "adapted its milieu" to incorporate both the positive reinforcements more often associated with behavior modification techniques and "detailed psychopharmacological assessment and treatment."[145]

We can also read Bettelheim's story as a cautionary tale about analytical frameworks and passionate commitments in biomedicine today. It reminds us that social and environmental contingencies affect the perceived efficacy of any therapeutic modality. Despite claims for universality and objectivity, biomedical knowledge can be both situated and pluralistic in practice, drawing on multiple and contradictory ways of thinking about disease and difference. Bettelheim's conviction that one might temper reason with love and his insistence that emotion stood at the heart of rational scientific practice might sound unfamiliar to practitioners of contemporary autism research.

Observers inclined to equate reliance on affect with the abdication of reason might even see the seeds of Bettelheim's downfall in the claim. Still, we should consider seriously his conviction that his methods worked and that affective work lay at the heart of their efficacy. "The daring heart must invade reason with its own living warmth, even if the symmetry of reason must give way to admit love and the pulsation of life." [146] While this might sound like an impractical demand to those committed to a view of biomedicine that divorces reason from affective commitments, it remains a reasonably accurate description of biomedical and therapeutic work in practice.

Psychoanalysis offered an explanation for autism that worked until it failed to cure. That failure notwithstanding, it founded research schools, generated funds for investigators, and offered a systematic means of comprehending previously inexplicable, severe disorders of development. An emphasis on the contingent rather than fixed factors in development recurs in contemporary discussions of both gene–environment interactions and therapeutic modalities. Sanders believes that "the accounts that describe reliable treatment are remarkably similar to the practices of the Orthogenic School with autistic children. Shock treatment, facilitated communication and the like come and go, but the need for an intense involvement of a whole environment over a long period of time remains." [147] She is not alone. Another psychoanalytically oriented clinician, Bertrand Ruttenberg, argued in 1976 that "among good programs—i.e., those which were sensitive to the behaviors and needs of the children and which were skillfully implemented by a dedicated and attentive staff—there was little evidence of differences in therapeutic effectiveness regardless of whether the therapy was behavior modification, education, psychoanalytically oriented relationship therapy, or activity therapy." [148]

As Bettelheim noted, at a time when his colleagues still believed him, love alone could not secure such intense involvement. The work required discipline and expertise. Structured therapeutic techniques and the caring and labor involved in creating them are the topic that I turn to next.

3

Expert Amateurs: Raising and Treating

Children with Autism

This is a love story, and it begins with a sensitive child. Benjamin ("Ben") Lettick was born on April 7, 1955. He was the fourth child of Amy and Birney Lettick of New Haven, Connecticut. Amy Lettick had trained as a schoolteacher before her marriage to Birney, a portrait artist. Their son Ben suffered from severe food allergies almost from birth. Amy Lettick took the susceptibilities of her youngest in stride. Dealing with the allergies of her three older children had armed her with strategies for treating him, including keeping a detailed record of diet, immunizations, and reactions. Her diary entries indicate the delicate balances that had to be achieved.

> Feb. 17 David—one pimple on cheek. Had liver today??
> Mar 17 Gave Sharon cooked carrot. Skin on arms & legs improved.
> June 7 S had ¼ c. raisins. <u>Terrible</u> hives all over body.
>   Gave benedryl.
>   No more raisins for anybody![1]

It soon became clear that Benjamin Lettick had developmental problems far beyond those of a typical, if delicate, child. Although he developed on schedule for the first six months, he then "grew very quiet" and began to sleep for most of the day. Lettick, trained in education, knew what normal behavior looked like. The "peppy, smiling, chubby baby" turned into an unsmiling child who no longer seemed to recognize anyone, including his mother.[2] At eight months, Ben's pediatrician told Lettick he suspected that her son was retarded and referred him to the Yale Child Study Center in New Haven for evaluation.

After the doctor's crushing assessment, Lettick was relieved when the director of the Autism Unit at the Child Study Center diagnosed Ben with autism. At the time most parents, Lettick included, had little understanding of the disorder save that it seemed better than the more serious and irreversible diagnosis of mental retardation. Ben received psychotherapy, the standard practice at the time, between the ages of two and a half and six, when his therapist recommended discontinuing the treatment. His behavior and responsiveness to people had improved, but he had failed to learn to talk, and it was unclear whether he understood spoken words at all.[3]

For Lettick, this admission of defeat by the staff at the Yale Child Study Center seemed more devastating than the original diagnosis, but it led her to learn more about autism and eventually to seek advice and training from Newell Kephart at Purdue University. Kephart, in turn, inspired Lettick to found a school and then a residential program for her son and others like him. Over the course of the next four decades, Lettick developed an educational program for Ben through her own research at the Yale University Library and information provided by other mothers of children with autism, many of whom were seeking help for their children through early versions of behavioral therapy. She helped found the National Society for Autistic Children (NSAC, later the Autism Society of America), and she founded Benhaven, one of the first lifespan-oriented residential programs for children and adults with autism.

Although Lettick's energy and determination were exceptional, her experiences were tied to those of many parents during the 1960s and 1970s who often found themselves with few resources other than each other in learning to treat their children. During the 1950s, parents of children diagnosed with mental retardation had successfully lobbied for special education classrooms and other forms of support in their efforts to keep their children at home and out of institutions, often against the recommendations of psychologists.[4] Parents of children with autism in the 1960s and 1970s faced many of the same difficulties, made worse because autism was still viewed as an emotional disorder rather than a cognitive disability. Several founded schools and treatment programs in response to the overwhelming lack of resources.[5] Lettick's work as an institution builder distinguishes her. However, she consistently described her efforts as a succession of pragmatic responses to Ben's needs as he grew older—in other words, as the understandable consequences of her commitment to her child.

Parents' accounts of their work during a period when the diagnostic category of autism was in flux identify their unique authority as caregivers and "amateur" therapeutic practitioners. They claim an expertise that is well defined, but never quite professional. The most successful behavior programs took place in highly controlled environments. Parents did the work of translating them into elements of daily life in domestic spaces. In many cases, this transformation of everyday familiarity into everyday authority began as an opposition to psychologists who ignored them and experts who offered only dire prognoses. However, even as parents were developing their own therapeutic strategies, psychologists were working to incorporate parents into the programs that they were designing themselves.

Lettick said that she and other parents were compelled to become "paraprofessionals."[6] This idea lies at the center of the practice of what is now called applied behavior analysis (ABA) and related behavioral therapies derived from operant conditioning, as well as other developmental education programs. In the 1970s, professionals in child psychology adopted the methodology of parental participation. Leo Kanner recognized that

> parents are beginning to be dealt with from the point of view of mutuality, rather than as people standing at one end of a parent–child bipolarity; they have of late been included in the therapeutic efforts, not as etiological culprits, nor merely as recipients of drug prescriptions and of thou-shalt and thou-shalt-not rules, but as actively contributing cotherapists.[7]

Amy Lettick never published the story of her son's development and her search for treatments, although she wrote several books about Benhaven.[8] Other parents did write about their own experiences of raising children with autism, using terms that are remarkably similar despite the distance of decades that separated them. Noah Jiro Greenfeld, the subject of Josh Greenfeld's memoir *A Child Called Noah*, was born a decade after Benjamin Lettick in 1966. Raun Kahlil Kaufman, the subject of *Son-Rise* and its sequel, was born in the early 1970s, and Catherine Maurice's memoir *Let Me Hear Your Voice* takes place in the mid 1980s—and these are only a representative sample of some of the most widely read books. These books show that the transformation of parents into technicians is far from straightforward. Indeed, they make visible some longstanding contradictions in the distinction between what Americans understand to be therapeutic expertise and what they call acts of love. Parents both gain and lose when they use the category of personal experience to emphasize their authority, just as there can be contradictions in therapeutic programs that train parents as "cotherapists" and "paraprofessionals," amateurs at research but experts on their own children.

The term "amateur" has been central to parents' accounts of their work. It serves at once as a demure renunciation of expertise and a claim about commitment and particularity of knowledge. Catherine Maurice recalled,

> Once when I sent a mother to one of the early-intervention programs in New York to try to recruit some therapists for her home program, she reported back to me that the director had informed her that it was "illegal and unethical" for "amateurs" to be attempting this kind of work.
>
> We parents *are* amateurs, in the true sense of the word: amateurs are lovers. We are lovers of our children, and until the professional community can offer us more effective programs, we will often have to take matters into our own hands.[9]

More than two decades earlier, Clara Claiborne Park wrote about the differences between parents and professionals as she reflected on her daughter Jessy's first eight years. When daily life constitutes a series of ongoing, experimental interventions, determining who is a reliable witness of a child's behavior or the efficacy of a treatment can be complicated.[10] Parents seem both materially and emotionally invested in the development of their own children, while professionals seem dispassionate and uninvolved. However, Park intimated, professionals' interest in autism as a clinical entity gave them commitments far more dangerous than the caring partiality of parents.

When Park wrote in 1967, psychiatrists and psychologists would "seldom welcome parents as co-workers" or see them as potential therapists because of the "handicaps inherent in their position," when "detachment is necessary for wise action." Nevertheless, Park continued, the handicaps of parents may be "counterbalanced by special advantages that even the most gifted psychiatrists cannot match." Park listed these advantages, including a familiarity with their child's developmental trajectory and current behaviors that rivaled any doctor's, the continuous therapeutic opportunities offered by the activities of daily life, and their own biological kinship with the child, including shared personality traits and milder forms of the same symptoms. Conscious that they were not professionals and constantly made aware of the variety and changeability of their child's behavior, the also had a "certain humility" that professionals often lacked.[11]

Park left the most important asset until last, not even quite including it in her list. "I have not dared to set down in my list of advantages a parent's love for his child. Love is not only not enough—we have almost been persuaded to admit that it is a disadvantage. Yet I cannot think that we are disqualified for working with our child because we love her. Detachment and objectivity are techniques too and can be learned."[12] Park reflected on her own experience interacting with professionals, noting that Bettelheim may have been right in claiming that "love is not enough"—certainly, and "one must know *how* to love as well." Love is a form of expertise or, in Park's words, a "technique" that is given the name of empathy, transference, or knowledge when it translated into expert terms. It is, above all, an attitude of reflecting on the needs of another and translating those inner states into facts that can be acted upon, and it is a skill that can be refined. Park wrote that "physicians of the soul do the thousands of afflicted children no service if they undermine the confidence of their parents in what they can accomplish by intelligent love. Intelligence and love are not natural enemies. Nothing sharpens one's wits for the hints and shadows of another's thinking as love does—as anyone who has been in love can testify," and she concluded that "love is a technique as well as an emotion." [13]

In a book about the daily operation of Benhaven, Amy Lettick included a talk on raising a severely disabled child at home. In choosing to keep one's child at home and with the family, parents were left with little support, isolated in their decisions about how best to care for their children.

> The last thing I want to say is that what *all children but particularly ours need is love.* About four weeks ago a young teacher came to school and she was telling us about her school. She said that the key word in their school, the word that guided them through everything, was the word "Love."
>
> I told her that that wasn't the key word in our school. The key word was "help."
>
> We were really both saying the same thing, except that I think that "Help" is more positive, a more positive way of expressing your love than just showing affection. Love can't really accomplish much unless it is fed into action.[14]

For Bettelheim, the insufficiency of love pointed the way to the reflexive and interactive healing processes of psychoanalytic principles applied in a therapeutic milieu. Amy Lettick's emphasis was similarly site specific and pragmatic. Love was essential, but it was ineffective without appropriate application and practice. Lettick reminded her audience that the techniques that helped children were acts of caring empathy backed by knowledge of a child's needs, not mere affection. Simple and unpracticed affection might actually cause harm. As Josh Greenfeld, another parent-turned-author concluded, "Love is caring enough to teach obedience."[15]

The work of parents entailed incorporating expert knowledge and research into daily routines. Commitment in the form of love helped justify shaping everyday life around therapeutic techniques, but it was not necessarily the substance of the treatments themselves. Like the work of counselors at the Orthogenic School, parents' work was characterized by situated efficacy. They achieved results through emotional and cognitive labor in particular settings, among specific communities.

Although many parents have written about professionals who resented their intrusion into expert domains, designers of treatment programs also emphasized the centrality of parental involvement in the daily tasks of treatment. Eric Schopler, who with Robert Reichler pioneered a therapeutic program during the 1970s that explicitly incorporated parents' insights, thought that a number of factors explained the reluctance of professionals to speak frankly with parents. Professionals may have intuited that parents would "resist" their psychoanalytic interpretations of parental culpability in their children's autism. They also believed that telling parents about "indications of brain damage" in addition to autistic symptoms would discourage them. Not least, professionals felt the need to preserve their status by maintaining terms of the art such as IQ scores as "top secret," even if IQ scores ideally correlate to performance in everyday life, something that is "usually no secret from parents anyhow." Knowledge about their child's condition and explicit involvement in their treatment enabled parents to "react, think, and feel more rationally about their child." Parents' initial dismay at their child's diagnosis caused far less harm than ill-advised "professional attempts to protect them."[16]

O. Ivar Lovaas's research at the UCLA Psychology Department's Autism Clinic beginning in the mid-1960s formed the direct or indirect basis for much of the work done on structured behavior modification with autistic children. For Lovaas and his team in the Young Autism Project, parents offset the "situationality" of children's gains, a liability of a largely clinic-based approach. Without including the home environment, children would never learn to generalize the skills that they were taught. Furthermore, parents were already a "child's primary language teachers."[17]

Martin Kozloff, arguing in 1973 for the importance of parent training, explained that "systematic efforts are made to teach parents to be teacher-therapists in programs for educating, treating, or socializing their children." Parental involvement was necessary for psychosocial development and treatment as were parents' "extensive and detailed *practical* knowledge of their children's strengths, impairments, capacities, learning needs and preferences." In the absence of "timely and adequate parent training," there was a danger that a child's impairments might worsen as a family's re-sources and strength wore thin. There were also simply not enough trained professionals to serve autistic children.[18]

As skilled practitioners who nevertheless lacked a professional iden-tity, parents have had to justify their credibility and authority in order to be taken seriously. They often used conventional, well-established meth-ods, for example, behavioral programs. Their work was informed by then current beliefs about normal bonding, child development, learning, and communication. The work also depended on highly specific knowledge of particular children. In this sense, successful behavioral programs required both affective commitment and "situated knowledge" formed through a close relationship with one child. This type of knowledge is by definition partial in both senses of the term, where partial refers to both an incom-plete point of view and the state of caring and being invested.[19] Although the content of parental expertise depends on context, the terms are re-markably similar: attention, the quotidian patterns of care, and the impor-tance of similarities among family members. Love is an advantage and a technique rather than a liability.

Life's Work

Amy Lettick saw her diary as a record not only of her son's growth but also of her own progress from young mother to parent of a child with autism to determined educator and eventual administrator. Ben Lettick, she wrote, was possibly the best-documented autistic child of all time.

> But there was a life of sorts outside of Ben. There were birthday celebrations, trips to the dentist, and dinner parties; I worked vig-orously as my husband's research assistant, and compiled his ex-tensive picture file, handled the billing for his art classes. I froze corn, polished silver, and ironed shirts. What is apparent, though, from the diaries, is that as the demands of caring for Ben became overwhelming, my husband and my other children had to take sec-ond place in my life, even in my thoughts. It never occurred to me that I had a choice; the others could help themselves, while Ben could not.[20]

Lettick's diary documented experimental care, research, and training—her "life's work"—produced at a time when little was known and even less was standardized about treating children with autism. She described Ben's development in terms of a series of authorities who exerted a formative influence on her life and her perception of her son's development. "The intense scrutiny and documenting of my existence over the past four decades was required of me by the three people who shaped my life."[21] The pediatrician Morris Krosnick had encouraged her to record every environmental variable in her household in order to manage her son David's extreme allergies. Sally Provence, a pediatrician at the Yale Child Study Center, had requested records of Ben's behavioral development. Newell Kephart, the director of the Achievement Center for Children at Purdue University had, starting in 1962, developed an educational program for Ben that required careful records of his daily activities.[22]

Lettick's journals chronicled "how little professional help was available in the decades following Leo Kanner's first article on autism." They also demonstrated "what could be accomplished by a low-functioning, classically autistic person with optimum education," and the cost of those accomplishments to the child's family.[23] Lettick's attitude was eminently pragmatic. She rarely speculated, in writing at least, about the cause of Ben's condition. She saw her role as one of enabling development and growth at whatever level was possible. The nineteenth and twentieth century ideal of scientific motherhood dictated that women turn to experts for advice on every aspect of child care. Lettick, like other mothers before her, was selective about the advice that she followed.[24] Ben's needs also meant that Lettick went beyond the mandate that she merely seek and follow expert guidance. She reinterpreted and adapted the information she found in order to develop methods that were suited to her child.

In her efforts to synthesize ongoing research on behavioral interventions that might help Ben, Lettick sought consultations with rising experts in the field. However, she also kept detailed reading lists and gained access to the Yale library, where she devoured books on educational methods for typically developing children as well as remedial educational techniques. In one of her few references to psychoanalysis she mentioned the one useful piece of advice from Bettelheim's *Love Is Not Enough*: keep a jar of candies available, from which the child can help himself freely. She didn't mention Bettelheim's complicated psychological rationale based on denial and fulfillment, but she did leave a jar of M&Ms out for Ben and noted his delight.

Lettick experimented with a range of educational techniques. She devised visual puzzles where Ben was required to match identical pieces in a row, exercises to increase his fine motor coordination, tactile routines that required him to manipulate forms, and a wide variety of techniques to teach Ben to form spoken consonants with the hope that he might eventually learn to speak. Although she speculated about Ben's responses to one educational trial or another and sometimes recorded that he was "having a bad day" (or that they both were), she rarely interpreted Ben's behavior in any terms other than pleasure, frustration, anger, or boredom. She persisted in working to develop Ben's verbal skills until, when he was eleven, she decided to have his hearing tested—none of his doctors had thought to check on this—and discovered that he had severe hearing loss, probably significant enough to prevent him from distinguishing speech as anything but "noise."[25] Lettick promptly refocused her teaching methods.

In the summer of 1961, a student in her husband's art class sent Lettick an article from the *Saturday Evening Post* by Rosalind Oppenheim, "They Said Our Child Was Hopeless."[26] By then, the staff at the Yale Child Study Center had concluded that there was no way to help Lettick's son. Oppenheim's article offered Lettick hope that she might teach herself to treat Ben, and she began corresponding with Oppenheim.[27] Although their relationship was not always personally close, they shared a series of troubling and revelatory experiences. For many of the same reasons that Lettick founded Benhaven, Oppenheim founded and directed two schools, the second of which she named the Bernard Rimland School for Autistic Children. She also wrote a book on teaching methods for parents and professionals.[28] Lettick would write of Oppenheim that "she was my first mentor, and a more capable one could not have existed."[29]

Oppenheim had trained herself as a teacher after finding Newell Kephart, a specialist at Purdue working on a treatment for brain-damaged children. Contrary to the beliefs of doctors influenced by psychoanalytic theory, Kephart said that Oppenheim would not "irreparably damage Ethan's psyche by making demands on him (advice which was, incidentally, diametrically opposite to everything we had been told by every clinician we had consulted prior to Dr. Kephart)."[30] Her son Ethan was six years old and nonverbal, but after using a "home-training program" designed to teach him pre-academic skills, the Oppenheims had discovered that he was capable of communicating by writing. After publishing her article, Oppenheim was "besieged by hundreds of letters from distraught parents from several continents who were seeking help." Professionals wanted to cite it. Oppenheim told Lettick, "I wish I had a secretary!"[31] Most inquiries she answered only once, but Lettick's enthusiasm, energy, and, above all, persistence led her to continue the correspondence.[32] Lettick described reading Oppenheim's response to her first letter as a transformative moment: "I put down Roz Oppenheim's wonderful letter, took Ben by the hand, walked him upstairs to the table in his bedroom and began his first classtime."[33]

Rosalind Oppenheim encouraged Lettick to attend Kephart's summer camp, which trained parents in behavioral techniques, and she reassured Amy when Ben's progress was slow: "Don't be discouraged by Ben's seeming lack of progress. Kep says all children have learning plateaus during which they seem to be standing still, or even regressing; but are actually consolidating their previous gains."[34] Lettick placed a great deal of weight on Oppenheim's advice and support, persisting in her efforts to gain access to Kephart at Purdue. This turned out to be a lengthy process, requiring her first to convince Sally Provence to write a referral to Kephart and then wait for Kephart to respond and agree to treat Ben.[35]

The week before the Letticks planned to travel to Indiana to visit Kephart, Rosalind Oppenheim warned Lettick that she might have misunderstood what Kephart could offer. While Kephart's techniques helped immensely in educating Ethan, Ethan's behavior and social skills were still far from normal. Oppenheim thought that she might not have written the article had she understood how slow progress would be:

> Learning to read and write, for Ethan, and, when it happens, for Ben, was no more remarkable than it is when a normal child learns to read and write. *Because this has nothing to do with their basic problem.* I hope you won't hate me for telling you this. But, oh God, what a letdown we suffered! This is not to imply, I hasten to add, that the situation is hopeless; but Ethan's social progress—while there *is* some—continues at what seems to us to be a snail's pace. He is still very deviant. [36]

While Ethan's testable performance might have improved, his ability to function socially did not—he was still autistic.[37] Ethan, moreover, was generally more responsive than Ben, and had considerable receptive language abilities to begin with. Where Ben tended to be lethargic, Ethan was hyperactive. Lettick almost cancelled the trip, writing that the letter "knocked the heart right out of me."[38]

Luckily, Kephart designed individualized programs geared toward increasing children's overall "flexibility" and skill in integrating sensory information, rather than their performance in any specific area.[39] The methods depended on a view of developmental domains as fundamentally related to each other. It was a perspective in keeping with Lettick's desire to see Ben acquire skills that he could take out of the classroom and into the outside world. The group in Indiana that the Letticks joined included two other autistic children, who were a recent research interest for Kephart. Lettick noted that Ben performed better than many of the other children, and she took Kephart's encouragement seriously. The Letticks returned from their visit to Indiana optimistic:

> Basically, what we came away with was a completely new understanding of why Ben acts the way he does and what we have to do. I realize that what I have been doing with Ben hasn't harmed him, but his needs go far, far, backward to much more basic behavior, and now of course I shall concentrate on those needs. Being fortified with understanding is the greatest strength we received.[40]

Lettick also felt that she now had the skills to act alone, "as though the cord tying me to Roz has been cut."[41] She began a wide correspondence, and she became part of a small but growing network of parent activists, including Bernard Rimland, who wrote to Lettick about a study of high-dose vitamin B6 that was recruiting participants through the new National Society for Autistic Children.[42] Years later, what most struck Lettick was the divergent paths that Ben's and Ethan's lives had taken, even though their mothers were equally determined and "she had the bright boy, I had the retarded boy."[43] After Oppenheim's death, Ethan was placed in a residential facility, where he regressed to the point that he interacted with no one and did not appear to recognize Lettick when she visited. Meanwhile, Ben was "flourishing" in adulthood, living at Benhaven and working at a supervised job, surrounded by people who "enjoyed, even loved him."[44]

The two mothers had both begun by contacting the same doctor, Newell Kephart, an expert on teaching children with diagnoses of brain damage. The amorphous category referred less to a discrete injury in an adult brain than to the recognition that an alteration early in development could lead to multiple disabilities later in life. For many parents of children given diagnoses of autism or "autistic tendencies" during the 1960s and 1970s, "brain damage" might have seemed the most adequate description of the difficulties that their children experienced, including developmental regressions and unusual combinations of strengths and deficits in cognitive abilities.[45]

Kephart's approach concentrated on "perceptual motor skills." He based his techniques on the premise that children's cognitive development occurred in parallel to their ability to coordinate the movements needed to explore and learn from their environments.[46] He thought that children who had developed atypically were often pressured by parents or schools to develop "splinter skills" that they memorized as a series of movements rather than integrated as organic reflexes.[47] Although Kephart's method deviated from the behaviorist approaches now standard in treating children with autism, it shared with them an emphasis on parents as "prime coordinators of and contributors to their child's development and learning."[48] He avoided technical descriptions of his methods and stressed the importance of training parents in general concepts that they could apply themselves.[49]

Not all experts offered the same level of hope and encouragement. Much of Lettick's daily work involved seeking teachers for Ben and then training them, an intellectually and emotionally demanding process. At one point, the Letticks met with a man at Southern Connecticut State College who claimed to be a psychologist who had recovered from autism through the help of yet another recovered autistic man.[50] At their initial meeting, the psychologist identified Lettick as "classically neurotic" and told her that she was pressuring her child to behave as a typical person when he was unable to conform to her expectations. Autistic children had to be met at their own level and in their own language. He spoke of rolling on the floor and growling and of his own lack of empathy for other human beings. The Letticks listened in fascination and dismay. After telling them that they were utterly unable to love or care for their son, he said that he had no time to treat Ben and that treatments took two years. They did not bring Ben back for an evaluation.

Ben had appointments at the Yale Child Study Center twice a week and was enrolled in their preschool for a time. As he neared the age of seven, Lettick discovered that Ben would no longer be eligible for treatment when his doctor casually asked Lettick about her plans for the future. The center had "no procedure for helping parents find successive placement, nor did they have lists of existing facilities elsewhere."[51] The Association for Retarded Children (now the ARC) was starting a chapter in New Haven, and a group of parents set up a day care center that Ben attended for a time, although Lettick was saddened to place Ben with "defective children" when his limitations seemed so different from theirs.[52]

Starting in 1962, Lettick worked with other parents to set up an autism class at the public school.[53] In 1966, the New Haven public school system hired a new teacher, Gilbert Freitag, for the autism class. Lettick found Freitag's behaviorism difficult to countenance. Although he had been highly recommended by Bernard Rimland, Lettick wondered whether Freitag knew anything about child development.[54] Lettick decided to start a new school as a nonprofit corporation, with a year-round schedule so as not to "leave too much of the day to regress in for children who don't know how to use free time or whose parents are not able or free to cope with their needs." The public educational system offered mainly frustrations and no residential schooling options apart from institutionalization for children who had graduated from elementary school and who could no longer live with their families. Lettick would, as she put it, turn her "remaining energies to creating rather than adapting."[55]

She envisioned the new residential program, Benhaven, as a developmentally organized environment. The goal for students was not normality but achievement and growth within the boundaries set by their disability. Lettick's choice of a name for the school echoed New Haven, Connecticut; the idea of a safe home for children like Ben; and the name of Newell Kephart's school, the Glen Haven Achievement Center, in Fort Collins, Colorado. It was to be a year-round facility, based on Kephart's ideas and practices, although Lettick differed with Kephart on the question of parent training.[56] Kephart felt that there was "no adequate substitute for parent participation in the training program," while Lettick believed it crucial to serve parents who might not have the ability or the time to fully participate or who divided their attention among many children. Other advisors to the school argued against parent volunteers, but Lettick disagreed. "The one basic difference between me and all my advisors is that in addition to being a teacher, I am a mother of a child like this. I don't intend that this shall be a handicap to the development of Benhaven. Rather I feel that my experience in this double capacity can contribute to the endeavor."[57]

Benhaven was an experimental site where, during a typical six months, behavioral programs for any given student might be tried and, if necessary, abandoned.[58] The tools used at Benhaven included diagnostic inventories imported from developmental psychology, forms for rating improvement, behavioral methods, and other "developmentally designed" psychoeducational approaches. Teachers set goals according to each child's abilities rather than a predetermined trajectory. A child might be taught sign language as an alternative to verbal speech. Employees sometimes had to stop students from engaging in self-injurious behaviors and occasionally used restraints.[59] One student had been expelled from all of his previous schools and arrived in restraints, requiring two grown men to control him. Behaven's treatment program, which emphasized his skills and downplayed restraints, helped him to leave as one of the school's first graduates.

Benhaven became "a place that everyone who works with severely handicapped people should see," and "an inspiration," but it could not become a home to all, and not all residential treatment programs reflected the values of an Amy Lettick.[60] From the outset, she envisioned her approach as one that could be replicated, and the National Society for Autistic Children agreed, naming her methods "essential reading" for people who worked with autistic children in any capacity.[61] She was open about both the strategies that worked and those that failed, earning her books a warm review in the *Journal of Autism and Developmental Disorders*.[62] In contrast to psychoanalytic treatment programs that emphasized relationships between children and staff, the Benhaven philosophy stressed "immediate work with the child, with the idea that through work, relationships will be formed."[63]

Lettick's honorary degree from Yale, a doctorate of humane letters awarded in 1975, made implicit and perhaps even wry reference to the legacy of training—from "training schools" for disabled children in the early part of the century to the promises of discrete trial training and the professional training offered by universities. The citation read:

> The haven you provided for autistic children is recognized as one of the most advanced schools for those so tragically impaired. You were not willing to accept the dehumanizing institutions available for such children. The accomplishment of Benhaven is the result of your extraordinary effort to train yourself, teach others and perfect existing knowledge about the autistic child. Through love and action you have earned the admiration of all who work in your field.[64]

Technologies of Change: NSAC and Behavioral Therapies

Bernard Rimland, an experimental psychologist with an autistic son, founded the National Society for Autistic Children (NSAC) in 1965 with a group of concerned parents, including Amy Lettick. The organization would be "a means for parents of autistic and schizophrenic children to meet and work for better schools and facilities for their children."[65] By promoting the idea that autism was incorrectly classified as a severe emotional disturbance (SED) when it was in fact an "organic" neurological disorder best treated through specialized educational programs, NSAC influenced a transition in the disease category of autism from psychological to neurological disorder. A large proportion of the early work of NSAC involved making the autism diagnosis visible to educators, legislators, and physicians.[66]

These efforts took place prior to the Education for All Handicapped Children Act of 1975 (renamed the Individuals with Disabilities Education Act [IDEA] in 1990) and other legislation that made developmental disorders a bureaucratically visible entity.[67] The laws extended the principle of equal protection or what the legislation termed a "free and appropriate public education," in the "least restrictive environment" possible for a given child. Parents played a role in their passage, motivated in part by the reprehensible and often debilitating conditions in institutions for the mentally and developmentally disabled. Despite the existence of NSAC, parents of autistic children lagged behind parents of children with other cognitive disabilities in their efforts to organize. One reason was the assumption of their culpability by a generation of medical professionals.[68] They banded together to secure educational supports, in response to the prospect of effective interventions, and because of the sense of accomplishment and agency they derived from therapies that worked.

Even though autism was not yet an entirely stable medical category, those diagnosed with the disorder had become an orphaned population in terms of care and support services. NSAC reflected the realization among parents that they comprised a population with shared experiences, among them an arduous journey through clinics and expert consultations en route to a diagnosis. Although psychiatrists began to develop standard guidelines for autism diagnosis by the late 1970s, the majority of autism diagnoses during that decade, as in the present, were based on clinical observation and judgment. The Society enlisted the help of a professional advisory board in crafting a new, standard definition of autism that was suited for use in schools and in writing legislation. In 1975, they successfully pushed for autism's inclusion in the Developmental Disabilities Act, procuring entitlements to developmental opportunities and education for their children.[69] Children with autism deserved the same services available to other developmentally disabled children. Protection alone was not enough. Autistic citizens had the right to education within the bounds of their capacities, and professionals and parents alike, under the influence of current research, saw those capacities broadening.

After he helped reshape research approaches to autism with his 1964 book *Infantile Autism*, Bernard Rimland became an important proponent of biomedical treatments. Rimland saw the founding of NSAC primarily as a means to promote behavior modification therapies based on the work of O. Ivar Lovaas, who was just then developing educational methods for use with autistic children. Rimland was willing to consider any treatment not premised on psychotherapy, and which made room for the neurological and biological differences of children with autism.

In the late 1960s, when Lovaas began his research on Skinnerian operant conditioning techniques for use with autistic children, many specialists

viewed behavior analysis as antithetical to the developmentalist progression of other structured learning techniques. The method treated skills in
isolation rather than as interlinked in cumulative developmental patterns.
Although applied behavior analysis (ABA) was becoming established as
a method for addressing problem behaviors in educational settings, it
met with significant opprobrium from within the educational and medical communities devoted to autism. Bruno Bettelheim described operant
conditioning disparagingly as "a method where small (or even severe)
punishments, and rewards, are used to induce the subject to do what the
experimenter wants him to do, and this without any consideration of why
the subject chose to do what he did, or not to do what he does not do."[70]

Parents oriented toward whatever might work and hungry for practical
advice worried less than others about theoretical inconsistencies. Lovaas's
techniques suggested that skills could be acquired separately, using positive and negative reinforcements to establish basic imitation and language
abilities. For children who had failed to acquire these skills in a typical
pattern, sometimes a counterintuitive progression worked better. Bernard
Rimland, although initially skeptical of operant conditioning techniques
because it seemed unlikely that children would generalize beyond the laboratory or classroom, became convinced that children could acquire skills
beyond those they were taught by therapists. They were literally learning
how to learn through techniques that parents could apply themselves.[71] In
1965, Rimland visited Lovaas's laboratory at UCLA and arranged a meeting with some parents of "autistic-type" children.

> It was the beginning of a worldwide movement for active and vig-
> orous parent participation in their children's training.
>
> As a result of that meeting, Dr. Lovaas set up an experimental
> workshop at UCLA in which the mothers were taught to use op-
> erant methods to teach their children speech, simple arithmetic,
> imitation, and other things. Before the one-hour daily sessions got
> underway the parents' letters to me were full of misgivings. Pro-
> fessionals had advised them for years to be permissive and lov-
> ing and to accept anything the children did, in the hope that they
> would, someday, somehow, realize that they were *really* loved and
> accepted.[72]

These new techniques produced "spectacular" results. Although none
of the children had been "made normal," many had improved in their
communicative abilities and had fewer destructive and ritualistic behaviors. Lovaas, "impressed and pleased at the skill and determination the

mothers showed in their work," invited them to lecture in his classes and made parent workshops part of his program.[73] Rimland immediately saw the promise of the technique and its mode of delivery, but he "felt that unless a grass roots (consumer's) movement of parents was started, it might take 20 years or more for behavior modification to filter through the walls of the ivory towers and begin to replace psychoanalysis and play therapy as the preferred treatments for autistic children."[74] At the founding meeting of NSAC, Rimland introduced the concept of behavioral treatment and went on to promote it in meetings across the country. However, it was not until 1987 that Lovaas published results on the use of discrete trials in treating autism and established ABA as a legitimate intervention for autism in the eyes of psychiatrists and policymakers.[75]

ABA used "discrete trial training," which required a child to perform a simple task in return for positive reinforcement in the form of applause, food, or a favorite toy. A child might initially be required simply to sit in a chair for a period of time or establish eye contact or respond to his or her name. If the child failed to complete the task, the therapist could give a physical prompt by guiding the child's hand to match a puzzle piece or deliver a requested object.[76] Tasks would then grow more complex. ABA primarily focused on language, drawing on B. F. Skinner's idea of language as a "stimulus function." Lovaas treated language as the basis for other social interactions. If children came to understand speech as a way to get what they wanted, they would begin to employ it spontaneously. Thus initial sessions often involved verbal prompts. Lovaas wrote that "we were interested in learning how the child's language might regulate his own behavior. In the back of our minds we had some notion that if the child learned to talk, somehow a conception of himself would emerge, that he might become more defined as a person, that he might show more self-control," a view of autism not entirely remote from psychoanalytic concerns with ego formation, although Lovaas's approach drew on learning theory instead.[77]

Throughout his work, Lovaas emphasized parents' participation. "We have been unable to help a child meaningfully in language development without the parent's active involvement."[78] Lovaas's handbook, *Teaching Developmentally Disabled Children: The ME Book*, became something of a bible for a generation of parents teaching themselves the techniques of behavioral analysis. The book had a warm and instructive tone: "You want to teach your child to listen more, to talk more, and to take more care of his personal needs." When Lovaas introduced new terms like "rewards" and "punishments," he repeated them so that readers would "understand them like an expert" by the time they had finished the book.[79] The book taught parents the technique of discrete trial training, guiding their efforts to employ contingent rewards in calculated rather than intuitive ways. The mother of one of the first children enrolled in Lovaas's Young Autism Project worried that she was expected to participate in the therapy when she had no professional training. Years later, she observed that while her son "seems to take his normality for granted," she did not. "Many years after his autistic behavior was extinguished, I find myself watching Drew, seeking opportunities to further his socialization."[80] She went on to earn a degree in learning disabilities and became a special education teacher.

If Oppenheim's 1961 *Saturday Evening Post* article showed that children with autism could be educated, the 1965 *Life* magazine article that made Lovaas's work visible to the American public had an even more immediate and far-reaching effect. While for many parents the story made education appear as a real possibility for their autistic children, the "Screams, Slaps and Love" of the title also made clear that Lovaas sometimes used violent aversive techniques—and demanded that the audience recognize those techniques as acts of loving intervention.[81] In a choice that Lovaas and his team perhaps should have anticipated, the editors selected photographs that showed "aversive events": a graduate student shouting only a few inches from a boy's face, his hand a blur as he moved to slap the child; a girl in a flowered dress cringing as her bare feet touched an electrified grid.[82] Lovaas and his team were surprised and dismayed at the editorial choices.[83] Immersed in their experimental work, they had not imagined how their techniques might look to observers. The *Life* article left a lasting impression, enough so that when Rimland began actively promoting behavior modification starting in 1966, "the hands would shoot up" and concerned audience members would demand his response to the images.[84] Even after he had discontinued the use of most aversives, an approving article in *Rolling Stone* in 1979 featured one of Lovaas's students using an "aversive no" delivered at a volume that made the reporter "jump a foot out of my chair."[85]

Many parents and therapists saw aversives as crucial to the care of autistic children, even with the risk that they might harm a child. Untreated, the child's behaviors might lead to far more severe injuries or death. Parents described children who dashed out into the street in front of cars and others who banged their heads ceaselessly and without discernable cause.[86] The debates within NSAC and among professionals illustrate how both groups understood the ethics of the emerging behavioral therapies. Their values and attitudes did not segment neatly across group lines, and instead suggest the centrality of experiential knowledge for individuals' decisions. In 1975 the board of directors of NSAC issued a white paper on behavior modification that gave "qualified support" to the use of aversive techniques to alleviate severely self-injurious behaviors. Responding to reports of abuses, the society adopted a "Position on the Abuse of Aversives" in 1985, stating that "many conscientious and concerned practitioners are aware that occasionally they must make judicious use of short-term, well-designed, and carefully monitored interventions that include aversive elements."[87] However, in 1988, the board of directors of the renamed Autism Society of America passed a resolution effectively calling for a ban on "aversive techniques" across the board.

This move provoked an extended letter-writing campaign by board members including Amy Lettick and Bernard Rimland, as well as by experts in the field such as Eric Schopler, former editor of the *Journal of Autism and Developmental Disabilities*, and Donald Cohen, director of the Yale Child Study Center. They argued that those who sought to ban these practices failed to understand the technical aspects of behavior modification. They suggested that critics, perhaps because of their lack of experience, did not recognize that even the daily routines for educating severely handicapped children would in some cases cause the children emotional distress, and that sometimes children had to be restrained. Schopler's support for the limited use of aversives mattered because his North Carolina-based program, Division TEACCH, emphasized the "culture of autism" and respect for the different ways that children with autism perceived the world. He suggested that those who opposed aversives made the same mistake as those who had once argued for psychotherapeutic treatment. They assumed that children with autism were "essentially normal" and therefore required only "normal experiences."[88]

In an exchange with Bernard Rimland in *The Advocate*, the newsletter of the Autism Society of America, Marcia Datlow Smith argued that "We have always had a technology of behavior change for even the most challenging behaviors. It has never been necessary to use strategies which are dehumanizing or cause discomfort or injury."[89] For Datlow Smith, a "functional analysis" of behavior in the context of a child's environment would allow practitioners to understand why problem behaviors occurred in the first place. "Misbehavior has a purpose," and identifying that purpose allowed therapists to address problems without resorting to aversives. Rimland disagreed. He countered that "the prohibitionists are mistaken in claiming that positive reinforcements *always* work. . . . Is a lifetime of blindness, of self-injury, or of being drugged insensible 24 hours a day—

often the real alternatives to aversives—more humane?" Although aversives could be misused, the results of "regulated and monitored" aversive techniques were lasting, were not to be confused with abuse, and in any event, "aversives are a fact of everyday life, quite unavoidable by any living creature," making the Autism Society of America resolution unnecessarily restrictive.[90]

The *Rolling Stone* reporter that Lovaas had startled with his "aversive no" wrestled with the idea that "conditioners" like Lovaas were merely imposing a "culturally relevant sense of order" on autistic children. After visiting families, special education classrooms, and speaking with Lovaas in Los Angeles, he came to a different conclusion:

> One transparent, unmystical giggle from one of these strange kids—one laugh that seems to exist in relation to something funny makes you see it: behaviorism as applied to autism is a stopgap, a methodology of convenience, but autism, like war, is hell, and until somebody produces that magic pill it seems to be all there is.[91]

Precisely because of their imperfections, behavioral techniques required parental support networks not only for knowledge about implementation but also for support and reassurance. With behavioral therapies, care became even more technical, the demands on the energy of therapists and parents even greater. Looking back on her daughter's early years, prior to the wide use of behavioral techniques, Clara Park described how "no one person, or family, could provide all that Jessy needed to grow. There was always someone else working with her in those days. . . . None had any training in special education or developmental psychology, but I claim for them the word 'therapist' without hesitation."[92] Behavioral therapies transformed some of those informal therapists into trained technicians. However, the alterations ran in both directions. Essentially laboratory techniques, behavioral therapies required social work to transform them into a viable intervention for use with disabled children.

Theorizing Child Development, Brain Injury, and Parental Work

From the start, biological theories of autism fit well with behavioral techniques. Even before researchers began to look for structural abnormalities in the brains of developmentally disabled children or to treat childhood disabilities through pharmacological therapies, books like Newell Kephart's *The Slow Learner in the Classroom* began with introductory chapters on neuroscience. Biological reasoning helped child psychologists establish their professional authority. Their approaches were methodologically diverse in ways that mattered to their designers and to parents, but the programs shared certain elements. They nodded to behaviorism in that they focused on discrete goals and did not assume specific mechanisms of neurological impairment. Their authors did not consciously avoid hypotheses about the neural or psychological basis for autism, but they also did not depend on them. They also shared an even more crucial element, which architects of behavioral programs recognized and documented as a clinical innovation: Parents played as large a part in therapy as the counselors had at the Orthogenic School in the 1950s and 1960s.

Ivar Lovaas had begun research on reinforcement techniques in 1961, and by 1966 he had enough data to report on the work in a peer-reviewed journal.[93] In their initial study, Lovaas and his team at UCLA found that all of the twenty children treated responded in some degree to behavior modification. Therapy worked better when it was practiced intensely over a longer period of time.[94] The UCLA group discovered something else in their follow-up research. Children treated in institutions improved, but their gains evaporated when they left the institution. There was an obvious solution.

> More and more we became involved in parent-training because the parents, as the child's therapists, could overcome these problems. That is, they could restructure the child's total environment and provide him with continuous treatment, which protected against the situational effects of reversibility.[95]

Lovaas realized some of the same things as Bettelheim, although their techniques were markedly different. Both spoke about the need for a "total environment" for treating children. In this case, the milieu was transported into the home. Lovaas saw other benefits in transforming parents into "explicitly trained cotherapists." The controversies surrounding behavioral therapies made it "absolutely essential, for both moral and legal purposes, that the parents be intimately familiar with how their child is treated." Parents who learned the techniques became "semi-professionals." In cases where parents placed their children in therapeutic group homes instead of providing therapy themselves, Lovaas referred to the caregivers as "*professional* parents."[96] Other behavior analysts likewise found that parents, nonscientists, could be trained in behavioral techniques with results superior to when children were treated in clinics isolated from their homes. Lovaas reached his conclusion alongside a growing number of other researchers and parents.

As a behaviorist, Lovaas thought that therapies should be used to eliminate problem behaviors in order to attain "normal functioning," not the more elusive "normality." His well-known 1987 study, portentously titled "Behavioral Treatment and Normal Intellectual and Behavioral Functioning in Young Autistic Children," involved an experimental group of nineteen compared with forty control children, all of whom had a clinical autism diagnosis consistent with the criteria in *DSM*-III. The researchers "sought to maximize behavioral treatment gains by treating autistic children during most of their waking hours for many years. Treatment included all significant persons in all significant environments."[97] Because the study demonstrated that a control group of children receiving less therapy had poor outcomes, and a follow-up study on the children receiving behavioral treatment indicated that they retained their skills, the publication helped justify wide implementation of Lovaas's methods. It did so despite Lovaas's warning that parents and teachers might find it difficult to achieve the level of intensity that his group had maintained in a laboratory setting with almost unlimited resources.

Many professional objections to the study focused precisely on this question of the relationship between success in the laboratory setting and in the far more complex environment of everyday life. Eric Schopler was concerned about Lovaas's use of aversive techniques and about the near-prohibitive expense of a forty-hour-a-week program. He warned parents to wait for definitive research on outcomes before demanding ABA programs under special education legislation.[98] Schopler and his colleague Gary Mesibov questioned the validity of Lovaas's 1987 study on several grounds, including the outcome measures, which involved IQ testing and placement in a classroom with typical children. These measures might have reflected a child's compliance on the one hand and school policy on the other, neither of which were relevant to the central communicative and behavioral features of autism.[99] Schopler and Mesibov also disagreed with Lovaas's criteria for subject selection and the composition of the control group.[100] Finally, they criticized Lovaas's willingness to move from his experimental results to the claim that autism did not have a basis in neurological impairment.[101] Despite their criticisms, the 1987 study established ABA as a gold standard for the treatment of children with autism.

During the late 1960s and early 1970s when Lovaas and his team at UCLA were developing their program, Eric Schopler and Robert Reichler were completing a pilot study and five-year experimental program based on related principles.[102] The University of North Carolina–based psychologists called their program Division TEACCH (Treatment and Education of Autistic and Communication-related handicapped CHildren). Although they designed their program only to test the efficacy of using parents as the "primary developmental agents" in educating children with autism, parents successfully petitioned the North Carolina state legislature for permanent funding.[103] The TEACCH system relied on "high external structures" organized around educational tasks, but unlike the program Lovaas had developed, Schopler and Reichler's program emphasized individualized developmental goals based on extensive diagnostic testing, the cognitive strengths of the child, and a nuanced understanding of the child's home and family environment.[104]

Like Kephart and Lovaas, Schopler and Reichler understood that parental work mattered to their program and that parents were the "primary experts" in the needs of their children.[105] Lovaas required that parents sign a formal "work-contract" that committed them to the program and its demanding schedule of therapy sessions. Schopler and Reichler were less regimented in their approach, opting for a treatment contract that allowed parents to define the focus of work. Treatments began by observing parents working with their child on an "organized activity" that would be similar to the tasks in the program.[106] Following this first session, parents and therapists took equal shares of the work. Along with a "parent consultant"—all staff members acted as both therapists and parent consultants, although not with the same family—parents observed therapists working with their child through a one-way screen, placing parents in literally the same position as professional clinical observers.[107]

Making the therapists try activities themselves kept them from suggesting tasks that sounded reasonable but were impossible to execute in practice. More important, the practice downgraded "the mystique and unfounded authority of the therapist who reports to parents from only private observations of the child" and allowed the parents to see the therapist, like them, suffer through failures, missteps, and frustrations.[108] In addition to the sessions observing therapists, parents developed and implemented home programs for their children, solving the problem of helping children—and their parents—generalize from the clinical and experimental setting. Martin Kozloff used a similar design for his parent-training program, including an "experimental" phase in a laboratory setting followed by a home program.[109]

Schopler and Reichler emphasized that their demonstrations were meant to help parents "develop a degree of self-consciousness inappropriate to normal child rearing. Indeed, they need to become experts on their own autistic child." Like Lovaas, they were impressed by the dedication of parents who drove up to four hours for visits, assiduously maintained daily logs, and often outdid trained therapists in the effectiveness of their work. Schopler and Reichler concluded that using parents as cotherapists and experts was not merely an expedient in the face of staff shortages.[110] Given confidence in their expertise, parents were often more capable than trained professional staff in working with their own children.

From Schopler's perspective, the stage had long been set for parents to participate fully as cotherapists for their children, even by treatment approaches that consciously excluded them. By identifying parents as the cause of their children's autism, Schopler argued, psychoanalytically inclined practitioners made observing and altering parental behavior through psychotherapy the focus of autism treatment for their children.[111] The experts in learning theory and behaviorism who arrived on the scene in the 1960s with experimental approaches to behavior modification identified children rather than parents as the target of intervention. However, many of the techniques they developed still demanded that parents alter their interactions with their children. Behaviorists worked with typical and brain-damaged children to establish methods for reinforcing behavior. In the process, they also established that parents made effective therapists. Despite the status of behavioral techniques as the province of skilled professionals, with training, parents might be in a position to surpass their efforts.[112]

Lovaas and his team had shown that in order for children to maintain the skills that they gained through behavioral programs and transfer them from the laboratory setting to their daily lives, parents had to become actively involved in therapy, even to the extent of setting agendas and carrying out experimental observations in their own homes.[113] These findings did not come out of the blue. Rather, they reflected a decade of experience by specialists in the wider field of mental health and children's behavior problems. Several factors had combined to increase involvement by parents in behavioral therapies. More children required services, and the number of trained mental health workers in a traditionally low-paid industry could not satisfy the demand. At the same time, behavioral therapies were becoming more intensive, leading researchers to consider the feasibility of using "nonprofessionals" in a range of mental health fields.[114] Researchers had first demonstrated that "untrained psychotherapists" like child-care workers and teachers could apply operant conditioning methods to treating autistic children in the early 1960s, and it was this work that directly inspired Lovaas's own research.[115]

Investigators also broadened the scope of behavioral therapies. They wanted to go beyond "contrived settings" in which "highly trained professional personnel" worked with children who were then left to their own devices when they returned home, and who often regressed. The evidence suggested that training had to be done in the "natural environment" for behavior change to take place, a finding that "inevitably leads to the parents." The techniques that had worked so well in the laboratory setting worked equally well in the home.[116] In some cases, parents could use the same social reinforcements that worked with their typical children, only systematizing their habitual responses to each of their child's actions. Investigators realized that generalization was not only a problem for the children. Parents might need help implementing techniques that they had learned in the laboratory.[117] Given an appropriate initiation into the techniques of behavioral therapy, however, even siblings could be trained as "behavior modifiers," with their parents acting as reliable experimental observers. Far from being unable to report objectively on improvements in their child, parents proved to be "at least as good as outside observers."[118]

In summary, a number of factors hastened the move from the clinic to the home and from expert personnel to parents as cotherapists. Clinicians cared about practical matters: children's ability to generalize skills in different settings, the pressing shortage of trained professionals to administer intensive therapy, and, later, the discovery that parents could indeed be expert, objective experimental observers of their own children. Learning theory, experimental psychology, and behaviorism had taught researchers to pay close attention to the naturally occurring "reinforcers" in a developmentally disabled child's environment. It was a short, if not always intuitive step to move from scrutinizing parents to engaging them as therapeutic practitioners who could be taught to behave in regularized and experimentally reliable ways.[119] Parents, as we have seen, were happy to receive guidance and support in their efforts to treat their children. Indeed, they worked hard to promote behavioral approaches.

Researchers sought to establish the validity of their techniques not only as therapeutic methodologies but also as components of general models. For parents, what they already knew to be effective from their experiences raising their typical children—knowledge about bodily states, preferences, and commonplace reinforcement and persuasion—formed the basis for a therapeutic relationship with their child. Not all parents had access to Newell Kephart, TEACCH, the Young Autism Project at UCLA, or any number of other site-specific programs, however, through which they might have learned the finer points of behavioral techniques. For the majority, their transformation into semiprofessionals and their incorporation of the techniques of behaviorism into their daily lives drew on more eclectic sources, working through trial and error.

Tales of Love and Labor

Accounts by parents make clear that expert knowledge and private life have continually intersected in the families of autistic children. Although some memoirs report startling transformations that could be compared to "conversion narratives," not all tell triumphant stories of total recovery.[120] Religion or spirituality plays a role in some, but they are mostly about hard work. A few examples among many published accounts illustrate the ways that parents have described their complicated roles as experts and caregivers, their views on the ethics of treatment, and the effort it took to transform laboratory techniques into practical interventions and homes into therapeutic environments.

Barry Kaufman describes his son, Raun, as a beautiful, seemingly typically developing child who regressed after a severe ear infection. Spinning objects fascinated him, and he grew increasingly remote. The Kaufmans became concerned about Raun's development while he was still quite young, and in the early 1970s they could not find programs willing to accept or even diagnose him at such an early age. Instead they began a vigorous process of self-education. They "contacted a dedicated specialist in behaviorism in California with a major university and a Federal grant to study and research autism"—probably Lovaas. They "investigated psycho-pharmacology. Psychoanalysis. Behaviorism. Vitamin Therapy. Nutritional analysis. The CNS (central nervous system) factor. The genetic theory. There were many opinions and non-opinions, many unsubstantiated theories and debatable assumptions."[121] They eventually turned to the Option Method, as taught by a "short, round, monk-like Friar Tuck sipping Coke and smoking one cigarette after another."

> As I listened, I felt a surging from within. Understanding a knowledge that always seemed to have been there, but that I had never really put into focus. As it crystallized rapidly for me, I began to recognize that my feelings and wants did come from my beliefs and that those beliefs could be investigated. And this pursuit of exposing and choosing beliefs was the subject of the Option Attitude:

"To love is to be happy with." It was not merely a philosophy, but a vision that would become the basis for our way of life and a foundation from which we would try to help Raun.[122]

Kaufman's book, published in 1976, is infused with the language of acceptance, withholding judgment, and consciously inspecting the origins of desires and needs. The Kaufmans brought in caregivers from among their extended community of yoga teachers, movement instructors, and mother's helpers. They became virtual members of the family. Resisting the idea that Raun's behaviors could be modified directly, the Kaufmans decided that the best intervention was to "join" Raun in his behaviors:

> Sometimes there would be as many as seven of us spinning with him, turning his isms into an acceptable, joyful and communal event. It was our way of being with him . . . of somehow illustrating to him that he was okay, that we loved him, that we cared and that we accepted him wherever he was.[123]

Kaufman contrasted this approach with the methods of behavior modification advocated by Lovaas and others, which, although effective as an "educational tool," failed as the basis for a rehabilitation program. "The behaviorist, at the outset, makes many judgments about an autistic or deviant child and his behavior. Some activities are categorized and labeled as 'bad' or undesirable while others are deemed good. The underlying reasons for the behavior would not be considered applicable in treatment."[124]

The Kaufmans designed an alternative, three-phase program. The first phase required an attitude of total acceptance that would accompany any attempt to communicate with Raun. They envisioned the second phase as a "motivational/therapeutic experience" designed to "show Raun that our world was beautiful and exciting." Suzi Kaufman directed the third phase of treatment, a summer of intensive intervention with Raun, putting in seventy-five hours a week and nearing exhaustion at times.

> Often, we were asked how we felt about being deprived of other activities and interests. The word "sacrifice" was even suggested. If a painter or sculptor begins a piece and works year after year on it, no one would ask him how deprived he feels.[125]

The Kaufmans periodically sought the advice of professionals, with disappointing results. None of the doctors knew the research that Kaufman had been able to locate on his own.[126] Kaufman was dismayed at their lack of familiarity with the work of researchers like Lovaas and Kozloff. And while they opted to go it alone and had markedly different ideas about the reasons underlying successful treatments, they also learned much from the research at UCLA and elsewhere, sharing with other programs an emphasis on positive reinforcement and intensive parental involvement.[127] Other parents, likewise, heard about the Kaufmans' method and took what they could use from it. While Judy Barron didn't think that the method would have worked for her son, in their joint memoir *There's a Boy in Here*, she and her son Sean remembered how watching a TV special on Son-Rise led them to have their first honest conversation about his autism and their feelings for each other.[128]

Josh Greenfeld reacted with some skepticism to Kaufman's widely read account, to which he referred indirectly:

> I read of a parent who claims to have cured his autistic son through love, by accepting the kid the way he was. But when I read closely I realized the kid wasn't too developmentally disabled—never had any toilet problems, for example; and that the autism diagnosis came from the parent himself. The number of miracle workers who are quick to generalize from a false specific is frightening. And the effect is cruel beyond words on other parents.[129]

Greenfeld's *A Client Called Noah* covered the period during which his son Noah was placed in what Greenfeld called the "Operant Conditioning Center (OCC)," an unnamed residential school in the Southern California desert outside their home in Pacific Palisades, where Greenfeld worked as a screenwriter. The Center was run by a "strict Skinnerian," who "carries operant conditioning to its nth degree, and evidently that sometimes gets her into a lot of trouble." As Noah's time at the Center lengthened, the Greenfelds became concerned that "OCC is too committed to a program bent on breaking the kids spiritually through aversives," some of which bordered on physical abuse.[130] In response to their inquiries, the Center's president gave the Greenfelds an ultimatum: remove Noah from the Center or agree not to contest the Center's use of aversive techniques. They removed Noah.

Catherine Maurice, the pseudonymous author of *Let Me Hear Your Voice,* adhered to the fundamentals of ABA in treating her two children. By the 1980s, the family had access to therapy aides who used the principles of behaviorism and discrete trial instruction but were not directly affiliated with the UCLA program. The approach had found increasing acceptance. Still, Maurice found professionals inclined to counsel resignation and acceptance, an attitude that she "wasn't buying," especially after her own "crash course" in autism and her growing skill at identifying targets for therapy and problem behaviors. She saw an important difference between herself and professionals.

> They, with their clinical distance, were comfortably resigned; I was torn apart. Worse, they could delude themselves, with their degrees and their windy verbosity, that they were "helping." I could afford no such pretensions.[131]

However, even after reading *The ME Book*, Ivar Lovaas's manual for parents, she found videos of ABA "dehumanizing" and avoided watching her daughter's therapy. She nevertheless found herself drawn into the routine.

> It was ironic that I had mentally castigated Bridget [her child's therapist] for doing just this, when she had asked me to draw up my lists, but here I was learning how to look at my daughter's weaknesses and daily note all her autistic behaviors, just as Bridget did in the session logs. This clinical objectivity about something that a month ago had caused me the most searing pain was rendered possible, I suppose, by the simple fact that she was making sure and steady progress on all fronts.[132]

Such splintering of opinion among parents regarding even a single category of treatment such as behavioral therapies suggests autism's heterogeneity as a syndrome. It also points to the difficulty of conveying the practicalities of a home-based program in a memoir intended to persuade rather than instruct. However, these disagreements should not be read as demonstrating the fundamental incoherence of parents' ideas and accounts, but rather as evidence of their resourcefulness and willingness to draw on a range of methods in developing the programs best suited for their own children and families.

A Nation of Caregivers

Parents from the 1960s to the present have encountered a bewildering proliferation of techniques and practices for treating autism, including a range of distinct methods broadly categorized as early intensive behavioral intervention (EIBI). Their advocacy groups, like parents themselves, have balanced an attitude of acceptance with one of aggressive treatment-seeking in the face of highly variable evidence. Children with autism respond inconsistently to treatments, necessitating an experimental approach in each case. Parents of children with autism have weighed their desires for recovery against the apparent contentment of their children. In doing so against a shifting landscape of treatment options, they navigate terrain as unfamiliar as the "research frontier" of reproductive technologies that Rayna Rapp memorably describes. Clara Park wrote that contrary to the claims then current in psychoanalytic theory, it was always clear that her daughter was happy. But Park still refused to "leave Jessy to her empty serenity."[133]

Like many others, the Parks came to behavior modification in the context of using other therapeutic strategies and found that it solved some problems beautifully and failed to address others. Within the field of disability studies, aggressive efforts to cure are often seen as normative efforts at social control on a micro level. Such a perspective assumes that enlightened accommodation and intrusive rehabilitative technologies are easily distinguished from each other. Critics often view disability as a social construct in the deepest sense, the failure of a society that demands excessive standardization and consistency from its citizens and penalizes those who fail to conform. As proxies and spokespeople for their affected children, parents who seek to apply behavioral or biomedical techniques make the opposite determination, that their children must want to become more interactive, communicative, and socially cognizant.

Daily life with a child with autism does not often assume a stable pattern. It is more frequently a matter of finding tentative workable arrangements in the context of chronic difficulties. Problem behaviors are brought under control with one approach just as new ones emerge, demanding alternative strategies. The onset of adolescence can present both social and biological challenges after a period of relative calm. In a broader national context, thresholds are crossed as educational systems become overburdened with children with complex social and cognitive needs. These processes can lead to the systematic abandonment of populations, especially those who "age out" of educational systems or other types of support. Amy Lettick founded Benhaven at the height of deinstitutionalization, a process begun in 1963 but that picked up speed with changes in medical entitlements brought about by Medicaid and Medicare and the growth of the mental patient's rights movement.[134] The absence or deterioration of both community and institutional supports leaves families as exclusive providers of ongoing care for disabled relatives. This structural failure to recognize the uncompensated labor of familial caregivers contributes to untold hardships on an individual level. The families of disabled children, like those who care for the chronically ill, the elderly, or people with severe mental illnesses, have few options for their continuing care.

Behavioral techniques for treating autism have been subject to continual criticism. Skeptical experts in other areas of autism research have questioned their ability to effect meaningful changes in developmental trajectories, while psychological and educational professionals have criticized the techniques for their harshness and failure to take into account the communicative or functional meanings of behaviors. Others have questioned the lack of standard certification for practitioners. Therapists, often students employed at low wages, frequently cannot stay with families for the full course of treatment, making outcomes uncertain. Self-advocates with autism and Asperger syndrome have called the techniques abusive. Indeed, self-advocates have targeted ABA in particular for withering criticism. In the United States, insurance companies often refuse to cover ABA as an "un-proven" treatment, although both the Autism Society and the National Academies of Science recommend twenty-five hours a week of ABA as a best practice for treating autism.[135]

Parents played a key role in developing behavioral therapy methods during the 1960s and through the 1980s through their advocacy, their participation in experiments, and through teaching themselves the techniques and teaching others about them. To a significant extent, those who developed these techniques did so with just this type of participation in mind. Indeed, the intensive approaches literally required the participation of parents in the therapeutic process, and the redesign of the home as a therapeutic environment. State-run Early Intervention programs continue to situate parents as ambiguously authoritative semiprofessionals, reiterating their right to serve as "service coordinators" for their children, while simultaneously framing families as "targets of intervention" and professional scrutiny.[136] Promoters of behavioral therapies have framed them as a means of transitioning children into educational settings, but that fact does not negate the intensity of demands on parents for the duration of their use.[137]

When insurers refuse payments for behavioral therapies, citing the failure to reproduce the rates of success in Lovaas's original studies, parents are left to pay out of pocket or seek treatment through the special education programs in their child's school district.[138] Some parents, frustrated with the lack of quality or consistency in the therapists that they employed, have earned master's degrees in behavioral therapy in order to run their children's programs themselves.[139] Children with autism are often eligible for treatment in a public educational setting through the 1990 Individuals with Disabilities Education Act. However, school districts may resist providing behavioral therapies like ABA because of the expense involved, as much as $40,000–$80,000 per child each year, and so parents have become experts of another kind, legal representatives for their children at the annual meetings required by law to settle the terms of a child's Individualized Education Program (IEP).[140] Although school districts argued that parents "lack professional experience and judgment and are 'emotionally invested in the outcome of the case,'" the Supreme Court ruled that parents had a legitimate personal interest in their children's education, rendering it both acceptable and constitutionally mandated that they be allowed to represent their children.[141]

Behavioral therapies, as everyday semiprofessional activities on the part of parents, established two important precedents in the history of the autism diagnosis and the population that it defined. By making parents technicians, they provided structural and pragmatic support for what parents had argued all along and what they would come to argue more energetically: Parents were experts on their own children, in terms of their individual symptoms and their idiosyncratic responses. By establishing that children with autism could be educated and that such practices could take place in the context of a theory of neurological difference and sensory atypicality as much as one of meaningful behavior, they provided a context for later developments.

In the ensuing years, an emphasis on surveillance, early identification, and intervention meant that parents spent less time seeking explanations before they were able to act. An increasingly standardized diagnosis and growing empirical support for treatment gave parents better guidance in their decisions about their child. And research in genetics and neuroscience provided a foundation for understanding children with autism as biologically different from typical children. However, parental knowledge remained central to daily life.

Parents Speak: The Art of Love and the Ethics of Care

Disability studies in the university emerged from the disability rights movement of the 1970s and 1980s. Conversations about autism are inevitably also about issues that have occupied both scholars and activists. They range from philosophical questions about defining disability and the ethics of treatment to policies regarding access to health care and living supports, deinstitutionalization and patient's rights, the Individuals with Disabilities Education Act (IDEA), and inclusive education.

A history of autism focused specifically on parental experience and knowledge cannot hope to incorporate all the lessons that disability studies teaches us, in particular, that we take seriously the accounts of people with disabilities themselves. As I mentioned in the introduction, there are many women and men with autism diagnoses who are capable spokespeople. A number of them are passionate advocates of neurodiversity, the concept of accepting and accommodating atypical cognitive styles and personality types as valuable elements of human difference.[1] Advocates insist on the importance of respecting the desires of the person with the disability, first and foremost, in policies and treatments directed at them, a position best expressed in the imperative "nothing about us without us."[2]

Many draw on their experience of autism to question not only policies but also psychiatrists' assumptions, maintaining, for example, that the diagnostic distinction between "low" and "high-functioning" autism is specious. This segmentation fails to acknowledge the range of strengths and weaknesses of any individual. Dividing the autism spectrum, needless to say, divides people. Self-advocates reject the claim that those able to communicate and live without assistance are not qualified to weigh in on interventions directed toward those who are unable to care for themselves. Self-advocates have routinely argued that attempts to ameliorate or cure autism are motivated by parents' self-interest. Parents, they say, long for a typical child who conforms to dominant standards of normal functioning. Their pursuit of cures can make them oblivious to their children's own desires or needs.[3] Self-advocates have also criticized federal allocations of research funds on similar grounds. Funding for studies of autism's causes and treatment eclipses outlays for research into services and supports.[4]

In making such claims, they invoke arguments from the disability rights movement.[5] The movement has tended to view medical discourse about disabilities suspiciously and with often well-deserved scorn. The dominant medical model of disability emerged from rehabilitation medicine for wounded soldiers that aimed to return them to their pre-injury level of functioning. As a consequence, many doctors learned to view disabilities against a concept of normality or normal functioning. Activists in the 1960s and 1970s began to challenge this concept of disability. It valued individuals only in terms of their productivity, framing disability in terms of barriers to participation in the workplace, and it automatically assumed that a disabled person was less than whole or complete. Disability studies offered an alternative, the "social model," which holds that the experience of disability emerges from a person's social and physical environment rather inhering in an individual. Accommodations in the built and human environments are the way to address disability. The burden should not be on the individual but on society, which effectively creates the experience of disability by failing to accommodate human variations.

In the United States, the history of autism cannot be written without reference to the history of cognitive disabilities more generally. The idea that parents caused their children's autism or that autism was a product of the child's will resembled other moral explanations for disability common in the nineteenth and early twentieth centuries. Although expressed in a psychotherapeutic language, the demand that both children and parents achieve a cure through self-understanding had much in common with earlier theories of intellectual disability that saw cognitive deficits as failures of character. The association that professionals drew between criminality and intellectual disabilities further stigmatized those conditions, and current arguments over the presence or absence of intellectual disabilities associated with autism attest to the persistence of that stigma.[6] Parents' work to create the National Society for Autistic Children (NSAC) and find effective treatment methods during the late 1960s and 1970s took place at a time when parents of children with many types of disabilities had begun to cooperate to obtain educational rights for their children. Current developments take place in a system defined by legislation enacted during the 1970s, including the Education for All Handicapped Children Act, which transformed the experience of many childhood disabilities.[7]

By focusing on interventions intended to cure, ameliorate, or reframe autism as a medical condition, my discussion may seem remote from the concern in disability studies with recognizing each individual's fundamental value as a whole person with a right to autonomy over decisions about his or her care. If anything, mine is an account of the relentless medicalization of autism. Parents adopted and integrated expert discourses from behaviorism, biochemistry, psychology, and genetics in their efforts to treat their children. In the process, their advocacy work centered more on raising awareness and funds than on examining the social factors that have contributed to the perception of autism as a severe disorder in need of treatment. I focus on caregivers because understanding how they make distinctions between their knowledge and that of professionals helps show how acts of love are part of biomedical work. This means telling a story about the shaping of autism through different sets of biomedical discourses and practices as opposed to a history of the social production of autism as a disability.

The "semiprofessional" parents who have intervened in the production of autism demonstrate facility with medical terminology and practices and argue for their own situated expertise on their children. They may be aware of self-advocates' arguments, but they also act knowing that their choices early on may affect their child's entire life. Some children with autism will become adults with the same needs and limitations that they had as children, while others will go on to live more independent lives. However, *all* children remain absolutely dependent on their caregivers and unable to express their needs with complete freedom, at least for their first few years. This is significant for thinking about the decisions that parents must make.

Chapters 2 and 3 identified a number of sites in which love has functioned as a form of practice or technique in interventions to address the syndrome of autism. I want to take a step back and revisit the idea of love as an introduction to the chapters that follow. Love relates to practical knowledge, the ethics of care, and concepts of "moral personhood," familial commitments, and dependence, themes I introduced at the beginning of this book. It also matters to treatment choices and to the ethics of interventions, all of which are central to the final three chapters on genetics research, biomedical interventions, and immunizations. Gail Landsman has described how

> mothers of disabled infants and toddlers also suggest that mothers, because of their commitment to their child rather than to a stated prognosis or to their own professional ego, have the passion and freedom to gather the *same* biomedical information as physicians do, and in some instances, to come to know more than a particular medical practitioner not only about their child but about their child's disability and treatment options.[8]

Throughout this book, I extend Landsman's insight by describing how caregivers have applied their expertise not only in providing therapies for the child in their care, but also in helping to shape research programs and treatment options within the biomedical community devoted to that child's diagnosis. Here I provide additional examples of how they have accomplished this and how professionals have responded.

I hope to accomplish two things by taking the time to discuss how parents think about treatment. The first is to draw attention to the practical forms of bioethical reasoning used by parents and practitioners in the course of everyday life and work. Disability studies can help draw attention to the practice of caregiving and affective work as central to biomedical practices and, therefore, crucial to debates about the ethics of those practices. The second goal is to show how studying the application of medical interventions matters for disability studies, a discipline that has traditionally been concerned with normative questions that are not always the focus of work by sociologists of science and medicine. To do this, I need to begin by discussing how experts have represented parents' ability to reason and make decisions.

The Demands and Desires of Parenting

As we have seen, parents of children with autism have been scrutinized nearly as much as their children. Psychologists and anthropologists studied them for clues about a child's "choice" of symptoms.[9] Beginning with Leo Kanner, experts also noted interesting parallels between parents' personalities and those of their children, although it was hard to determine whether these shared traits reflected common genetic factors or parents' reactions to their child's unusual behavior and emotional remoteness. Behavioral therapists sought to harness parents' knowledge, but focused on the therapeutic interaction rather than on the minutiae of daily life with an autistic child. Professionals finally realized that therapies could take place within households rather than the laboratory, but homes came with their own set of pitfalls. Behavioral programs often broke down under the stress and, at moments, chaos of daily life.[10]

Stress is a recurring theme in writing about these parents. Researchers distinguish it from the predictable stress of raising a child with a severe disability.[11] Young children with autism often appear typical to onlookers, who then tend to blame parents for their children's "misbehavior."[12] Some researchers think that raising a child with autism is uniquely taxing because the children have a difficult time relating socially and emotionally.[13] If part of parents' stress stems from their children's difficulties with social reciprocity and part from stigma, a significant portion comes from managing behavioral issues, including problems with eating and sleep and emotional outbursts.[14] Parents of children with autism report more extreme experiences of isolation and loneliness than do parents of children with other developmental disabilities. The loneliness is no doubt reinforced when doctors tell them that their child can learn to mimic appropriate behaviors but will never share feelings with them, and that what they believe about their child's sociability and capacity to interact with them is an illusion.[15]

Given the levels of parental demands and stress, it is not surprising that even sympathetic researchers characterize much of what parents do as coping strategies. Their turns to religion or use of support services and, in particular, their activism are ways of coming to terms with a harrowing diagnosis and uncertain prognosis.[16] There is a cost, however, to seeing such actions as determined exclusively by parents' involuntary reactions to their child's symptoms rather than by their intelligence or beliefs—a mistake similar to seeing every act carried out by a child with autism as a symptom of the disorder: It robs conscious actions of their value and intentionality. As Gail Landsman explains, when parents disagree with doctors about applying the label of developmental "delay" rather than "disability" to their child, they are not denying the obvious but making a strategic choice about their own level of investment. Their choice to believe that their attention and nurturance can continue to shape their child's development yields concrete results.[17] It is no accident that parents describe their own actions as those of knowledgeable observers and rational actors.

Parents Speak

In 1974, the *Journal of Autism and Childhood Schizophrenia*, then the only journal devoted exclusively to research on autism, began publishing a section called "Parents Speak." It ran for slightly over a decade, until 1985. It was a remarkable column, coming at a time when the majority of research that focused on the parents of children with autism did so only in order to assess the parents' level of pathology and identify exactly how parents had caused their child's disability.[18] In the course of the column's life, contributors used their own experiences to identify significant characteristics of autism that researchers would not investigate for another three decades. More important, they demonstrated that alongside their technical acumen, they were willing to address problems relating to the ethics of treatment. In contrast, practitioners without autistic children tended to define those ethical problems as outside their area of concern, when they acknowledged their existence at all.

The influence of Eric Schopler, the new editor-in-chief, was evident in the decision to begin "Parents Speak." He had to defend the choice to at least one skeptical reader who feared that "the scientific level might well be lowered as a result."[19] As a founder of Division TEACCH, Schopler favored an ecological approach to autism predicated on seeing parents as cotherapists with professionals. The first editor of the column, Mary S. Akerley, then president of the National Society for Autistic Children (NSAC), wanted to encourage dialogue as a way to counteract the increasing specialization among autism researchers, often at the expense of a comprehensive view of the child in their care. She valued parents' perspectives in particular because "their observations, interpretations, and suggestions for research and/or treatment are perhaps more likely to represent the problems of the autistic child than the specialized professional concerns."[20]

It turned out that parents had quite a bit to say. One discussed the "Near-Normal Autistic Adolescent," a "subgroup of autistic persons with unique problems and needs, not previously given separate attention." [21] These young people were often hungry for social interaction but unsure of how to seek it. David Park, Clara Claiborne Park's husband and Jessy Park's father, described trying operant conditioning with his daughter, years before the publication of Lovaas's 1987 study on efficacy.[22] In another article, Park marveled at the mathematical complexity of his daughter's scheme to order her world. Working to understand the "entirely personal kind of meaning" of these intellectual structures might, at the very least, provide a source of shared interest and conversation with an autistic child that could help them to develop speech.[23] Parents debated the use of aversive techniques and reviewed books and memoirs by other parents. There was even a selection of poems about children with autism.[24] Throughout, they insisted on the irreducible importance of their own observations as a kind of data that experts were incapable of providing.

The column also provided a forum for parents to suggest directions for research and treatment, often before professionals showed interest in the same areas. Parents noticed responses in their own children that seemed like promising avenues for investigation. In a 1975 column titled "Hunches on Some Biological Factors in Autism," Ruth Christ Sullivan wondered whether there might be a connection linking rheumatoid arthritis, celiac disease (an immune reaction to wheat protein), and autism, as the three seemed to run in families. She was particularly interested in the gastrointestinal symptoms that parents reported in their children.[25] A section of a column titled "Why Do Autistic Children. . .?" commented on the routine observation that children with autism seemed much calmer, more communicative, and better oriented when they were running a fever. Might this be a clue to some underlying biological mechanism of the disorder? Only decades later would researchers systematically investigate these connections, in both cases finding that the parental observations were largely correct.[26]

The column also became a place to explore the ethics of treatment. At one point, Mary Akerley proposed the subtitle "Values in Conflict," since so many of the entries dealt with the often wrenching process of weighing a child's health against his or her freedom, or a child's needs against those of the family.[27] One article about the successful use of a diet to treat a child's "cerebral allergies" occasioned short commentaries by Eric Schopler, the Nobel Prize–winning chemist Linus Pauling, an allergist, and a psychiatrist on the responsibilities of practitioners and national organizations like NSAC in publicizing promising but unproven treatments.[28]

As editor, Mary Akerley took the opportunity to suggest some ways that the doctor–patient or, more accurately, the doctor–parent relationship might be improved. In the mid-1970s, long after researchers had putatively abandoned psychogenic theories of causation, psychological professionals still had the unsettling habit of blaming parents for their children's autism. Others sought to protect parents by delaying diagnosis, withholding prognoses, and discouraging them from doing their own research. Most parents, Akerley pointed out, were doing their own research anyway. Doctors needed to understand that "hard as it is to live with one's mistakes, it is infinitely more terrible to have to live with someone else's." She also called for professionals to take a more active role alongside parents in advocating for services for autistic children.[29] Professionals responded approvingly to the column, although few believed that the criticisms applied to them. Rather, they described other "incompetent" psychiatrists who "would not survive in most of our therapeutic programs," or doctors who had unsuccessfully treated their patients in the past.[30]

The column also brought parents into debates that originated on the research pages of the journal. One of the most anguished discussions of the period concerned the use of negative reinforcement or "aversives" in treating children with intractable behavior problems including self-injury, aggression, and running away—sometimes into traffic. A 1976 review article on the use of shock in autism treatment triggered responses, often heartfelt, from both parents and professionals that continued for two years.[31] One of the most telling came from a North Carolina parent who had been forced to place her son in an institution. She wrote, "Every 10 days I make the 200 mile trip to visit him. I have glimpsed competence. Risk/benefit?"[32] A decade later, as activists called for full rights and education for people with cognitive disabilities, professionals took up the appropriateness and content of sex education. Parent respondents reminded readers that they were already making decisions about what their children needed to understand about sex and providing the instruction themselves, at home.[33]

In 1977, Ruth Christ Sullivan took over the editorship of the "Parents Speak" column, leading off with an article by Katharine Sangree Stokes about "Planning for the Future of a Severely Handicapped Child." It was an issue that was largely absent from the journal and neglected by experts on the whole. Nonetheless, Christ Sullivan reminded readers, Stokes spoke to a concern "that parents (and truly concerned professionals) talk about when they are speaking with their hearts."[34] Like other parents, Stokes had "worked to find, to support, and to create the necessary educational and social opportunities" for her child. Although these were the immediate concerns, she wanted to address the thinking "that occupies parents in the long nights after their more immediate cares are set aside."[35]

Stokes questioned the readiness of any institution to provide what the family setting did for her son, namely, connecting with and valuing him as an individual. For instance, a school's efforts to teach her adult son age-appropriate behaviors might actually work against his interests. She imagined a situation in which an otherwise dangerous encounter with a police officer unaware of his condition might be mitigated by his thumb-sucking.[36] Other parents chimed in, suggesting that the best possible environment for their children might not be one that superficially appeared normal, but rather one that provided for their particular developmental needs in ways that allowed them to continue to grow and learn. An autism label served their children only in some contexts. It might sometimes be useful to "consider efforts to unlabel our children."[37] One of the respondents, Clara Park, concluded that those who helped her daughter grow were "those who take her where she is, responding warmly to both woman *and* child, continually alert to the possibilities for normalization, but recognizing their limits, and warmly responding to her simple humor and guilelessness, her charm."[38] The care that parents and other primary caregivers provided was profoundly difficult to replicate in a standard or conventionalized format. Nevertheless, they knew that someone would eventually have to learn to do their work for them.

Deinstitutionalization and "normalization" were important trends in the care of children with autism and other developmental disabilities during the 1970s. Professionals wrote about these issues in the pages of the journal, but parents also weighed in, urging researchers to recognize the gulf between daily realities and the ideal of disabled children experiencing the typical rhythms of daily life rather than the artificial routines of institutions.[39] In this instance, career employees of treatment centers and others who worked with autistic children on a daily basis also commented. The portrait of normalization as a rigid and prescriptive set of practices offered by Gary Mesibov, a psychologist, had failed to take into account the flexibility of such programs in practice.[40]

Community care came up again in the 1980s as the column became a place where the "autism family" could air opposed views on the desirability of deinstitutionalization and the degree to which the approach made room for the individualized programs that seemed to work for many severely affected children. Christ Sullivan summarized the responses to a new NSAC resolution in favor of closing residential institutions.[41] Amy Lettick, who had founded Benhaven in 1967, opposed it, pointing out that for many children with autism, the best, least restrictive environment was not necessarily the one with the least structure.[42] Ivar Lovaas and Corinne Fredricks, another parent, believed that the resolution provided important support for the movement toward group homes where people with developmental disabilities could live alongside other members of the community, having new experiences and learning skills that they would never have acquired in an institution.

The long run of columns in the *Journal of Autism and Childhood Schizophrenia/Journal of Autism and Developmental Disorders* revealed parents eager to share their knowledge and ideas in an academic forum, aware that they had data that clinicians and researchers didn't possess. That information came in part from parents' ability to see their children as whole persons and to observe them throughout their daily lives. Although parents wanted treatments, they were also the first to promote the then-controversial view of autism as a static condition to be dealt with by recognizing the value of their child's unique attributes and, where feasible, accommodating their special needs. Others were the first to suggest interventions that became standard practice. This focus on everyday life and a child's immediate needs shows parents, through their entanglement with their child, charting a complicated course between treatment and acceptance.[43] Finally, the contributions to the "Parents Speak" column remind us that many who contributed were also professionals who had entered the field in part due to their experience as parents.

The social role of parent provides no assurance that a person will make the best of all possible decisions for his or her child, nor does it make that individual a better authority than the child on questions about that child's own condition. It certainly does not grant a person sudden and effortless medical and neurological expertise. What the identity can signify is a very specific and intimate understanding of a child's physical and emotional character, born of years of close observation and experience. In most cases, it also signifies insights gained as a result of the special attentiveness that comes from love. Parents learn to understand their child both as an individual and as a member of their family unencumbered by assumptions about what the child's particular diagnosis or symptoms may mean. As Gail Landsman explains,

> In one's own home, alone with the child and apart from the stresses of "competitive mothering" or medical diagnoses, a mother comes to understand her child as simply himself/herself, neither terribly unusual nor comparable to other children on any scale that makes sense.[44]

Landsman's insight is particularly relevant to questions about the ethics of treatments designed to ameliorate the symptoms of autism. Those debating the ethics of interventions tend to assume that the choice is between two alternatives, to act aggressively to cure the disorder or to respect the integrity of autistic personhood by eschewing treatment altogether.[45] This yields little practical advice for those considering treatments designed to ameliorate elements of autism but unlikely to cure it. Landsman's interviews with mothers of children with a range of disabilities also demonstrate that few see the choices so starkly. Most of the women that Lands-man spoke with effortlessly negotiated the tensions between apparently opposed perspectives.[46] They saw their child as a complete person, worthy of value and respect, not despite but in terms of his or her disability. At the same time they were committed to working to increase their child's opportunities for pleasure and new experiences in ways that often involve efforts to alleviate some of their impairments.[47] Their position, and that of many parents of children with autism, is not far from more recent writing in disability theory. Scholars like Tom Shakespeare now argue that the social model of disability unfairly disregards both the reality of bodily suffering and the fact that impairments do inevitably alter individual experience, sometimes in painful ways.[48]

Contemporary Developments

As we have seen, for parents of children with autism, experimentation is central. I describe the types of parental knowledge that have mattered in the context of a series of successive, competing, and often incommensurable arguments about autism's causes and about the correct course of treatment. I do so largely for ease of exposition. In reality, parents range across theories, practices, and paradigms in treating their children. Their approaches reflect a kind of biomedical syncretism, where they are behaviorists one moment, biochemists another, and homeopaths later, often unconcerned about the degree of fit among rival theories. Their choices can seem irrational to experts who proceed from theory to treatment, but they reflect a pragmatic logic rooted in caregiving and defined by practice. Even more than other professional groups that treat children with autism, parents are technicians first, although some may become theorists. Their attitude toward their children is caring, but it is also experimental—as most childrearing is.

The relationship between affective commitment and specific, practical knowledge unites places as disparate as the Orthogenic School at the University of Chicago and Defeat Autism Now! conferences. The young female counselors at the Orthogenic School were "repeatedly bitten, kicked, defecated upon or otherwise abused," but they tolerated these behaviors out of devotion to the students and a belief that they had provoked them, at least in part.[49] Similar motives drive parents who, decades later, administer taxing schedules of nutritional supplements and detoxification agents to their children. Both therapies raise troubling ethical questions, at least for some. Parents and counselors consider their affective commitment an advantage, while critics say that devotion blinds them to consequences. Love is never enough, but those parents and counselors might argue that at times it, or other forms of affective knowledge, accounts for the difference in decisions that are otherwise too hard to make. Medical practitioners and even some sociologists see parents' choices as reactive, motivated by their despair at a diagnosis. Parents have a more subtle understanding of the knowledge and values that they bring to determining the right course of action. Despite their frequent need to choose among undesirable alternatives in order to care for their children, they indeed weigh the ethical consequences of their actions.

Recognizing parents' ethical agency is crucial because parents often have to make decisions for children who are unable to do so for themselves. Such choices are sometimes shaped by parents' hopes for a typical child but more often by deep appreciation of their child's individuality and unique strengths. Parents also understand that while some adults with autism lead lives in which they experience their autism as a source of strength rather than a liability, many more of them, the majority, remain dependent on extensive services and support, often in highly restrictive environments where they have limited autonomy.[50] In a sense self-advocates represent another set of experts that parents may call on for inspiration. I take up some of their arguments in the next chapter on genetic and neurological models of autism.

Although the number of individuals diagnosed with autism is increasing, the vast majority of people in the United States and elsewhere are neurotypical. The task for most of us in the years ahead, as researchers, educators, journalists, neighbors, and voters, is to learn how to interact with autistic people in an ethical and honest fashion, even if their perceptual and emotional worlds are different from ours. Parents have longer experience in this task than the rest of us. When we stop thinking about them as limited by their commitments to and love for their children and start thinking of them as rational actors whose knowledge is enhanced by the attentiveness that love encourages, it seems clear that they represent one community that has already thought long and hard about the ethics of treatment, the desirability of normalization, and the difficulty of balancing respect, protection, and care.[51] The rest of us are compromised, too, by our anxieties, commitments, and desires. Parents have thought more than many of us about what these feelings do and the help that they might provide in the production of knowledge.

The remainder of this book considers different perspectives on autism treatment, theories of etiology, and the implicit and explicit ethical concerns that influence both theory and professional practice. As parents enter into professional areas of authority they do so by claiming that their love helps them determine how best to understand and treat their children. These claims about love are strong and sometimes risky.

Two

Brains, Pedigrees, and Promises:

Lessons from the Politics of Autism Genetics

Patricia Stacey is a memoirist who attributes her son's recovery from autism to "floor time," an intensive program of early behavioral intervention. Like many parents' accounts, Stacey's story of her child's diagnosis and treatment includes an explanation of autism's causes. In her version, seemingly unaffected parents exhibit, in milder form, the same behaviors and sensitivities as their children. Autism "runs in the family."[1] When Stacey describes how a therapist's passing comment about her tendency to "space out" during sessions with her son helped her recognize her own sensory oversensitivities and defensiveness, she is speaking to a wider community of parents for whom genetic claims make obvious sense. "Sometimes the children we are working with are just exaggerated versions of their parents," her son's therapist observes.

> Time and again when I have been talking to women with children with autism, I hear a resonant story. I heard nearly the same story twice from two different mothers who had never met. The couple goes to a lecture on autism or visits a therapist shortly after their child receives a diagnosis. The couple learns that people with autism have systematic minds, like things in certain orders, have trouble with transitions—that people with autism are not social—that they may be good with math and music, or they are highly visual. The husband walks out of the classroom, or office, and says, "My God, they've just been describing me."[2]

That shock of recognition concerning the heritability and genetic nature of autism comes at a moment when the category has been rendered relatively stable through standardized behavioral screening tools and an entry in the *Diagnostic and Statistical Manual of Mental Disorders*. It probably could not have happened at an earlier moment. Parents might have noted similarities between themselves and their children in passing, but they and their children's doctors would not have shared an understanding of autism as a genetic syndrome of unknown origin, among the "most heritable" of disorders of its kind.[3] For parents to raise millions to fund genetic research and donate blood and tissue samples from themselves and their children to fuel that research, autism first had to become a genetic disorder. That process occurred in tandem with diagnostic standardization. However, clearer diagnostic boundaries were not sufficient to make autism visible as "genetic." That process required that researchers learn to exchange psychological explanations for genetic ones, while characterizing the disorder in terms of broadly defined behavioral symptoms that could be identified in family lineages. They had to exchange their reservations about the existence of environmental causes for certainties about prenatal origins and faith in evocative animal models of behaviorally similar syndromes.

Organizational spokespersons, self-advocates, and relatives of people with autism work in a landscape shaped by the history of autism genetics. Autism has become genetic, but it has become so in the wake of the long history of theorizing about autism as a form of organic affective deficit in those diagnosed or as caused by a deficit of emotion in their parents. In the present, acts of speaking for people with autism are often legitimated by the idea of heritability as much as by claims of parental caring and involvement. Likewise, when self-advocates speak from the perspective of their identities as autistic people, they ground their claims in presumed neurological and genetic likeness to other autistic people. The idea of genetic similarity in autism research and advocacy provides ethical legitimacy and entitlement. In stories such as this one, where individuals choose one definition of a disorder (as "genetic"), thereby excluding others (for instance, theories of environmental etiology, psychological frameworks, or purely behavioral descriptions), it is important to acknowledge the workings of desire. Self-advocacy groups and parents are not merely pawns, expressing the genetic optimism of scientists because that is what they have been told to believe. They want autism to be genetic and they invest financially and emotionally in a definition of it as such.

Genetics provides an effective vocabulary for expressing responsibilities and experiences of membership that develop out of love, friendship, and loyalty. These connections have been established in a number of ways. Parent groups and researchers reframed autism as a neurological and genetic condition during the 1960s as an alternative to psychogenic theories of autism. In the 1990s, parent groups began to dispute the proper organization of research on biological materials from themselves and their children. Two of these groups were able to mobilize the partiality associated with their status as parents as an asset as they constructed new institutions for producing facts about autism genetics. In the process, they mobilized representations of ideal scientific practice drawn both from scientists' accounts and from popular representations of science to demand acceptable behavior from the scientists that they sought to enlist.

In the present, advocates for autism and Asperger syndrome (AS) accept a genetic and neurological definition of the syndrome, but protest the use of behavioral and sometimes medical interventions. Even as they embrace genetic characterizations of autism, they fear the possible outcomes of genetic research applied to prenatal testing or treatment. They argue that aggressively seeking interventions devalues autistic traits and tendencies. Autism represents a type of neurological diversity that becomes a disability only due to discrimination and stigma.

Advocates' efforts to define an "autistic culture" and "autistic voices" remind us that genetic identities are only as fixed as the meanings attached to them. For instance, it is not entirely clear what it means to be "a little autistic" when psychiatrists or genetics researchers use the term in casual conversation to describe a family member of a child with full-spectrum autism. That researchers and increasingly the general public understand what this means, that "a little autism" grants one a certain attention to detail combined with more limited social skills, reflects a social consensus crucial for the shaping of identity and relationships.[4] Put slightly differently, the presumed genetic status of autism permits certain kinds of kinship relations—seeing a relationship of likeness between "high" and "low" functioning autistic individuals or recognizing similarities between parents and children with autism—as well as expressions of commitment and obligation, while excluding others. Meanwhile, brain research and genetics research in autism work synergistically, each contributing to an explanatory framework in which autism is a genetic disorder that affects the brain and cognition exclusively, effectively precluding research on mid-level explanations focused on disease mechanisms.[5] Who gets caught up in the genetic relations of autism, then, becomes a question of research politics, with both practical and ethical consequences.

Making Autism a Genetic Disease

Since the 1960s, disease has been largely conceived of in genetic terms, reflecting the gradual "realization of an idea," in Susan Lindee's words, "that all human disease is a genetic phenomenon subject to technological control."[6] Genetics is also understood in a particular way, in which genes are not multiple, interacting sources of vulnerability but discrete sites for potential therapeutic intervention.[7] Peter Conrad has called this "the mirage of genes."[8] "Genes for" complex psychiatric disorders are increasingly the focus of corporate, government, and activist attention. "Gene talk" in expert discourse helps to heighten public expectations.[9] This "genetic" status of many contemporary disorders required social and intellectual work. Acknowledging the labor required to link a disease primarily to genetic knowledge, as opposed to physiological or behavioral knowledge or the "familial knowledge" of caregivers, does not deny the reality of genetic causes for disorders.[10] It simply takes into account the multiple possible ways of describing a disorder and the active choice of genetics as the preferred explanation. Disorders become genetic through research programs that help to certify them as such.

While the tendency of autistic traits to run in families has been of interest to researchers since the category was first described, research into the heritability of autism constituted a relatively small proportion of work through the 1970s. Since the mid-1990s, autism genetics has enjoyed a massive increase in prominence via private and government-funded research programs.[11] From its origins in a series of twin studies, research has come to focus successively on sibling pairs and multiplex families, and more recently on full-genome scans paired with candidate gene studies. Researchers operate with the implicit assumption that high-throughput genetic research will eventually yield results.[12] The vast majority of these studies rely on families in which multiple members have autism diagnoses, despite the fact that the vast majority of autism cases—about 90 percent— are sporadic, meaning that they occur in families in which there was no prior history of the disorder.[13] Publications in autism genetics have transformed autism from a disorder with hereditary components to a complex genetic disorder, a shift that has impacted the direction and funding of autism research. The change reflects an increasing focus on psychiatric genetics in general and a deepening conviction that autism treatment is necessary, that it will involve the use of pharmaceuticals, and that developing these techniques depends on locating autism genes.

Familial Tendencies

Speculation about the relationship between familial traits and autism has a history as long as that of the diagnosis. Depending on the perspective of the expert who observed them, what looked like affective distance on the part of parents was a causative factor in autism or evidence of underlying genetic likeness in parents. As we saw in chapter 1, Leo Kanner observed that parents of children with autism were often highly educated and seemed aloof and removed. In a 1960 *Time* magazine profile, he described parents as "just happening to defrost long enough to produce a child," although he later regretted that characterization.[14] Kanner's ideas shaped the way that child psychiatrists and psychologists first understood and treated autism in the 1950s and 1960s. The idea that parents might have caused their child's autism offered the hope that it might be treated. The allure of psychology eclipsed the study of heredity, with its uncertain prospects.

In 1964, Bernard Rimland published *Infantile Autism*, the first point-by-point refutation of the psychogenic theory of autism. The book reflected mounting skepticism among many psychologists, if not among the pediatricians and other health-care professionals that had been trained on their earlier work, of the idea that parental rejection—or even outright mistreatment—was an important causal factor in autism. Rimland revisited Kanner's original characterizations of his eleven cases and their parents, suggesting that these observations offered clues to a genetic etiology. Rimland argued that "despite the presence of a few borderline cases . . . the evidence overwhelmingly supports Kanner's unprecedented early report that the parents of autistic children form a unique and highly homogeneous group in terms of intellect and personality."[15]

Genes promised parents, Rimland included, both exculpation and the prospect of targeted medical intervention, the kind of therapeutic specificity on which modern medical knowledge is premised.[16] Psychological experts had thought that genetic reasoning precluded interventions into children's behavior and development. The growing promise of behavioral therapies helped to separate the practice of successful treatment from psychological theory. Rimland played a role in this shift as well, founding the National Society for Autistic Children (later the Autism Society of America) in 1965 with the aim of promoting behavioral therapies.

Psychologists like Bruno Bettelheim saw little difference between causal theories that implicated genetics and parental psychopathology. Since parents caused harm to their children through the operation of unconscious processes of rejection, whether their faulty genes or their flawed psyches damaged their children didn't affect parents' culpability. Treatment remained the same. For parents, however, the moral valence of genetic theories appealed more than their psychogenic equivalents. By the 1970s, the most influential researchers in the field agreed that "such parental abnormalities as do occur are at least as likely to result from pathology in the child as the other way around."[17] As researchers largely rejected the idea of parental attitudes playing a role in triggering autism, their certainty about the heritability of autism increased. Twin studies provided the justification for describing autism in genetic terms, but familial tendencies toward autism were the means through which these genes would be identified. The fact that the majority of autism cases are sporadic, with no previous family history, was a methodological hindrance, not an indication of potential limitations in the genetic framework. Some parents embraced a view of autism's genetic underpinnings. Others held back, observing that even when there is no family history of mental illness or cognitive disorders, "this diagnosis is like a metal detector, beeping on harmless bits of trash that appear more tantalizing when underground."[18]

Producing Certainty

Twin studies played a crucial role in convincing researchers of the hereditary nature of autism, although they said little about the mechanism through which genetic differences resulted in the behavioral syndrome. The impetus for these studies came from a number of published case reports of monozygotic, or identical, twin pairs that were concordant for autism, meaning that both twins fit the requirements for diagnosis. The results seemed suggestive enough that in the 1971 inaugural issue of the *Journal of Autism and Childhood Schizophrenia*, Michael Rutter and Lawrence Bartak allowed that that there might be a "genetically determined type of autism that constitutes a small subgroup of autistic disorders." They also thought that the evidence weighed "rather against a decisive hereditary element."[19] Others agreed. A 1976 review article argued against a significant genetic contribution to autism, although the authors were fairly certain that autism was caused by biological factors, perhaps pre- or postnatal brain injury.[20] At the time, it seemed possible that autism could be caused by a rare spontaneous mutation, although the under-100-percent concordance in monozygotic twin pairs seemed to contradict this, or by an interacting set of genes, but that so few family members of autistic children were affected made this seem unlikely.

By 1977, Rutter and Susan Folstein's study of twenty-one twin pairs had found a 36-percent concordance rate for autism in monozygotic twins. This finding hardly served as evidence that hereditary factors explained all cases of autism, although when researchers asked whether nonautistic identical twin siblings of children with autism had any kind of cognitive or social impairment, they found higher rates of concordance. These milder traits would later become important for theories of a "broader autism spectrum." At the time, Rutter and Folstein concluded that "the hereditary influences are concerned with a variety of cognitive abnormalities and not just with autism," noting that although the nonautistic twin siblings were more likely to have "delays or disorders in the acquisition of spoken language," it was impossible to draw "firm conclusions" on the heritability of "social and emotional difficulties." Rutter and Folstein also thought that the higher autism rates in twins might reflect their increased likelihood of perinatal complications. They had observed that when they took account of such "biological hazards" as delayed breathing or congenital abnormalities in cases where both twins did not have autism, the sibling with autism invariably was the one who had suffered the complication.[21] It seemed possible to researchers that autism might only develop after an experience that rendered children especially vulnerable. It might be a consequence of delayed development but not necessarily itself a developmental disorder.

During the 1980s, geneticists began conducting twin studies using broadened concepts of an "autism spectrum," including participants who tested within the typical range for IQ. They found concordance rates above 90 percent in monozygotic twins. Still, in 1986, an article on the early developmental backgrounds of autistic and mentally retarded children emphasized their preconception histories, including parental exposure to chemicals and maternal viral infections. "To the extent that not only direct infection by the mother but mere exposure to viruses, either in the workplace or in the household, can have an adverse effect on the developing embryo and fetus, we need much more research in this critical area," the authors argued.[22] Autism had yet to become a "genetic disease" as late as 1991, when Susan Folstein, the coauthor of the important 1977 twin study, wrote in a review article that "autism is a behavioral syndrome with multiple etiologies. Within the subgroup where hereditary factors play a significant role it is likely that there is genetic heterogeneity as well."[23]

By the late 1990s, twin studies had given way to other approaches designed to locate susceptibility genes, although researchers continued to cite concordance rates from earlier twin studies as evidence for the heritability of autism. Researchers argued for the use of affected-sibling-pair research designs and candidate gene studies, most of them focused on genes associated with the central nervous system.[24] Changes in diagnostic practices, meanwhile, reflected attempts by researchers to produce behaviorally (and presumably genetically) homogeneous populations for research. The ADI-R and ADOS, diagnostic tools developed during the mid-to-late 1990s, offered promise for creating standardized populations for genetic studies. Researchers also adopted the concept of a "broader autism phenotype," arguing that in family studies this approach might "increase the power to find genes" by allowing researchers to take into account family members who did not quite meet the criteria for autism.[25] Geneticists knew that siblings of children with autism had about a 4.5-percent chance of developing the disorder themselves.[26] Broader criteria would help researchers make use of the similarity among family members. They could also use new tools for genetic analysis, including automated sequencing, linkage studies, and full genome scans.

These new efforts also met with limited success. A review article in 2001 found that the eight published whole-genome scans for autism available at the time "yielded a fairly large number of suggestive linkage signals, only a few of which overlap from one study to the next."[27] An accompanying figure made the point clear: when signals from the majority of studies were collated, candidate loci appeared on all but three chromosomes. Nevertheless, the authors believed that "on the basis of the past few decades of research, genetic factors have clearly emerged as the most significant aetiology for autism spectrum disorders." Based on candidate gene studies combined with animal models and studies of human brain tissue, "we can afford to be optimistic that important progress will soon be made in our understanding of this most puzzling of conditions."[28] Even if autism disease genes had "proven elusive" to researchers who now admitted that autism was unlikely to be caused by any single genetic mutation, researchers tended to view the problem as an "impasse," which they would surmount through the use of ever-more-innovative techniques.[29] Another review of the molecular genetics of autism simply stated that "autism is one of the most heritable complex disorders, with compelling evidence for genetic factors and little or no support for environmental influence."[30] Yet by 2008, even the most successful studies using genome scans of multiplex families could use their findings to explain 1 percent of autism cases at best.[31]

Although researchers maintain a genetic focus in autism research for multiple reasons, at least one is the conviction that genetics will lead to treatment. "Locating susceptibility genes is the first step in developing medical and genetic interventions for individuals with autism, and ultimately it is hoped that genetic findings may lead to the development of new and more effective drug treatments for autistic individuals.[32] This ever-receding genetic horizon is not unique to autism research. Adam Hedgecoe has described how limits to genetic explanations are incorporated into the discourse of genetics in Alzheimer's disease research in what he has called a "narrative of enlightened geneticization," in which findings that apparently contradict the idea of Alzheimer's as a genetic disease are simply built into the dominant framework.[33] Most recently, researchers have looked to copy number variations, small segments of the genome that are reproduced or deleted, to explain the preponderance of cases of sporadic autism. Other teams have looked at families with a high degree of intermarriage to implicate a set of genes involved in brain development and language.[34] Although the findings are suggestive, none offers the prospect of a single explanation for autism. Rather, they raise the possibility that different cases of autism are likely to be associated with different genetic factors.

As further evidence suggests that multiple genes and genetic pathways may contribute to autism, experts often invoke an "additive model" popular with researchers working on mental illnesses, in which the number of atypical genes that an individual has determines how much they are affected by a disorder. Siblings of children with autism show "subsyndromal" impairments of social responsiveness.[35] Within this discourse, genetics goes hand in hand with the expectation of future treatments. Genes are made to seem fundamental. Other points of entry into the pathophysiology of autism, in contrast, come to seem less reliable and less worthy of investment.

Meanings from Mice: Rett Syndrome and Animal Models

Based on the limited findings in autism genetics, one might have expected parent groups to grow skeptical of the promise of therapeutic targets in the near future. However, the opposite was true. Financial support for research on autism genetics from parent groups like the National Alliance for Autism Research and the Cure Autism Now Foundation ballooned during the 1990s. Successes in other disorders held out the promise of genes for autism, sometimes even appearing on the timelines of autism genetics research used by parent organizations in their educational materials.[36]

A number of genetic disorders are associated with autistic features in some individuals, including Fragile X syndrome, tuberous sclerosis, and neurofibromatosis. By far the most significant of these is Rett syndrome. Huda Zoghbi, a researcher at Baylor College of Medicine, identified a gene for Rett syndrome, MECP2, in 1999 while funded by the International Rett Syndrome Association.[37] Rett syndrome is a relatively recently described disorder, first identified in a 1966 case series of twenty-two children.[38] It only affects girls, and it is characterized by a period of typical development followed by a rapid and often extreme loss of motor and communication skills around age two. Rett syndrome is a pervasive developmental disorder, linked diagnostically to autistic disorder, Asperger syndrome, childhood disintegrative disorder (CDD, a severe neurodegenerative condition), and pervasive developmental disorder not otherwise specified (PDD-NOS).

As with autism, the parents of children with Rett syndrome became aggressive and savvy advocates for research into their children's condition. The International Rett Syndrome Association (IRSA) consisted of a group of dedicated, tireless, and, in their own telling, somewhat obsessive parents. IRSA provided funding for Dr. Zoghbi, who, through a series of hunches and experiments, isolated the gene for Rett syndrome in 1999. Two factors aided Zoghbi in her investigation. The first was the existence of one family with heritable Rett syndrome—most cases are caused by spontaneous mutations, making linkage studies difficult. She was also aided by the knowledge that the syndrome was likely to be caused by a gene involved in the form of gene regulation called methylation, an epigenetic process that selectively activates or inactivates portions of the genome.

After they identified the gene, Zoghbi and her colleagues produced a mouse model for the syndrome. In order to produce a reliable laboratory organism, the model featured an important deviation from the syndrome in humans. Rett syndrome is only seen in girls because the MECP2 gene is on the X chromosome. Boys with the genotype generally do not survive beyond birth, because they experience the full impact of the mutated gene. In girls, the phenomenon of X chromosome inactivation—common to all women—makes the expression of Rett syndrome highly variable. Because each cell has only one active X chromosome, all girls with Rett syndrome have at least some cells in their bodies with functioning copies of the gene.[39] In contrast to the syndrome in humans, when researchers created the mouse model they introduced a nonfatal "knockout" of the gene in male mice, thus limiting the variability of the phenotype. "Male mice have consistently more severe symptoms than female mice and more uniform symptoms," making the severely affected male mice a better testing ground for "new medications or therapies."[40] A characteristic trait of girls with Rett syndrome is their almost continuous hand-wringing; the icon for IRSA was a line drawing of clasped hands. The trait was poignantly reproduced in the model mice.[41]

Dr. Zoghbi gave a keynote address at the 2002 International Meeting for Autism Research. Her speech left few doubts about the ideological power of the successful hunt for MECP2 for autism researchers. While she spoke, a video of Rett model mice was projected onto a large screen. The mice stumbled off a balance rod that wild-type mice can navigate without difficulty. An unseen researcher then dangled them by their tails and the mice began wringing their forepaws. Many in the audience gasped. The video froze for a few seconds on the final frame of the Rett mice with paws clasped together, as Dr. Zoghbi continued speaking, noting that in most cases members of her laboratory can reliably genotype knockout mice by picking them up by their tails and observing their behavior.[42]

Despite its appeal as a herald of promised advances in autism genetics research, the relevance of Rett syndrome research for autism is not entirely clear. Like many disorders in which epigenetic factors play a role, the route through which mutation leads to disorder in Rett syndrome is still unknown. Researchers cannot explain why a gene involved in so many physiological pathways seems to affect primarily neurological function without causing other major systemic problems in affected girls.[43] Because in Rett syndrome phenotypes vary as a result of X-inactivation, different girls and even different tissues in individual girls have varying levels of the damaged gene, whereas genes on the X chromosome have not been significantly implicated in autism. Another major source of phenotypic variation is the multiple spontaneous mutations that can occur in MECP2, leading to subtly different symptoms.[44] Still, a preponderance of cases of Rett syndrome —around 85 percent— occur as a result of mutations in MECP2, making it close to a monogenic disorder. This scenario is unlikely in autism, where genetics researchers suspect that the heterogeneity of the condition stems in part from a pattern of multiple, interacting genes.

Zoghbi's success, though significant, has yet to lead to specific therapies for affected children. It also offered few investigative techniques that could be incorporated into autism research. The gene was not found through the relatively blunt instrument of linkage or genome-wide association studies, the two favored forms of genetics research in autism. In linkage studies, samples from families with high rates of autism are screened for markers that indicate portions of the genome that are inherited consistently from generation to generation. The identified sites indicate places to seek out candidate genes. In association studies, many samples are screened in search of any genetic variant present in affected children but absent in a control population. In both methods, researchers proceed without any precise idea of the locations of genes of interest. In contrast, Dr. Zoghbi already had a good idea of the type of gene involved in the disorder. Although the genetic test for Rett syndrome does not offer any information to guide treatment, it nonetheless gave parents some measure of relief—"once we had the gene, they could see it was not their fault"—in an equation where the existence of a defective gene definitively exonerated parents from guilt and worry.[45]

Autism organizations encouraged Zoghbi to pursue further research in autism genetics, hoping that the success with Rett syndrome might be replicated. The Cure Autism Now Foundation awarded Zoghbi a $100,000 "genius grant" for autism research, but, according to one report, it might have been the $2.2 million grant from the Simons Foundation that "actually prompted Dr. Zoghbi's foray into autism research."[46] James Simons, a mathematician turned hedge-fund manager, and Marilyn Simons, parents of a girl diagnosed with a "mild form of autism," decided to use their considerable wealth to promote autism genetics research after bringing together a group of "renowned academic figures" and determining that the "one solid lead" in autism research was the results of twin studies.[47]

The appeal of Rett syndrome as a model genetic disorder and a symbol of the desires of autism genetics researchers increased with a 2007 report on success in reversing neurological deficits in a mouse model of Rett syndrome. In this case, researchers engineered mice to have their MECP2 genes conditionally silenced by an allele that could itself be inactivated with timed injections of the drug tamoxifen. If the symptoms of Rett syndrome were due to the inactivation of the gene during development, causing irreversible damage to neural architecture, then reactivating the gene would have had little effect in mature mice already showing symptoms. Instead, the researchers observed what they called "robust phenotypic reversal, as activation of MECP2 expression leads to striking loss of advanced neurological symptoms in both immature and mature adult animals."[48] In other words, genetic neurological disorders that affect children early in their development may carry the potential for reversibility. They are not, strictly speaking, developmental disorders marked by permanent changes in brain architecture.[49]

Although the researchers cautioned that the results "do not suggest an immediate therapeutic approach to RTT," the families speaking in videos on the Rett Syndrome Research Foundation Web site made the potential connection to therapies explicit. One father said that he would be delighted to teach his daughter to walk at the age of fifteen, given the opportunity.[50] Reports of the experiment in the news followed the lead of the families by further broadening the applicability to autism spectrum disorders in general. A headline on the *Scientific American* Web site read "Reversal of Fortune: Researchers Erase Symptoms of Autism Spectrum Disorder."[51]

Meanwhile, researchers have continued their attempts to construct a plausible mouse model for autism in all of its behavioral features, many of which are inconveniently human in character. Despite the "long and illustrious history" of rodent models for human neuropsychiatric disorders, it is not easy to create mouse analogs for communication difficulties, lack of a theory of mind, or failure to engage in imaginative play, nor has it proven easy to design tasks to test these capacities in mice.[52] Some models involving selective gene "knockouts" have succeeded in mimicking specific behavioral abnormalities such as "impaired social learning," but animals with these features often turn out to have clearly visible neuropathology of a kind rarely associated with autism in humans.[53] When researchers have attempted to use primates to study the importance of specific brain structures in autism, results have been similarly disappointing. The amygdala seemed to be an important component of the "social brain" that might be impaired in people with autism, but primates with damage to this structure did not behave in ways that fully supported that conclusion.[54]

Neurological Difference

Studies of the brain in autism consistently failed to locate any specific impaired structures, even on a microscopic level. Nevertheless, researchers still imagined that impairments in autism would eventually correlate to damaged brain structures. Studies of brain tissue during the 1990s indicated that cells in the cerebellum might be missing in the brains of people with autism, but the original research team eventually concluded that they had been mistaken.[55] Scientists have also speculated about the potential role of mirror neurons in autism, referring again to primate studies. Findings in humans have indicated structural abnormalities in the mirror neuron system, which seems to play a role in understanding and imitating the actions of others, forming "a possible neural substrate of empathy."[56] This ability to comprehend the actions of others as though they were our own is what psychologists have referred to as a "theory of mind." [57] However, the connections linking these structures and their specific malfunctions to any set of genes have yet to be determined.

Many researchers working on brain research in autism assume that findings in the brain tissue of people with autism should, like the ideal genetic findings, locate specific domains that are structurally atypical. However, one of the most reliable findings in the brains of people with autism is that they seem to experience a period of rapid early brain growth and then a slowing down that leads to a statistically higher brain volume in young children with autism, concentrated in the white matter of those portions that developed after birth.[58] This pervasive change does not lend itself to any simple genetic interpretation and has inspired some scientists to begin thinking in terms of disrupted developmental systems and chronic disease processes rather than malformed structures.[59] The neurological differences involved in autism seem literally to pervade the brains of affected people.[60]

When researchers use imaging techniques such as functional MRI or psychometric tests from social and cognitive psychology to study brain function, their results seem to support the finding of pervasive, nonspecific brain changes. People with autism may have an atypical excitation/inhibition ratio, a measure of brain activity that relates to the ability to screen out irrelevant information. Many have difficulties shifting their attention on cognitive tasks and perform better when their attention is focused rather than divided, perhaps as a paradoxical result of their difficulties screening out irrelevant stimuli.[61] The psychologist Simon Baron-Cohen distinguishes between "empathizing" and "systemizing," with systemizing seen as a function of autistic strengths that can co-occur with a deficit in empathizing.[62] Researchers have wondered whether these findings might relate to altered patterns of brain connectivity due to brain overgrowth during early development, leading to a pattern of overconnectivity between neurons in smaller regions and underconnectivity over larger expanses.[63] Some researchers note that this pattern of cognition shades easily into autism "endophenotypes," or characteristics associated with autism but not diagnostic of the syndrome, such as the ability to focus on one task to the exclusion of others. These patterns are present within the cognitively typical population and might relate to genetic models of a "broader autism phenotype."[64]

Brain research in autism requires its own system of tissue repositories and sample sharing protocols. Since individuals with autism have a normal lifespan, brains can be difficult for researchers to acquire. Even researchers who succeed in obtaining brain tissue contend with sample sizes far smaller than would be acceptable in many other areas of research, especially given the acknowledged variability among people with autism. Scientists must collaborate to acquire material for research. The LAD-DERS clinic outside Wellesley, Massachusetts, an interdisciplinary autism research and treatment clinic, "works closely" with the Harvard Brain Tissue Resource Center, a brain donation program and repository, which is in turn partnered with the Autism Tissue Program, funded by the National Institutes of Health and the parent organization Autism Speaks.[65]

Beyond supporting the Autism Tissue Program, parents have made fewer attempts to influence brain research relative to their work funding genetics. This could be due to the difficulty of obtaining research materials compared to genetics research or because researchers had already established a system for sharing samples. Although autism researchers have tended to present brains as the site of pathology, they have not presented them as likely points of direct intervention, and that may also have made the stakes in brain-based research seem less high. They present visible brain pathology as the product of prenatal developmental processes, rather than as resulting from an ongoing process of chronic illness. Despite evidence suggesting that brains retain elements of plasticity, or the ability to heal, into adult life, many people view brain pathology as less alterable than genetic abnormalities.

Although researchers have had trouble finding localized structural changes, autism has retained its identity as a genetic disorder of the brain. Those few findings that are produced, from unusual activation of the amygdala to differences in the mirror neuron system, assume an almost iconic value.[66] Like findings in genetics, they invite multiple interpretations on both a functional and ethical level. Opponents of treatment see pervasive brain differences as evidence of fundamental differences in autistic brains that should be treated as a form of "neurodiversity." Advocates concerned about environmental causes welcome evidence that inflammatory processes may trigger the behavioral differences seen in autism. Brain researchers and social psychologists focus on the possibility that the malfunctioning systems in autistic brains might yield insights into the nature of social knowledge, learning, or even gender.[67]

Parenthood, Pedigrees, and Partiality in Autism Genetics

In a 2003 speech, Jonathan Shestack, who founded the Cure Autism Now Foundation (CAN) with his wife, Portia Iverson, spoke about fatherhood and autism. He implicitly referenced histories of parent-blaming as he explained his devotion to research:

> Dov is now eleven, and I'm still trying to figure out how best to love him. All the ways they teach men to be—loud, fast, aggressive—aren't effective with an autistic kid. You come home from the office and make a big commotion, looking for a big reaction, like you're the greatest, most fun dad, but that's just not going [to] get you any closer. They say autistic kids don't imitate very well, but their parents imitate quite well and after a couple of years of non-responsiveness sometimes you just sort of check out.

Shestack more easily expresses his commitment to his son through advocacy than through conventional expressions of paternal devotion: "That's what I know how to do for Dov. That's how I know best to love him."[68]

Genetics operates as a powerful resource for parent organizations. It provides leverage with autism researchers and the ability to speed sluggish research timelines. The authors of a 2004 review in *Pediatrics* admonished, "Parents need to understand that they and their affected children are the only available sources for identifying and studying the elusive genes responsible for autism," but the urging was unnecessary.[69] Parents of children with autism had taken up the idea of genetic research and embraced their unique position to foster that research nearly a decade earlier, with the founding of the New Jersey–based National Alliance for Autism Research (NAAR) in 1994 and the California-based CAN in 1995. Both organizations committed millions to autism research over the following decade. More important, both groups exploited the identities of their members as parents to influence the direction of genetics research in autism. CAN believed that "with enough determination, money and manpower, science can be hurried." Science meant genetics, and genetics signaled the means to repair families as much as it was a sign of familial likeness.[70]

The founders of CAN, Portia Iverson and Jonathan Shestack, are Hollywood insiders who bring a certain charisma and aptitude for pitching a story to their work in autism advocacy. They founded CAN in 1995, shortly after their son, Dov, was diagnosed. Shestack and Iverson realized that they could shift researchers' priorities by leveraging control over genetic materials and the social networks of parent autism communities to influence researchers. HIV/AIDS treatment activists had used similar strategies in the 1990s, and Iverson and Shestack drew inspiration from the Los Angeles–based Pediatric AIDS Foundation in particular.[71] Elizabeth

Glaser, who founded the organization in 1988, argued that in a context of funding neglect for AIDS research as a whole, researchers had ignored the fact that the virus developed and progressed differently in children. CAN also followed a number of groups that had organized in the 1990s around the goal of locating disease genes, including the Dysautonomia Foundation, Inc., PXE International, and the Hereditary Disease Foundation.[72]

All of these groups understood that professional researchers would not necessarily share their priorities or interests. Realizing this, they made use of their funds and human contacts to create novel institutions. Parents demanded that scientists adhere to the standards of "good research" and the ideal of researchers as driven by the altruistic goals of broadening knowledge and treating illness, rather than by their desire for recognition or commercial gain. As observers of scientific practices often note, day-to-day behavior often deviates from the scientific norms of disinterestedness and communal sharing of data.[73] Such lapses dismayed Iverson and Shestack.

Controlling the Coin of the Realm

The founding of CAN's Autism Genetic Resource Exchange (AGRE) in 1997 is one of the more visible success stories in autism research and advocacy. According to most accounts, Portia Iverson and Jonathan Shestack met with experts and determined that genetics offered the most promise in autism research. They also learned that effective genetic research would require DNA samples from at least 100 multiplex families, that is, families with two or more family members with the condition. This requirement proved difficult because families with one case of the disorder are more common. When they began contacting genetics researchers, they discovered that "as as group, the scientists had collected DNA from the necessary 100 families. Individually, however, no single team had DNA from anywhere near that number." The researchers refused to share their samples. Shestack explained that "everyone wanted to be the first to find the genes—their careers depended on being first—and they didn't want anyone else to get a competitive advantage."[74]

The solution was to control "the coin of the realm: DNA." Iverson and Shestack formed their own gene repository, using their status as a parent organization to reach and recruit families. They eventually produced a sample of over 400 multiplex families, more than four times the original requirement.[75] By the summer of 2006, the collection totaled 12,000 families.[76] The acronym for the Autism Genetic Resource Exchange, pronounced like the word "agree," makes explicit CAN's objective of accelerating collaborative work on shared samples. Qualified researchers could access AGRE's samples, including purified DNA, serum samples, and immortalized cell lines approximately at cost. A team that included pediatricians, geneticists, and neurologists gathered phenotypic information through home visits designed to minimize inconvenience to the families. AGRE supplied the results to participant researchers via a built-to-purpose database, the Internet System for Assessing Autistic Children (ISAAC), designed by the father of a child with autism. Private donors contributed more than $6 million to the project, which also received a substantial grant from the National Institute of Mental Health in 2002.

AGRE was set up as a necessary destination for genetic researchers who wished to work with the best possible samples.[77] In the process, CAN made researchers behave in ways that matched the interests of parents. By 2004 the National Institutes of Health (NIH) followed suit by requiring that grant recipients provide "explicit details" on their plans for sharing materials with other researchers.[78]

Where CAN/AGRE chose to exploit parental networks to create a material resource in the form of a genetic repository, the genetics initiative headed by NAAR used a different strategy. The Autism Genetics Cooperative (AGC) incorporated the professional and social worlds of the scientists into the architecture of their program. The desire for recognition and the fear of preemption by competing researchers mattered to genetics researchers in the same way that speed and treatment targets mattered to parents. The founders of NAAR, like the founders of CAN, reasoned that the combined effects of the NIH funding structure, academic career trajectories, tenure considerations, and the increasing commercialization of genetic information had created a climate of intense competition and secrecy. In an attempt to overcome this barrier, NAAR directly addressed the culture of autism genetics research, using its status as a parent organization as a tool for organizing scientific work. For NAAR, research was better organized by those with personal, indeed affective and familial, stakes in the outcome than by the purportedly neutral scientific collective.

In the words of one staff member, NAAR-AGC acted as an "honest broker" for autism geneticists.[79] NAAR selected twenty-two international sites that included the most experienced researchers with the objective of encouraging them to pool their samples and work collaboratively. Researchers attended an annual, invitation-only retreat in Atlanta, Georgia. Several ground rules set the tone for the meetings. Researchers could only present unpublished work, discussions were strictly confidential, and researchers agreed to respect priority, meaning that if an individual had staked out a particular area of research, other participants would not encroach on that area. The organizers insisted on democratic participation, meaning that junior researchers worked alongside more experienced colleagues.[80]

The organizers established an atmosphere of trust among members, although it took about four years. Although it was made up primarily of parents, NAAR nonetheless developed credibility as an organization capable of promoting collaborative research insulated from the routine pressures of scientific careers. It emphasized its status as an "honest broker," gaining the confidence of researchers and fostering trust among them. The resulting arrangement served the interests of both the parent organization and the scientists.

In different ways, CAN and NAAR turned their identities as parent groups to their advantage in acting on and reshaping the social worlds of scientists. They capitalized on their cultural and biological role as parents by acting as brokers and intermediaries, transforming family connections, biological likenesses, and emotionality into a resource. For both CAN and NAAR, the partiality that comes with parenthood was an asset rather than a liability. Although experts on advisory boards ensured that proposals were evaluated based on the standards of the research community, parents added an essential component of affective investment. [81] They evaluated proposals not only in terms of the work's scientific interest, but also for its potential to improve the lives of their children.

With support from the NIH, the NAAR-Autism Genome Project (AGP) Consortium launched in 2003. The project incorporated most of the major autism genetics research networks, including AGRE, into a consortium, or a "collaboration of collaborations."[82] Having altered the terrain of autism genetics research, the initiatives of CAN and NAAR were effectively absorbed into the normal practices of government-funded research. In 2005, NAAR announced that it was merging its operations with the newly formed Autism Speaks. In 2006, CAN followed suit, bringing its gene bank AGRE with it. As of February 2006, the three groups had merged into a single entity.[83]

Meanwhile, genetics researchers adapted their language to reflect the unpromising results of the multiple genome scans that they had conducted on the newly abundant genetic material. They recognized that the time had come to "give up" on finding a single gene for autism.[84] By 2004, the NAAR Autism Genome Project began to refer to "autism susceptibility genes," contributing to an "inherited risk of autism" that implicitly worked together with environmental factors to create autistic symptoms.[85] For parents and researchers with commitments to genetics research, the failure to produce results has been a function of genetic complexity, technological lags, and the breakdown of collaboration in the quest for ever-larger sample populations for research. It is not a problem with the underlying assumptions guiding the research. Parents could make researchers cooperate by helping to reorganize research programs and sample-sharing. They imagined that the complexity of the genetics would yield to high-throughput technologies, improved sample sizes, and alternative genetic models.[86]

Making Use of Genetics: Kinship along the Spectrum

For organizations that have invested in genetic research, the question has been not whether a cause for autism can be found, but how long it will take. Their certainty contributes to fears on the part of adults with autism that people like them will eventually be eliminated through prenatal testing and selective abortion. The concerns are not unfounded.[87] Bioethicists worry that future genetic tests for autism could lead parents to choose against having a child who might have become a future version of Bill Gates, Thomas Jefferson, or Lewis Carroll, who all retrospectively seem to "fit the profile" for Asperger syndrome.[88]

Organizations like CAN, NAAR, and the Autism Society invoke broken family relations in their fundraising appeals, reinforcing the idea that children with autism are, like the changelings in fairy tales, fundamentally unlike their typical family members.[89] A Web site sponsored by the Autism Society of America featured family photographs torn into two pieces, isolating one child.[90] These popular images of alienation are nevertheless at odds with the genetic research programs that the organizations sponsor, since such research often makes use of the existence of autistic traits in direct family members. Many parents recognize these traits in themselves and obtain diagnoses only after their child is found to have autism.[91] Like the parents of children with other disabilities, parents of children with autism spend a great deal of time thinking about the ways that their children resemble them and explaining that resemblance to the world.[92]

Genetic research has so far failed to produce information with concrete implications for screening or treatment and it has done little to illuminate the underlying biological mechanisms of autism. When parents, the popular media, and self-advocates use genetics as support for their arguments about the nature of autism, they make little use of ongoing linkage or association studies. Instead, they draw on a wider set of genetic discourses, although they may not do so consciously. These include ideas about the relationship between modern life and genetic degeneration, notions of kinship that go beyond shared lineages, and fears of eugenics programs.

Autism, Asperger Syndrome, and Autistic Cousins

An emerging autism self-advocacy movement uses genetics as a basis for an entirely different kind of appeal than that made by parents. For those who describe themselves as supporters of neurodiversity, the genetically defined population with an autism diagnosis matters to a set of claims about representation and entitlement. By emphasizing kinship across the spectrum, adults with autism can argue for recognition as spokespeople and biologically ideal translators for children who may seem unlike their parents.[93]

Autism self-advocacy as a visible social force emerged as a result of at least three factors. A resurgence of professional interest in the Asperger syndrome diagnosis and the broader autism spectrum in the 1990s led more adults and people with "higher functioning" forms of autism to be diagnosed. The growth of Internet mailing lists made communication among people with autism easier. And an already established framework of parent organizations allowed connections to be formed among people "on the spectrum."[94] Although what self-advocates call the neurodiversity movement originated partly in parent organizations, by the early twenty-first century self-advocates had become increasingly critical of these groups.

In 2005, when the Autism Society of America, which called itself "The Voice of Autism," launched a new campaign for early diagnosis and treatment, complete with a Web site, "Getting the Word Out," self-advocates with autism responded indignantly.[95] The Web site www.autistics.org changed its slogan to "The Real Voice of Autism," arguing that people with autism ought to speak for themselves and that a diagnosis rather than familial connections was the more significant requirement for spokespersons.[96] Amanda Baggs, another self-advocate, posted a parody of the site and those of other organizations that used images of suffering in their fundraising. She scored points in noting that the images of stricken families used on the site were not real families with autistic children but instead stock photographs of models posing as sad children and miserable parents.[97] The parody was only one instance of an ongoing conflict in which parents of children with autism and self-advocates battle over who gets to "speak for" autism, and most importantly, what that speech says about the value of autistic persons and the meaning of their symptoms.

Jim Sinclair's essay "Don't Mourn for Us," written in 1993, continues to express the sentiments of a segment of the autism community. He writes that the sadness that parents experience upon their child's diagnosis and their subsequent search for a cure reflect "grief over the loss of the normal child the parents had hoped and expected to have," but that to focus on this grief is damaging.

> Push for the things your expectations tell you are normal, and you'll find frustration, disappointment, resentment, maybe even rage and hatred. Approach respectfully, without preconceptions, and with openness to learning new things, and you will find a world you could never have imagined.[98]

Sinclair does not merely claim genetic-cum-ethnic kinship with children with autism. He downplays their ties to their parents, explaining that parents must first accept that their child "is an alien child who landed in my life by accident," someone who is "stranded in an alien world."[99] Meanwhile, adults with autism also have children, and they reflect on the connections that result from a shared diagnosis and biology. They can offer their children "something fundamental" as parents and advocates: "the capability—and importance—of pointing out *meaning* in autistic behavior, sensory and aesthetic sensibilities, cognitive patterns, and emotional processing—and of asserting their legitimacy."[100]

Advocates base their arguments on a framing of autism as neurological and genetic rather than contingent and environmental.[101] In some cases, they are vocal critics of hypotheses of environmental etiology. They are often joined by parents who resent professional and media portrayals of autism as a tragedy. These parents focus on acceptance and accommodation, arguing through advocacy groups and research that nonautistic parents of children with autism need to learn to adapt to their children rather than the reverse.[102] The self-advocacy community has forced the question of legitimate representation for the genetically different. They demand that genetic likeness, which is presumed to unite the population that shares a diagnosis of autism, trumps familial relations in the contest over who gets to speak for children with autism. They may reshape not only how autism is represented but also the normal practices of autism research and treatment.

Many of the implications of these new ways of valuing people will only be worked out through practices that require intense, intimate relationships among people. One way requires inviting autistic people to participate in designing research programs. Others involve learning to create spaces, both professional and casual, where people with autism can have their differences accommodated and even valued. Jim Sinclair founded the annual Autreat in 1996 to provide a space for autistic people from any point on the spectrum where they were not expected to " 'act normal' or to behave like a neurotypical person."[103] The Internet provides another social space in which autistics (the preferred term for many self-advocates) arrange dating or interact at a pace and in a medium that is less intrusive and overwhelming in emotional or sensory terms.[104] For children, schools have been created that encourage the "perseverations" of their "Aspie" pupils, while their families may come to embrace their shared autistic traits.

There are also parents who find no contradiction between identifying with their child's autism diagnosis and trying to help their child recover or participating in genetics research.[105] They credit their persistence, ability to synthesize information, and broad knowledge of technical literature to an autistic attention to details bordering on the obsessive. Genetics researchers note with pleasure that unlike "ADHD parents," "autistic parents" show up on time for appointments. Their studies take into account the existence of relatives with "communication difficulties" or "social impairments," or the fact that some parents of children with autism have "distinct" ways of judging emotions from facial expressions.[106] Hans Asperger, after all, speculated about the similarities between the children that he studied and their mothers, describing the way one mother-and-child pair walked down the street as though they did not know each other.[107] By the late 1950s, researchers were noting that the fathers of many autistic children were "obsessive, detached and humorless individuals," accomplished in their professional lives but uncomfortable with social encounters.[108] Later researchers emphasized the number of engineers among the fathers and grandfathers of children with autism, speculating that the "assortative mating" of computer engineers in places like California's Silicon Valley led to locally increased autism rates.[109] Hearing the theory, one journalist worried that the "hidden cost" of the growing technology industry "may be lurking in the findings of nearly every major genetic study of autism in the last 10 years."[110]

In some forms of childhood disability such as Down syndrome, the visible physical differences between parents and children can disrupt the experience of kinship. In autism, genetic kinship is defined in terms of disability.[111] Within the parent community, jokes about the milder symptoms of autism that many parents exhibit are common. Their more serious conversations touch on familial histories of autoimmune syndromes, allergies, and other characteristics that might have acted as risk factors for their children. At the same time, researchers can turn those similarities against parents, accusing them of symptomatically "perseverating" on unproven treatments and cures—although researchers have also been known to accuse colleagues of acting on autistic impulses if they don't agree with the focus of their research.[112]

Autism's Genetic Futures

Both parent organizations and self-advocates are eminently pragmatic in their efforts to promote their interests. Their allegiances, in the end, are to specific goals of representation, accommodation, or treatment, not to broadly conceived research programs in genetics or psychology. During the 1970s and 1980s, parents learned to invest their time and energy in behavioral therapies for their children even as they explored the potential of megavitamin therapies and dietary modifications. During the 1990s and early 2000s, parent organizations diversified their investments, waiting for genetic therapies in the long term while focusing in the short term on addressing the pathophysiology of possible genetic difference using a similarly broad range of interventions. The majority of parents are committed to no perspective on autism as strongly as they are devoted to the idea that their children can be helped in some way.

For this reason, the differences between self-advocates and parent advocates are more ethical than epistemological. They are characterized as much by disputes over appropriate courses of action as they are by disagreements about the biological facts of autism. Ideals of neurological diversity and acceptance do not mesh well with research programs devoted to eventually treating or eradicating neurological disabilities. In contrast, as we have seen, the genetic models that are used to support both advocacy for neurological diversity and research on neurological disability display similar themes and invoke similarly linear models of causation.

As genetic knowledge develops beyond the more reductive or deterministic models that characterized earlier expectations of finding an "autism gene," the social groups that reference genetics may need to reconsider using it as a basis for claims about community or representation. Direct lines between genetics and identity will seem far more contingent. For example, the ethical implications of genetic identities will become uncertain as researchers become more knowledgeable about how genes and environments interrelate.[113] In addition, forms of autism may be found to share common molecular mechanisms with other seemingly unrelated disorders, bringing children into new relations of surveillance and care.[114] Self-advocates who understand their autism as a benign genetic variation may also need to see their present identities as shaped by their past experiences and surroundings. Parents who count on intensive behavioral therapies and medical interventions as a way of treating intractable symptoms of the disorder might have to allow that other elements of autism will prove to be fixed and settled from birth, and could even present advantages or sources of pleasure for their child.[115]

The idea of autism genetics has been used to claim that the disorder is an untreatable constant in human populations that ought to be accepted and not treated. It is also seen as a way of repairing kinship ties in affected families or as the path to a cure in the near future. All of these ways of thinking view genetics as a determinant of disorder, and disorders as unified wholes for which treatments are either useless or fully curative. The perspective leaves little room for complex causation or for treatments that modulate some traits and leave others alone. Meanwhile, autism genetics has been a waiting game tied to the future prospects of research.

In reality, few parents can wait for definitive answers. Some push for increases in funding for translational research that has the ability to act as a bridge between studies of disease mechanisms and treatment applications.[116] In the absence of a satisfying explanation for autism, many others become experimenters and investigators. In doing so, they do not necessarily deny the plausibility of genetic studies—in fact, many are convinced that genes play a large role in autism susceptibility. However, they believe that genotypes are merely the starting point for developmental processes that take place in response to an environment. Processes that are controlled by genes can still be modulated through individualized treatments. This plasticity is nowhere more evident than in disorders diagnosed in childhood, where early intervention has the potential to literally reshape the neurology and biology of a syndrome.[117]

My next chapter is about the choice of parents to take on the task of trying to shape their child's development. These parents have come to regard their children's behaviors in terms of underlying biological processes. They have incorporated this perspective into their daily life, restructuring their schedules, diets, attention, and habits into the work of caring for their children through biomedical interventions. They do this without the factual certainty that genetics has promised but not yet delivered.

5

Desperate and Rational: Parents and Professionals in Autism Research

In fact, the journey grows longer than expected—and
steeper—
            and perplexing
How many times have you, now almost nine, sent us back to our
            lovers' laboratory
Dark with dashed expectations, challenging us to let go and try
again?
                                        —Jack Zimmerman[1]

Jack Zimmerman is the husband of Dr. Jacquelyn McCandless, the author of *Children with Starving Brains*, a guide to biomedical treatments for autism spectrum disorders. In the poem that prefaces McCandless's book, Zimmerman addresses his granddaughter Chelsea, the subject of those "dashed expectations" and the inspiration for their "lovers' laboratory." Zimmerman's and McCandless's focus on treating an individual child, the affective and rational challenges of treatment, and the idea that the process of healing is a "journey" are all components of a perspective they share with an international network of doctors and parents. Although McCandless entered the world of autism treatment after a lengthy career in anti-aging medicine and psychiatry, the couple joins evangelical Christians, functional and integrative medicine practitioners, parents with nursing degrees, and university-based pharmacologists in their efforts to transform the syndrome of autism. The laboratory that they describe is both private and connected to hundreds of similar places. These include commercial testing sites, the homes of individual parents, the collaborative hum of a doctor's listserv, and lone researchers trawling medical databases for useable entries late into the night.

In this chapter, I describe the production of biomedical knowledge in one parent-practitioner community. I discuss the process of persuasion and affective involvement whereby parents and new practitioners come to take part in the practice of treating autism. I emphasize the ways that social relations based on affect alter vision, create trust, and change measures of therapeutic success. Such a community neither arises spontaneously nor remains entirely stable over time. Members come and go, and they identify with its main premises to varying degrees. However, despite the fact that biomedical treatments for autism are considered to be "alternative" practices, this community does not operate "outside" the forms of expertise and representations of biological systems accepted by conventional practitioners. What makes them distinct is a conscious shift in perspective as opposed to an appeal to a different knowledge system altogether. They are an experimental community within biomedicine.

The treatments employed by this community remain controversial, but parents of children with autism are exploring them at increasing rates. Between 30 percent and 74 percent of all parents use alternative treatments.[2] Investigators report different rates depending on the scope of their survey instruments. Some include a wide range of treatments under the umbrella designation of complementary and alternative medicine (CAM). Even when a broad definition is used, parents seem to turn to "biologically based" treatments about 70 percent of the time they go outside the treatments defined as "conventional" or "mainstream." Parents of younger and more severely impaired children appear more inclined to explore a range of treatments.[3]

Biomedical treatments encompass a range of conventional and unconventional therapies, all premised on the idea that autism is a treatable medical condition. In using the term "biomedical," participants emphasize that these interventions employ biomedical models of physiological systems. At the same time, they distinguish biomedical interventions from treatments focused on altering behaviors alone (e.g., applied behavior analysis), and from approaches that focus on single bodily systems (e.g., the gastrointestinal tract) without recognizing that different parts of the body share common regulatory mechanisms and biochemical pathways. Since metabolic processes can be described in conventional scientific terms, community members would distinguish efforts to manipulate them from, for instance, homeopathy, although many families explore such treatments as well.

Members of the community that uses these methods speak in terms of "recovering" and "curing" autism, ideas that contradict established models of autism as a lifelong condition. Their practices also involve a fragmenting of the diagnostic category that, if taken seriously, might be quite disruptive to established research programs. Because it is defined behaviorally, autism is a syndrome, a set of related symptoms. It is not a single disease with a known pathophysiological mechanism. Observable autism symptoms may be secondary to a range of other underlying causes, rather than associated with a single, definitive disease process.[4] Autism may not be only one disorder. Individuals running carefully constructed research programs that assume an underlying biological homogeneity in autism might find such a statement difficult to accept.

The Food and Drug Administration (FDA) has currently approved only one medication as a treatment for autism, risperidone, an atypical antipsychotic marketed as Risperdal by Johnson & Johnson. The medication is not considered to treat the "core" behavioral symptoms of autism, but rather the "irritability" associated with the condition in children. Most practitioners recognize that its metabolic and psychiatric side effects, including often-dramatic weight gain, make it far from ideal.[5] The paucity of approved medical treatments coupled with the severity of many cases of autism and its categorization as a lifelong condition almost inevitably lead members of the medical profession and the journalists who consult them to question the ethical standing and emotional state of those making claims about treatment or recovery.

To speak of treating autism, let alone curing the disorder, is to invite accusations of desperation on the part of parents and charlatanism on the part of practitioners. A *New York Times* cover story in December 2004 read "Autism Therapies Still a Mystery, But Parents Take a Leap of Faith." It opened with the line, "Desperate parents of autistic children have tried almost everything—hormone injections, exotic diets, faith healing—in the hope of finding a cure." Experimenting with alternative treatments made it difficult to ascertain the benefits of more established forms of behavioral therapy. An expert in the field said that the use of alternative treatments was a "grief response."[6] Another article, "Desperate Parents Seek Autism's Cure," in the *Providence Journal* in August 2005 quoted an internist at the National Center Against Health Fraud as saying, "It's a group of people preying upon the desperate."[7] A third described autism as a battle, "parents vs. research," and noted expert concerns about "a raft of unproven, costly, and potentially harmful treatments—including strict diets, supplements and a detoxifying technique called chelation—that are being sold for tens of thousands of dollars to desperate parents of autistic children as a cure for 'mercury poisoning.'"[8] A 2004 *Boston Globe* story quoted the director of a noted residential treatment center who, despite having said he understood "why 'desperate' parents might consider various treatments" beyond behavioral therapy, explained, "We don't see these kids as experimental guinea pigs for the latest cure *du jour*. . . . We want parents to be informed advocates for their kids, and to choose wisely."[9] Doctors tell reporters that parents are "willing to believe anything" as an alternative to "expensive and difficult" behavioral treatments.[10]

When physicians write for their peers, they explain parents' use of alternative treatments as "an attempt to gain a sense of control over their child's chronic illness or disability and to improve quality of life," or as a form of "stress reduction" in the face of a severe diagnosis. While they emphasize respect for parental choices, they also underscore the importance of the pediatrician as a "medical home" and the site of primary care.[11] They worry that alternative treatments may be harmful and that support for them is based on practitioners' "subjective" reports rather than peer-reviewed studies.[12]

Yet despite the prevalent view that parents who use alternative treatments are irrational, ignorant about their child's condition, and too easily persuaded by false claims, a 2006 survey found a mild association between the use of CAM and higher parental education level, longer time since diagnosis, and a greater degree of disability.[13] Those who use biomedical treatments may have more time and ability to learn about the diagnosis. Parents talk about desperation too, but they portray themselves as emphatically reasonable, at once skeptical and willing to experiment. Their accounts emphasize experience. A mother speaks with other parents, and

> they give me copies of exotic recipes, show me cupboards full of pure honey, molasses, and nuts, freezers full of game meats and bizarre flours. By nightfall, Jonah is off all milk, butter, cheese, bread, crackers, pasta, and cookies. Five days after our talk with Jane, we have begun the gluten-free/casein free diet with sheer desperation as the catalyst.[14]

When physicians write for parents, they draw sharp boundaries between "sound, systematic, and well-conducted research," and "hype, dramatic claims, and wishful thinking," as Laura Schreibman does in *The Science and Fiction of Autism*.[15] Schreibman's examples of theories and treatments that "waste time, money, and emotional energy" range widely, from the psychogenic theory of autism and facilitated communication to biomedical treatments, but she explains to readers that "the principles of science" will enable them to distinguish these from legitimate research. Like other doctors, she uses secretin, a pancreatic hormone that had once seemed like a promising therapy but failed to show benefits in clinical trials, as an example of how resources can be misspent following up on parents' hunches.[16] One "need not be a scientist" to separate reliable claims from false ones, but her readers had best rely on the judgment and systematic analyses of people other than themselves.[17] Some of these critical physicians are themselves parents. Michael Fitzpatrick, a general practitioner whose teenage son has autism, accuses parents who opt for biomedical treatments of resisting the idea that no one is to blame for their child's disability. Practitioners who offer the treatments are opportunists and parents who focus on their children's medical symptoms harm the cause of autism acceptance by using "metaphors of toxicity and disease" to describe their child.[18]

Parents describe their use of biomedical interventions in caring for their affected children as an act of love. There are costs in doing so. If knowledge of the affective, the anecdotal, and the everyday lends efficacy to treatments for autism, it also makes it difficult to translate them into conventional medical terms and to replicate their effects.

The Autism Research Institute, Defeat Autism Now!, and Biomedical Interventions for Autism

Most parents who seek biomedical treatments for autism learn about the techniques from the Autism Research Institute's publications and Defeat Autism Now! (or DAN!) conferences.[19] The Autism Research Institute is neither the largest nor the best-funded of the parent groups involved in research on the autism spectrum disorders, and it is one of several that advocate biomedical interventions. However, it is the only one that not only promotes but also develops the techniques. It has therefore become broadly identified with biomedical treatments for autism by both parents and practitioners.[20] Understanding Defeat Autism Now! is crucial for understanding the ways in which families with autism intervene in medical knowledge production and the complicated ways in which familial, scientific, therapeutic, and professional interests converge in an organization that seeks to recruit practitioners as well as parents.

Defeat Autism Now! conferences are a project of the Autism Research Institute (ARI) in San Diego, California, founded by Bernard Rimland, who also cofounded the National Society for Autistic Children (renamed the Autism Society of America). Rimland was a Ph.D. in experimental psychology and spent his career in the Navy, working as the director of the Personnel Measurement Research Department at the Training Research Laboratory in Point Loma, California. As a parent of a child with autism and a scientist, Rimland represented the paradigmatic parent activist, using his set of prior skills in autism research while ironically and publicly referencing his own "autistic" tendencies. In his experience, "parents of autistic children are often people able to concentrate deeply," an ability that served them well in research careers.[21]

The story of Bernard Rimland's entry into the field has been told many times. His son Mark cried constantly from birth and did not speak a meaningful sentence before the age of eight. Mark cared less about who was taking care of him than whether they were wearing a "certain flowered dress," so Rimland's wife, Gloria, ordered them from a catalog for his grandmothers to wear while they babysat.[22] Gloria remembered reading about children like Mark in one of her textbooks, and Rimland "went out to the garage, found the dusty box of old college texts, and there, five years after I had earned a Ph.D. as a research psychologist, I saw the word 'autism' for the first time."[23] Rimland obtained behavioral therapy for his son and maintained that this was largely responsible for his significant improvements. Nevertheless, as early as 1972 in an article promoting operant conditioning therapies for autism, Rimland noted that "the ultimate answer to the problem of severe behavior disturbances in children—and adults—will come from the biochemistry laboratory, in the form of a drug or a special diet, like the one for phenylketonuria (PKU)." In other words, an intervention tailored to a disorder's underlying biological mechanisms could prevent symptoms of the disorder from appearing.[24]

Rimland formed the National Society for Autistic Children in 1965 in part to promote applied behavior analysis (ABA), then being developed by O. Ivar Lovaas at UCLA. As we have seen, proponents of psychotherapeutic treatments regarded ABA as a form of conditioning tantamount to abuse, but Rimland saw promise in the techniques. He also began his own research program, leading to the publication in 1964 of *Infantile Autism*, which won the Appleton Century Psychology Series publishing award. Rimland's work earned praise for offering a fresh perspective in a field in which experts' lack of interdisciplinary knowledge kept them from drawing on new research.[25] Rimland challenged the psychogenic theory of autism promoted in the work of Kanner, Bettelheim, and others, proposing an alternative theory of etiology and directions for future research.

In 1967, two years after founding NSAC, Rimland set up the Institute for Child Behavior Research, later the Autism Research Institute (ARI), as a clearinghouse for treatment-based research. He began publishing the *Autism Research Review International*, a review of promising and new treatments, to which many parents subscribed over the years.[26] To this end, Rimland spent decades refining diagnostic measures of factors left out of the standard definition of autism. The original Autism Behavioral Checklist he included in *Infantile Autism* asked about developmental regression, pregnancy complications, and the child's eating habits, in addition to questions about behavioral symptoms.[27] His instructions for a system of monitoring and ambition to develop individualized care have become part of the practice of the Defeat Autism Now! community.

The idea of treating mental and developmental disabilities using nutritional supplements did not begin with Defeat Autism Now! conferences or even ARI. Roger J. Williams's work on "biochemical individuality" and the variability of patients' nutritional needs inspired Rimland to frame autism as a chronic illness, as did Linus Pauling's idea of a "molecular disease" that could be treated through nutrient supplementation.[28] In practical terms, parents and practitioners began experimenting with high doses of B-vitamins for autism during the 1960s, following studies of phenylketonuria patients and controversial attempts to use nutritional supplements to treat Down syndrome.[29] Elsewhere, experiments with megadoses of vitamin B3 seemed promising in treating adults with schizophrenia.[30] Despite equivocal results in the syndromes studied and the resistance of medical organizations, parents and practitioners remained interested in experimenting with nutritional therapies in autism.[31]

Rimland began investigating megavitamin therapies and orthomolecular medicine through his Institute for Child Behavior Research in San Diego. During the mid-1960s, parents had begun contacting him about the therapy.

> Even though few of the parents were acquainted with each other and each was trying quite a variety of vitamins, the same small group of

vitamins was being mentioned again and again. As the number of parent-experimenters grew, it began to include more parents whom I knew personally to be intelligent and reliable people. At that point I contacted a number of doctors in California and on the East Coast who had been experimenting with vitamin therapy. The combined information from the doctors and parents convinced me that I could not, in good conscience, fail to pursue this lead.[32]

Rimland conducted his initial study on megavitamins with the help of parents in the National Society for Autistic Children. Linus Pauling advised on the project. While the long-term affiliation between ARI and Kirkman Laboratories, which manufactured the vitamin mixture, might represent a conflict of interest to some, Rimland noted that of "all 26 vitamin manufacturers in the *Thomas Register*," Kirkman was the only company willing to experiment with autism treatments. His results suggested that when combined with magnesium to prevent deficiencies associated with high doses of B6, the therapy helped a subset of children.[33] The fact that only some children responded to any treatment suggested problems with current psychiatric nosology:

> I am firmly convinced that very little progress may be expected in finding cause and treatment for mental illness in children until the total group of children now loosely called "autistic," "schizophrenic," "psychotic," or "severely emotionally disturbed" can be subdivided in a scientific way into smaller homogeneous subgroups. . . . I believe the children loosely called "autistic" or "schizophrenic" actually represent a dozen or more different diseases or disorders, each with its own cause.[34]

This multiplicity of causes might correspond to an equally large number of interventions that would be effective for only some children. Although Rimland preferred to evaluate treatments through parent responses rather than eliminate an option merely because it was unfamiliar, he was hardly indiscriminate in his support of therapeutic techniques. For example, he disputed the claims of those who promoted "facilitated communication" as a means of enabling people with autism to use language. The technique, developed first to help people with cerebral palsy, required a facilitator to support the arm of a person with autism while they typed. Rimland argued against the approach in the *Autism Research Review International* and later published an article suggesting that it involved a significant degree of prompting on the part of the facilitator that its supporters confused with independent action on the part of autistic children.[35] Research by others corroborated the finding.

Rimland convened the first Defeat Autism Now! meeting in Dallas, Texas, in January 1995, with Sidney Baker, a physician with a background in functional medicine and Jon Pangborn, an industrial biochemist and parent of a child with autism. The Dallas meeting helped to define the Defeat Autism Now! mission: to go beyond merely describing autism to "identify treatments—safe treatments—for which there is credible evidence of efficacy." Once found, "an attempt would be made to find why they work, so their efficacy could be improved."[36] Those among the thirty or so participants at the first Defeat Autism Now! meeting remember it as exhilarating, a moment when physicians from research universities shared the floor with alternative medicine practitioners experimenting with promising therapies, and where parents of autistic children, many of them also scientists, were taken seriously. Defeat Autism Now! elevated the commitment to listening to parents to the level of principle. Rimland observed that "as the years went on, I continued to find, repeatedly, that the parents, especially the mothers, were remarkably effective at identifying treatments that were helpful to their autistic children. They were also very observant in detecting factors that caused their children to become worse."[37]

Following the conference, Rimland and Baker published a brief report in the *Journal of Autism and Developmental Disorders*. Developing effective interventions would require physicians to consider the potential of alternative treatments for which there existed "abundant clinical evidence," despite the difficulty of testing them in placebo-controlled studies. The Defeat Autism Now! group saw a number of interrelated factors contributing to autism, among them food allergies and intolerances, microbial infections, and immune dysregulation. The interventions they advocated in 1996 included

> gluten- and casein-free diets; avoidance of allergenic foods; antifungal, antimicrobial, and antibacterial drugs; normalization of bowel flora; improvement in gut mucosal nutrition and permeability; biochemical support with nutrients that are important in intermediary metabolism (B6, Mg) and in detoxification chemistry (sulfur amino acids, reduced glutathione, treatment of phenosulfotransferase deficiency).[38]

This set of treatment types, individualized for each child, has, with the exception of an increasing emphasis on detoxification, remained much the same. Pangborn, Baker, and Rimland all grew more concerned about rising rates of autism diagnoses in the mid-1990s and began to emphasize the possibility that immunizations could be triggering the disorder. A decade later, most Defeat Autism Now! practitioners and conference speakers tended to treat vaccines as one among a range of environmental causes, an opinion shared by many parents. Rimland maintained that his own son, a successful artist whose whimsical paintings are exhibited in a gallery next to ARI's headquarters, differed from the younger children who accounted for the recent increase. That is, he did not regress and did not appear to have suffered ill effects from vaccines.

Bernard Rimland passed away in 2006 after a long illness. He earned wide and well-deserved recognition for having transformed the professional perspective on autism.[39] Stephen Edelson took over as director of ARI. Edelson, referred to Rimland as a graduate student in the 1970s by Rimland's friend Ivar Lovaas, had become the director of the Oregon affiliate of ARI, the Center for the Study of Autism. He had spent many years working with Rimland in assessing various treatments, and remembered him as "not just a professional mentor but also a kind and generous friend."[40] Rimland's death came at a transitional time for ARI/Defeat Autism Now!, as other founding members moved closer to retirement. It served to emphasize the need to train new practitioners and publicize the dual messages of autism's treatability and the role of biochemical individuality in the disorder.

Despite the stability of ARI's commitment to promoting systematic medical evaluations and collaboration with parents in designing treatment programs, Defeat Autism Now! conferences have evolved to reflect parents' new concerns and the shifting research agendas of its members and the autism research community at large. By the end of the first decade of the twenty-first century, many presenters emphasized the interactive effects of multiple environmental and genetic factors. Ten years earlier a majority might have argued that vaccines alone accounted for the bulk of new autism cases. ARI/Defeat Autism Now! had drawn the line at the understanding of autism promoted by the neurodiversity community, which rejects the idea that autism should be treated. Lately they have begun working to reconcile the two approaches by addressing the medical problems that adults with autism report and by engaging directly with some self-advocates.[41] As of 2011, the organization announced that it would refer to future meetings as "ARI conferences," partly because so many self-advocates objected to the Defeat Autism Now! name.[42] However, Defeat Autism Now! practitioners resolutely see autism as a treatable result of chronic medical conditions. They believe that improvement and sometimes recovery are both desirable and possible.

An Experimental Community: Biomedicine as Practice

ARI organizes twice-yearly Defeat Autism Now! conferences along with periodic parent or practitioner training workshops in cities across the United States. Both parents and practitioners attend conferences, rubbing shoulders during sessions, at coffee breaks, and in the exhibitor hall. At the center of the Defeat Autism Now! conferences and the broader parent community that they inspire is the Defeat Autism Now! guide, *Biomedical Assessment and Treatment Options for Autism Spectrum Disorders*. It has grown from a spiral-bound sheaf of suggestions distributed at the first meeting in Dallas to a commercially produced manual that parents and practitioners take home from conferences along with a "syllabus" of the PowerPoint slides from presentations. Presenters urge parents to share the guide with their children's doctors.

The Defeat Autism Now! treatment method involves an explicit, though often individualized, set of tests and regimens, which proceed stepwise through levels of difficulty and sometimes cost. More complex treatments require monitoring by a medical professional. The first stage is an elimination diet, removing foods that parents and doctors have associated with sensitivities in autistic children. Two popular diets are the gluten-free/casein-free (gf/cf) diet and the specific carbohydrate diet (SCD). In some cases, a practitioner will feel that a child might do well on a diet designed to address an overgrowth of yeast (*Candida albicans*) by eliminating sugar, yeast-containing foods, and dairy products. They may supplement that diet with antifungal medications like Nystatin or Diflucan. Many parents report that such diets ameliorate typical symptoms such as "stimming" (self-stimulatory behavior like hand-flapping) and acting "drunk" or "silly." They also improve their child's level of awareness and visibly result in improved physical symptoms. "His skin is smoother too—the small white bumps on his cheeks are gone. His fiery cheeks faded with the diet, but now he isn't really red-cheeked at all. . . . We've come to realize how sharply his behavior deteriorates when he gets sugar."[43]

The second stage aims at repairing metabolic processes through nutritional supplements. Defeat Autism Now! doctors speak of an "emerging picture" of the biochemistry of autism. They do not believe that the children they treat have nutrient deficiencies. Rather, they use supplements to promote or "drive" metabolic processes that may be slower or less effective in children with autism because of problems at multiple points in a reaction. For example, a child might have a functional but slower form of an enzyme required to metabolize nutrients like vitamin B6.[44] These problems may be caused by oxidative stress, the overproduction of reactive oxygen species, molecules that can kill or injure cells. They could also be caused by environmental factors combined with genetic predispositions. In some cases, doctors will also prescribe antiviral medications and treatments designed to support children's immune systems, such as intravenous immunoglobulin (IVIG). They use these drugs because of concerns about persistent measles virus infections acquired from vaccines and because of symptoms that seem generally consistent with immune dysregulation, such as recurring ear infections.[45]

Chelation (pronounced key-LAY-shun), the third stage of treatment in the guide, is also the most contentious. Originally developed as a treatment for acute heavy metal poisoning, it involves the oral, transdermal, or intravenous administration of molecules with a selective binding affinity for heavy metals, which are then excreted in urine along with the captured metals.[46] The process is time-consuming and unpleasant. Treatments take place throughout the day, during which parents need to measure and monitor their child's urine to ensure that metals are being excreted. Only certain doctors, usually those with a background in functional or environmental medicine, will oversee chelation treatment because of the risks involved. At some level, most who offer the treatment believe in a mercury or heavy metal hypothesis of autism etiology. While a majority of Defeat Autism Now! doctors maintain that autism involves some form of toxic etiology, many have shifted in their public statements from describing autism as a vaccine-caused epidemic to emphasizing heterogeneous causes and symptoms, effective treatments, and outcomes.

Laboratory and clinical studies of nutrition and metabolism in children with autism seem to confirm parents' routine reports of improved functioning and behavior and the remission of allergies and gastrointestinal problems after beginning biomedical treatment. Some recent studies suggest a biological basis for altered immune responses to certain foods in children with autism. Additional studies point to the presence of oxidative stress and impaired methylation, both of which can slow the removal of toxic substances from bodies. Others have found potential functional impairment or even genetic vulnerabilities in detoxification enzymes such as methionine synthase or glutathione transferase. Still others highlight evidence of recognized pathological processes, including neuroinflammation and overt gastrointestinal pathologies.[47] Defeat Autism Now! doctors see in these studies children with bodies unable to sustain the daily burdens of metabolizing and removing complex modern foodstuffs and toxic environmental substances—who retain rather than excrete elements that are harmful to their bodies.[48]

For the parents associated with Defeat Autism Now! these biomedical interventions entail laborious experimentation and therapeutic trials followed by incremental improvements and occasional sudden leaps in functional behaviors. A parent quoted in the Defeat Autism Now! treatment guide says that the most important thing "is daily record keeping."[49] Parents track the treatments that they have tried, recording minute variations in their child's mood, behavior, and physical symptoms in thick binders with elaborate charts. One parent posted her recording method to the ARI Web site as an example to others. She monitors eleven variables, from stool quality to eye contact, using a five-point scale to rate responses to twenty separate treatments. She explains that this strategy helps her with the different kinds of attentiveness and sensitivity required by biomedical treatments because it "allows me to adjust one treatment at a time without rushing into different things. It also allows me to see subtle differences over a relatively long period of time and helps me go back and ask: 'When did I see that behavior last?' "[50]

Motherhood often involves this type of intense care and watchfulness. In this sense, parents using biomedical treatments take part in a longstanding U.S. culture of childrearing. Historians and sociologists have documented the tendency of American mothers in particular to seek expert scientific advice. The time-consuming practices that Defeat Autism Now! doctors recommend—or that parents discover on their own—become a type of biomedical "intensive motherhood." As Sharon Hays points out, women accept that the emotional rewards of mothering will compensate for the sacrifices of time and energy.[51] Love is both the impetus and the outcome. Christina Adams makes the point even more plainly. The mothers of some children with autism diagnoses become not mere mothers but "Autism Mommies."

> This is a slender tier of women who do everything that sounds remotely reasonable. They do the diet. They draw vials of blood from

their children and test it for signs and deficits, like oracles looking
to foretell the future. They run twenty-five- or thirty-hour-a-week
home programs, and send their kids to the special ed classroom
twice a week to keep the school district happy. They make the immediate round of specialists, trudge to occupational and speech
therapy twice a week. They share gf/cf recipes, educate relatives,
and generally walk the intervention treadmill for years.[52]

Like many parents, Adams sees her entry into intensive motherhood as a
transformation by choice and necessity. It is a full-time job driven by love,
but accomplished through reason and experience, because "This is our
work. Everything else vanishes."[53]

Defeat Autism Now! conferences act primarily to disseminate knowledge about biomedical treatments. Advocacy for services and support play
a secondary role at best. Parents share experiences and encourage others.
Still, the circulation of knowledge in the Defeat Autism Now! community
is political in that it involves an active choice about how to conceive of
autism. That choice is informed by more than the facts that medical authorities can provide by citing studies or arguing from expertise. It com-
prises personal craft knowledge about the specifics of interventions. The
Defeat Autism Now! community sees diets as a form of targeted biomedical intervention because they address the pathophysiology of the disorder
rather than the symptoms alone. In this sense diets are more appropriate treatments than psychopharmaceuticals. However, parents undertake
diets not because the underlying rationale is convincing but because the
results reinforce the practice. This framing of an experimental approach
in which parents are the technicians as a pathway to an authentic understanding of autism is reflected in discussions among doctors and in pro-
motional literature.

Beyond the Defeat Autism Now! conferences and guide lies a broader
constellation of message boards, discussion groups, and newsletters. Doctors use one listserv to share insights, seek guidance on difficult cases
(withholding identifying information about patients) and how to interpret unexpected laboratory results, and circulate references to journal articles. A group closely connected to Defeat Autism Now! is a Yahoo-based
listserv called the Autism Biomedical Discussion Group (ABMD), with
over 5,000 members. A parent set up the list in early 2000 to share information about using the pancreatic hormone secretin as a treatment for
autism, and it later expanded to cover the range of biomedical interventions.[54] Not all participants on ABMD are parents. Doctors told me that

they tracked the list for information about possible treatment side effects or the general tenor of parent discussions and concerns.

The listserv discussions occasionally reference key texts that circulate within the biomedical treatment community, including Karen Seroussi's *Unraveling the Mystery of Autism and Pervasive Developmental Disorder: A Mother's Story of Research and Recovery,* which promotes elimination diets, and Lynn Hamilton's combined memoir and handbook, *Facing Autism: Giving Parents Reasons for Hope and Guidance for Help.*[55] Lisa Lewis's *Special Diets for Special Kids* guides readers through dietary modifications and Stephen Edelson and Bernard Rimland's *Treating Autism* includes parent testimonials about their children's sometimes-tentative improvements.[56] A fifth book, Jacquelyn McCandless's *Children with Starving Brains*, details her journey from psychiatrist to autism treatment specialist as a result of her granddaughter Chelsea's diagnosis.[57] McCandless's book is sold at Defeat Autism Now! conferences and members consistently reference it as central to their approach. McCandless and her husband, Jack Zimmerman, use the language of love as one explanation for what they see as a reciprocal process of healing opposed to the conventional medical model of treatment:

> The children with starving brains challenge our capacity to love— particularly in regard to the qualities of patience and perseverance, devotion beyond the usual parental call of duty and the capacity to think and act creatively "out of the box." Often, it is only after a profound challenge to our capacity to love, such as the rearing of an ASD child, that we come to realize how much more there is to discover about loving.[58]

While Seroussi and Hamilton both say that treatment led to their children losing their diagnoses, McCandless offers a more guarded appraisal of her granddaughter's progress.[59]

Crossing Over

> I was once a "very mainstream" physician. I did everything by the book. I was taught, "if it is not a drug, it doesn't work," and "parents know absolutely nothing." And I truly believed this.[60]

The organizers of Defeat Autism Now! conferences see them as a means to recruit and train new doctors and parents. For many years, ARI maintained a registry of clinicians offering biomedical treatments, but it abandoned the practice in 2011 because it was too difficult to review each applicant to ensure that he or she was reliable and had the requisite training. ARI now suggests that parents contact local support groups for referrals.[61] As is the case in many medical or scientific communities, parents decide to trust practitioners based on their physical presence; their self-presentation, including signs of their devotion to research; and their commitment to evaluating evidence in a disinterested manner. Parents' trust also hinges on how well a doctor can muster facts on demand and demonstrate mastery of the specialized language of biomedical treatment. Conferences and meetings help build this trust.

The daily routine of monitoring and care trains parents to view their children's symptoms as mutable via interventions. The same methods affect practitioners through seeing children "actually respond" for the first time since beginning to treat children with autism. Their experiences with parents and patients lead to membership in the group. Onstage at a banquet held at a Defeat Autism Now! conference, one father offered "the top ten reasons that you know that you are the parent of an autistic child": You cheer when your child has a normal bowel movement. You have alarms installed in your home to alert you when someone has *left* rather than entered without warning—a reference to the ordeal of lost or missing children shared by many parents—and you find that you have packed for a trip with only the things that your child needs. You are also able to "sit for hours listening to scientific theories—and understand it." Others in the room nodded and, despite the heartwrenching details, laughed along with him.[62]

One of the most vivid accounts of parenting a child with autism while immersed in biomedical interventions is the comic "The Chelation Kid" by Robert Tinnell and Craig Taillefer. Many of the strips deal with the skepticism that accompanies biomedical treatments, first on the part of the father when his wife suggests that they explore alternatives in treating their son, and then on the part of the therapists, teachers, and doctors who work with their son. When a doctor advises them to stop using nutritional supplements and continue on only the gf/cf diet, their child is transformed from the relatively calm and happy "Chelation Kid" to the angry and violent "Autism Lad."[63]

Defeat Autism Now! treatments depend on a network of commercial laboratories with specialized tests for measuring baseline and posttreatment levels of various enzymes, nutrients, antibodies, and heavy metals.

A typical set of tests will check for allergies, nutrient levels, and both immediate and delayed allergic reactivity.[64] Conventional practitioners tend to regard these tests skeptically. At worst, they exploit parents desperate for information, and at best they are too poorly standardized an instrument to be useful. Insurance companies often fail to cover the costs of laboratory work. Nevertheless, Defeat Autism Now! doctors argue that genetic vulnerabilities in conjunction with environmental triggers might cause a variety of symptoms. These complex responses may not be visible at thresholds conventionally recognized as indications of disease processes. From this perspective, doctors have been quietly characterizing the biochemistry of autism for at least two decades. One researcher explained that

> it is IMPORTANT, if present models are to change, that concrete data about the chemistry of those with autism is made a public record. Professionals with whom I have shared my own daughter's chemical workup have been miffed by what they've seen, because this sort of workup is not usually done; since these sorts of results are unfamiliar they are viewed as only a curiosity when they are seen individually. How can a neurologist become convinced he needs to know about his patient's immune/metabolic status unless the results of a great many of these workups are put to public inspection? [65]

At one Defeat Autism Now! conference, I attended a meeting organized to introduce "mainstream" practitioners from the local community to the framework promoted by the Autism Research Institute. The Defeat Autism Now! practitioners each gave short presentations on the metabolic and nutritional differences between individuals with autism and typically developing children. They suggested that in principle it was possible to intervene at these points of variation to produce behavioral changes. Each presentation focused on a different metabolic system. During the question period, one audience member, an experienced chemist but not a Defeat Autism Now! doctor, asked for a sheet of butcher paper and demonstrated how the various implicated biochemical pathways formed an interlocking series of reactions. One could intervene at various points in order to produce effects throughout the entire body. The point is one that Defeat Autism Now! practitioners regularly make, but the chemist came up with it on his own after hearing the presentations on single disease mechanisms. The presentations hardly addressed treatment philosophy. They reported pathological findings, and the chemist made the connection himself. If this practitioner chose to become involved in Defeat Autism Now!, he would have found a dispersed community united less by their association with Defeat Autism Now! than by their interest in alternative treatment methods, their practical attitude of experimentation, and their individual commitment to that particular vision of bodies as dynamic convergences of fundamentally interlinked systems.[66] The rest is open for discussion.

Defeat Autism Now! doctors and families focus on treating children and on converting qualified practitioners to their vision of autism. With increased experience, doctors and families also work a process of transformation on themselves. This is not indoctrination into an "irrational" nonscientific belief system. Rather, it means joining a community acutely aware of how social relationships help to define the boundaries of rationality, of the difficulties inherent in translation and proof, and of how expectations and prior assumptions can govern how experts read scientific texts, seeing some connections and overlooking others. Reflexivity is the dubious privilege of a marginal group. People who face continuous questions about their decisions build up arsenals of sources and arguments and become skilled at explaining why they believe what they do. Defeat Autism Now! practitioners struggle with the conflicting demands of treating children based on parent reports, maintaining credibility and certification, and establishing biomedical facts legible and credible to regulatory agencies and medical associations.

While I have argued that shared practical and affective dimensions of autism treatment rather than a specific theory of etiology unite this emerging community, a collective vision of autism as a treatable and mutable syndrome does indeed emerge from these practices. The vision is a practical one. It involves attending to dimensions of the disorder that could be described as medical rather than behavioral. These include skin ailments, levels of stimming and self-injury, exacerbations of gut disturbances, and variations in mood, all of which may be correlated with different dietary or other biomedical regimens. Tracking these associations leads parents and practitioners to reframe the diagnostic category. The same Defeat Autism Now! researcher quoted earlier expressed this idea well in an e-mail to a parent that focused on funding genetic research on autism.

> You and I probably would agree about the need for autism to become a diagnosis of biochemical certainty rather than one built

around behavioral things that may change as people respond to a whole host of different sorts of therapy. I think that the only thing you and I may see differently is what may be the fastest and most effective method at getting to a "physical marker" which could replace current methods of diagnosis. I very much feel that studying the measurable factors in the immune, endocrine and metabolic systems would yield faster results, as opposed to looking at something as incredibly large as the human genome, and looking at only those persons from multi-incidence families who may not represent at all those whose autism appears without precedent in a family.[67]

While it is possible to seek genetic analogs for behavioral characteristics, the search for metabolic biomarkers by doctors who insist that "every child is biochemically unique" points to a reframing of both disease concept and research practice. Seeking explanations for autism at the level of cellular signaling involves a choice of perspective, away from a monolithic diagnosis and toward autism as a "final common outcome" (a perspective that, ironically, genetic research may also eventually adopt). In similar fashion, research programs that look to treatment response to identify potential disease mechanisms revise the investigative process by enrolling caregivers' observations and designing studies around the work of community-based clinicians.[68]

The Heart of the Matter: Commitment, Trust, and the Work of Recovery

At my first Defeat Autism Now! conference, I experienced what many other newcomers feel. I was utterly overwhelmed. I didn't know whom or what to trust.[69] First-time parents sometimes leave the room in tears during a lecture, overcome by the prospect of healing a child diagnosed as untreatable or else by the onslaught of biochemical jargon and PowerPoint slides.

One of the premises of the field of science studies is that contemporary science and biomedicine are built on trust as well as claims to truth. If I wanted to understand the Defeat Autism Now! community, it followed that I needed to learn how practitioners' claims were persuasive. As I spent more time at Defeat Autism Now! meetings, I realized that the problem involved not unwavering trust in medical authorities as much as persuasion, followed by provisional commitments. Parents can decide to try one intervention, rather than accept a wholesale shift in viewpoint. I started to spend less time squeezing myself into huddles of doctors and more time chatting with moms in the lobby, asking them why they tried biomedical interventions. One parent showed me a photograph of her dreamy-eyed daughter. When she first considered biomedical treatments her friends said that only the desperate would try diets and supplements. She said that she reached that point when her daughter, who had taken to wandering out of the house mid-winter in her nightgown, tried to jump out of their car into traffic.

Parents certainly grow skeptical when experts cannot solve their most pressing concerns, but doubts about conventional forms of medical authority are something of a tradition in the United States. The transition from home- to hospital-based care followed on doctors' claims that medical treatment required expert knowledge and extended training, what Paul Starr terms the "legitimate complexity" of American medicine.[70] Recipe books for special diets, an emphasis on home-based care, and mistrust of medical professionals by parents who would rather do their own research are predictable and enduring responses to the limitations of accepted treatment modalities and the difficulty of contending with symptoms that conventional models of disease do not recognize or acknowledge.[71] While the rationales for biomedical interventions are often as complex as those for conventional treatments, the mode of interaction between practitioners and parents is decidedly different. Defeat Autism Now! doctors depend on parental reports, and this compels them to regard parents as collaborators as much as clients. Parent reports are something to be taken seriously and shared with colleagues, because it is through them that doctors can evaluate interventions and learn about the behavioral effects of different treatments.

Their acknowledged debt to parents' observations of their children and their descriptions of parents as competent technicians and insightful partners in treatment can put Defeat Autism Now! doctors at odds with the prevailing public depictions of "autism parents." The image of the desperate parent often trumps the professional identities of researchers, practitioners, or reporters. Members of the Defeat Autism Now! community accept that observations of one's own child, professional practices, and clinical experimentation often run together. Elsewhere, researchers will go to significant lengths to downplay the fact that their research follows upon their own child's diagnosis, especially when the work might be associated with a "hysterical" parent's belief about vaccines or environmental toxins. Parents are acutely aware that their status compromises their claims for objectivity and disinterestedness. Objectivity, understood as the ability to evaluate experiments without any personal stake in the outcome, is what theorists have called a technique of social position, a way of seeing that has historically been associated with certain identities and not with others.[72] At different moments, women, employees, parents, or anyone else whose well-being was too tightly dependent on another person have been seen as unreliable observers. Some parent-researchers operate within mainstream science by insulating their public, professional identities from their roles as parents. Others situate themselves outside the center of scientific culture, citing eclectic educations, the demands of parenting, or a deeply felt critique of conventional medicine.

In 1964, a reviewer of *Infantile Autism* noted Rimland's comparison between his perspective and that of an observer putting an eye to a keyhole and finding a magnified landscape beyond.

> Yet maybe because he has come from the other side of the door the author has been able to see things which were obscured to those in the room, obscured in part because they were too close to the problem, in part because doctrinaire viewpoints prevented them from perceiving the obvious, and in part because their obscure notions of genetics, neurophysiology, motivation and cognition did not permit them to make use of the latest research findings from these rapidly expanding sciences.[73]

If theorizing autism treatment requires a view "from the other side of the door," then accepting the idea of complete recovery from those treatments requires a still greater shift, even as many researchers have begun to accept that a small percentage of children do in fact lose their autism diagnoses.[74] A 2004 video produced by ARI, "Recovered Autistic Children," featured a series of children interacting with their parents and speaking directly to the camera. Not all of the children would be likely to meet a diagnostician's standard of developmental typicality, but the parents in the video seemed thrilled nonetheless about how far their children had progressed. For some parents, recovery promises a respite from behaviors that disrupt daily life, the parts of autism that prevented them from "having a family," in the words of one parent. They might refer to chronic physical problems like diarrhea or eczema as the real source of discomfort to the child, far more disabling than a lack of social reciprocity. Or they might accept the premise that recovery is possible for some children but see their own use of biomedical treatments as simply one more way that they are working to improve their child's prospects for a good life.[75] Parents also highlight changes too subtle to record in a standard interview like "the length of their sentences, their empathy and sense of humor," traits that are so tightly woven into the fabric of family interactions and the individual quirks of a personality that it may take an intimate to register them.[76]

Visceral Issues: "Sick Kids" and Diagnostic Vision

The complexities of symptom identification, interpretation, and diagnostic modes of seeing involved in alternative treatment practices come together in the case of gastrointestinal issues in autism. Other examples would serve the same purpose: vitamin B6 and magnesium, or subcutaneous injections of methyl-B12, or the elimination diet laid out in *Special Diets for Special Kids* by Lisa Lewis. Members of the medical community consider each approach equally dubious. Adherents have had an equally hard time establishing the existence of a specific pathological mechanism and the efficacy of the corresponding treatments. This is partly because all of these treatments, depending on a functional approach to physiological systems, do not involve the clear correlations between brain chemistry and behavior that the broader medical community expects to see in autism treatments. It is also because only a subgroup of children seems to respond to each treatment. This confuses analysis when investigators base their studies of treatment efficacy on an assumption that all cases of autism are caused by the same underlying biology.

The broader medical community is only now coming to accept that children with autism can experience significant gastrointestinal symptoms, although they disagree about whether these symptoms represent a distinct diagnostic category of "autistic enterocolitis," as some doctors associated with Defeat Autism Now! have contended.[77] Doctors have arrived at this recognition of the reality of digestive symptoms often despite, not because of, a long history of parents complaining about allergies and gastrointestinal issues in their children. According to the testimony of parents in the on-line biomedical discussion group and at conferences, often the first—and sometimes the only—effect of an elimination diet is that their child finds relief from chronic diarrhea or constipation. Researchers who want to confirm the reports confront the additional problem of identifying a disease process, which may not be visible without invasive diagnostic exams, in children who do not communicate well.

Some physicians are willing to treat children empirically, that is on the basis of reported symptoms and without medical evaluations that can require procedures like colonoscopies. The problem is that in general a clearly defined set of symptoms must be present to justify invasive tests. Patients need to report that they have cramps, or they need to have bloody stool or unexplained weight loss. Often children with autism present none of these indicators, and doctors are more likely to consider their bowel issues consequences rather than causes of the child's neurological disturbance. A child might simply be refusing to defecate or be experiencing stomach upset as a result of stress. Likewise, the physicians are likely to view self-injurious behaviors as an isolated problem, rather than a result of underlying physical discomfort. The problem of gastrointestinal illnesses in autism literally had to acquire diagnostic visibility.

In 1998, Andrew Wakefield, a gastroenterologist at the Royal Free Hospital in London, published a paper with colleagues describing a novel intestinal pathology in children with autism and developmental regression.[78] Although the paper was discredited and eventually withdrawn by the journal (an episode I discuss in chapter 6), doctors have since increasingly accepted that gastrointestinal issues could affect the behavior of individuals with autism spectrum disorders. These symptoms may be due to allergies, food intolerances, inflammatory processes, behavioral issues, or functional problems with the gastrointestinal tract.[79] However, taking gastrointestinal symptoms seriously requires a change in perspective. Without this, members of the Defeat Autism Now! community have argued, they are literally invisible.

When I first met one pediatric gastroenterologist at a Defeat Autism Now! conference, he preferred to avoid explicit speculations about the causal relationship between gut pathology and regressive autism. He suggested that stress associated with the inability to communicate might be the cause of the problems parents reported.[80] Certainly, many of the children he treated had exceptionally difficult gastrointestinal symptoms. At a subsequent meeting, having spent more time with the Defeat Autism Now! community, he remained skeptical about the existence of any distinct gastrointestinal condition associated with autism. However, he was convinced of the need to teach pediatricians to look for medical issues underlying a host of behavioral problems. He showed a video clip of a child screaming and writing on the floor, pressing his hands into his stomach.[81] An audience primed to the underlying condition reacted as expected. That is, they responded empathically to a case of agonizing pain, visibly expressed, where others might have said that the child was merely "tantrumming."

Another gastroenterologist illustrated his talks with photographs that parents provided of their own children angling their bodies over chairs and placing pressure on their abdomens, behaviors that would be dismissed as "posturing" or forms of stereotyped behavior by an uninitiated audience. He talked about the limitations of conventional gastroenterologists when they encounter these kids in their practices. Their training dictates that gastrointestingal disorders will follow a recognizable pattern, including persistent diarrhea or rectal bleeding, and so they fail to recognize important signs like growth retardation and don't even think to ask parents about constipation.[82] In some cases, parents have to work hard to find doctors willing to use techniques like colonoscopies or X-rays to examine superficially healthy children, although it is often these techniques that yield the definitive visual evidence of pathology that many practitioners refer to when they explain why they began considering gut issues in their patients with autism. Diagnostic moments like this require both empathy and detailed knowledge. Without them, it is as if professionals literally cannot see a child's pain.

Symptoms of children with autism that are dismissed as comorbidities or "just the autism" by many conventional practitioners can also be reinterpreted as food sensitivities that lead in turn to gastrointestinal disturbances. Although many doctors are primarily attuned to the acute immune-mediated allergic reactions that children can have to problem foods (think peanut allergies), many parents are more concerned about food sensitivities and intolerances. These conditions may not be mediated by the same immune responses as typical food allergies or may not involve immune reactions at all. At one conference I joined a group of young mothers from Louisiana while they talked among themselves, mainly about their children's bowel problems. One participant confided, "If you hang around autistic parents enough, all we talk about is poop." For a community that understands their children's problems to arise at least partially from gut dysfunction, the specifics of foul-smelling bowel movements and chronic diarrhea or constipation are important observational diagnostic tools that are a special province of parents. Parents share the common currency of experience, filtered through their conviction that these experiences can be interpreted in medically significant terms.

The first step toward embracing a biomedical framework is learning to view children with autism as suffering from physiological dysfunctions that can affect their entire bodies, as opposed to purely neurological problems manifested mainly in behaviors. In conversations with practitioners about deciding whether to incorporate biomedical treatments into their practices, many referred to the threat of liability for using "unproven" treatments. Even recommending elimination diets as a treatment for autism can lead to losing one's license to practice medicine. Vitamin and mineral supplementation carry a lower risk, while chelation and intravenous therapies are higher risk. The riskiest move in personal terms may be altering the way one weighs available information in treating a condition that is supposedly localized in and expressed by the brain and its dysfunctions.[83]

The case history becomes an important way of learning to see autism differently, that is, to see children with autism as "sick kids" who are in need of treatment. Martha Herbert is a pediatric neurologist at Massachusetts General Hospital who, although not a Defeat Autism Now! doctor, has emphasized thinking about the brain in autism as often "downstream" of other physiological problems. She described her own shift in perspective:

> A key transition in my own understanding of this disorder has been taking careful and thorough medical histories of my autistic and other neurobehavioral patients, and taking their physical complaints seriously. These complaints, once one learns to ask about them, turn out to be so common that it has become impossible for me to ignore them or assume that they are less important than the behavioral features. These children cannot be assumed to have nothing more than brain and behavior problems, since so many of them are also physically ill. A critical question is whether—and if so how—these things are related.[84]

Doctors associated with Defeat Autism Now! are converts if only in the sense that their diagnostic perspective is dramatically different from the one that they learned in medical school. This change can complicate their sense of identity as doctors.[85] They emphasize the importance of listening to parents for clinical insights and research suggestions.[86] Some see themselves as part of a movement with the objective of altering medical practice in order to improve the prospects for children with autism and other neurodevelopmental disorders. Others emphasize the disciplinary and investigational aspects of their work as neurologists, psychiatrists, gastroenterologists, or immunologists, thereby maintaining their identities as specialists and primary researchers, even if, like Martha Herbert, they draw on insights from biomedical approaches. Those who are less concerned with institutional status may come increasingly to identify themselves as "DAN! docs." These are not a homogeneous group by any means.

At one conference, I joined a conversation between two doctors whom I had known for several years. One explained how he had become interested in nutritional medicine after traditional training in pediatrics and medical genetics. He had gone to school in the 1960s and acquired the habit of questioning conventional wisdom. This might have primed him to listen when a family returned to his office with a child that he had known years before, a small boy with severe autism. The child was thriving, nearly typical in behavior. The parents said that the child was on an elimination diet and asked him to watch a video of the child being fed a piece of pizza. Within hours, the child "went to pieces," giggling and running in circles, shedding his clothes. Later still, he was curled in a fetal position on the floor, moaning. In the background, offscreen, it was possible to hear his father saying that he knew that it hurt, but they had to make this video so that the doctors would know that they were telling the truth. The doctor showed me a copy of the video on his laptop. It was indeed hard evidence to ignore.

Biomedical Pluralism, Invisible Labor, and the Practice of Love

The combination of compromised witnessing and daily attentiveness associated with biomedical interventions in autism suggests a problem that must be dealt with in discussing contemporary illness-based communities in general. Sociologists of medicine and science have underscored the importance of social position in the construction of credible witnessing. They have documented how hard it can be to establish lay expert claims to knowledge. Clumsy descriptive terms like "semiprofessional" and "amateur" remind us that parental knowledge always seems unreliable, compromised, and partial, never more so than when parents make forays into more technical aspects of biomedicine or when practitioners rely on their reporting of technical details to establish their own claims to truth.[87] Because parents have a primary commitment to their child rather than to generalizable knowledge, their understanding is not only colored by their emotional involvement. It is also limited to their subjective observations of one child. But as we have seen, that partiality, attention to individual variation, and unwavering commitment may also have a lot to do with the efficacy of biomedical treatments for the families that have chosen to use them.

Just as some versions of "biosociality" seem to discount the active work that renders certain disease categories "genetic" in the first place, the concept of biosociality can also make social organization around disease categories appear spontaneous, as though illnesses themselves cause communities to form. We tend to naturalize the forms of labor and care associated with chronic illness. We also ignore how the decision to manage it experimentally, using unproven medical interventions, may produce an experience of membership and belonging. It is important to recognize these as choices based on reason and experience, rather than passive reactions to any particular diagnosis. What types of language are appropriate to the rich circulation of techniques, information, craft knowledge, inquiry, and passion that attend membership in these groups? If this is not scientific investigation, but it takes place inside of biomedicine—if it is standardized practice on bodies, but is not legitimate science—then what is it? Doctors and parents refer to their work as "biomedical interventions" because they identify it with techniques and models drawn from biomedicine's system of reason and rationality.

Deciding to value treating metabolic processes over identifying genes, environment over "innate biology," development over hardwiring, and cell over protein entails a shift in perspective and emphasis that renders certain processes more or less visible, certain interventions more or less possible, but that does not negate any specific approach. Defeat Autism Now! practitioners seamlessly incorporate genomics, psychopharmacology, and behavioral therapies into their practices. They may do so as a result of their education and background, of witnessing the effects of treatment, or out of a desire to help affected children. For parents, therapeutic pragmatism is one after-effect of engaging in the practical operations associated with learning to manage the disrupted biochemistry and difficult behaviors of their children. Members of the Defeat Autism Now! community have tried to reach other researchers and clinicians by using the techniques of contemporary biomedicine: peer-reviewed articles, clinical trials, published case reports, and readily legible theories of pathological mechanisms. The persuasive power of such techniques can only do so much against the resistance of autism, as a category, to resolve into a clear population in biological terms.

Psychiatrists can promise at least the prospect of a specific treatment for many of the disorders that they see in their practices, and this expectation is an incentive to produce accurate and clearly defined diagnoses. [88] Autism diagnoses using techniques like the ADOS and ADI or early screening methods like the CHAT have become standardized at least partly in the interest of developing treatments, but the monolithic definition of autism may in fact hinder the identification of successful therapies. Directed efforts to destabilize rather than refine the category, supported by unlikely alliances of functional medicine practitioners, not-for-profit research institutes, nutritional supplement manufacturers, maverick researchers, and independent laboratories, have encountered marked resistance from investigators whose research programs depend on the stability and reality of autism as a "true" population.

The efforts of parents and professionals using biomedical treatments to reframe autism as a chronic illness rather than a fixed genetic and neurological condition are, in some sense, aided by the absence of generally recognized biomarkers for autism. No genes or distinctive patterns of metabolites or dysmorphology have been consistently identified to establish children with autism as a visibly separate population. The work that constructs autism as a stable population occurs largely at the level of behavioral observations, diagnostic questionnaires, and checklists. Even researchers working outside of the world of biomedical interventions have become frustrated by the heterogeneity within the diagnostic category of autism. They have hinted at the need to consider the possibility that not one, but multiple forms of pathophysiology lead to the behavioral syndrome known as autism. As Martha Herbert and others put it, there is not one "autism" but multiple "autisms."[89] These might involve different genetic backgrounds as well as different patterns of onset and metabolic markers. Those who made the testimonies of parents part of their data set came to this conclusion earlier and more emphatically.

In one world, parents sit with their child in a doctor's office somewhere in the United States, hearing a diagnosis that they have probably already suspected. They are told that the term describes a mostly fixed and lifelong condition with a neurological basis, which will someday, through the efforts of academic research and the pooling of genetic material, become susceptible to pharmacological interventions or prenatal diagnostic screening. They are directed toward early intervention programs and behavioral therapies. They may be encouraged to take part in one of the autism genetics initiatives currently in progress. Time passes, the child's behavior deteriorates, life becomes unmanageable, and the parents enter another world, seeking help through handbooks, the Internet, or exchanges with other parents. In this other world, parents trade diet tips and learn to administer vitamin injections. They attend conferences and talk tentatively about improvements and recovery. There are few reports of miracles, but considerable optimism. In both worlds, parents' massive efforts of attention, monitoring, care, and observation are described as acts of love.

While it might seem that this story describes parents gradually accumulating experience and knowledge about autism, the subjective experience of moving from a conventional framework to a biomedical framework for understanding autism entails a more radical shift in perspective. The experience of joining a community devoted to biomedical treatment can involve learning to see familiar phenomena through different eyes. It's not unlike those random-dot stereograms that resolve from a mass of disconnected pixels into pictures of dolphins and palm trees if you stare hard enough. Learning to see in this new way requires physical effort, the affective labor involved in the private, home-bound work of treatment and care, and committing to an experimental attitude that yields results only sparingly and often without the comfort of expert support.

Making this claim, that learning to see autism in biomedical terms involves both reinterpreting daily life and transfiguring one's own beliefs about autism as an entity, requires that I take a position about what autism really is. The doctors and researchers involved with Defeat Autism Now! want to recruit colleagues and supporters with the objective of changing medical practice in tangible ways. A sympathetic description of them that takes seriously their claim that really listening to parents, taking case histories, and thinking about the individual before the syndrome can all work to change the clinical entity of autism means that I am necessarily participating in their system of values and judgments.

The psychologist Erich Fromm wrote that our preoccupation with romantic love leads us to regard love as a state of being, when it ought to be regarded as an art or a practice. It is one that demands techniques that might be familiar to parents: "discipline, concentration, and patience."[90] For Fromm, the practice of love required "rational faith," based on a productive and future-oriented focus on the potential of the object of love, be it one's child, oneself, or, he suggested, the subject of a scientific investigation.[91] Maybe it is all three. Passionate investment is characteristic of scientific practice, but it is also not far from parenting, especially at a moment in which intensive motherhood has become common practice, to sometimes problematic and sometimes transformative ends.

6

Pandora's Box: Immunizations, Parental Obligations, and Toxic Facts

The November 2003 "Autism Summit" conference of the Interagency Autism Coordinating Committee occupied a large lecture hall in the new Washington Convention Center in Washington, D.C. Heads of the three major autism advocacy organizations joined the rest of the audience to watch presentations on research, advocacy, and education. Officials from the National Institutes of Health (NIH), geneticists, database administrators, parents, and legislators listened to the speakers attentively and mingled in the building lobby. I had been spending a lot of time thinking about the concept of risk as I followed the ongoing debates about the appropriate management of the National Immunization Program (now the National Center for Immunization and Respiratory Diseases [NCIRD]), vaccine safety, and autism. Parents and public health officials routinely talk about the relative risks associated with vaccines in children. One side in the debate connects the risk of developing autism with vaccines. The other side stresses the higher risk associated with the diseases that vaccines are designed to prevent and the risk to the public health and confidence in immunization programs that could result from sustained public discussions about autism and vaccines.

One speaker momentarily confused me by projecting a slide that divided NIH-funded projects by level of risk—"low," "moderate," and "high." In an area where studies often involve children, wasn't risk to research subjects rigorously controlled? That was when I realized that the presentation referred to projects "at risk" of not being completed.[1] Many of the studies described in speeches and presentations were as yet unfunded, existing only as proposals and potentialities. At best, Congress had authorized funds for the general purpose of research in a given area, but had not yet appropriated them. As it turned out, that risk that research will remain frozen at the discussion stage in the absence of meaningful support or funding also affects arguments about autism and vaccines.

The Interagency Autism Coordinating Committee (IACC), which organized the Autism Summit, coordinates all autism-related activities of the various member agencies of the U. S. Department of Health and Human Services, including the Centers for Disease Control (CDC), the Centers for Medicare and Medicaid Services, the NIH, and the FDA. The IACC was initially authorized by the Children's Health Act of 2000 and renewed in accordance with the Combating Autism Act of 2006. In addition to coordinating the autism spectrum disorder–related work of different agencies and facilitating information-sharing between groups, it provides a public forum "for discussions related to ASD research, screening, education, and interventions" at its committee meetings.[2] The broad range of activities and participants represented at the IACC meetings and the Autism Summit, where even the most banal laboratory research is scrutinized for political undertones, makes controversy inevitable.

The organizers of the Autism Summit designed the meeting along the lines of a scientific conference, but it operated more like a market. Presenters sold their rival projects to the audience as more urgent and thus more deserving of scarce funds and attention than others. As speaker after speaker emphasized the "bipartisan" nature of autism, I saw approaches to a neurodevelopmental condition transformed into commodities. Since advocacy groups, politicians, government administrators, and judges, like parents themselves, do not have the luxury of waiting for closure on debates about the cause or treatment of autism before they act, facts alone do not necessarily determine their choices. Needless to say, each of these constituencies interprets evidence differently. Many parents and at least some clinicians grant the most weight to personal, subjective, and experiential knowledge. Those who make immunization policy or measure the health outcomes of immunizations, in contrast, see good knowledge as objective, abstract, and based on large population samples. The different sides in the debate do not disagree with each other's arguments. They find them unfathomable.

The organizers may not have intended it, but the issue of childhood immunizations surfaced repeatedly at the Autism Summit. The Indiana Republican congressman Dan Burton's talk featured video clips showing neural cells in a petri dish retreating and degenerating when treated with thimerosal, a solution of approximately 49 percent ethylmercury that was used as a preservative in multidose vaccines until 2001. Representative Burton is a prominent advocate of theories that link autism cases to thimerosal, and he has stated in public that vaccines caused his grandson's autism.[3] The slides he used conveyed the idea of autism overtaking a brain at the cellular level—the neural cells seemed literally to recoil as they reacted to the solution.[4] Some scientists in the audience squirmed. While dramatic, Burton's presentation had little standing based on their standards of proof. The cells in solution seemed a poor substitute for a child receiving a vaccine.

Other presentations, held in breakout sessions the day after the packed plenaries, argued the case for environmental causes of autism with more subtlety. One researcher's talk covered example after example of the dangers associated with low doses of environmental toxins when combined with genetic susceptibility and exposure during a vulnerable developmental period. He then turned to the ways that persistent infections could be implicated in neurological disorders. In the final portion of his talk, he described a study of the measles, mumps, and rubella (MMR) vaccine and autism, mentioning in passing that he didn't feel strongly about the subject or outcome of the study. Unlike some other presenters, he wanted the audience to know that he hadn't made up his mind.[5] As the audience filed out, the presenter remained to answer questions. Behind him, his final slide featured an image of a woman lifting the lid of a chest to peek inside. The name of his study, the Pandora's Box Program, appeared above the picture.[6] Although the slide served mainly to provide his contact information, it wasn't hard to imagine a connection between his talk and his choice of name, an allegory about unintended consequences.

That idea, presented as ambiguous afterword in a talk that was a model of rigor and restraint, also happened to reflect the sentiments of many parents of children diagnosed with autism. They are certain that the world has become a dangerous place as a result of human activities and that their children are paying the price. Their children began life developing typically and regressed into autism as a result of their childhood immunizations, in some cases helped along by severe allergies, too many courses of antibiotics, or environmental toxins like lead and arsenic.

On the whole, these parents do not receive a particularly sympathetic hearing in scientific, policy, or media circles, although they do receive a great deal of attention.[7] Critics portray them as people grasping at an otherwise implausible explanation out of anger, disappointment, and frustration at their child's disability. They point out that language delays often become visible around the age that children receive a number of vaccines, leading parents to mistakenly identify immunizations as the cause of their child's autism. Indeed, many parents do want an explanation that will indicate not only how their child acquired autism, but how to treat the condition. Parents are also angry, not only at the possibility that they might have prevented their child's disorder, but also at the inadequacy of educational accommodations, the failings of insurance companies, and the lack of support services.

A preponderance of evidence suggests that vaccines are not responsible for the upsurge of autism cases over the past two decades, although the matter is not closed and may never be. Still, parents who nonetheless believe that vaccines caused their child's autism are not impaired, in denial, or unable to comprehend statistical correlations. Their individual experiences and observations contradict the claims of scientists and the evidence against an association between immunizations and autism. There is much that we can learn from the claims that parents make and little to be gained by ignoring them.

Parent Advocacy and Vaccine Fears

The modern public health systems in the United States, Great Britain, and most other industrialized nations rely on childhood immunizations. Although they administer and enforce them differently, all of these countries have programs to ensure that children are vaccinated against diseases that were some of the worst killers and causes of permanent disability during infancy and childhood. These diseases included measles and rubella (German measles), mumps, pertussis (whooping cough), and tetanus. Despite the great gains in health associated with immunization campaigns, these public enterprises have also inspired public suspicion and fear since their inception. During the nineteenth and early twentieth centuries, women's groups campaigned against vaccination as an unwelcome government intrusion into the private sphere of family life and an unhealthful violation of children's bodies.[8] Victorian methods of immunization were not nearly as safe or as hygienic as contemporary methods, and activists produced pamphlets with chilling photographs of children allegedly disfigured by vaccines.[9]

Like many debates over the appropriate use of technologies, arguments about vaccination have never been about the technique alone. They have also reflected anxieties about entrusting the health of one's family to authorities. In nineteenth-century England, the antivaccination movement engaged antivivisectionists, supporters of women's suffrage, and religious dissenters. Early activists emphasized that mothers knew more than vaccination enforcers about the health and needs of infants.[10] Contemporary parents may place more trust in medical professionals, but they react strongly if they believe that this trust has been violated. As one mother explained, when she first gave birth to her son, she understood an implicit division of labor: "My job is to love him; your job is to keep him well." After her son developed autism and she became convinced that his immunizations had played a role, her understanding changed, "my responsibility as his mother expanding to include advocacy—even activism—along with love."[11]

Contemporary parents concerned about the link between neurodevelopmental disorders and immunizations share some of their predecessors' mistrust of authority, but it is not the act of immunization itself or the loss of privacy that motivates them. They also rely less on sensational imagery and more on the language of science in articulating their concerns. During debates in the 1980s about risks associated with the diphtheria, pertussis, and tetanus (DPT) vaccine, activists like Barbara Loe Fisher, the cofounder and president of the National Vaccine Information Center, found success with a strategy of couching reservations about vaccines in terms of concerns over lapses in the vaccine safety and monitoring system.[12] In their role as autism advocates, parents have published journal articles and authored white papers on public health policy, and they have succeeded in recruiting scientists and medical practitioners to their cause.

Bernard Rimland, a cofounder of the National Society for Autistic Children (renamed the Autism Society of America) and founder of the Autism Research Institute (ARI), was not initially concerned about vaccines and never implicated them in his son's autism, which was present from birth. The published handbook of methods recommended by doctors associated with ARI's Defeat Autism Now! project mentions vaccines as one of many possible factors involved in autism. It emphasizes the value of immunizations and focuses instead on practical approaches to autism treatment.[13] However, after hearing the concerns among a newer generation of parents, Rimland began to focus on vaccines as a possible cause of autism. Defeat Autism Now! conferences featured talks devoted to immune dysfunction and detoxification. In the years before his death in 2006, Rimland took to asking the audience at Defeat Autism Now! meetings for a show of hands on whether their children had regressed and whether they believed that their child's regression had been caused by one or more vaccines. Rimland would look to the back of the room to be certain that the response was noted or filmed by any reporters present.

Professional epidemiologists would argue that Rimland's poll, based on an association of like-minded parents, is just the kind of nonsystematic measurement that has led to fears about vaccines in the first place. Public health officials worry that parental concerns about immunizations are a type of mass hysteria, where yellow journalism and opportunistic medical professionals fuel the fears of vulnerable and impressionable parents. Their concerns are only heightened when news programs, determined to report on controversies, devote equal time to antivaccine activists and their critics within the medical profession or when popular television programs feature a "ripped from the headlines" story of an autism–vaccine trial, with the lawyer for the parents positioned clearly on the side of good.[14]

When parents describe their own understanding of their child's regression in terms of vaccines, they often reference their growing awareness of news reports and organizations promoting the association. That the association only occurred to them after hearing other reports doesn't matter. One parent recalled leaving her house for an autism conference:

> Before I left I went through Connor's photo album. I did this soon after he was diagnosed, but perhaps I was too close to him and too ignorant of autism to recognize dramatic changes. This time, I saw it: Connor at 11 months, smiling for the camera, looking into his daddy's eyes, touching his mommy's hair. Connor on his first birthday, after his morning visit to the doctor's office and MMR vaccinations, no longer looking at anyone, no longer smiling. And perhaps the most revealing picture: Connor walking on his toes, one of the most common behaviors in autism. Within a day he had changed.[15]

Although each parent has a unique account of their child's regression, published theories about autism and vaccines generally propose two different possible etiologies, sometimes presented in combination. The first theory, relating to the connection between autism and MMR vaccine, has received slightly more attention in the U.K. Theories linking autism and the preservative thimerosal, produced by Eli Lilly and Company since the 1940s and containing 49.6 percent ethylmercury by volume, have received more attention in the United States.[16] Many parents believe that the combination of vaccines, or "two hits," triggered their child's regression. A mercury-containing vaccine weakens the immune system of children with a genetic susceptibility. When followed by an MMR vaccine that, because of the child's vulnerable state, leads to a chronic measles infection and intestinal inflammation, it can produce the behaviors and cognitive symptoms characteristic of autism. Parents are certainly well versed in the evidence in support of various theories; however, what they more often talk about are their child's complex and difficult-to-manage medical symptoms, the temporal association of those symptoms with vaccines, and the importance of detoxification, dietary changes, or anti-inflammatory medications in their child's treatment.

The MMR Vaccine and Autism as a Chronic Disease

The idea that the MMR vaccine might be associated with autism emerged prior to concerns about mercury as a preservative. In 1998, a team of researchers headed by Andrew Wakefield, a gastroenterologist at the Royal Free Hospital in London, published a paper in the British medical journal *Lancet* about a group of twelve children with regressive autism. Their parents had brought them in for consultations related to their painful gastrointestinal symptoms, although the article also noted that a number of the parents had connected their children's symptoms to the MMR vaccine. Colonoscopies revealed that the children had chronic gut inflammation and a set of symptoms that Wakefield began to term "autistic enterocolitis."[17]

Wakefield would have been primed to see a connection between the measles vaccine and gut disturbances in these children. His previous research had looked at a possible connection between measles and Crohn's disease, a chronic bowel disorder with autoimmune components.[18] The new research made him an ardent advocate of a theory linking autism to the MMR vaccine. Following the publication of the article, he held a press conference at which he suggested that parents seek out single shots rather than the combined MMR vaccine for their children.[19] His continuing willingness to go public made him a hero to many parents and an outcast among his colleagues, culminating in his departure from the Royal Free Hospital in 2001.[20] In February 2004, the *Lancet* issued a public retraction of its decision to publish Wakefield and his coauthors' article, stopping short of actually retracting the article from the published record. The editor explained that a previously unrevealed "fatal conflict of interest" had come to light, leading the editor to regard the findings of the study as "entirely flawed."[21] A few days later, the *Sunday Times* revealed that Wakefield had received support from the Legal Aid Fund, an agency that provided financial support for families engaged in litigation against vaccine manufacturers. The association may have compromised the referral process for the *Lancet* study.[22]

By 2007, Wakefield had joined Thoughtful House, a Texas clinic founded by parents. He continued to conduct research on the potential role of the measles vaccine as a causative agent in autism spectrum disorders.[23] He also continued his public role as advocate, testifying before congressional committees on the associations among the MMR vaccine, enterocolitis, and autism, and serving as an expert witness in lawsuits against the pharmaceutical industry.[24] He spoke with intensity and conviction about the importance of listening to parents. Meanwhile, immunization rates in the U.K. began to decline, and Wakefield and two of the coauthors of the *Lancet* study faced the prospect of losing their medical licenses. In January 2010, the U.K.'s General Medical Council reprimanded Wakefield for unethical conduct, including medically unnecessary investigative procedures performed on the children in his study.[25] The *Lancet* then retracted in full the article that they had partially retracted in 2004.[26] In May 2010, Wakefield lost his license to practice medicine. He promised to continue his research nonetheless. "These parents are not going away. . . . The children are not going away. And I am most certainly not going away."[27] In January 2011, the journalist who wrote the initial *Sunday Times* exposé reported that Wakefield also appeared to have fabricated details of his initial cases. The story received wide coverage.[28]

Wakefield was neither the first researcher to link viruses to autism nor the only one to argue that autism involved abnormal immune responses. Doctors generally accept that there are connections between maternal exposure to rubella and autism in children, and there is some evidence linking autism to other viruses, as a result of either chronic or acute infections.[29] Studies have found evidence of autoimmune reactions in autism, including the presence of antibodies against the brain in children's blood. At least one lab associated autoantibodies with the presence of measles virus antibodies, although this finding has been strongly contested.[30]

Scientists know that molecules associated with inflammation called cytokines also have a role in neural signaling and brain development. They seem to be elevated in children with autism, especially in those who experienced a developmental regression, suggesting that regression may be tied to an inflammatory process. Researchers have hypothesized that children who later develop autism have an abnormal innate immune response that might make them react to immunizations in idiosyncratic ways.[31] Of more interest to practitioners concerned about potential environmental causes is accumulating evidence of "an active neuroinflammatory process" in the brains of children with autism.[32] Inflammatory processes are often associated with infections. That observation encourages practitioners who might otherwise be skeptical to consider the possibility that some as-yet-unidentified infectious process could lead to the symptoms that parents attribute to the MMR vaccine.

Wakefield's supporters asked why enrolling children whose parents believed that their autism was vaccine-related constituted a source of bias, when, for example, journals routinely publish papers by experts who receive funding from pharmaceutical manufacturers. Had Wakefield acted unethically by misinterpreting his own results? The multiple coauthors and peer-review process presumably protected him. Was the problem the funding that Wakefield received from lawyers who were directly interested in supporting their clients' cases? The study's coauthors maintained that ongoing research supported their initial findings, yet the retraction led many to assume that all of the article's claims had been rejected.[33] In fact, ten of the thirteen authors of the original article had issued a highly unusual partial retraction, or "retraction of an interpretation." They maintained that the original findings of an "unexpected intestinal lesion" in children with autism were valid but sought to make clear that "no causal link was established between MMR vaccine and autism."[34] Few commentaries noted that the new disease entity remained a source of concern, as did the more general question of whether children with autism had gastrointestinal symptoms that required treatment. In the end, Wakefield's credibility was compromised because he was seen as allied with parent groups rather than the research community.

Wakefield crossed a line by making a policy recommendation as a bench scientist, a choice that disturbed many of his colleagues. He consistently maintained that the new pathological entity he identified was real, as was its association with measles virus.[35] For many of his medical colleagues, this alone was enough to discredit him and his associates. Research in 2008 failed to replicate Wakefield's findings of measles virus in the gut tissue of children with autism and enterocolitis, meaning that the laboratory that evaluated Wakefield's samples might have inadvertently contaminated the materials.[36]

None of this mattered much to parents. That is, theories implicating MMR in autism seemed to offer concrete possibilities for treatment and an explanation for their children's gut disturbances and even for apparently unrelated behavior problems. Children could be treated with antivirals, restriction diets, and anti-inflammatory medications, and parents reported that they saw improvements. Because the broader medical community rejected the theory guiding these treatments, research on their effectiveness has been slow to arrive.

Thimerosal and Detoxification

The second theory connecting the onset of autism to vaccinations concerns thimerosal, an ethylmercury-based preservative used to prevent contamination in multidose vaccines and flu shots. Thimerosal was not considered highly toxic when it was first developed in the 1920s, although manufacturers acknowledged by the 1970s that some consumers had severe reactions to high concentrations of the substance.[37] The convenience and apparent safety of thimerosal kept it in production through the 1990s, even as parents began to report concerns. In 1999, an FDA team tallied the amount of mercury that a child would have received following the recommended vaccine schedule and found that the total easily exceeded the maximum safe dosage for methylmercury, another form of mercury, as set by the Environmental Protection Agency. There was no standard for exposure to ethylmercury, the kind in thimerosal. A vaccine safety expert at Johns Hopkins University admitted his surprise at the finding because "what I believed, and what everybody believed, was that it was truly a trace, a biologically insignificant amount."[38] While he believed that the possible association between mercury and developmental delay ought to be investigated, he did not believe that there was any association with autism.

Since the 1990s, evidence has increasingly linked methylmercury, the type of mercury associated with environmental contamination, to neurodevelopmental disorders. Reports on historical incidents in which populations received accidental exposure to high levels of environmental mercury through contaminated food or pollution present disturbing evidence of brain damage, severe cognitive deficits, and developmental delays.[39] Lower exposures to mercury over time can affect intelligence, and it is possible that there are long-term effects on motor skills and attention, which are poorly measured by IQ tests. Even prenatal exposures seem to cause problems.[40] Toxicologists have found that individual responses to methylmercury vary, and that even pollution that doesn't necessarily affect food supplies can have significant effects.[41] Specifically, methylmercury is a potent developmental neurotoxin, especially dangerous to developing brains. The FDA monitors mercury levels in commercial fish and shellfish and recommends that women who are pregnant or planning to become pregnant, nursing mothers, and young children limit their consumption of fish with higher levels of mercury in their tissues.[42]

These emerging associations may have encouraged parents to consider a connection between the ethylmercury in vaccines and developmental disorders.[43] Beginning in 2000, parents formed a number of organizations focused specifically on mercury in vaccines, most prominently The Coalition for SafeMinds (Sensible Action for Ending Mercury-Induced Neurological Disorders), Moms Against Mercury, and Generation Rescue.[44] Older organizations like the National Vaccine Information Center, which were concerned with the phenomenon of vaccine injury more broadly, joined forces with parents of children with autism after those parents sought them out. Although ARI describes its primary mandate as one of promoting clinical research and treatment, speakers focused on both thimerosal and MMR toxicity have found a warm reception at Defeat Autism Now! conferences. Members of all of these groups have played a role in making the thimerosal debate part of public discourse and therapeutic practice, from running an early listserv called "Chelating Kids" to funding published studies of hair mercury levels and encouraging congressional and IOM hearings. Almost any account of the origins of public unease about thimerosal in childhood vaccines cites parents as the first and most vocal proponents of this view. Medical practitioners and laboratory researchers signed on later, as parents actively recruited them to the cause.

In 2001, Sally Bernard, Lyn Redwood, Albert Enayati, and Teresa Binstock, three parents of children with autism and an independent researcher with a diagnosis of Asperger syndrome, published a paper in the journal *Medical Hypotheses* that argued that regressive autism might be a "novel form of mercury poisoning." The authors observed that victims of mercury poisoning and individuals with autism shared symptoms such as lack of pain perception and odd behavior. The effects of low-dose mercury exposure even appeared to parallel the sex ratios found in autism. The spread of autism spectrum disorders also seemed to follow the increasing use of thimerosal-containing vaccines in the United States, with the first reported cases of autism emerging shortly after the introduction of thimerosal-containing vaccines.[45] Although the article was not published in a peer-reviewed medical journal and autism researchers criticized its central claims, it became a rallying point for parents who already suspected a causal association between their child's regression and their immunizations.[46]

Those concerned about thimerosal received a boost from investigative journalist David Kirby's 2005 book *Evidence of Harm*, which followed the stories of a number of founding members of SafeMinds from the moment they first noticed problems with their children's development to their transformation into political activists. Kirby emphasized parents' sense of betrayal at their discovery that the CDC had misjudged the true amount of ethylmercury that children received cumulatively through their vaccinations. He portrayed the researchers and clinicians associated with Defeat Autism Now!, who were willing to explore the link and consider possible mechanisms of toxicity, as sympathetic allies of parents.[47]

The CDC has never found any association between thimerosal and autism spectrum disorders. Rather, it has produced a number of epidemiological studies demonstrating a lack of association between thimerosal-containing vaccines and developmental disorders. The destructive potential of ethylmercury, the form of mercury used in thimerosal, is difficult to characterize. Many scientists argue that the substantial evidence against methylmercury does not apply to ethylmercury, the form in thimerosal, which differs in a small but very significant way in its chemical composition. The reality is that the biological activity of ethylmercury is not well understood. Toxicity estimates have drawn mainly on studies of exposure to methylmercury.[48] We know relatively little about the differences in the ways that bodies respond to the two forms of mercury, differences that could render thimerosal either more dangerous than organic mercury or entirely benign.[49]

Evaluating those studies that have focused on ethylmercury is complicated. Disputes over results have turned on the putative affiliations and loyalties of those interpreting them. Investigators sympathetic to the claims of parents have gradually built a theory about the relationship between thimerosal and neurodevelopmental harm, although many of them are conscious of maintaining their credibility and refrain from making any direct claims about vaccines and autism in their published work. It is up to the press, to parents, and to practitioners to guess at the work's practical implications.

Some studies have directly examined the toxic effects of thimerosal on neural cells. Exposure can lead to a process that looks much like apoptosis or "programmed cell death." A healthy body normally uses apoptosis in the process of development and in removing dead or aging cells. If thimerosal causes cell death that mimics apoptosis, it may not leave the clear evidence of injury that investigators would otherwise expect with a toxic exposure— this was the research that caused such a dramatic reaction at the Autism Summit in 2003.[50] Thimerosal may also act to inhibit intercellular signaling at concentrations even lower than those that are lethal for cells in culture.[51] Subgroups of children may be genetically vulnerable to thimerosal toxicity because of differences in the metabolic pathways devoted to detoxification and managing oxidative stress, a source of cellular damage.[52]

One major way that genes are regulated is through the selective attachment and removal of methyl groups, methylation and demethylation. Researchers have connected a number of diseases, including cancer, autoimmune diseases, and neurodegenerative disorders, to problems with DNA methylation. Thimerosal, like the two known developmental neurotoxins ethanol and lead, appears to affect an enzyme, methionine synthase, which plays a significant role in methylation and in the manufacture of glutathione, another chemical important in mercury detoxification.[53] When researchers exposed neural cells to toxic levels of thimerosal they found depleted levels of glutathione, lending further weight to the hypothesis.[54]

Although critics invariably point to the limits of any attribution of symptoms of autism to animal models, a well-publicized 2004 study found that a strain of mice that had been engineered with a tendency to develop autoimmune conditions appeared far more vulnerable than typical laboratory mice to behavioral and brain structure changes resulting from injections of thimerosal during crucial developmental periods.[55] A 2007 study found that thimerosal itself was capable of altering immune responses.[56] That the susceptible mice were those with a genetic vulnerability fueled claims that children who developed autism reacted differently to mercury than typical children, although a later study failed to reproduce the findings.[57] Several studies funded and in some cases coauthored by parents found significantly lower rates of mercury in first baby haircuts of children with autism compared to those of typical children. Children with autism might have a reduced capacity to excrete mercury, but other groups of investigators have disputed that result as well.[58]

Mercury and Detoxification Therapies

The findings from laboratory studies suggest to some researchers the beginnings of a plausible integrated picture of autism as a chronic illness induced in vulnerable individuals by even relatively low doses of thimerosal. These potential mechanisms have inspired practitioners to experiment with biomedical treatments based on the affected metabolic pathways. In some cases, they have also served as post hoc justifications for treatments that practitioners were already using to address suspected cases of toxic exposures to thimerosal. They include supplementation with either glutathione or methylcobalamine, methyl-B12, which parents usually administer to their children through subcutaneous injections. Both chemicals are part of the methionine synthase pathway that is affected by thimerosal. The treatments are intended to increase rates of methylation in affected children by providing extra doses of substances in order to drive chemical reactions.

By far the most notorious treatment for thimerosal toxicity is chelation, a therapy commonly used to treat individuals suffering from the acute effects of heavy metal poisoning. It works by chemically binding toxins so that the body can excrete them. Although dimercaptosuccinic acid (DMSA) is the best known of the chelating agents, doctors have also used other substances, including ethylene diamine tetraacetic acid. EDTA is sold as edetate calcium disodium under the brand name Versenate. The Autism Research Institute's mercury detoxification consensus statement does not mention or advocate EDTA, but this meant little to critics when, in a widely covered incident, a doctor inadvertently caused the death of a five-year-old boy by giving him an infusion of edetate disodium, another form of EDTA.[59] Although investigators concluded that he had used the substance in error, the doctor eventually faced a charge of involuntary manslaughter. Critics of detoxification therapies saw the tragedy as further evidence that practitioners and parents who opt for these interventions do not have the best interests of affected children at heart.[60] Self-advocates with autism, appalled by the incident, said it proved that pro-cure parents would willingly risk the lives of their offspring in exchange for the prospect of normal development. Even if the doctor had administered the correct substance, the procedure still carried risks.

News that the National Institute of Mental Health (NIMH) had decided to fund a clinical trial of chelation as part of a study of novel treatments buoyed proponents of detoxification therapies. The NIMH initiative aimed at better understanding autism subtypes such as regressive autism.[61] Critics warned that that the safety and potential utility of DMSA was not established enough to warrant a trial, although thousands of parents were already treating their children with it. Then, an institutional review board refused to approve the trial after the release of a new study showing that DMSA might cause lasting cognitive harm if prescribed unnecessarily. To the dismay of a number of advocacy organizations, in July of 2008 the NIMH cancelled the trial.[62] Nevertheless, parents continue to pursue chelation. They are encouraged by laboratory reports that show high rates of mercury and other heavy metals in their children, especially after an initial "provocation" with a chelating agent, although some results show the same levels in typically developing children following provocation.[63]

Parent advocacy groups like SafeMinds have proved particularly skilled at recruiting supporters from within the medical professions and the government. They have targeted those already suspicious of immunizations because of their own children's medical problems, lawmakers opposed to government interference in private life, and people who distrust experts or pharmaceutical manufacturers. Republican congressman Dan Burton was one early recruit. His grandson developed autism following his childhood immunizations, and Burton became a convinced opponent of mercury in vaccines as well as a supporter of disabilities-related legislation. A second Republican in Congress, Dave Weldon, a medical doctor, signed on as well. Weldon had spoken publicly about his belief in the importance of immunizations but warned that "the failure to get answers to the many questions concerning vaccine safety is beginning to undermine public confidence" in the CDC and immunization program.[64]

Supporters spanned party and ideological lines. The environmental lawyer and member of the first family of the Democratic Party, Robert F. Kennedy Jr., wrote an impassioned article in *Rolling Stone* about the thimerosal controversy, which came down largely in support of parents. The controversial radio host and political independent Don Imus championed *Evidence of Harm*, the book by David Kirby about vaccines and autism.[65] Critics charged both Kirby and Kennedy of opportunism, speculating in Kennedy's case that he might pursue tort cases against vaccine companies. Kirby allegedly just wanted the free publicity.[66] Meanwhile, Rick Rollens, the former secretary of the California State Senate, who believes his son's autism is vaccine-related, helped raise more than $5 million to fund the MIND (Medical Investigation of Neurological Disorders) Institute, an autism research center at the University of California, Davis.[67]

Parents are not a homogeneous group. Those who implicate immunizations in autism take that position for a variety of reasons. Many others remain skeptical of hypotheses that environmental factors, including childhood immunizations, play a role in autism. They ally themselves with medical authorities in their interpretations of the symptoms and probable causes of autism, and they focus on educational services and accommodation, in line with self-advocates. Some help to fund research on the genetics and neurobiology of autism but have largely refrained from criticizing or seeking to influence scientists' underlying assumptions about the biological underpinnings of the disorder.

To some parents, however, it is hardly necessary to test for a possible connection between vaccines and autism. They know through experience that an association exists. They worry less about a study's design than whether its conclusions support their beliefs and can be used to mobilize support for alternative treatments and vaccine policy reform. Even the most sympathetic researchers tend to interpret their results conservatively. They care more about what those findings can tell them about disease mechanisms than their implications in the vaccine debate. Parents, in contrast, see published articles as political tools.

Testimony versus Epidemiology

In February of 2004, as the news was breaking about Andrew Wakefield's potential conflict of interest and as the *Lancet* issued its first retraction, the Institute of Medicine (IOM) in Washington, D.C., convened a meeting of its Immunization Safety Review Committee. It was held in a spacious lecture hall at the National Academies of Science building and, like the Autism Summit a few months earlier, it was open to the public. A wide range of interested parties attended—young women wearing jeans and "Moms Against Mercury" T-shirts, lawyers and epidemiologists, laboratory scientists who looked distinctly uncomfortable on stage, congressional interns, and reporters with notepads. The participants had assembled to address the question of the relationship between immunizations and autism. The committee, which was composed of experts in immunization, public health, and pediatrics, although not necessarily specialists in autism, sat at the front of the room and listened to a full day of presentations before retiring to write its report.

Wakefield's absence from the hearings stood out. Other researchers, especially those sympathetic to him, cited his work as evidence of the potential danger of the MMR vaccine. The experts who presented at the meeting reflected two distinct research traditions and, not coincidentally, the two main positions in the controversy. The majority, who did laboratory work using blood samples and animal models and who reasoned from the perspective of biochemistry, molecular biology, and toxicology, tended to argue that the risk associated with immunizations had yet to be conclusively determined. One toxicologist with little background in autism research seemed surprised by the contentiousness of the hearing. Ethylmercury was quite possibly a developmental neurotoxin, with its precise level of toxicity not yet established. The problem clearly required further research. The epidemiologists insisted the opposite, that their population studies demonstrated that immunizations with the MMR or thimerosal-containing vaccines carried negligible risk. No correlation existed between immunizations and autism spectrum disorders. The two sides turned out to be debating two different, if related, questions.

Released four months later, the final committee report made clear which question the panel considered relevant. Although noting cases of autism in which children had regressed and that autism was a complex, heterogeneous disorder, it concluded that no credible evidence existed to connect autism with immunizations. Although scientists conducting laboratory research in vitro had suggested some potential, biologically plausible mechanisms, the findings were not sufficiently strong, and it was more important that research funds be "channeled to the most promising areas." [68] Opponents of the decision saw the statement as an explicit attempt to close down debate. The decision dismayed parent groups. Committee members seemed to have let their concern about the integrity of a powerful public health program override any reservations they might have had about the effect of vaccines on individual children. [69] To the more disillusioned parents, the decision also reflected a willingness to bend to the desires of pharmaceutical companies and bureaucrats in the CDC concerned about their public images.

It was not the first time that the IOM had tackled the issue of public mistrust of childhood immunizations, nor was it the first time that parents had felt cheated by a committee that had ignored crucial evidence. Three years earlier, in 2001, the IOM had called two separate meetings of the Immunization Safety Review Committee on the topics of the MMR vaccine and autism and thimerosal-containing vaccines and autism. Their report, issued in 2001, found no direct evidence of thimerosal leading to developmental disorders or other neurological symptoms in children, but that the hypothesis warranted further study. They had drawn similar conclusions about the MMR vaccine. [70] Parent groups began to respond by challenging the methods and findings of the studies upon which the IOM had relied.

SafeMinds, the most forceful promoters of the mercury–autism hypothesis, worried that scientists at the CDC had suppressed positive epidemiological results. The organization had obtained transcripts of a June 2000 IOM scientific meeting at the Simpsonwood Retreat Center in Norcross, Georgia. The attendees discussed the preliminary results of a study using data from the Vaccine Safety Datalink, a database created through a partnership between the CDC and several private health maintenance organizations (HMOs). The study's authors met with other experts in epidemiology and immunizations to confirm their interpretation of the results and to address possible flaws in advance of meetings of the IOM review committee and the CDC's Advisory Committee on Immunization Practices.

At the closed session, the authors presented their analysis of the data, which associated thimerosal with a risk for some neurological disorders. After a tense discussion, the authors decided to exclude some groups from the sample and add others, which resulted in the weakening of thimerosal effects in the revised models. They brought younger children who were less likely to have been diagnosed into the analysis. One decision in particular concerned parents in SafeMinds. In massaging the data (or, as the authors understood it, improving the model) the researchers had excluded from the sample children who had received little or no exposure to thimerosal at an age when children typically receive the majority of their shots. The authors reasoned that these children were from atypical families. If the families had been unwilling or unlikely to have them vaccinated, they were probably also unwilling or unlikely to bring them in for a developmental evaluation. In other words, the low rate of neurological disorders in the sample resulted from underdiagnosis rather than from low exposure to thimerosal.[71]

It is possible to read the transcripts and construct an account of the meeting that differs from that of SafeMinds. Paul Offit, a University of Pennsylvania professor of vaccinology and author of *Autism's False Prophets*, finds an instance of routine scientific practice. Researchers commonly have their findings and methods critiqued by panels of their peers prior to publication.[72] Parents focused on the negotiations recorded in the transcripts and the decision to revise the sample set. It convinced them that CDC officials had made protection of the nation's vaccination program a priority even at the cost of exposing children to a potent developmental neurotoxin.

Decisions to include or exclude sets of children from epidemiological studies can reflect underlying ideas about the nature of reliable research and about disease mechanisms. Many epidemiological researchers assume that a good study should answer the question: were previously healthy children more likely to develop autism if exposed to either thimerosal or the MMR vaccine? Thus, the strongest evidence against an association between autism and immunizations comes from population-level studies that compare children who received vaccines with those who did not. Since 2000, epidemiologists have conducted a number of these studies on several data sets in the United States, Denmark, and Canada, and the majority failed to demonstrate any association.[73] Based on a study design that seeks to eliminate confounding factors, researchers exclude children likely to have other underlying health conditions. From the perspective of parent advocates, such decisions make no sense. Children with underlying vulnerabilities—genetic conditions, preexisting health problems, family histories of illness—are more likely to be harmed by vaccine-related exposures. Excluding these children from the sample set only proves that researchers are not really listening to their ideas about the causes of autism.

During the IOM meeting in February 2004, when toxicological and laboratory analyses of potential vaccine toxicity clashed with epidemiological analyses of their evident safety, it became evident that participants understood the idea of a "conflict of interest" in very different ways. The formal requirement that presenters disclose their potential financial conflicts might have seemed like a rule with self-evident justification to the many who understood conflicts of interest as arising from private and, in particular, corporate funding for research, while viewing their own government funding as a primary safeguard of disinterested and objective scholarship. At the meeting, however, some participants who had obtained seed funds from parent organizations implied that employment by the CDC or funding through that agency constituted a far more egregious conflict of interest. It did not matter that one branch of the CDC oversaw the national immunization program and another the safety evaluations of vaccines. These participants and their supporters took conflict to mean any affiliation that might lead the investigator to favor a particular set of results over others. In other words, parent groups viewed financial ties as only one of many possible impediments—including institutional, ideological, or political commitments on the part of an individual investigator—to the ideal of "good science."[74] The dispute may have led the CDC to restructure the offices responsible for safety monitoring of vaccines in the following year.[75]

Any possibility of measuring the relationship between immunizations and autism rates depends on the availability, integrity and, ultimately, reliability of different databases. Countries with nationalized health care have more readily available records of immunizations, including adverse outcomes. In the United States, most researchers rely on the Vaccine Adverse Events Reporting System database and the Vaccine Safety Datalink. In 1990, in accordance with a legislative mandate that the CDC monitor the post-market safety of vaccines, the Immunization Safety Branch of the Epidemiology and Surveillance Division of the National Immunization Program established the two databases.[76]

The Vaccine Adverse Events Reporting System database (VAERS) is a voluntary reporting system in which primary care practitioners, patients, and insurance companies can register adverse events associated with immunizations.[77] Epidemiologists do not have a particularly high regard for the quality of the VAERS data, both because reporting is voluntary, which leads to underreporting of incidents and poor identification of cases, and because no standardized criteria exist for reporting symptoms. In one instance, following publication of an article that used the VAERS data, the American Academy of Pediatrics issued a statement declaring that that the data were never intended for use to test hypotheses about connections between immunizations and illnesses.[78] At best, the VAERS database could aid in the post-market monitoring and oversight of vaccines and might occasionally serve to identify issues for further study. Mark and David Geier, a father-and-son team that has turned out a steady stream of epidemiological studies on vaccines and autism, have relied almost exclusively on the VAERS data.[79] Most epidemiologists ignore their work because of its methodological problems. The willingness of parents to hold up work by the Geiers only reinforces critics' belief that parents do not understand the mechanics of reliable research design.

The second database, the Vaccine Safety Datalink (VSD), is a collaborative project run by the CDC and a consortium of HMOs. Participants voluntarily report on a broad set of variables in their patient populations that can then be correlated with vaccination schedules. The VSD data suffer some significant shortcomings of their own. The HMOs have historically used different reporting systems with poorly standardized measures to report health outcomes, and no method exists to distinguish differences in health care utilization, income levels, and other significant variables among populations in the various HMOs. The VSD also includes detailed information on variables that could be linked to individual patients, including geographic location, genetics, and exact dates and times of doctor visits and procedures. As a result, the CDC tightly restricts access to the data, requiring that potential researchers submit a formal proposal in addition to obtaining the approval of an institutional review board before they begin their study. Researchers must travel to the Research Data Center (RDC) in Atlanta in order to access the data. The many inconsistencies in the data also make it difficult to interpret and, the CDC suggests, subject to misinterpretation by ill-informed or poorly trained researchers.

Parent organizations did not find those arguments convincing. Although they have differed on the importance of investigating the relationship between autism and vaccinations, they have agreed on the desirability of greater public access to the VSD data and the need for further safety research on vaccines in general. A joint statement issued in 2003 by organizations including the Autism Society of America, the Cure Autism Now Foundation, SafeMinds, and the Autism Research Institute demanded that the VSD "must be made available to all qualified research scientists in a timely manner. The current practice of restricting access to the database to a limited group of possibly biased individuals is not acceptable."[80]

Accounts and Explanations

Parents may be more sympathetic than researchers to the idea that vaccinations affect specific vulnerable populations because of their experiences with the medical complaints of their own children. Critics have suggested that parents create retrospective narratives about vaccines only after hearing similar claims from others or after watching news reports that, some say, overrepresent the potential role of vaccines.[81] However, to read accounts by parents of their child's precipitous developmental regression following a set of immunizations or to read the transcripts of the Autism Omnibus Proceedings of the U.S. Court of Federal Claims is to appreciate the degree to which parents' testimonies reflect their intimately observed understanding of the onset of symptoms. The accounts also reflect their utter certainty, retrospectively, about the cause of their child's illnesses.

Parents tell stories of acute reactions to vaccines, including clear declines in overall health, which began with enough of a delay following a child's immunizations that doctors reject any association between the two. Parents, however, insist on the connection. According to one parent, "eleven days after Ryan's DPT he had a sudden, rapidly rising fever (to 105°) and a stiff neck and body. He screamed and pitched for 24 hours, having convulsions, his eyes rolling."[82] Another writes that "shortly after his 18-month shots, RJ seemed to shut down right before our eyes. His first words stopped abruptly and he wouldn't do anything to communicate except point and grunt. He stopped interacting, smiling, and laughing altogether."[83] Another remembers that

> two years ago, shortly before his second birthday, our son William went to his doctor's office and received a standard set of "catch-up" shots. . . . During the following summer William suffered from constant diarrhea, unexplained bumps and welts, reduced speech, bloating, binge eating, bloody lesions, "croup attacks," and lost interaction and eye contact.[84]

Other parents describe their growing certainty in the wake of medical tests that confirmed for them that their children suffered from an environmental illness caused by the immunizations that they had received:

> So you see, I've had some successes here and there, and I've gained much knowledge, but I have a lot more to think about. We just received test results showing that the kids have antibodies to almost all of their brain proteins and neurotransmitters. They have anti-

bodies to myelin, serotonin and receptor sites, catecholamines and neural axon filament proteins. You cannot tell me that these children are just psychologically involved; they are *systematically ill.*[85]

The nutritionist ordered a hair test to see how Augie was metabolizing minerals. The test results showed that Augie's mercury level was literally "off the chart," and that he also had some aluminum in him. . . .Dr. Zbylot then gave us the name of another doctor who specialized in chelation, and that doctor started Augie on a very low dose of DMSA. Augie remained on DMSA in varying doses for a year and a half. Each time we gave it to him, we thought we saw him take a little developmental jump forward.[86]

Many doctors dispute the validity of unorthodox or unfamiliar tests that examine antibody levels, measure amounts of organic acids in the blood, look for the possibility of yeast overgrowth, and calculate the amount of heavy metals excreted following chelation treatments. For many parents, those same laboratory printouts provide documentary evidence of the foreign substances that their children harbor as a result of their vaccines and of the real physical changes that underpin their behavioral regressions. The situation of these parents resembles that of other communities brought together by their experience of disorders that doctors do not universally recognize as "real" disease entities with characteristic patterns of onset. Examples include multiple chemical sensitivity and Gulf War syndrome, among other environmental illnesses.[87] Even though epidemiologists and parents agree on the existence of autism as a valid and generally recognized disease entity, this agreement counts for little. Parents view gut symptoms, body rashes, food intolerances, and an inability to concentrate as important ways that the disease manifests in their children, whereas researchers persist in describing autism in terms of impairments or abnormalities in communication, behaviors, and social reciprocity.

Many of the public health and policy experts who arbitrate on issues of vaccine safety recognize experimental biomedical treatments as "complimentary and alternative treatments" but not as practices intimately bound up with the vaccine issue. For many parents, however, the two are closely connected. Part of the significance of these treatments for parents is the role that they play in a causal narrative, one that ends with the prospect of healing. What matters is that, instead of having to depend on the instructions of medical personnel, parents take an active role in monitoring their child's condition. Many parents first learn to understand their child's autism as a chronic disease. They later begin to see it as a result of immunizations, based on their successes with treatments or meeting other parents with similar concerns.

Detoxification therapies appear to work, as evidenced by the toxins excreted from their children's bodies, the repair to their compromised digestive and immune systems, and their behavioral improvements. Providers of specialized therapies operate on the assumption, based on clinical observations or on laboratory work, that children with immune over- or underactivity, gut disturbances, and inflammation differ in clinically important ways from children with heavy metal toxicity, oxidative stress, and impaired methylation capacity.[88] Parents talk about "mercury kids" being "zoned out" and "spacey," possibly as a result of their chronic yeast infections, while "measles kids" have chronic diarrhea and gastrointestinal pain, weak immune systems, food sensitivities, and obsessive symptoms.

To parents, the CDC is as incapable of recognizing these distinctive illnesses as it is the risks associated with vaccines. One parent explained that he believed that CDC officials were quite conservative and careful in their initial approval of new vaccines—it was what came after they were introduced to the market that troubled him. Although officials were cautious about adding new vaccines to the schedule, they paid little attention to the possibility of cumulative effects or interactions among vaccines. Vaccine critics worry in particular about the neglect of chronic diseases in post-market monitoring practices. Bernadine Healy, a former head of the NIH, came forward in 2008 with her concerns that the CDC might prefer epidemiological studies as a way of identifying possible adverse effects of vaccines, even though they had a more limited ability to tease out vulnerable subgroups. Although she recognized that many colleagues would criticize her for saying it, she was inclined to be thankful for the vaccine court, where even concerns about widely accepted practices could receive a hearing.[89]

Defining Science in Court

About a year before the strange confluence of political and medical discussions at the November 2003 Autism Summit, angry references to the Homeland Security Act appeared on parent listservs. Members took aim not at the act itself but at a rider attached to it, designed to limit litigation in cases of vaccine injury. The National Vaccine Injury Compensation Program (VICP), begun in 1988, already restricted litigation on vaccine injuries, but parents could still bring legal cases against vaccine manufacturers outside the structure created by the National Childhood Vaccine

Injury Act. They used a loophole that allowed them to focus on thimerosal, a preservative, rather than on the vaccine itself. They could sue vaccine manufacturers over their use of thimerosal without first bringing their cases before the VICP.

These civil suits also offered some recourse for children who had found their cases excluded under the three-year statute of limitations set by the VICP, a considerable number given that many parents did not draw an immediate connection between vaccines and their child's illness. Authorities designed the rider to insulate the pharmaceutical industry from litigation on the grounds that protecting the national vaccine supply took priority, an argument that parents considered to be transparently flimsy. Congress eventually dropped the rider from the bill. The uproar helped to publicize the parents' concerns and also suggested how much manufacturers would have liked to shut down the ongoing discussions about autism and vaccines.

The Office of Special Masters of the U.S. Court of Federal Claims, colloquially the "vaccine court," is an unusual institution. It exists exclusively to hear cases brought to the VICP. "Special masters" rather than career judges preside. They are lawyers vested with provisional judicial powers in order to execute the requirements of the Vaccine Injury Compensation Act.[90] The VICP was brought into being through activism by parents who believed that their children had been injured by the whole-cell pertussis vaccine used in the DPT shot in the 1980s. When companies reported a vaccine shortage due to the burden of lawsuits related to this concern, Congress passed the National Childhood Vaccine Injury Act of 1986 (NCVIA), which established the VICP. In 1990, in accordance with the requirement that the CDC monitor post-market safety of vaccines, the Immunization Safety Branch of the Epidemiology and Surveillance Division of the National Immunization Program also established the two key databases, the VAERS and the VSD.

The VICP turned out to be a lucky legislative move for the CDC and vaccine manufacturers, and a Pyrrhic victory for parent advocates of injury compensation.[91] By incorporating parents' objections and arguments about vaccine safety into the very fabric of vaccine-related legislation, lawmakers effectively silenced them and all but ended the possibility of large-scale civil suits against vaccine manufacturers. Congress created the VICP explicitly as a "no-fault alternative" to tort litigation on vaccine proceedings. While parents benefited from a standardized hearing and compensation process, vaccine manufacturers gained a "less adversarial" legal process, in which findings that children were owed compensation did not lead to penalties for manufacturers.

In the summer of 2007, that is, eighteen years after its creation, the VICP finally began to hear cases brought by the families of children with autism. These constituted the Omnibus Autism Proceeding, a series of "test cases" to determine the validity of parents' claims. At the time, there were over 5,000 cases related to autism filed under the VICP, none of which had gone to trial.[92] The court selected the test cases in order to examine the evidence for claims about injuries caused by the MMR vaccine, thimerosal-containing vaccines, or a combination of the two. The testimony brought into sharp focus the many conflicts that pitted parents concerned about vaccines and the minority of doctors that allied with them against the majority of other medical practitioners concerned with autism. Many families attended the open sessions, while others listened in via teleconference or later downloaded and read the transcripts. They already knew the arguments if they had been following discussions of vaccines and autism through Defeat Autism Now! conferences, parent listservs, or other publications.

The first autism case heard by the Office of Special Masters involved Michelle Cedillo, a then twelve-year-old girl with multiple health problems. She had been a healthy and sociable toddler before receiving thimerosal-containing vaccines followed by the MMR vaccine. Her parents claimed that she regressed dramatically, became nonverbal, and developed a variety of severe medical problems including inflammatory bowel disease. But some of Michelle's otherwise unexplained and self-injurious behavior, which included repeatedly hitting herself in the chest, began to abate once she received treatments for a stomach ulcer and gut inflammation. Parents in other test cases told similar stories.

All of the families also produced videotapes of their children before their first birthdays, and these videos played a major role in the hearings. For the parents, they represented clear evidence that their children had developed typically up until a sudden and dramatic regression. The lawyers representing the government's case brought witnesses in to reinterpret the tapes. The witnesses explained that they saw early signs of autism that the parents failed to identify. Why? Parents lacked special training. They did not have a typically developing child as a reference point. They were "actually compensating in their behavior [for] the lack of response in the child, but they are not aware of that."[93] One expert witness pointed to Michelle Cedillo's "hand regard," a type of self-stimulatory behavior, as evidence that her autism predated her vaccinations. Theresa Cedillo disagreed. It was only Michelle blowing kisses. "He's referring to where she pulls her hand back to look at it, but what you're probably not aware is that my mom, her grandmother, had been teaching her to blow kisses. Of course, when babies blow kisses, you know, she was just doing that."[94]

As the Omnibus Autism Proceeding began, an epidemiologist and a professor of psychiatry participating in an NIH-funded autism program appeared as guests on *Talk of the Nation*, a National Public Radio call-in show. The two specialists assured listeners of vaccines' safety. Minimal evidence existed to prove an association with autism.[95] They feared the adverse consequences of parents refusing to vaccinate their children. In the United Kingdom, where compliance with vaccination is voluntary, the rate of immunizations with the MMR vaccine declined following public concerns about its safety, and this could have contributed to a measles outbreak in 2007.[96]

The speakers on the program, like many of their colleagues, may also have worried that listeners would not understand how evidence was used in the vaccine court. In the Omnibus Autism Proceeding, the claimants only had to demonstrate that a "preponderance of evidence" supported their case, not that it was true "beyond a reasonable doubt." The standard conforms to civil law but seems markedly looser than that supplied by conventional use of evidence in court cases.[97] The families needed to prove to the court's satisfaction that their argument was plausible for their particular case. They had no need to demonstrate that immunizations caused autism as a general rule, the standard that would apply within most of the scientific community. Nevertheless, they served as "test cases" for the latter, wider claim.

One caller asked the radio guests whether the studies used to reject the claim that immunizations caused autism had been conducted by groups affiliated with either vaccine manufacturers or government agencies charged with overseeing immunization programs. The guest assured the caller that "of course" there were no connections, although the claim may have been based on his own convictions rather than certain knowledge. The CDC had relied on a set of Danish studies. The advocacy organization SafeMinds argued that many of the lead researchers had ties to vaccine manufacturers.[98] The problem is that it is quite difficult to find researchers with adequate expertise in the area of vaccine safety that are not in some way affiliated with either the government or a vaccine manufacturer.

The Omnibus Proceedings provided a perhaps unintended forum for both sides to explain what they understood to be sound science. On the plaintiff's side, the expert witnesses talked about the importance of entertaining all possible theories of causation in the interest of treating children and of crediting parents' understandings of their own child's development, regression, and recovery. "It's not scientific certainty," a lawyer for Michelle Cedillo explained, "because, frankly, the science is in dispute."[99] An epidemiologist appearing as a witness for the plaintiffs argued that existing studies would not have been able to identify a small set of children with "clearly regressive autism" if such a group existed. For that reason the studies refuting a link between autism and vaccines might not apply to the test cases.[100]

The lawyers representing the Department of Health and Human Services responded by distinguishing between "good science" and "junk science," as defined by the Supreme Court. "What has no place here are experts at the margins of legitimate science" whose theories were no better than guesses.[101] In the hearing regarding the thimerosal causation theory, a lawyer for the Department of Health and Human Services declared that

> there is no scientific debate. The debate is over. There's no scientific controversy. The only controversy is the media controversy, propelled by those groups who were founded on the premise that vaccines cause autism or by those groups who promote and advocate experimental therapies for autism such as chelation. The credible scientific community has already spoken on this issue and has rejected it.[102]

In conclusion, the respondents warned that the Special Masters' decisions would be taken as guides not only by the vaccine court, but by parents in general, who might look to them as they decided whether their own children should receive vaccines.[103]

Parents grew hopeful after the 2008 finding by the vaccine court for Hannah Poling, a child with autism that was related to a mitochondrial disorder. The court had accepted that the disorder might have been triggered by vaccines.[104] Then, in February 2009 the vaccine court ruled against the arguments of the first three test cases and the theory that MMR vaccine and thimerosal-containing vaccines could together lead to autism.[105] In March 2010 the court ruled against the second three test cases on the theory that thimerosal alone could cause autism, effectively concluding the proceedings.[106]

Throughout the series of test cases, the lawyers for the Department of Health and Human Services questioned the credibility of the expert witnesses who supported the theories that vaccines could cause autism. They challenged the witnesses' qualifications to speak on toxic injury or neurological malfunction given that many of them were pediatricians rather than clinical researchers. The Special Master for the Cedillo case concluded his decision by observing that the parents sincerely believed that Michelle had been injured by vaccines, but had been "misled by physicians who are guilty, in my view, of gross medical misjudgment."[107]

Paul Offit, a vaccine expert present at the hearings, suggested that Michelle Cedillo's lawyers had established an antagonistic tone early on in the hearings by alleging that the government had stood "shoulder to shoulder" with vaccine manufacturers.[108] By the conclusion of the hearings both sets of lawyers were decidedly confrontational. Everyone involved took pains to acknowledge the devotion and care on the part of the parents as entirely distinct from their efforts to demolish the arguments of the parents' allies. No one was questioning whether the parents were attentive, responsible, and devoted to their children. For the parents the distinction might not have been so clear. The witnesses whose competence was being called into question were also the doctors that they had chosen to trust, and who were treating their children with what the parents saw as definitive success.

Risk, Particularity, and Responsibility

The beliefs that parents hold about vaccine injuries and autism spectrum disorders matter to them for their explanatory power. The vaccine hypothesis validates a course of treatments, but it also identifies a cause of their children's condition, answers the question of who or what is to blame, and opens up the issue of compensation, including support for their children's continuing care. Officials worry instead about the consequences for the health of present and future generations if the courts or the medical research communities ultimately side with parents. Public health professionals see vaccination programs as victims of their own success, where declining rates of infectious diseases have made parents complacent. Complications from diseases like measles can be life-threatening or disabling.[109] The solution is more and better information delivered through a trusted government body.

Sociologists of medicine are concerned with recent trends in vaccine use as well, but their analyses challenge those of the public health officials on a number of grounds. First, parents of typical children don't differ all that much from parents of children with autism when it comes to evaluating risk and the possibility of harm. Both act rationally, in ways consistent with the way they understand their obligations. Second, the focus on reassuring the public through information campaigns cannot solve the problem of trust in interactions with medical authorities. Parents see the choice to vaccinate, especially when there is no way to know with absolute certainty about the associated risks, as a "leap of faith" of the type that takes place in the context of any close relationship between two trusting individuals. A general mistrust of government that may seem initially unrelated to medical issues compounds the problem.[110] Third, doctors miss something important when they dismiss all objections of vaccines as problems of misunderstanding or "bias." Many parents come to their decisions as a result of broader ideological commitments to holistic medicine or attachment parenting.[111]

For many mothers and fathers, good parenting constitutes a type of "moral imperative" that obliges them to seek out additional information and not take authorities' assurances as fact.[112] Many groups that are critical of vaccinations want to encourage parents to come to conclusions for themselves, and the statements of parent groups reflect this sense that "the process of education and learning is more important than the eventual decision and that trust, (or at least blind faith) is . . . itself a source of risk."[113] Immunizations remind parents how much they must, as citizens and consumers, trust in "systems of expertise" that can potentially fail.[114] Many parents emphasize their child's particular vulnerability to vaccines and the need to conduct case studies on specific populations. Even if epidemiological findings offer convincing evidence of a lack of association, "these findings in and of themselves lack the rich meaning offered by the narrative accounts found in parents' description of their children changing."[115]

Sociologists also point to the problems created by the perceived divide between the assumed rationality of medical professionals and the emotionality of parents. Indeed, doctors and nurses themselves have expressed reservations about the demand that they express absolute certainty when they tell parents that vaccines are safe, rather than admit the complexities of the issue.[116] Doctors also do not have an "exclusive claim to rationality" in their concern about the potential for disaster if a child goes unvaccinated. Parents too engage in a style of "worst-case" thinking when they worry about autism or other adverse outcomes of vaccines.[117] Rather than viewing parents who choose not to vaccinate as part of an "antivaccination movement" with the potential to seriously undermine public health programs, it might be more reasonable to understand them as "vaccine critics." They do not necessarily oppose vaccines but demand more research on safety and on the potential existence of vulnerable populations. By cultivating respect between the two sides and recognizing the claims to rationality of each, there is a better chance of creating the trust that underpins decisions to vaccinate.[118] In some cases this is easier said than done, and public health experts and researchers have reason to be discouraged and angered when they receive threats or find their work misrepresented.[119]

The CDC and the public health community will have to work harder to solve the problem of the decline in vaccination rates. To claim that immunizations carry absolutely no risk or to contrast the risk in choosing not to vaccinate with the risk of contracting a disease like measles can have the effect of lessening parental confidence. Parents understand that herd immunity protects their child. If a disease were to appear, it would probably be contained because most people have been vaccinated. Educational messages instead ought to emphasize the idea of vaccination as a social responsibility. Those parents unwilling to expose their child to any risk are effectively threatening others, and public health officials are correct that such decisions are both unsafe and unfair.

The public also needs better information about the safety research built into vaccine development, even if drawing attention to safety can have the unintended effect of raising concerns about risks. Parents of children with autism have highlighted some problems with the way that the CDC has worked in the past. A critical one is the markedly smaller amount of resources devoted to post-market research and vaccine safety. Another is the appearance of conflicts of interest in research on vaccine safety. The CDC needs to vet authors of the studies it funds and consider rejecting those that have plausible conflicts, including connections to vaccine manufacturers. The increased costs will return dividends in the form of restoration of public trust in immunizations. Officials have fallen into the habit of assuming that public trust is a given, something inherent in the authority of medical experts, rather than something earned and assiduously maintained.

Parents of children with autism, at least some of them, differ from other parents in their conviction that immunizations brought on their child's disability. They are witnesses to an adverse reaction to a vaccine or set of vaccines. Public health officials therefore have little to gain and much to lose by disputing their accounts, or, worse, questioning their sanity. Parents are not all driven by desperation. In some cases, their testimony needs to be questioned as part of an investigative process, as in the case of Michelle Cedillo, where her baby videotapes potentially contradicted her parents' account of her first year's "typical" development. However, the arguments of parents have served to highlight problems with standard claims about the onset and progression of autism, and they have led researchers to pay greater attention to symptoms that may hold significant clues to the disorder's underlying causes and mechanisms.

The Limitations of Certainty

When parents talk about thimerosal or the MMR vaccine, they employ an alternative framework for thinking about etiologies and disease mechanisms for autism. The terms do not imply a static condition or an exclusively genetic form of causation. Parents see the MMR vaccine and thimerosal either as distinct causes or as part of a cumulative series of "hits" to the bodies of children with an underlying genetic predisposition. They link theories about the synergistic effects of vaccines with concerns about antibiotic overuse, perhaps as a result of chronic ear infections brought on by an impaired immune system. They implicate maternal illnesses; Rho-Gam injections; environmental mercury, lead, and arsenic; and organophosphate pesticides, to name just a few of the possible environmental factors that have been suspected of causing autism. Epidemiologists have been unable to rule out environmental factors as a partial cause of the continuing increase in autism rates.[120] Therefore, it is important to take these concerns seriously, as impossible as it may be to determine with any certainty the effects of such a broad set of potential causative factors and associated disease mechanisms.

It is easy to dismiss the arguments for all of the reasons enumerated by critics—the frustration and anger of parents trying to raise children with disabilities in a social climate that provides too little meaningful support, the negative or at best ambiguous results of epidemiological studies, the division among parents themselves when it comes to the question of autism's cause or causes, and the antagonism of many adults on the autism spectrum to hypotheses that link autism to environmental factors. In practice, though, respectful dialogue ought to be possible. Indeed, the situation demands it because all of these groups—parents, self-advocates, researchers, and clinicians—need to share their particular insights to arrive at the best ways to understand, respect, and nurture people on the autism spectrum.

Parents concerned about vaccines have pointed to features of autism that might otherwise have received little attention and which may have significant implications for treatment regardless of their relevance for understanding causation. Prior to 1999, a handful of articles made passing reference at best to a subgroup of children who seemed to lose skills over time. No researchers devoted themselves to identifying unique features of this group. Beginning around 2001, an increasing number of articles began to deal explicitly with regression in autism and ask whether or not children with the "regressive phenotype" shared distinctive biological or behavioral features. Likewise, following Wakefield's 1998 study, more published studies focused on gastrointestinal symptoms in autism as a problem worthy of attention, even apart from any possible association with the MMR vaccine.[121]

Parental testimony has also provided valuable clues to those clinicians and laboratory researchers who are now thinking about autism as a chronic disease. In many cases parents have pointed researchers toward paths that would have been invisible without their intimate knowledge of the bodies and behaviors of affected children. For these researchers, worries about appearing to validate the concerns of vaccine critics and the tendency to dismiss parental reports of successful treatments as "desperate foolishness" act as barriers to serious consideration of autism's underlying neurological and biological mechanisms.[122] The polarization of opinion that has characterized so much discussion about the possibility of a genuine increase in autism cases and the role of environmental factors can lead investigators to neglect very real and potentially promising avenues of research. Conversely, those researchers who were attentive early on to the possibility that environmental factors played a role in autism have cleared a path for investigators from a wide range of backgrounds and institutional affiliations who are studying intermediate mechanisms in autism, rather than focusing exclusively on genes, brain structure, and behavior. Their findings suggest that oxidative stress and neuroinflammation, which can be caused by toxic agents, infections, or autoimmune processes, can act early on to disrupt neurodevelopment, playing a significant role in some cases of autism.[123]

It seems unwise, unreasonable even, to dismiss the claims of parents who are so specific in their delineation of the physical symptoms that affect their children, the ear infections, the gut symptoms, the allergies, and the insensitivity to pain. Not all parents have the technical vocabulary, the social authority and status, and the scientific expertise to articulate these concerns in ways that pass muster in the world of formal academic publications or even committee hearings at the National Academies of Science or in Congress. It would be a great mistake, however, to conclude, as many writers have, that because their explanations are not always theoretically consistent or because they place too much weight on hypotheses and speculation as opposed to peer-reviewed publications, it follows that their experience contains nothing of value. Those observations and informal trials can, in their attention to symptomatic particularities and individuality, help researchers incorporate some of the passionate particularity of parental commitment and love into their own devotion and commitment to research programs and experimental facts.

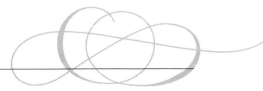

What the World Needs Now:
Learning About and Acting on Autism Research

None of the debates that I describe in this book has ended. Despite periodic promises that researchers are "closing in" on a comprehensive understanding of autism's causes, the distance still appears formidable.[1] Many researchers now agree with parents that although autism is a useful term for describing a common behavioral syndrome, it is one that offers few insights into the particular biology of individual children. It may say even less about adults because, in addition to the biological and cognitive differences among them, they have been shaped by experiences over a lifetime. For the foreseeable future, both the facts about autism and the politics of treatment will remain contentious.

In this conclusion, I return a last time to the question of love as both a subject and a method for research on autism. I revisit the evidence for its centrality to the work of producing knowledge about autism and in particular the importance of parents' caring as a source of insights about children. I then turn to the issues that these arguments raise about knowledge production in the field of science studies. I conclude by discussing how we can move forward from here to include other neglected voices in autism research, in particular people on the autism spectrum.

Love at Work

Certain researchers have devoted themselves to predicting the onset of autism in its earliest stages. They analyze social behavior using videos of the younger siblings of children with autism, deemed "high-risk" infants because of the genetic contributions to the syndrome.[2] Some of the children are only a few months old. The researchers have become connoisseurs of babies' smiles and gurgles. They talk about "beautiful joint attention" behaviors and "gorgeous" social gazes. They are learning to distinguish among subtle indicators of derailed development and to predict future pathology before a formal diagnosis is possible. With earlier diagnoses, interventions might be initiated at ever-younger ages.

Work like this represents the cutting edge of research, combining standardized diagnostic instruments, behavioral studies, epidemiology, genetics, and brain imaging. It promises early treatments and support. It also reminds us that, despite the practical and epistemological differences among the many programs developed over the past half century, autism research and treatment are syncretic processes.[3] Technicians identify subjects of genetic research using cognitive measures. Biomedical treatments take place in the context of structured behavioral therapy programs through which parents track and record the progress of their child. In addition to the functional interdependence of these programs, they all demand affective as well as intellectual and financial resources.

Some may argue that I have perseverated on love, conjuring it where there really is nothing more than the routines of medical research and treatment. They would be wrong. Love is a vexed term that is nonetheless central to a discussion that ranges from the mechanisms of social movements to the daily preparation of meals and to state-level education and early intervention programs. My choice arose from some concern that the technical vocabularies of science studies, while useful, can alienate some readers and obscure a relatively clear point. I also respect the categories of my actors and the work that they do. Love captures the social processes at work in contemporary biomedicine so well because it is common property.

Autism research depends on it. Love has been incorporated into those diagnostic instruments that demand the attentive, detailed knowledge of caregivers. Emotional work kept the Orthogenic School running during Bruno Bettelheim's tenure as director, and it was part of what made parents some of the most effective behavioral therapists. Parents have argued for its importance in the criteria for selecting research projects. It matters to all those biomedical treatments that rely on parents. It also shapes the vaccine debate, in ways that may be dangerous but are even more risky when ignored. Biomedicine is increasingly important to arguments about citizenship, entitlement, and governance, so it is crucial that we do our best to understand how it works and what can be done to improve it. Love is a central, if often overlooked, component of biomedical knowledge. It is also part of work in the social sciences. Neglecting my own affective responses would be akin to placing myself impossibly outside of this system.

Guidelines for Caring

In the 1990s, academics across the United States and Europe launched what became known as the "science wars," that is, a set of debates about who has a right to weigh in on the conduct and content of scientific research and on the conceptual tools to be used in their analysis. Did it make sense to bring the methods of literary studies to scientific texts? Could an anthropologist suggest that scientists, like members of other social and professional cultures, hold beliefs shaped by their values in addition to the incontrovertible evidence of the material world? While I entered the field of science studies after the dust had settled, I benefited enormously from the hostilities, above all from Donna Haraway's questioning how "commitment, anger, hope, pleasure, knowledge, and work all come together in the practice of love we call science? And science studies?"[4]

One consequence of this project is that some of my own writing has become part of the phenomena that I describe, simply through my commenting in print on activist strategies and research priorities. There is no consensus on the rules for social scientists working on a contested illness. We do know that representations are potent instruments for shaping reality.[5] Studying autism made me ask whether good scholarship in science and technology studies can include statements about appropriate action.[6] It also made me question how my own affective commitments to friends, informants, and colleagues colored my interpretations. Researchers often confront this question as members of the communities that they are studying, as I would be, for instance, if a family member or I had an autism spectrum diagnosis. Did I have the right to argue for what I thought best, in addition to representing what I believed was true? What was an appropriate ethical position for a researcher investigating a condition that has had such power to shape lives and families?

Many social scientists have come to believe that one obligation of scholarship in contemporary professional and activist communities is faithful representation of and engagement with their technical and political arguments.[7] While many of the professionals and advocates I studied are less vulnerable than other, more marginal populations, they have a stake in my findings and the ability to appraise the ways in which a positive representation benefits them. It is easy to become involved in the "projects and interests" of the researchers that we study. We can lose sight of what Paul Rabinow has described as "the ethical task [of] finding the mean" between identifying with our subjects as scientists and becoming an uncritical promoter of research agendas or technological products.[8] With communities that include parents and patients who can be simultaneously savvy and vulnerable, we need to consider what obligations our relationships produce. There is no real option of deferring affiliations until after completing our research.[9] Scientific work involves interpersonal relationships, and in order to comprehend these relationships we have to form some ourselves.

A secondary part of work at home is the additional requirement—long recognized by cultural anthropologists—to contribute to the community studied. Subjects of ethnographic research increasingly expect a reciprocal investment from ethnographers. When they offer themselves as willing subjects of research, they want to know what the knowledge generated by this research can do for them. They may ask what they can expect in exchange for serving as research subjects, contributing their time, instructing the researcher, and offering potentially risky revelations. Those in large clinical trials customarily receive compensation for contributing their time to the projects. For families with members affected by a genetic disorder, participation holds out the promise of an eventual treatment or cure. It is harder to portray the ultimate deliverables of research in the social sciences in the same hopeful light.

At one point, I imagined producing a handbook for health-based social movements. Activists for research reform borrow strategies from other kinds of movements. I would survey the most productive approaches used by a range of groups, including autism advocates. Many of the advocates I had interviewed were self-conscious about their role in creating knowledge about autism and presenting their ideas using a language valued by those setting research policy. I gave up the idea. I wasn't enough of a participant or insider to write compellingly about strategy. Instead, as a sympathetic outsider, I could strive to portray the members of these communities in a comprehensive and contextualized way.

Our choices are not always limited to joining those we study or eschewing all involvement. For instance, social scientists are uniquely positioned to promote dialogue among groups that are otherwise at odds.[10] At various points in my research I served as an informal translator among activist groups, between activist groups and scientists, and among scientists in different disciplines. Now, at the end of a long research project, I have joined an ongoing conversation about autism research, doing my best to raise questions as a researcher and also as a caring person where I think that the choices being made are wrong ones.

Rights, Wrongs, and Awkward Alliances in Autism Research

We measure the efficacy of actions in biomedicine by using bodies and minds. Doing so exposes men and women to potentially tragic risks. Even interventions that carry a minimal possibility of bodily harm, like behavioral therapies, can have irreversible, life-altering consequences. Thus, those who serve as spokespeople for communities or for particular forms of treatment exercise tremendous power. The stakes are high for those faced with the choice of whom to believe. When geneticists design a research program or funding agencies support a particular line of inquiry or parents decide on one intervention over another, they are all choosing whom to trust regarding what is best for people with autism.

Central to both feminist epistemologies of science and theories of autism treatment is a view of empathy as a learned skill—something to be struggled for and achieved laboriously, partially, and imperfectly. Autism is a uniquely good place to listen in on conversations about the role of affect in biomedicine and about the ethics of empathy. It is, however, far from the only place where these conversations take place. They happen every time children develop in ways different from what their parents expected and the parents seek out experts for guidance. These exchanges are especially tough since parents, doctors, and at times policymakers all must make decisions affecting children who may not be able to communicate fully their own thoughts and desires, and who are, by definition, changing every day.

Mark Osteen, in confronting this problem, has proposed what he calls "empathetic scholarship." Researchers should try "speaking *with* those unable to communicate entirely on their own," by "combining rigorous scholarship with the experiential knowledge" acquired through kinship and friendships with autistic people.[11] As a matter of both method and ethics, in writing about disabilities like autism it is important not only to acknowledge but also to build those relationships so critical to knowledge production.[12]

Treatments for autism cannot be understood apart from their specific historical and social contexts, just as autism must be understood as having evolved over time through communities constituted by practice. Each of the techniques that I have described is a site of ethical and technical controversy where the boundaries between the two are often hard to make out. I focused on what participants have had to say about various therapies rather than just the theories of etiology that informed them, since theories are never sufficient to describe the full range of experiences that constitute treatment.

When I write about pluralism in American biomedicine, I am making essentially the same argument. Different ways of engaging with autism are site specific and involve practices that are *both* affective and rational, but these practices are not "alternative," if by alternative one means opposed to biomedical reason. Positioning unconventional medical practices outside of mainstream medicine invites analysts to ignore or to diminish them—as "culturally bound" or a product of desperation rather than research and rational evaluation. Contests over autism treatment are nearly always arguments over what counts as medical knowledge and who can produce it. For this reason, ethical debates do not occur in parallel to but as a constitutive part of biomedical choices and contests. What do we talk about when we talk about love—especially in regard to biomedicine? One thing is ethics—the ethics of communication, of position, of dependence, responsibility, obligation, and commitment.

One issue that almost everyone involved with autism agrees on is the need for better services for people with autism across the lifespan. Currently, insurance companies cover educational and behavioral treatments only inconsistently if at all. Parents pay for treatments, including nutritional supplements and the expenses associated with special diets, out of pocket. Although the law requires school districts to provide appropriate educational supports, in practice, as many parents know, these vary widely by region. As a result, families are often forced to move in search of better services. Educational services also evaporate once a child ages out of the school system around age twenty-one. Even parents of young children fear for the future of their children were they to die or become ill and incapable of caring for them. Parents of adult children face the additional, continuing trial of finding stimulating occupations and care for people who may need constant and watchful supervision.

The neurodiversity movement has made a difference in several areas. Many national autism advocacy organizations understand that they cannot adequately represent the needs of people with autism without including people with autism diagnoses in their decision-making and on their supervisory boards. Adults with autism who serve in executive positions may not be representative of the full spectrum of people with autism, but that is not a justification for exclusion. If they cannot speak for children and adults unable to communicate their own wishes, their demands for changes in conventional representations of autism and in the services that the national organizations push for are different enough from existing priorities to make their inclusion not only ethical but also productive.

Self-advocates, together with parent activists, have contributed to changing public awareness and popular representations of autism. People with autism continue to be the subject of misunderstanding and discrimination in public and in the workplace. Strangers still stop parents in the street to offer suggestions about managing their child's "misbehavior" and teenagers with autism face exclusion by their peers. Nonetheless, more people now understand the basic facts about autism and are prepared to learn more. The impact on research priorities may be even greater in the long run. While the opposition of self-advocates is unlikely to halt studies on autism genetics, biomedical treatments, environmental causation, or behavioral therapies, some researchers are now listening to people with autism when designing new research projects, asking what aspects of the experience of autism ought to be considered and which areas might be of interest to them and useful in their daily lives.

More inclusive research and public awareness will not, however, solve all the ethical dilemmas that surround autism. The most unsettling of them stem from the reality of dependency and of suffering that can't be ameliorated by changes in the social or physical environment. All children with autism and those adults who are most severely affected rely on others for their care and for the decisions that impact their treatment. The particular theory of autism that their caregivers subscribe to, as I have shown, matters to the choice of treatment, including the decision not to intervene. No specific form of treatment, however, necessarily follows from a view of autism as genetic, biochemical, psychological, a benign form of neurological diversity, or the result of an injury. Many genetic conditions are labile, susceptible to all manner of nutritional and pharmacological interventions, whereas many injuries are just as "fixed" as genetic errors.[13] In other words, the degree to which beliefs about fundamental causes and mechanisms of autism do continue to guide treatment is further evidence—if any is needed—of the ethical and social valences of scientific and biomedical facts.

Parents who want simultaneously to love and heal their children are old hands at finessing the fact that caring requires that we believe incompatible things at the same time. That is, parents can accept the value and importance of their child's obsessions and the beauty of their different ways of experiencing the world around them, even as they work to free them from restrictions that their impairments impose on them. As Clara Park observed, parents often learn, after all, that they "can have it both ways." At the beginning of her memoir of her daughter's adult years, Park writes that

> the world we share, the only world we had to offer that wordless baby, is our common world of risk, frustration, loss, of unfulfilled desire as well as of activity and love. We could not leave Jessy to her empty serenity. We would not, as was often recommended in those days, institutionalize her "for the sake of the other children," to spend her days somewhere in a back ward, rocking. We would keep her with us, entice, intrude, enter where we were not wanted or needed.[14]

Caring for her reminds the Parks that just as Jessy's autistic traits can contain things of value for both Jessy and the people that surround her, the world of typical behaviors and sociability is not an entirely good or desirable place. It contains no assurance of right action or a superior understanding of reality compared to their daughter's "secret life." Yet, despite grappling with the possibility that they are stepping in where no change is wanted or needed, the Parks persist in framing their obligation in terms of providing the best possible circumstances for their daughter to flourish. Perhaps that tentativeness is part of the moral of these love stories. Devotion is ideally an experimental procedure. It is especially so when, as parents often feel in the case of autism, it impels us to consider the object of our love as both a biological being, subject to manipulation and harm, and a person, precious and complete in his or her own right.[15]

NOTES

Note on Sources and References

I consulted the Bruno Bettelheim Papers at the Special Collections Research Center, University of Chicago Library; and the Amy L. Lettick Papers at the Manuscripts and Archives Collection, Sterling Memorial Library, Yale University.

In order to provide ease of access to readers, in the notes to this book I have included full citations to both archival sources and published primary sources that I cite a single time. The notes also contain short references to secondary sources. These sources are listed in the bibliography. Readers interested in finding a general guide to secondary literatures (e.g., in the social sciences) can consult the bibliography.

Introduction

1. Rose (1983, 83).
2. Haraway (1997a, 124).
3. Slogan on a T-shirt, CafePress, http://www.cafepress.com/buy/autism/-/pv_design_details/pg_4/id_9298831/opt_/fpt_/c_360/.
4. It can also refer to a type of person (e.g., "autistic child") or a syndrome that a person has ("child with autism"). Throughout this book, I observe the convention of "person-first" language advocated by the disability rights movement when referring to children with autism in the present, but I use the terminology appropriate to any given historical period when describing children in that period. In keeping with the preference of most self-advocates in the present, I do not use person-first language when referring to them.
5. There is a growing body of anthropological scholarship that does focus on informal practices of care with children with autism. See, in particular, Park (2008) and Solomon (2010).

6. Bruno Bettelheim cited Freud's statement that "Psychoanalysis is in essence a cure through love," in *Freud and Man's Soul* (New York: Knopf, 1983). Cited in Zelan (1993, 97).

7. Park (1967, 188).

8. Park (1985, 115).

9. Lenny Schafer, "Autistic Children Murdered: Outrage vs. Sympathy," *Schafer Autism Report* 10, no. 89 (May 23, 2006).

10. Alexandra Wood, "Mother's Bridge Death Plunge with Her Son Was an Act of Love, Say Sisters," *Yorkshire Post,* May 22, 2006, http://www.yorkshiretoday.co .uk/ViewArticle.aspx?SectionID=55&ArticleID=1517218. Alison Davies jumped off a bridge into the River Humber with her son, Ryan. Ryan was diagnosed with Fragile X syndrome, which is often associated with autism; news coverage referred to both diagnoses.

11. Cammie McGovern, "Autism's Parent Trap," *New York Times,* June 5, 2006. The full quote read "In mythologizing recovery, I fear that we've set an impossibly high bar that's left the parents of a half-million autistic children feeling like failures."

12. Josh Greenfeld, the author of three books (1970, 1978, 1986) about his son Noah, who has autism, has said that "We're always on that edge of violence when we're on that edge of intense concern and intense love or intense— whatever word you want to use," and mentioned that he wanted to write about that impulse so "once I've said them, I can't do it" because he would be accountable. Greenfeld was quoted in a 1978 *60 Minutes* interview. "Noah's Story," http://www.cbsnews.com/stories/2000/05/09/60II/main193439 .shtml#1978.

13. Park (1967, 194–95).

14. Merton (1973); Mulkay (1976); Shapin (1994).

15. Daston and Galison (1992); Daston (1992, 609).

16. Shapin (1996).

17. For example, Haraway (1989, 1991, 1997b), Rose (1994), and Keller (1983, 1992).

18. Cowan (1983); Wajcman (1991). Gibbon (2007, 92–94) provides an insightful analysis of gendered "care work" in the context of testing for genes associated with increased risk of breast cancer. On gendered divisions of caring labor, see Gilligan (1982).

19. For example, Baron-Cohen (2003).

20. According to the Women's Bureau of the Department of Labor, the top five occupations for women in 2009 were secretaries and administrative assistants, registered nurses, elementary and middle school teachers, cashiers, and nursing, psychiatric, and home health aides. United States Department of Labor, Women's Bureau, "20 Leading Occupations of Employed Women: 2009 Annual Averages," http://www.dol.gov/wb/factsheets/20lead2009.htm.

21. Keller (2007, 355–56).

22. Bérubé (1996, xviii, 145–46, 249); Kittay (2001, 560–61, 567–68).

23. For example, adults with autism may arrive at moral judgments by applying rules or a repertoire of models of people's behaviors. Kennett (2002, 352).

24. But for a discussion of some of these questions, see Barnbaum (2008).

25. Stacy Clifford (2006, 131–32), writing as the sibling of a person with severe autism, argues that just as people with autism strive for "local coherence" as a way of coping with an otherwise chaotic perceptual world, caregivers should think about solutions to the ethical questions of caregiving "at the local level, contextualized into the local realities of dependency situations."

26. MacIntyre (1999). Also see Nussbaum (2006).

27. Kittay (1999, 557–79).

28. A "philosophy of the limit" is Eva Feder Kittay's term for the types of decisions that women must make, quoted in Rapp (1999, 3, 308–9).

29. Frankfurt (2006, 40–43, 2–5, 24–26).

30. Ibid., 3.

31. Fromm (1956, 93,103).

32. Kittay (1999, 172–73).

33. A rough estimate, based on the fact that as of 2002 the Department of Education reported that there were 120,000 children with autism being served under the Individuals with Disabilities Education Act (IDEA). Because the CDC reported in 2009 that approximately one in 110 children in the U.S. has an autism spectrum disorder, "hundreds of thousands" might in fact be closer to millions. U.S. Government Accountability Office, "Special Education: Children with Autism" (January 14, 2005), http://www.gao.gov/products/ GAO-05-220, Autism and Developmental Disabilities Monitoring Network Surveillance Year 2006 Principal Investigators and Centers for Disease Control and Prevention (CDC), "Prevalence of Autism Spectrum Disorders— Autism and Developmental Disabilities Monitoring Network, United States, 2006," *MMWR Surveillance Summaries* 58, no. 10 (2009): 1–20.

34. On the silencing of parents in encounters with health professionals, see Noah Feinstein, "Silenced by Science? Parents of Autistic Children Finding Their Voice" (paper presented at the Society for Social Studies of Science, Vancouver, British Columbia, November 2006).

35. Bourdieu's (1975/1999, 19) description of science as a system of productive labor, the outcome of which is "the objective truth of the product," and of scientific careers as a "competitive struggle" for authority are reflected in much of autism research, but the field has not always progressed steadily toward increasing autonomy or independence from external interests.

36. Murray (2008).

37. These accounts can be found in Johnson and Crowder (1994).

38. Bettelheim (1959, 117). See the thoughtful critique of Bettelheim's analysis in Jurecic (2006, 8–10).

39. The specific phrase comes from an interview with Francesca Happe conducted on June 21, 2005, although others echoed the general observation.

40. Ferguson (1996, 25). Ferguson noted that populations seen as "chronic" and "unteachable" were particularly neglected in historical work on disability. There have been notable exceptions since he wrote, in particular Trent (1994) and Noll (1995).

41. Some scholars contrast biomedicine with other, non-Western knowledge systems, an assumption that fails to recognize the many differences in how biomedicine is practiced in different places. In fact, biomedical knowledge often has to accommodate or incorporate other adjacent or prior ways of knowing about the world, what Susan Lindee (2005) calls "moments of truth" in biomedicine. On the rise of molecular biology following World War II, see de Chadarevian (2002).

42. Rosenberg (2002).

43. Kay (1993, 2000); Luhrmann (2000).

44. Dumit (2003).

45. Epstein (1996).

46. Apple (2006).

47. On the tension between trust in scientific authority and traditions of lay participation in biomedicine, see Starr (1982).

48. Hays (1996, 9). In making the connection between Hays's work and parenting children with autism, I draw on Stevenson (2008, 199).

49. The classic text exploring the historical contingence of "childhood" as a category is Ariès (1962).

50. Murphy (2000, 88; 2006) has described how people suffering from multiple chemical sensitivity (MCS) come together not due to their symptoms, which vary, but due to their shared experience of bodies that don't fit the explanatory frameworks that their doctors have to offer them. Also see Kroll-Smith and Floyd (2000). Brown, Zavestoski, McCormick, Linder, et al. (2001) describe how disputes over Gulf War syndrome have followed similar lines.

51. Brown, Zavestoski, McCormick, Mayer, et al. (2004, 54–55). Also see discussions of myalgic encephalitis and Lyme disease in Aronowitz (1998). Dumit (2000) describes some contested illness categories as "the new socio-medical disorders," which are characterized by their "biomental" nature, causal indeterminacy, biosocial organization, legal explosiveness, therapeutic heterogeneity and diversity, interrelationships between categories, and the disputed use of brain imaging techniques in establishing their "objectivity."

52. Bourdieu (1984, 479) uses the term to describe struggles over the identity of groups and particular social practices.

53. Apart from the finding that in the United States, autism is more frequently diagnosed among children in higher-income families, relatively little research has been done on how the experience of the diagnosis differs across socioeconomic contexts. See Maureen S. Durkin, Matthew J. Maenner, F. John Meaney, Susan E. Levy, et al., "Socioeconomic Inequality in the Prevalence

of Autism Spectrum Disorder: Evidence from a U.S. Cross-Sectional Study," *PLoS One* 5, no. 7 (2010): e11551. There is a growing body of work, however, on autism in different cultural contexts. Grinker (2008) describes how families in India, Korea, and South Africa often must oppose social and institutional norms in order to obtain diagnoses and treatment for their children. Also see Daley (2002, 2004). Shaked (2005) and Shaked and Bilu (2006) describe how mothers use religious discourse strategically to push for their children's inclusion in the Jewish ultraorthodox community. Ochs and Solomon (2010, 74–76) observe intersections among cultural, sociological, and symptomatic aspects of a child with autism's experience of sociability.

54. More research is needed on the exact relationships among income, education, and choice of therapies. Here I refer to three things: first, the finding that use of alternative treatments for autism is very high overall, perhaps as high 74 percent or even 92 percent of all children diagnosed; second, that this seems to be consistent across income levels; and, third, that mothers with a range of educational levels are willing to question doctors' developmental prognoses. See Ellen Hanson, Leslie A. Kalish, Emily Bunce, Christine Curtis, et al., "Use of Complementary and Alternative Medicine among Children Diagnosed with Autism Spectrum Disorder," *Journal of Autism and Developmental Disorders* 37, no. 4 (2007): 628–36, 628; John W. Harrington, Lawrence Rosen, and Ana Garnecho, "Parental Perceptions and Use of Complementary and Alternative Medicine Practices for Children with Autistic Spectrum Disorders in Private Practice," *Developmental and Behavioral Pediatrics* 27, no. 2 (2006): S156–61, S160; and Landsman (2009, 6).

55. Fleck's (1979) account of how syphilis stabilized as a disease category and Jack Pressman's (1998) work on the emphatic—if temporary—adoption of psychosurgery are only two of the best accounts of this type. On studying the achievement of closure on matters of scientific fact more generally, see Latour (1988).

56. Rabinow (1996).

57. Hacking (1998, 1999, 2007) has called this tendency of populations to shape and be shaped by medical categories "dynamic nominalism" or the "looping effect," a phenomenon that he has suggested applies to autism spectrum disorders. As he has observed (1999, 170), no two instances of "making up" people are the same.

58. On the concept of genetic citizenship, see Heath, Rapp, and Taussig (2004).

59. In the absence of predictive testing for autism risk, parents do not enter into the type of potentially coercive relations with genetic counselors and other professionals that Rose (2007, 27–29, 73–76, 217) describes as an "ethopolitics" that influences conduct by appealing to people's "sentiments, beliefs, and values." However, what Rose calls "somatic experts" do have authority in the field of autism, through advising, for example, on the crucial importance of early intervention as a future-shaping technology (e.g., Leiter [2004]).

60. Amsterdamska and Hiddinga (2004) have argued that provisions in American disabilities legislation encouraged practitioners to emphasize autism spectrum disorders' status as developmental disorders.

61. My use of "partiality" and "situated knowledges" depends on Haraway's (1991, 183–202) foundational use of the terms.

62. In addition, advocacy for one's own child often leads to work that is better described as social activism. Ryan (2009, 52).

63. Marcus and Fischer (1986) advocate "multi-sited ethnographies" for studying cultural practices that occur at multiple scales, locations, and levels of organization, such as commodities markets and biomedical research. The method works well for examining the tight connections between local and global economies of knowledge production and the "emergent forms of life" made possible by new sciences and technologies. Also see Marcus (1998), and for considerations of the potential applications of ethnographic techniques in science studies, see Fischer (1999; 2000).

64. Nader (1972); Forsythe (1999, 7).

65. Two examples are Haddon (2004) and Moon (2003).

66. Belmonte (2008, 168–69); The Gray Center for Social Learning and Understanding, http://www.thegraycenter.org.

67. This claim has been made more than once, but I am thinking in particular of Joan Didion's (1990, 11) observation that stories are both essential and an "imposition" of meaning upon the overwhelming clutter of images and events that constitute "actual experience."

Part One
Chapter 1

1. See, for instance, any of the essays in Rosenberg and Golden (1992).

2. Hacking (1999; 2007, 303–4; 2009a) has applied his own analysis to autism spectrum disorders, describing how people with autism are and are not like other "kinds of people." Autistic autobiographies, Hacking argues, have helped develop a language to describe what is distinct about autistic experience.

3. Frith (1991, 1).

4. "Medicine: The Child Is Father," *Time,* July 25, 1960.

5. For instance, Lane (1979), Happe (1994), Houston and Frith (2000), Frith (2003), and Waltz and Shattock (2004).

6. Rosenberg (2002).

7. "An observer even slightly trained in ethology cannot help seeing such 'experiments by nature' happen all the time to autistic children." Tinbergen and Tinbergen (1983, 75).

8. Kanner (1943, 250).

9. Neumärker (2003); Leo Kanner, *A History of the Care and Study of the Mentally Retarded*, (Springfield, IL: Charles C. Thomas, 1964), 143.

10. Kanner first worked in South Dakota, then moved to Johns Hopkins University, where he spent the rest of his career. Neumärker (2003); Edwards Λ. Park, "A Child Psychiatric Clinic in a Paediatric Department," *Canadian Medical Association Journal* 38, no. 1 (1938): 74–78, 76.

11. Leo Kanner, "Co-Editor's Introduction," *Nervous Child* 2 (1943): 216.

12. Rose Zeligs, *Glimpses into Child Life: The Twelve-Year Old at Home and School* (New York: W. Morrow & Co., 1942), quoted in Kanner (1943, 217).

13. Bleuler also coined the term "schizophrenia" in 1908, to describe the disorder that had previously been called "dementia praecox." Kuhn and Cahn (2004).

14. Trent (1994).

15. Grob (1994); Hale (1978, 303–4).

16. Kanner (1943, 217).

17. Leon Eisenberg, "Preface," in *Childhood Psychosis: Initial Studies and New Insights,* by Leo Kanner (Washington, DC: V. H. Winston & Sons, 1973), xi.

18. Kanner (1943, 249, 219, 221–22).

19. Ibid., 222–24, 226, 239–40.

20. Kanner (1943, 242, 248).

21. "Nevertheless, the usefulness of Kanner's original observation persists today when many of the other diagnostic formulations have faded into obscurity. This is precisely because Kanner relied on careful and systematic clinical observations rather than on theoretical dicta." Eric Schopler, Michael Rutter, and Stella Chess, "Editorial: Change of Journal Scope and Title," *Journal of Autism and Developmental Disorders* 9, no. 1 (1979): 1–10, 2.

22. Kanner (1943, 250).

23. Ibid., 249–50.

24. For a discussion of Bleuler's understanding of psychopathology and the sense in which he used the term "autism," see Kuhn and Cahn (2004, 364).

25. Asperger wrote in Austria during World War II, in the shadow of Nazi eugenics programs, and Frith (1991, 90) has suggested that this inspired him to downplay the idea that the syndrome was a disabling condition. Asperger (1944/1991, 38).

26. Ibid., 41.

27. Aperger (1944/1991, 88).

28. Leo Kanner, "Problems of Nosology and Psychodynamics in Early Infantile Autism," *American Journal of Orthopsychiatry* 19 (1949): 416–26, 425.

29. Leo Kanner, "To What Extent Is Early Infantile Autism Determined by Constitutional Inadequacies?" in *Childhood Psychosis: Initial Studies and New Insights* (Washington, DC: V. H. Winston & Sons, 1973), 69–75, 75, revised from the original published in D. Hooker and C. C. Hare, *Genetics and the Inheritance of Integrated Neurological and Psychiatric Patterns* (Baltimore, MD: Williams and Wilkins, 1954, 378–85); Leo Kanner and Leon Eisenberg,

"Early Infantile Autism, 1943–1955," *American Journal of Orthopsychiatry* 26 (1956): 556–66, 561.

30. Ruth Christ Sullivan, "Presentations from Experts in the Field" (round-table discussion), The Autism Summit Conference: Developing a National Agenda, Washington, DC, November 19–20, 2003; Warren (1984, 109).

31. Kanner (1971, 141).

32. Wing (1993, 63).

33. Leo Kanner, "Problems of Nosology and Psychodynamics in Early Infantile Autism," *American Journal of Orthopsychiatry* 19 (1949): 416–26, 420.

34. C. B. Ferster, "Positive Reinforcement and Behavioral Deficits of Autistic Children," *Child Development*, 32 (1961): 437–56.

35. *Diagnostic and Statistical Manual of Mental Disorders*, 2nd ed. (Washington, DC: American Psychiatric Association, 1968), 35; Leo Kanner, "Follow-Up Study of Eleven Autistic Children," *Journal of Autism and Childhood Schizophrenia* 1, no. 2 (1971): 119–45, 141. Interestingly, in 2009 researchers again proposed a connection between childhood schizophrenia and autism, noting the high degree of comorbidity between the two conditions, with many cases of childhood-onset schizophrenia initially receiving diagnoses of pervasive developmental disorder. Judith Rapoport, Alex Chavez, Deanna Greenstein, Anjene Addington, et al., "Autism Spectrum Disorders and Childhood-Onset Schizophrenia: Clinical and Biological Contributions to a Relation Revisited," *Journal of the American Academy of Child and Adolescent Psychiatry* 48, no. 1 (2009): 10–18.

36. Eric Schopler, Michael Rutter, and Stella Chess, "Journal of Autism and Childhood Schizophrenia. Change of Journal Scope and Title," *Journal of Autism and Developmental Disorders* 9, no.1 (1979): 1–10.

37. Michael Rutter and Lawrence Bartak, "Causes of Infantile Autism: Some Considerations from Recent Research," *Journal of Autism and Childhood Schizophrenia* 1, no. 1 (1971): 20–32, 24.

38. Michael Rutter, "Autism Research: Prospects and Priorities," *Journal of Autism and Developmental Disorders* 26, no. 2 (1996): 257–75, 257.

39. Nadesan (2005) provides a more thorough analysis in her history of the social construction of the autism diagnosis.

40. Tinbergen and Tinbergen (1983, 12).

41. Rimland (1964, 87–92).

42. Leo Kanner, "Foreword," in Rimland (1964, v).

43. Rimland (1964, 149).

44. Ibid., 151, 155.

45. Margaret S. Mahler and Manuel S. Furer, "Child Psychosis: A Theoretical Statement and Its Implications," *Journal of Autism and Childhood Schizophrenia* 2, no. 3 (1972): 213–18, 214.

46. Frances Tustin, "Revised Understandings of Psychogenic Autism," *The International Journal of Psychoanalysis* 72, no. 4 (1991): 585–91. Tustin began writing on autism in the late 1960s and published a book-length study, *Autism*

and Childhood Psychosis (London, UK: The Hogarth Press, 1972). See also Nadesan (2005, 99–101).

47. For example, researchers at the Yale Child Study Center conceptualized the anxiety that children with autism experienced in terms of "the persistent possibility of ego disorganization" in a 1987 paper. Sally Provence and E. Kirsten Dahl, "Disorders of Atypical Development: Diagnostic Issues Raised by a Spectrum Disorder," in Donald J. Cohen, Anne M. Donnellan, and Rhea Paul, eds., *Handbook of Autism and Pervasive Developmental Disorders* (Silver Spring, MD: V. H. Winston and Sons, 1987), 677–89, 682.

48. O. Ivar Lovaas, Laura Schreibman, Robert Koegel, and Richard Rehm, "Selective Responding by Autistic Children to Multiple Sensory Input," *Journal of Abnormal Psychology* 77, no. 3 (1971): 211–22, 211; Laura Schreibman, "Effects of Within-Stimulus and Extra-Stimulus Prompting on Discrimination Learning in Autistic Children," *Journal of Applied Behavior Analysis* 8, no. 1 (1975): 91–112; Robert L. Koegel and Arnold Rincover, "Some Detrimental Effects of Using Extra Stimuli to Guide Learning in Normal and Autistic Children," *Journal of Abnormal Child Psychology* 4, no. 1 (1976): 59–71; Barry S. Reynolds, Crighton D. Newsom, and O. Ivar Lovaas, "Auditory Overselectivity in Autistic Children," *Journal of Abnormal Child Psychology* 2, no. 4 (1974): 253–63; Laura Schreibman and O. Ivar Lovaas, "Overselective Response to Social Stimuli by Autistic Children," *Journal of Abnormal Child Psychology* 1, no. 2 (1973): 152–68.

49. O. Ivar Lovaas, "Contrasting Illness and Behavioral Models for the Treatment of Autistic Children: A Historical Perspective," *Journal of Autism and Developmental Disorders* 9, no. 4 (1979): 315–23, 318; O. Ivar Lovaas and Tristram Smith, "A Comprehensive Behavioral Theory of Autistic Children: Paradigm for Research and Treatment," *Journal of Behavior Therapy and Experimental Psychiatry* 20, no. 1 (1989): 17–29.

50. Michael Rutter and Lawrence Bartak, "Causes of Infantile Autism: Some Considerations from Recent Research," *Journal of Autism and Childhood Schizophrenia* 1, no. 1 (1971): 20–32, 25.

51. Susan Folstein and Michael Rutter, "Infantile Autism: A Genetic Study of 21 Twin Pairs," *Journal of Child Psychology and Psychiatry* 18, no. 4 (1977): 297–321, 308.

52. Partly because in the 1970s so few cases of autism were diagnosed, it was hard to find many instances where there were multiple cases in one family. This seemed to argue against genetic involvement. D. R. Hanson and I. I. Gottesman, "The Genetics, If Any, of Infantile Autism and Childhood Schizophrenia," *Journal of Autism and Childhood Schizophrenia* 6, no. 3 (1976): 209–34.

53. A single 1975 study used the older technique of pneumoencephalography to image the brains of eighteen children with autistic behavior, a surprising choice given that the procedure was notoriously painful and quite dangerous. Stephen L. Hauser, G. Robert DeLong, and N. Paul Rosman, "Pneu-

mographic Findings in the Infantile Autism Syndrome. A Correlation with Temporal Lobe Disease," *Brain* 98, no. 4 (1975): 67–88.

54. Christopher Gillberg and Pal Svendsen, "Childhood Psychosis and Computed Tomographic Brain Scan Findings," *Journal of Autism and Developmental Disorders* 13, no. 1 (1983): 19–32; Gary R. Gaffney and Luke Y. Tsai, "Brief Report: Magnetic Resonance Imaging of High Level Autism," *Journal of Autism and Developmental Disorders* 17, no. 3 (1987): 433–38. Others researchers produced evidence that there were asymmetries between the size of structures in the left and right hemispheres of autistic brains, although findings were inconsistent. The earliest report on brain asymmetries in autism was Daniel B. Hier, Marjorie LeMay, and Peter B. Rosenberger, "Autism and Unfavorable Left-Right Asymmetries of the Brain," *Journal of Autism and Developmental Disorders* 9, no. 2 (1979): 153–59; and the later study that failed to replicate the finding was Judith M. Rumsey, Helen Creasey, Jennifer S. Stepanek, Robert Dorwart, et al., "Hemispheric Asymmetries, Fourth Ventricular Size, and Cerebellar Morphology in Autism," *Journal of Autism and Developmental Disorders* 18, no. 1 (1988): 127–37.

55. Margaret Bauman and Thomas L. Kemper, "Histoanatomic Observations of the Brain in Early Infantile Autism," *Neurology* 35 (1985): 866–74, 871. Also see Margaret L. Bauman, "Brief Report: Neuroanatomic Observations of the Brain in Pervasive Developmental Disorders," *Journal of Autism and Developmental Disorders* 26, no. 2 (1996): 199–203.

56. Eric Courchesne, R. Yeung-Courchesne, G. A. Press, J. R. Hesselink, et al., "Hypoplasia of Cerebellar Vermal Lobules VI and VII in Autism," *New England Journal of Medicine* 318, no. 21 (1988): 1349–54.

57. Simon Baron-Cohen, Alan M. Leslie, and Uta Frith, "Does the Autistic Child Have a 'Theory of Mind'?" *Cognition* 21, no. 1 (1985): 37–46. The group built on Premack and Woodruff's concept and Alan Leslie's application of the idea to developmental theory. David Premack and G. Woodruff, "Does the Chimpanzee Have a 'Theory of Mind'?" *Behavioral and Brain Sciences* 4 (1978): 515–26.

58. On executive function and autism, see Sally Ozonoff, Bruce F. Pennington, and Sally J. Rogers, "Executive Function Deficits in High-Functioning Autistic Individuals: Relationship to Theory of Mind," *Journal of Child Psychology and Psychiatry* 32, no. 7 (1993): 1081–1105. On weak central coherence, see Amitta Shah and Uta Frith, "Why Do Autistic Individuals Show Superior Performance on the Block Design Task?" *Journal of Child Psychology and Psychiatry* 34, no. 8 (1993): 1351–64.

59. Ibid., 1353.

60. Lorna Wing, "Sex Ratios in Early Childhood Autism and Related Conditions," *Psychiatry Research* 5, no. 2 (1981): 129–37, 129; Leon Eisenberg and Leo Kanner, "Childhood Schizophrenia: Symposium, 1955. VI. Early Infantile Autism, 1943–55," *American Journal of Orthopsychiatry* 26, no. 3 (1956): 556–66, 560.

61. For example, researchers theorized that autistic girls' relatively superior early social development was aided by higher expectations from parents, while their later difficulties resulted from their "difficulty negotiating peer relationships that rely heavily on conversation." John D. McLennan, Catherine Lord, and Eric Schopler, *Journal of Autism and Developmental Disorders* 23, no. 2 (1993): 217–27, 225. On current efforts to provide support for girls with autism, see Emily Bazelon, "What Autistic Girls Are Made Of," *New York Times*, August 5, 2007.

62. Kristin Bumiller (2008, 972–74, 977–78) provides a more extended analysis of the role of gender in autism research and advocacy, arguing that the neurodiversity movement, in arguing for acceptance of autistic traits, also argues against normative gender expectations built into autism research and treatment.

63. Nichols, Moravcik, and Tentenbaum (2009, 21, 24, 26–27).

64. Asperger (1944/1991, 84–85). Asperger thought that autism might be "an extreme variant of male intelligence."

65. Baron-Cohen (2003); Simon Baron-Cohen, "The Cognitive Neuroscience of Autism: The Psychology and Biology of a Complex Developmental Condition," *Journal of Neurology, Neurosurgery, and Psychiatry* 75 (2004): 945–48; Simon Baron-Cohen and Matthew Belmonte, "Autism: A Window onto the Development of the Social and the Analytic Brain," *Annual Review of Neuroscience* 28 (2005): 109–26.

66. Susan L. Smalley, Robert F. Asarnow, and M. Anne Spence, "Autism and Genetics: A Decade of Research," *Archives of General Psychiatry* 45, no. 10 (1988): 953–61.

67. Geraldine Dawson, "Defining the Broader Phenotype of Autism: Genetic, Brain, and Behavioral Perspectives," *Development and Psychopathology* 14, no. 3 (2002): 581–611.

68. Catherine Lord, Cory Shulman, and Pamela DiLavore, "Regression and Word Loss in Autistic Spectrum Disorders," *Journal of Child Psychology and Psychiatry* 45, no. 5 (2004): 936–55.

69. For instance, some researchers argue that even regressive autism produces visible signs in infants, implicitly denying parents' claims that their children were developing typically before developing autism, and that the dramatic quality of their regression is central to the syndrome. Rebecca Landa commented on "progression" versus "regression" in autism at an NIH Interagency Autism Coordinating Committee (IACC) meeting on May 9, 2006, in Washington, DC. Also see Rebecca J. Landa, Katherine C. Holman, and Elizabeth Garrett-Mayer, "Social and Communication Development in Toddlers with Early and Later Diagnosis of Autism Spectrum Disorders," *Archives of General Psychiatry* 64, no. 7 (2007): 853–64.

70. Michael Rutter, "Diagnosis and Definition of Childhood Autism," *Journal of Autism and Childhood Schizophrenia* 8, no. 2 (1978): 139–61, 140.

71. Juliet Harper and Sara Williams, "Age and Type of Onset as Critical Variables in Early Infantile Autism," *Journal of Autism and Childhood Schizophrenia* 5, no. 1 (1975): 25–36.

72. Emily Werner and Geraldine Dawson, "Validation of the Phenomenon of Autistic Regression Using Home Videotapes," *Archives of General Psychiatry* 62, no. 8 (2005): 889–94.

73. See Dan Olmstead, "The Age of Autism: Backward," UPI, May 4, 2005, http://www.upi.com/Science_News/2005/05/04/The_Age_of_Autism_Backward/UPI-18211115179500/.

74. Kanner (1943, 225, 239, 237, 236).

75. Edward R. Ritvo, B. J. Freeman, Carmen Pingree, Anne Mason-Brothers, et al., "The UCLA-University of Utah Epidemiologic Survey of Autism: Prevalence," *American Journal of Psychiatry* 146, no. 2 (1989): 194–99, 199. The authors found that their rate of 4 in 10,000 was "remarkably close" to those found by a range of studies from different countries dating from 1966 to 1984.

76. L. A. Shieve, C. Rice, C. Boyle, S. N. Visser, et al., "Mental Health in the United States: Parental Report of Diagnosed Autism in Children Aged 4–17 Years, United States, 2003–2004," *Morbidity and Mortality Weekly Report* 55, no. 17 (2006): 481–86; Autism and Developmental Disabilities Monitoring Network Surveillance Year 2002 Principal Investigators, "Prevalence of Autism Spectrum Disorders—Autism and Developmental Disabilities Monitoring Network, 14 Sites, United States, 2002," *Morbidity and Mortality Weekly Report* 56, no. SS-1 (2007): 12–28; Gillian Baird, Emily Simonoff, Andrew Pickles, Susie Chandler, et al., "Prevalence of Disorders of the Autism Spectrum in a Population Cohort of Children in South Thames: The Special Needs and Autism Project (SNAP)," *Lancet* 368, no. 9531 (2006): 210–15 ; Eric Fombonne, "Epidemiology of Autistic Disorder and Other Pervasive Developmental Disorders," *Journal of Clinical Psychiatry* 66 Suppl. 10 (2005): 3–8.

77. On increased rates of hospital admissions for a number of childhood psychiatric disorders, see David Mandell, William W. Thompson, Eric S. Weintraub, Frank DeStefano, et al., "Trends in Diagnosis Rates for Autism and ADHD at Hospital Discharge in the Context of Other Psychiatric Diagnoses," *Psychiatric Services* 56, no. 1 (2005): 56–62.

78. A typical argument is made in Eric Fombonne, "Is There an Epidemic of Autism?" *Pediatrics* 107, no. 2 (2001): 411–12.

79. Paul T. Shattuck, "Diagnostic Substitution and Changing Autism Prevalence," *Pediatrics* 117, no. 4 (2006): 1438–39. An important related argument, put forward by Eyal, Hart, Onculer, Oren, et al. (2010), is that the perceived increase resulted from the convergence of changing diagnostic standards for autism, the deinstitutionalization of children previously diagnosed with mental retardation, changes in developmental disabilities legislation, and parent activism.

80. For example, Morton Ann Gernsbacher, Michelle Dawson, and H. Hill Gold-smith, "Three Reasons Not to Believe in an Autism Epidemic," *Current Directions in Psychological Science* 14, no. 2 (2005): 55–58.

81. Victor Lotter, "Epidemiology of Autistic Conditions in Young Children. I. Prevalence," *Social Psychiatry* 1, no. 3 (1966): 124–37, 125, 133–34.

82. Lorna Wing and Judith Gould, "Severe Impairments of Social Interaction and Associated Abnormalities in Children: Epidemiology and Classification," *Journal of Autism and Childhood Schizophrenia* 9, no.1 (1979): 11–29, 13; Interview with Lorna Wing on June 10, 2005; Eric Schopler, "On Confusion in the Diagnosis of Autism," *Journal of Autism and Childhood Schizophrenia* 8, no. 2 (1978): 137–38.

83. Wing (2001, xiii–xiv, 14–16); Lorna Wing and Judith Gould, "Severe Impairments of Social Interaction and Associated Abnormalities in Children: Epidemiology and Classification," *Journal of Autism and Childhood Schizophrenia* 9, no. 1 (1979): 11–29, 27. In referring to "unwritten rules," I am thinking of a book by two adults with autism, Temple Grandin and Sean Barron, *Unwritten Rules of Social Relationships: Decoding Social Mysteries through the Unique Perspective of Autism* (Arlington, TX: Future Horizons, 2005).

84. On the lack of empirical support for claims about the association between autism and mental retardation, see Meredyth Goldberg Edelson, "Are the Majority of Children with Autism Mentally Retarded?" *Focus on Autism and Other Developmental Disabilities* 21, no. 2 (2006): 66–83. Individuals with autism may also perform significantly better on tests that showcase their cognitive strengths, such as Raven's Progressive Matrices. The test demands that the subject recognize patterns and infer rules, and it is considered an excellent measure of fluid intelligence (the ability to solve problems and reason). Michelle Dawson, Isabelle Soulieres, Morton Ann Gernsbacher, and Laurent Mottron, "The Level and Nature of Autistic Intelligence," *Psychological Science* 18, no. 8 (2007): 657–62, 658.

85. Leo Kanner and Leon Eisenberg, "Early Infantile Autism, 1943–1955," *American Journal of Orthopsychiatry* 26 (1956): 556–66, 557. This is also discussed in Lorna Wing, "The Definition and Prevalence of Autism: A Review," *European Child and Adolescent Psychiatry* 2, no. 2 (1993): 61–74.

86. Michael Rutter, "Diagnosis and Definition," in *Autism: A Reappraisal of Concepts and Treatment* (New York: Plenum Press, 1978), 1–25.

87. Lorna Wing, "The Definition and Prevalence of Autism: A Review," *European Child and Adolescent Psychiatry*, 2, no. 2 (1993): 61–74. The *DSM-III* also specified that schizophrenic features must be absent in patients in order to qualify for an autism diagnosis.

88. For example, Ralph Savarese's memoir, *Reasonable People: A Memoir of Autism and Adoption* (New York: Other Press, 2007).

89. Warren (1984, 103–5).

90. Mary S. Akerley, "Parents Speak: The Politics of Definitions," *Journal of Autism and Developmental Disorders* 9, no. 2 (1979): 222–31, 230–31.

91. Warren (1984, 105).

92. D. Arn Van Krevelen, "Early Infantile Autism and Autistic Psychopathy," *Journal of Autism and Developmental Disorders* 1, no. 1 (1971): 82–86, 83; Lorna Wing, "Asperger's Syndrome: A Clinical Account," *Psychological Medicine* 11 (1981): 115–29. On the use of Asperger syndrome diagnoses in Japan and Europe, see Kohei Inose and Masato Fukushima, "Asperger's Solitary Ally: Psychiatric Debate and the Educational Policy on Autism in Postwar Japan" (presentation at the Society for Social Studies of Science [4S], Pasadena, CA, October 2005); and Lorna Wing, "Reflections on Opening Pandora's Box," *Journal of Autism and Developmental Disorders* 35, no. 2 (2005): 197–203. Bruno Bettelheim, an Austrian, was aware of Asperger's work during the 1960s, according to Jacquelyn Sanders (personal communication, November 27, 2005).

93. Lorna Wing, "Asperger's Syndrome: A Clinical Account," *Psychological Medicine* 11 (1981): 115–29, 118, 121; Asperger (1991).

94. Wing, "Reflections on Opening Pandora's Box," 198.

95. Asperger (1944/1991, 77).

96. Wing, "Asperger's Syndrome: A Clinical Account," 117.

97. On the variations in everyday diagnostic practices, see Victoria Shea, "Letter to the Editor: Lumpers, Splitters, and Asperger Syndrome," *Journal of Autism and Developmental Disorders* 35, no. 6 (2005): 871–72. The relationship of Asperger syndrome to autism continues to be debated, with some structural brain imaging studies suggesting that the disorders may be behaviorally similar but anatomically distinct. See Linda J. Lotspeich, Hower Kwon, Cynthia M. Schumann, Susanna L. Fryer, et al., "Investigation of Neuroanatomical Differences between Autism and Asperger Syndrome," *Archives of General Psychiatry* 61, no. 3 (2004): 291–98.

98. For an analysis of these changes, see Kirk and Kutchins (1992) and Kutchins and Kirk (1997).

99. American Psychiatric Association, "Pervasive Developmental Disorders," in *Diagnostic and Statistical Manual of Mental Disorders*, 3rd ed. (Washington, DC: American Psychiatric Association, 1980).

100. Fred Volkmar, Joel Bregman, Donald J. Cohen, and Domenic V. Cicchetti, "*DSM*-III and *DSM*-III-R Diagnoses of Autism," *American Journal of Psychiatry* 145, no. 11 (1988): 1404–8, 1405; Lynn Waterhouse, Lorna Wing, Robert Spitzer, and Bryna Siegel, "Pervasive Developmental Disorders: From *DSM*-III to *DSM*-III-R," *Journal of Autism and Developmental Disorders* 22, no. 4 (1992): 525–49.

101. American Psychiatric Association, "Pervasive Developmental Disorders," in *Diagnostic and Statistical Manual of Mental Disorders*, 3rd ed., rev. (Washington, DC: American Psychiatric Association, 1987). The *DSM*-III-R defi-

nition included only "pervasive developmental disorder not otherwise specified" (PDD-NOS) along with "autistic disorder" under the umbrella of "pervasive developmental disorders," eliminating the categories of "infantile autism—residual state," "childhood onset developmental disorder—residual state," and "atypical disorder" altogether.

102. Volkmar et al., "*DSM*-III and *DSM*-III-R Diagnoses of Autism," 1405.

103. American Psychiatric Association, "Pervasive Developmental Disorders," in *Diagnostic and Statistical Manual of Mental Disorders*, 4th ed. (Washington, DC: American Psychiatric Association, 1994).

104. Susan Dickerson Mayes, Susan L. Calhoun, and Dana L. Crites, "Does *DSM*-IV Asperger's Disorder Exist?" *Journal of Abnormal Child Psychology* 29, no. 3 (2001): 263–71.

105. American Psychiatric Association, "American Psychiatric Association: *DSM*-5 Development," http://www.dsm5.org/ProposedRevisions/Pages/proposedrevision .aspx?rid=94#. Also see Roy Richard Grinker, "Disorder out of Chaos," *New York Times*, February 9, 2010.

106. Simon Baron-Cohen, "The Short Life of a Diagnosis," *New York Times*, November 9, 2009. For one geneticist's objections, see David A. Greenberg, "Letter to the Editor," *New York Times*, February 14, 2010.

107. Claudia Wallis, "A Powerful Identity, A Vanishing Diagnosis," *New York Times*, November 2, 2009; Jon Hamilton, "Asperger's Officially Placed within Autism Spectrum," National Public Radio broadcast, http://www.npr.org/ templates/story/story.php?storyId=123527833&ft=1&f=123527833.

108. Maureen S. Durkin, Matthew J. Maenner, F. John Meaney, Susan E. Levy, et al., "Socioeconomic Inequality in the Prevalence of Autism Spectrum Disorder: Evidence from a U.S. Cross-Sectional Study," *PLoS One* 5, no. 7 (2010): e11551, 7. The authors do not rule out "the possibility that factors associated with socioeconomic advantage might be causally associated with the risk for developing autism."

109. Lorna Wing, personal communication, June 10, 2005.

110. Craig J. Newschaffer, "Commentary: Investigating Diagnostic Substitution and Autism Prevalence Trends," *Pediatrics* 117, no. 4 (2006): 1436–37. Michael Rutter made much the same claim, concluding in his review of the epidemiological literature that "a true rise over time in the incidence of ASD cannot be entirely ruled out," Michael Rutter, "Incidence of Autism Spectrum Disorders: Changes over Time and Their Meaning," *Acta Paediatrica* 94, no. 1 (2005): 2–15, 13.

111. Mark Blaxill reviewed the epidemiological literature published up to the point of his article, comparing the stated diagnostic criteria used in each of the studies. M. Blaxill, "What's Going On? The Question of Time Trends in Autism," *Public Health Reports* 119, no. 6 (2004): 536–51.

112. For the exchange in the *Journal of Autism and Developmental Disorders*, see Lisa A. Croen, Judith K. Grether, Jenny Hoogstrate, and Steve Selvin, "The

Changing Prevalence of Autism in California," *Journal of Autism and Developmental Disorders* 32, no. 3 (2002): 207–15; Mark F. Blaxill, David S. Baskin, and Walter O. Spitzer, "Commentary: Blaxill, Baskin and Spitzer on Croen et al. (2002), 'The Changing Prevalence of Autism in California,'" *Journal of Autism and Developmental Disorders* 33, no. 2 (2003): 223–26; and Lisa A. Croen and Judith K. Grether, "A Response to Blaxill, Baskin and Spitzer on Croen et al. (2002), 'The Changing Prevalence of Autism in California,'" *Journal of Autism and Developmental Disorders* 33, no. 2 (2003): 227–29.

113. On the concept of therapeutic specificity, see Rosenberg (1992). Lakoff (2005, 10–14) discusses the importance of therapeutic specificity to psychiatrists in particular, and the concept's effects on the evolution of the *DSM* and psychopharmacology. On biological psychiatry as a dominant approach, see Luhrmann (2000).

114. Martha Herbert (2005a, 2005b) has suggested the concept of multiple "autisms." For parent reports of medical problems, see, for instance, Edelson and Rimland (2003).

115. On the importance of recognizing that autism may not only contain biological subgroups but also multiple behavioral syndromes, see Francesca Happe, Angelica Ronald, and Robert Plomin, "Time to Give Up on a Single Explanation for Autism," *Nature Neuroscience* 9, no. 10 (2006): 1218–20.

116. Any research group or practitioner who wishes to use the ADOS or ADI in published research must purchase them from Western Psychological Services, which in addition to publishing the tests also runs the required training sessions.

117. Catherine Lord, Susan Risi, Linda Lambrecht, Edwin H. Cook, et al., "The Autism Diagnostic Observation Schedule-Generic: A Standard Measure of Social and Communication Deficits Associated with the Spectrum of Autism," *Journal of Autism and Developmental Disorders* 30, no. 3 (2000): 205–23, 206.

118. Ann Le Couteur, Michael Rutter, Catherine Lord, Patricia Rios, et al., "Autism Diagnostic Interview: A Standardized Investigator-Based Instrument," *Journal of Autism and Developmental Disorders*, 19, no. 3 (1989): 363–87; Catherine Lord, Michael Rutter, Susan Goode, Jacquelyn Heemsbergen, et al., "Autism Diagnostic Observation Schedule: A Standardized Observation of Communicative and Social Behavior," *Journal of Autism and Developmental Disorders* 19, no. 2 (1989): 185–212.

119. Ibid. (187, 192–93). The authors write that "first, the ADOS is an *interactive* schedule. What is standardized in the ADOS are the contexts that provide the background for all observations and, more specifically, the behaviors of the examiner, not the sample."

120. Once trained in this way, screeners can enable colleagues at their site to "establish reliability" under their guidance, but only if they are in daily contact. University of Michigan Autism and Communication Disorders Center, "Es-

tablishing Reliability on the ADOS," http://www.umaccweb.com/education/adosreli.html.

121. Catherine Lord, Michael Rutter, and Ann Le Couteur, "Autism Diagnostic Interview-Revised: A Revised Version of a Diagnostic Interview for Caregivers of Individuals with Possible Pervasive Developmental Disorders," *Journal of Autism and Developmental Disorders* 24, no. 5 (1994): 659–85.

122. Molly Helt, Elizabeth Kelley, Marcel Kinsbourne, Juhi Pandey, et al., "Can Children with Autism Recover? If So, How?" *Neuropsychology Review* 18, no. 4 (2008): 339–66; Herbert (2009).

123. The AQ was reproduced in Carolyn Abraham, "Is There a "Geek" Syndrome?" *Globe and Mail*, October 12, 2002.

124. Simon Baron-Cohen, Sally Wheelwright, Richard Skinner, Joanne Martin, et al., "The Autism-Spectrum Quotient (AQ): Evidence from Asperger Syndrome/High-Functioning Autism, Males and Females, Scientists and Mathematicians," *Journal of Autism and Developmental Disorders* 31, no. 1 (2001): 5–17, 5.

125. See, for instance, Nelkin and Tancredi (1994).

126. On the "silencing" of parents during encounters with professionals concerning their child's autism diagnosis, see Feinstein (2006).

127. Martha R. Herbert, "Neuroimaging in Disorders of Social and Emotional Processing: What Is the Question?" *Journal of Child Neurology* 19, no. 10 (2004): 772–84.

Chapter 2

1. Pollak (1997); Richard Bernstein, "Ideas and Trends: Accusations of Abuse Haunt the Legacy of Dr. Bruno Bettelheim," *New York Times,* November 4, 1990. Not all accounts of Bettelheim's tenure are as critical as Pollak's. More favorable ones include biographies by Sutton (1996) and Raines (2002), and a memoir by Stephen Eliot (2002, 53), a former student at the school.

2. See, for instance, Robert Coles, "A Hero of Our Time," *New Republic* 156, no. 9 (1967): 23–24; the assessment of Bettelheim and the counselors as "heroes" in Peter Gay, "Books: *Per Ardua,*" *New Yorker,* May 18, 1968, 160–73; Jacquelyn Sanders, quoted in Martin Weil, "Pioneering Psychologist Bruno Bettelheim Dies; Scholar Known for Imaginative Techniques in the Study of Children," *Washington Post,* March 14, 1990; and Robert Coles, quoted in Jacobsen (2004, 216).

3. Freud's statement to Jung is quoted in Karen Zelan, "Bruno Bettelheim, 1903–1990," in *Prospects: The Quarterly Review of Special Education* (Paris, UNESCO: International Bureau of Education) XXIII, no. ½ (1993): 85–100, 98.

4. Herman (1995). On the importation of psychoanalysis to America and the early history of the profession, see Hale (1978), and see Lunbeck (1994) on the

gendered division of labor involved in establishing psychiatric reasoning as a form of American cultural common sense. Luhrmann (2000) discusses psychoanalytic training in American medical schools and its gradual displacement by biological psychiatry.

5. See, for instance, Alfred Hitchcock's *Spellbound* (1945), which features Freudian analysis and dream sequences designed by Salvador Dalí. Hollywood's fascination with psychoanalysis proved to be enduring. The director Woody Allen featured Bettelheim playing a version of himself in the 1983 film *Zelig*. On the expanding ranks of clinical professionals during the postwar period, see Herman (1995, 259).

6. Herman (1995, 259).

7. On the history of parenting advice manuals, see Grant (1998) and Stearns (2003).

8. The ideology of scientific motherhood gave women responsibility for their families while simultaneously demanding that they turn to expert advice (Apple 1995, 176, 178). Watsonian behaviorist principles dominated expert advice before psychoanalytic ideas were introduced to the United States. Apple (2006, 83–85).

9. Leo Kanner, *In Defense of Mothers: How to Bring Up Children in Spite of the More Zealous Psychologists* (Springfield, IL: Charles C. Thomas, 1941); Benjamin Spock. *Dr. Spock's Baby and Child Care* (New York: Simon & Schuster, 1945/1998), 1–2.

10. Coles, "A Hero of Our Time," 23.

11. Sutton (1996, 199–200).

12. "As he later told the story, his advice was, 'There's only one thing to be done with that school: burn it down.'" Sutton (1996, 222).

13. Bettelheim's obituary in the *New York Times* stated that Bettelheim was held for "almost two years," but Bettelheim said that he was in the two camps for "approximately one year." Daniel Goleman, "Bruno Bettelheim Dies at 86; Psychoanalyst of Vast Impact," *New York Times*, March 14, 1990; Bettelheim (1943, 417).

14. Sutton (1996, 244); Roazen (1992, 225).

15. Bettelheim (1987, 199–201).

16. Jacquelyn Sanders, personal communication, December 10, 2005.

17. Roazen (1992, 233); Raines (2002, 488). During the 1950s, the question of who would be entitled to offer psychotherapy was far from settled, especially between psychologists and psychiatrists. The matter was further complicated by uncertainty over what, exactly, psychotherapy entailed. Buchanan (2003, 226).

18. Sutton, (1996, 223).

19. On the transition in the school's population, see Gayle Janowitz, quoted in Jacobsen (2004, 202–3).

20. Alan Dundes (1991, 80) notes that while Bettelheim might be credited with bringing the psychoanalytic treatment of fairy tales to "the attention of the

general public," he both failed to consult relevant sources in the folklore literature and failed to cite sources from which he borrowed substantially, specifically Julius E. Heuscher's *A Psychiatric Study of Fairy Tales: Their Origin, Meaning and Usefulness*, published in 1963 by Charles C. Thomas. Dundes notes that while Bettelheim mentioned Heuscher in a footnote, he appears to have "borrowed" entire passages.

21. Ivar Lovaas commented on this during "Presentations from Experts in the Field" (roundtable discussion), The Autism Summit Conference: Developing a National Agenda, Washington, DC, November 19–20, 2003.

22. Bettelheim (1943, 420–21).

23. For a discussion of the problem of retrospectively discussing therapeutic efficacy in psychiatric disorders, and the argument that "efficacy" must be understood not only in terms of biological mechanisms but also in terms of social, professional and institutional interests, see Braslow (1996) and Pressman (1998, 194–235).

24. See for instance Kramer's (1993/1997) speculations about how treating patients with SSRIs caused him to view the specifics of his patients' lives differently.

25. Rosenberg (1992, 2002) describes how, as medicine became increasingly committed to a scientific ideal over the course of the nineteenth century, therapeutic specificity became increasingly important. However, in psychoanalysis, nosology could be less important than general theories about the causes of psychological distress. Bettelheim thought that extensive considerations of diagnoses and even abstract discussions of psychodynamics ran the risk of distracting staff members at the Orthogenic School from the real, emotional, problems at hand concerning the children in their care. Bruno Bettelheim, "Psychiatric Consultation in Residential Treatment: Workshop, 1957. 1. The Director's View." *American Journal of Orthopsychiatry* 28, no. 2 (1958): 256–65, 262.

26. Eliot Fremont-Smith, "Children Without an 'I,'" *New York Times*, March 10, 1967.

27. Carol Kleiman, "A Total Commitment to Children," *Chicago Tribune*, January 22, 1967.

28. For an analysis of Bettelheim's rhetorical strategies, see Severson, Aune, and Jodlowski (2008, 72–74). Because of his lack of ease with English, Bettelheim relied on the help of an editor, Ruth Soffer Marquis, to produce finished work. (Raines, 173–76). Nevertheless, he was committed to accessible writing: "He was determined not to get bogged down in highly technical and overly specialized questions, not to write in jargon." Fisher (1991, 256). Jacquelyn Sanders, likewise, remembers that he "not only wrote without jargon, he talked without jargon—he would say that if you can't explain something so that ANYONE can understand it, then you don't understand it yourself" (personal communication, December 10, 2005).

29. Jacquelyn Sanders wrote that controversies about the book "clouded a more fundamental contribution to the study of personality development focusing on the significance of the relationship between parent and child for the child's development of self. Bettelheim also pointed to the problem of parental preoccupation and indifference which he and other critics believed unique to our own time, and which had important implications for the child's subsequent adjustment." Bertram J. Cohler and Jacquelyn Sanders, "Obituary: Bruno Bettelheim, (1903–1990)," *International Journal of Psychoanalysis* 72 (1991): 155–58.

30. Stearns (2003, 39) describes how expert discourse about psychological risks, changes in the environmental context of children's development, and the displacement of adult anxieties about their own lives contributed to the growth of the concept of the "vulnerable child" during the twentieth century. For changes in labor and insurance policies that placed increasing weight on children's physical wellbeing and protecting children from risks, see Zelizer (1985).

31. Letter from Amy Lettick to M. J. Shodell, dated January 11, 1967. "Shodell, M.," Box 2, ACC 92-M-41, Amy L. Lettick Papers, 1920–2006, Yale University Library Special Collections, New Haven, CT (henceforth, "Lettick Papers"). Margaret Shodell, the director of the Nassau Center for Emotionally Disturbed Children, had written to accept a position as an advisor to Benhaven in a letter to Amy Lettick dated January 3, 1967. "Shodell, M.," Box 2, ACC 92-M-41, Lettick Papers. Mira Rothenberg was another noted promoter of psychotherapeutic techniques for treating children with autism, as chronicled in her book *Children with Emerald Eyes: Histories of Extraordinary Boys and Girls* (New York: The Dial Press, 1960).

32. Barron and Barron (2002, 111).

33. J. K. Wing, "Family and Society: The Empty Fortress" (review), *British Journal of Psychiatry* 114, no. 511 (1968): 788–91, 789–90; Zelan (1993, 93). Wing also noted that the methods of counselors at the school "seem very similar to those used by other workers and adopted by sensible parents."

34. My discussion of Jacquelyn Sanders's reflections on treating autistic children at the Orthogenic School relies on Sanders (1996), email correspondence with Dr. Sanders, and an interview conducted on April 3, 2003, in Chicago, IL.

35. Michael Rutter, "The Influence of Organic and Emotional Factors on the Origins, Nature and Outcome of Childhood Psychosis," *Developmental Medicine and Child Neurology* 7, no. 5 (1965): 518–28, 521–22, quoted in Bernard Rimland, "Freud Is Dead: New Directions in the Treatment of Mentally Ill Children," *Distinguished Lecture Series in Special Education* (Los Angeles: University of Southern California, 1970), 33–48, 44. Adapted from a lecture presented to chapters of the National Society for Autistic Children in various cities, 1967–1970.

36. Bettelheim's description of autism for a Collier's Encyclopedia entry was similarly detailed. Bruno Bettelheim, letter to Miss Barbara Crowell, Life Sciences Department, Colliers Encyclopedia, September 15, 1971. Bruno Bet-

telheim Papers, Special Collections Research Center, University of Chicago Library, Chicago, IL (unprocessed; henceforth, "Bettelheim Papers").

37. Bruno Bettelheim and Emmy Sylvester, "Physical Symptoms in Emotionally Disturbed Children," reprint in folder marked "The Psychoanalytic Study of the Child" (probably *Psychoanalytic Study of the Child* [New Haven: Yale University Press, 1948 or 1950]), Bettelheim Papers. Elsewhere, Bettelheim interpreted sensory disturbances such as preferring one sensory modality (seeing, hearing, touch, etc.) over others in terms of lacking a "body ego" and having poorly integrated ego functions. Bruno Bettelheim, second interim report to Mr. Joseph McDaniel Jr., Secretary, Ford Foundation, July 17, 1958, folder marked "Ford Foundation Reports," Bettelheim Papers.

38. Gay, "Books: *Per Ardua*," 169.

39. Zelan (1993, 85).

40. René A. Spitz, *Dialogues from Infancy: Selected Papers* (New York: International Universities Press, 1983); Lucy Freeman, "Emotions of Baby Held First to Gain," *New York Times,* May 14, 1949.

41. Leo Kanner, "Problems of Nosology and Psychodynamics in Early Infantile Autism," in *Childhood Psychosis: Initial Studies and New Insights* (Washington, DC: V. H. Winston and Sons, 1973), 61, 59. Originally published in *American Journal of Orthopsychiatry,* 19 (1949): 416–26, 425, 424.

42. The investigators reported that although they "did not ask our subjects if they felt helpless and/or hopeless, their posture and lack of activity seemed to indicate an attitude of 'giving up,'" in addition to "profound and persistent behavioral abnormalities" that lingered after the experiment. Harry F. Harlow and Stephen J. Suomi. "Production of Depressive Behaviors in Young Monkeys," *Journal of Autism and Childhood Schizophrenia* 1, no. 3 (1971): 246–55, 247, 253.

43. Harry F. Harlow and William T. McKinney Jr., "Nonhuman Primates and Psychoses." *Journal of Autism and Childhood Schizophrenia* 1, no. 4 (1971): 368–75, 371.

44. Bettelheim (1967, 32, 74–75). Donna Haraway's (1989, 231–43) treatment of Harlow's experiments using terrycloth "false" mothers situates the peculiar cruelty of Harlow's experiments within the context of biological theories of both motherhood and gender as reproduced within primatology.

45. Bettelheim (1943).

46. Bettelheim (1967, 68, 129). Bettelheim wrote in an earlier article that "severe as the impact of the mother may be, the child also responds all along in terms of his nature, his personality." Bruno Bettelheim, "Childhood Schizophrenia; Symposium, 1955. III. Schizophrenia as a Reaction to Extreme Situations," *American Journal of Orthopsychiatry* 26, no. 3 (1956): 507–18, 508.

47. Bettelheim (1967, 385, 401).

48. Ibid., 403. Bettelheim thought that if "certain neural systems are not appropriately stimulated within a specific period of life, they may suffer permanent

impairment," a suggestion that his opponents might have agreed with in content if not in implications. Bettelheim (1967, 401).

49. Elsewhere, Bettelheim wrote that "as long as those who hold the view that schizophrenia is organic in nature do not present us with methods of therapy that are more successful than those based on psychoanalysis, it is justified if, for the time being, we neglect the organic factor, about which we can do nothing as yet, and concentrate instead on that psychological understanding and treatment which yields some quite worth-while results." Bettelheim, "Childhood Schizophrenia; Symposium, 1955. III. Schizophrenia as a Reaction to Extreme Situations," 508.

50. Zelan (1993, 93).

51. Bettelheim (1967, 410, 412).

52. Pollak (1997, 10).

53. Bettelheim (1967, 404).

54. Bettelheim, first interim report to Mr. Joseph McDaniel Jr.; Bettelheim, second interim report to Mr. Joseph McDaniel Jr., 2.

55. Bettelheim (1959, 117).

56. Ibid., 127.

57. Bettelheim (1959, 122, 124).

58. Critics have argued that Joey's sophisticated imaginary world suggests that he would not be given an autism diagnosis in the present. Grinker (2008, 81–82) suggests that the children described in *The Empty Fortress* might, indeed, have been victims of severe child neglect, rather than children with autism.

59. "Joey" was a pseudonym but the paintings were reproduced in Bettelheim's book and were easily recognizable.

60. Bettelheim (1967, 125).

61. A "liminal action of the autistic child—and most of their actions are liminal or subliminal—evokes ambivalence, or a negative response in the caretaker. To this the child responds with massive withdrawal." Ibid., 126.

62. Herman (1995, 313).

63. Matthews (1967, 61–62); Lemov (2005, 127); Gifford (1991).

64. Herman (1995, 259) "During the years after 1945, ordinary people sought therapeutic attention more insistently than ever before and for more reasons than ever before" (257).

65. Ibid., 82–83.

66. Herman (1995, 257, 259, 82–83, 238–39). The official name of the GI Bill was the Soldiers' Readjustment Act of 1944.

67. Bruno Bettelheim, *Dialogues with Mothers* (New York: Free Press of Glencoe, 1962).

68. Bettelheim (1987, xi and 17).

69. Ibid., 4–5.

70. See Molly Ladd-Taylor and Lauri Umansky, "Introduction," in Ladd-Taylor and Umansky (1998).

71. Of course, mother-blaming and the idea of "bad" mothers extended before and after the 1950s and 1960s in America. Ladd-Taylor and Umansky (1998, 2) argue that it is important to ask why mothers in particular have been the focus of public discourse about a range of social and economic problems. Jennifer Terry's (in Ladd-Taylor and Umansky, 1998, 169–90) survey of "momism" in psychiatric discourse during the 1950s focuses on the claim that dissatisfied or overvigilant mothers caused their children to become homosexuals, but these beliefs were related to arguments about "failures of development" more generally.

72. Wylie produced a vitriolic and psychologically inflected critique of what he perceived to be the effects of mothers who attempted to control their male offspring. Philip Wylie, *Generation of Vipers* (New York: Rinehart, 1942). On the acceptance of "momism" within the psychiatric establishment and on emerging feminist critiques in the late 1960s, see Herman (1995, 278–79, 281–84).

73. Irving Kaufman, Eleanor Rosenblum, Lora Heims, and Lee Willer, "Childhood Psychosis: 1. Childhood Schizophrenia: Treatment of Children and Parents," *American Journal of Orthopsychiatry* 27, no. 4 (1957): 683–90, 685, 683, 684.

74. There are a number of poignant, firsthand accounts in the documentary *Refrigerator Mothers* (Kartemquin Films, 2002).

75. Donald R. Katz, "The Kids with the Faraway Eyes: The Strange Secret World of Autism," *Rolling Stone*, March 8, 1979, 48–53.

76. Barron and Barron (2002, 247).

77. As Bettelheim wrote, "It is the parents who, in our opinion, make a significant contribution to the development of the autistic disturbance in their children." Bruno Bettelheim, second interim report to Mr. Joseph McDaniel Jr.

78. Not all of the families in Henry's book had autistic children; some are given no specific diagnosis. Henry (1971, 195).

79. John M. Townsend, review of *Pathways to Madness* by Jules Henry and *On Sham, Vulnerability and Other Forms of Self-Destruction* by Jules Henry, *American Anthropologist*, New Series 77, no. 3 (1975): 623–24, 623.

80. Bettelheim, second interim report to Mr. Joseph McDaniel Jr.

81. Ibid.

82. Eric Schopler and Gary B. Mesibov, "Professional Attitudes toward Parents: a Forty-Year Progress Report," in *The Effects of Autism on the Family,* eds. Eric Schopler and Gary Mesibov (New York, Plenum Press), 11.

83. Henry (1971, 298).

84. Horace Judson, "Five American Families (Review of *Pathways to Madness* by Jules Henry)," *Time*, March 12, 1973.

85. H. A. Gould, "Jules Henry, 1904–1969," *American Anthropologist*, 73, no. 3 (1971): 788–97, 788, 792.

86. The term comes from an obituary for Bettelheim. Rudolf Ekstein, "Bruno Bettelheim (1903–1990)," *American Psychologist* (October 1991). Bettelheim

260   Notes to Chapter 2

wrote that "if residential treatment makes any sense, it must come about through the creation of a milieu that is therapeutic in its totality, in all aspects and not just some of its aspects." Bruno Bettelheim, "Training the Child-Care Worker in a Residential Center," *American Journal of Orthopsychiatry* 36, no. 4 (1966): 694–705, 695. The fact that residents could leave freely but visitors required permission to enter is repeated in several accounts, among them Daniel Goleman, "Bruno Bettelheim Dies at 86; Psychoanalyst of Vast Impact," *New York Times,* March 14, 1990; and Gayle Janowitz, quoted in Jacobsen (2004, 208).

87. Bruno Bettelheim, letter to Miss Barbara Crowell, Life Sciences Department, Collier's Encyclopedia, September 15, 1971, Bettelheim Papers.

88. Zelan (1993, 85); Bruno Bettelheim and Emmy Sylvester, "A Therapeutic Milieu," *American Journal of Orthopsychiatry* 18 (1948): 191–206.

89. Earl Saxe and Jeanetta Lyle, "The Function of the Psychiatric Residential School," *Bulletin of the Menninger Clinic* 4, no. 6 (1940): 162–71; Fees (1998).

90. Jacquelyn Sanders explained how counselors were hired as child-care workers and "research assistants" in a personal communication, December 10, 2005. As an attitude on the part of the teachers in the school, participant observation (called a "marginal interview" by Fritz Redl, a colleague of Bettelheim's) meant a kind of critical or interpretive distance that did not preclude interaction. It was "interpretive in character but does not need to interfere with the momentary activity of the group or individual." Bettelheim (1950, 35). I have also drawn on Raines's (2002, 178–90) excellent explanation of the milieu at the Orthogenic School.

91. Helen Robinson, an "eminent professor involved in remedial reading," used the students in research before Bettelheim's arrival. Jacquelyn Sanders, personal communication, December 10, 2005.

92. Sanders (1996).

93. Counselors and therapists spoke out about how Bettelheim used to slap children when they were dangerous to themselves or others. He said that it was "utterly necessary that the kids feel secure in the school and that to feel secure from one another, which was the hardest thing to arrange, there had to be absolutely enforced rules about their not hurting one another." Robert Bergman, interviewed in Jacobsen (2004, 195). Also see the comments from "Stephen Eliot," a former student at the school, also quoted in Jacobsen (2004, 210), and Richard Bernstein, "Ideas & Trends; Accusations of Abuse Haunt the Legacy of Dr. Bruno Bettelheim," *New York Times,* November 4, 1990.

94. Sanders (1996, 2).

95. Ibid., 2–3. Sanders's phrase is that she "watched with breaking heart" as the children were sent away.

96. Zelan (1993, 93).

97. Raines (2002, 266–67).

98. Bettelheim (1967, 89–90); Bruno Bettelheim, "Training the Child-Care Worker in a Residential Center," *American Journal of Orthopsychiatry* 36, no. 4 (1966): 694–705, 705.

99. Gayle Janowitz, interviewed in Jacobsen (2004, 203).

100. Bettelheim (1974, 5).

101. Jacquelyn Sanders, personal communication, December 10, 2005.

102. At the time, the diagnosis of "childhood schizophrenia" and "infantile autism" would have been virtually interchangeable among most practitioners. According to Jacquelyn Sanders, "the most widely accepted notion was that, though there may be some organic propensity or predisposition, there was a significant component of environmental etiology. The firmness of this assumption was reflected in the nature of the grant awarded to Bettelheim by the Ford Foundation. Its purpose was not an investigation into autism, but an exploration of normal development." Sanders (1996, 6).

103. "The Unhappiest Children," Ford Foundation Annual Report (1958?), 26, Bettelheim Papers.

104. Sutton (1996, 303–4).

105. Jacquelyn Sanders, personal communication, December 10, 2005.

106. Bruno Bettelheim, "Psychiatric Consultation in Residential Treatment: Workshop, 1957. 1. The Director's View," *American Journal of Orthopsychiatry* 28, no. 2 (1958): 256–65, 262.

107. Bettelheim (1974, 4). For descriptions by former students, see Eliot (2002) and the semifictionalized account by Lyons (1983).

108. Bertram J. Cohler and Jacquelyn Sanders, "Obituary: Bruno Bettelheim, (1903–1990)," *International Journal of Psychoanalysis* 72 (1991): 155–58; Robert Bergman, quoted in Jacobsen (2004, 195).

109. Tomes (1981).

110. Sanders (2005).

111. Bruno Bettelheim, "Training the Child-Care Worker in a Residential Center," 697.

112. Zelan (1993, 86).

113. See Jacquelyn Seevak Sanders, "Defending Bruno Bettelheim," *The New York Review of Books* 50, no. 18 (November 20, 2003). Sanders was writing in response to Robert Gottlieb's description of her apparently ambivalent relationship with Bettelheim in Robert Gottlieb, "The Strange Case of Dr. B," *The New York Review of Books* 50, no. 3 (February 27, 2003).

114. Gayle Janowitz, interviewed in Jacobsen (2004, 207).

115. Zelan (1993, 85). On staff meetings, Bettelheim's teaching methods, and reports of Bettelheim treating counselors, see Raines (2002, 191–201).

116. Bettelheim, "The Role of Residential Treatment for Children; Symposium, 1954. 8. Staff Development in a Treatment Institution," *American Journal of Orthopsychiatry* 25, no. 4 (1955): 705–19, 711–15.

117. Bettelheim (1967, 129).
118. Bruno Bettelheim, "The Role of Residential Treatment for Children: Symposium, 1954. 8. Staff Development in a Treatment Institution," 706–7, 709–11.
119. Jules Henry, "The Culture of Interpersonal Relations in a Therapeutic Institution for Emotionally Disturbed Children," *American Journal of Orthopsychiatry* 27, no. 4 (1957): 725–34, 734.
120. For an example of the sociological critique of state hospitals in the early 1970s (approximately a decade after Henry wrote about this, but conditions had only worsened), see Rosenhan (1973). For a retrospective consideration of the political economy of deinstitutionalization in the 1960s and early 1970s, see Mechanic and Rochefort (1990).
121. Charles Wenar, Bertram A. Ruttenberg, M. L. Dratman, and Enid J. Wolf, "Changing Autistic Behavior: The Effectiveness of Three Milieus," *Archives of General Psychiatry* 17, no. 1 (1967): 26–35, 35.
122. Jules Henry, "The Culture of Interpersonal Relations in a Therapeutic Institution for Emotionally Disturbed Children," 727.
123. Ibid., 728.
124. Sanders (1989, xiii).
125. Bettelheim (1967, 412).
126. Some of Rimland's wide-ranging interests can be seen by exploring the archived issues of the *Autism Research Review International*, which Rimland edited beginning in 1987. Rimland was willing to report on and at least consider most potential theories or treatments, although he was skeptical of some. See archived issues online at http://www.autism.com/ari/newsletter/index_a.asp.
127. The phrase is from Park (1967, 190).
128. Bernard Rimland, "Freud Is Dead: New Directions in the Treatment of Mentally Ill Children," *Distinguished Lecture Series in Special Education* (Los Angeles: University of Southern California, 1970): 33–48.
129. Bernard Rimland, letter to Bruno Bettelheim, March 22, 1965, Bettelheim Papers.
130. Sanders (1996, 11).
131. Bruno Bettelheim, letter to Bernard Rimland, March 25, 1965, Bettelheim Papers.
132. Bruno Bettelheim, letter to Bernard Rimland, April 9, 1966, Bettelheim Papers.
133. Bernard Rimland, letter to Bruno Bettelheim, April 25, 1966, Bettelheim Papers.
134. Bruno Bettelheim, letter to Bernard Rimland, April 29, 1966, Bettelheim Papers.
135. Steve Silberman, "The Geek Syndrome," *Wired* 9, no. 12 (2001); Bruno Bettelheim and Alvin A. Rosenfeld, *The Art of the Obvious* (New York: Alfred A. Knopf, 1993), xv.

136. Ibid., 141–42. Bettelheim is referring to *The Laziness of the Heart* (trans.) by Jacob Wasserman, which recounts the story of Kaspar Hauser, a socially deprived child who became a celebrity of sorts in nineteenth-century Germany.

137. Gary B. Mesibov, "A Tribute to Eric Schopler," *Journal of Autism and Developmental Disorders* 36, no. 8 (2006): 967–70. 968.

138. Ibid., 968; Eric Schopler and Robert J. Reichler, "Parents as Cotherapists in the Treatment of Psychotic Children," *Journal of Autism and Childhood Schizophrenia* 1, no. 1 (1971): 87–102.

139. Eric Schopler, "New Publisher, New Editor, Expanded Editorial Policy—Goal: An Improved Journal," *Journal of Autism and Childhood Schizophrenia* 4, no. 2 (1974): 91–92, 91.

140. Buchanan (2003, 225).

141. Mira Rothenberg, *Children with Emerald Eyes: Histories of Extraordinary Boys and Girls* (New York: The Dial Press, 1960); Virginia M. Axline. *Dibs: In Search of Self* (New York: Random House, 1964).

142. According to Jacquelyn Sanders, Bettelheim was very popular in France, and she was invited to speak in Columbia, Argentina, France, and Italy on the basis of Bettelheim's reputation and her association with him. Jacquelyn Sanders, personal communication, December 10, 2005. Also see Chamak (2008a, 81, 85).

143. Karen Zelan, *Between Their World and Ours: Breakthroughs with Autistic Children* (New York: St. Martin's Press, 2003). Also see Raines (2002, 267–70).

144. Sanders (1996, 12).

145. "Treatment Methods," Web site for the Sonia Shankman Orthogenic School, http://orthogenicschool.uchicago.edu/treatment/ (accessed June 13, 2006; no longer available).

146. Bruno Bettelheim, quoted in Zelan (1993, 90).

147. Sanders (1996, 17).

148. C. Wenar and Bertram Ruttenberg, "The Use of BRIAC for Evaluating Therapeutic Effectiveness," *Journal of Autism and Childhood Schizophrenia* 6, no. 2 (1976): 175–91, 175.

Chapter 3

1. Excerpted entries from Amy Lettick's diary, 1953, 5–7, folder marked "Diaries of Amy Lettick, 1953, 1955–1957: transcription, 1991," Box 1, ACC 92-M-79, Amy L. Lettick Papers, Manuscripts and Archives, Sterling Memorial Library, Yale University, New Haven, CT (henceforth, "Lettick Papers," with finding information).

2. Amy L. Lettick, *Ways and Means* (Tempe, AZ: The Behaven Press, 1998), 1.

3. Sally Provence, letter to Newell Kephart, March 27, 1962, folder marked, "Kephart, Newell C.," Box 2, ACC 92-M-41, Lettick Papers.

4. See James Trent's description of this process in Trent (1994, 225–68), and for an excellent brief history of parent activism around services and education, see Leiter (2004).

5. Lettick was not the only mother to found a treatment program. In addition to Lettick's correspondent Rosalind Oppenheim, who founded the Rimland School for Autistic Children in 1971, Ruth Christ Sullivan founded the Autism Training Center at Marshall University in Huntington, West Virginia, in 1983. See http://www.marshall.edu/coe/atc/about_us/history_of_atc/default .asp and http://www.rimland.org/history.htm.

6. Lettick (1979a).

7. Leo Kanner, "Follow-Up Study of Eleven Autistic Children." *Journal of Autism and Childhood Schizophrenia* 1, no. 2 (1971): 119–45, 145.

8. She did circulate a short, self-published account of her experiences to colleagues and friends, which she kindly shared with me. Lettick, *Ways and Means.*

9. Maurice (1993, 307).

10. On identifying reliable witnesses for experiments as an enduring problem, see Shapin (1999).

11. Park (1967, 179, 180–86).

12. Ibid., 188. Park is referring to Bettelheim's *Love Is Not Enough* (Glencoe, IL: Free Press, 1950).

13. Park (1967, 195).

14. Lettick (1979a, 303–4).

15. Greenfeld (1986, 138–39).

16. Eric Schopler, "Toward Reducing Behavior Problems in Autistic Children," *Journal of Autism and Childhood Schizophrenia* 6, no. 1 (1976): 1–13, 6.

17. "The parents, of course, greatly expanded the efficiency of the project in a number of ways." Lovaas (1977, 184, 3).

18. Kozloff, (1998, 11–12).

19. On "partial perspectives" see Haraway (1991, 183–202).

20. The record included not only daily classroom sessions, but also videotapes and voice recordings. "Amy Lettick's Diaries: Introduction," folder marked "Diaries of Amy Lettick, 1953, 1955–1957: transcription, 1991," Box 1, ACC 92-M-79, Lettick Papers.

21. Ibid.

22. Ibid. Benjamin Lettick was a client at Newell C. Kephart's Achievement Center for Children from 1962 to 1969. Lettick, *Ways and Means*, foreword.

23. "The Daily Records of a 6-Year Educational Program Designed for a Severely Autistic Boy" (Manuscript), Milford, Connecticut, 1990, Folder 19, Box 1, ACC 92-M-79, Lettick Papers.

24. Apple (2006, 123–25).

25. Lettick, *Ways and Means*, 45–46.

26. Rosalind C. Oppenheim, "They Said Our Child Was Hopeless," *Saturday Evening Post* 23 (June 17, 1961): 56–58.

27. Amy Lettick, "Notes for Speech at Dinner in Honor of Rosalind Oppenheim, Evanston, Ill., Dec. 9, 1990, 20th Anniversary of Rimland School," folder marked "Oppenheim," Box 2, ACC 92-M-41, Lettick Papers.

28. Lettick, *Ways and Means*, 34–35; Oppenheim (1974).

29. Lettick, "Notes for Speech at Dinner in Honor of Rosalind Oppenheim."

30. Oppenheim (1974, 34).

31. Ibid., 10; Letter from Rosalind Oppenheim to Amy Lettick, May 28, 1962, Box 1, ACC 92-M-79, Lettick Papers. Clara Claiborne Park (1967, 188) was also inspired by Oppenheim's article.

32. Oppenheim regularly apologized to Amy Lettick for lapses in the correspondence, or for simply taking too long to reply—at one point she reassured Amy that "you are the only mother I am corresponding with regularly." Letter from Rosalind Oppenheim, May 28, 1962, folder marked "pgs. 306–399," Box 1, ACC 92-M-79, Lettick Papers.

33. Lettick, "Notes for Speech at Dinner in Honor of Rosalind Oppenheim"; Amy Lettick, diary entry, October 27, 1961, folder marked "pgs. 1–103," Box 1, ACC 92-M-79, Lettick Papers.

34. Letter from Rosalind Oppenheim, May 28, 1962, folder marked "pgs. 306–399," Box 1, ACC 92-M-79, Lettick Papers.

35. Dr. Provence did eventually provide a referral for Benjamin, in a letter to Newell Kephart dated March 27, 1962. Folder marked "Kephart, Newell C," Box 2, ACC 92-M-41, Lettick Papers.

36. Letter from Rosalind Oppenheim, October 18, 1962, folder marked "pgs. 400–483," Box 1, ACC 92-M-79, Lettick Papers.

37. Parents continue to remark upon this distinction. See, for instance, Iverson (2006).

38. Amy Lettick, diary entry, October 23, 1962, folder marked "pgs. 400–483," Box 1, ACC 92-M-79, Lettick Papers.

39. Kephart (1960, 83–84).

40. Amy Lettick, "Our Trip," Nov. 11, Nov 17, 1962, folder marked "pgs. 400–483," Box 1, ACC 92-M-79, Lettick Papers.

41. Ibid.

42. The treatment under investigation became Super Nu-Thera™, a product still available from Kirkman Laboratories. Bernard Rimland, Institute for Child Behavior Research, letter to Vitamin Study Parents and Physicians, folder marked "Rimland, B.," Box 2, ACC 92-M-41, Lettick Papers.

43. Lettick, *Ways and Means*, 35.

44. Ibid, 45.

45. Lettick, *Ways and Means*, 36.

46. An announcement for the 1969 schedule of a "Workshop for Teachers and Therapists Conducted under the Supervision of N. C. Kephart Ph.D." offered "practical experience in the diagnosis of perceptual motor problems and in teaching to the diagnosis." Folder Marked "Kephart, N. C.," Box 2, ACC

92-M-41, Lettick Papers. A film series produced by the Purdue University Department of Education proceeded from *Atypical Child in the Classroom* (Film 1) through *Motor Development I* (Film 2), *Laterality* (Film 6), *Body Image* (Film 7), *Perceptual Processes I* (Film 8), and *Teaching Generalization I* (Film 12), and concluded with *Time* (Film 20). Folder marked "Kephart, N. C.," Box 2, ACC 92-M-41, Box 2, Lettick Papers.

47. Kephart (1960).

48. "The Passing of a Giant: N. C. Kephart" *The N. C. Kephart Glen Haven Achievement Center Feedback* 3, no. 2 (Spring 1973). Kephart died on April 12, 1973. He continually emphasized the participation and knowledge of parents, arguing that "too often, the parent is the most forgotten element in the entire complex. We forget that he has the same problems we have but he has them in greatly magnified intensity. Whereas we have this child for a few hours a day in a limited and controlled situation, he has him twenty-four hours in all kinds of situations and all types of demands. Much valuable information can be gained from parents and much valuable aid in the child's handling can be obtained from them if one can only learn to communicate." Quoted in publication from N. C. Kephart Glen Haven Achievement Center, folder marked "Kephart, N. C.," Box 2, ACC 92-M-41, Lettick Papers.

49. Sylvia Kottler, foreword to "The Daily Records of a 6-Year Educational Program Designed for a Severely Autistic Boy."

50. Lettick related the incident in a letter to Rosalind Oppenheim, October 11, 1962, folder marked "Diary," folder marked "pgs. 400–483," Box 1, ACC 92-M-79. Lettick Papers.

51. Lettick, *Ways and Means*, 22.

52. Ibid., 22. As Benjamin matured, Lettick came to describe him as mentally retarded as well as autistic. The ARC, founded in 1950, was a coalition of parent groups that had been gathering since the 1930s as a means of support and activism for education for children with intellectual disabilities.

53. Amy Lettick, diary entry, Wednesday, June 6, 1962, folder marked "pgs. 306–399," Box 1, ACC 92-M-79, Lettick Papers.

54. Amy Lettick, diary entry, Wednesday, Sept. 21, 1966, "Original Journal, 1966, July 28–Nov. 30," Folder 17, Box 1, ACC 92-M-79, Lettick Papers.

55. She planned for the board of her school to consist of Dr. Kephart, Mrs. Margaret Shodell of the Nassau Center, and Dr. Carl Fenichel of the League School in Brooklyn. Amy Lettick, draft letter, undated, folder marked "Kephart, N.C.," Box 2, ACC 92-M-41, Lettick Papers.

56. Lettick, *Ways and Means*, 37

57. Ibid., 44–45.

58. Lettick wrote, "We believe that an intensive, driving dynamic program involving measurement, diagnosis and adjustment of techniques is the force that propels our children on the roads we would have them travel." Amy L.

Lettick, "The Philosophy behind Benhaven's Program," folder marked "All Writings, 1931–69," Box 3, ACC 92-M-79, Lettick Papers; Lettick (1979a).

59. Lettick (1979b).

60. Gary Mesibov, review of *Benhaven Then and Now* and *Benhaven at Work, Journal of Autism and Developmental Disorders,* 10, no. 2 (1980), 248–50, 248.

61. Lettick, *Ways and Means,* 51.

62. Mesibov, review of *Benhaven Then and Now* and *Benhaven at Work.*

63. Lettick, "The Philosophy behind Benhaven's Program."

64. Quoted in the *Connecticut Jewish Ledger,* March 29, 1975.

65. "Rimland Family Year-End Newsletter: 1968," folder Marked "Rimland, B.," Box 2, ACC 92-M-41, Lettick Papers. The British equivalent of the NSAC, the National Autistic Society, was founded two years earlier, in 1962.

66. Sula Wolff (2004, 205) writes that in both the U.S. and the U.K., "the greater awareness of the condition is largely attributable to the activities of parent organisations."

67. The Education for All Handicapped Children Act, PL 94-142, became the IDEA, PL 105-17, in 1990. "History: Twenty-Five Years of Progress in Educating Children with Disabilities through IDEA," Washington, DC: U.S. Office of Special Education Programs, http://www2.ed.gov/policy/speced/leg/idea/history.html.

68. Eric Schopler and Robert Reichler argued that parents of children with autism were slower to form advocacy groups because of their presumed guilt. Schopler and Reichler (1971, 89).

69. Mary S. Akerley, "The Politics of Definitions," *Journal of Autism and Childhood Schizophrenia* 9, no. 2 (1979): 222–31. The Developmentally Disabled Assistance and Bill of Rights Act, PL 94-103, was passed in 1970, amended in 1975, and amended again in 1978 to focus on functional limitations rather than specific diagnoses.

70. Bruno Bettelheim, letter to Miss Barbara Crowell, Life Sciences Department, Collier's Encyclopedia, September 15, 1971, Bruno Bettelheim Papers, Special Collections Research Center, University of Chicago Library, Chicago, IL.

71. Rimland (1972, 576).

72. Ibid., 582.

73. Ibid., 583.

74. Bernard Rimland, "Parents Speak: A Risk/Benefit Perspective on the Use of Aversives," *Journal of Autism and Childhood Schizophrenia* 8, no. 1 (1978): 100–104, 101.

75. O. Ivar Lovaas, "Behavioral Treatment and Normal Educational and Intellectual Functioning in Young Autistic Children," *Journal of Consulting and Clinical Psychology* 55, no.1 (1987), 3–9. In current usage, some parents and practitioners distinguish between ABA in general and the "Lovaas technique," meaning intensive ABA methods involving discrete trial training as they are applied to autism and other developmental disabilities.

76. Lovaas (1981, 9).

77. Lovaas explained that the operant learning theory upon which he based his work was premised on the idea that "aspects of the child's environment must acquire certain stimulus functions which serve to regulate the occurrence of his verbal behavior." Lovaas (1977, 11, 13).

78. Lovaas (1977, 3).

79. Lovaas (1981, 9).

80. Johnson and Crowder (1994, 177).

81. "Screams, Slaps and Love: Surprising, Shocking Treatment Helps Far-Gone Mental Cripples," *Life* 58, no. 18 (May 7, 1965): 90–101.

82. Ibid. Aversives were a fairly routine part of experimental practice. In one study, "pain was induced by means of an electrified grid on the floor upon which the children stood. The shock was turned on immediately following pathological behaviors. It was turned off or withheld when the children came to the adults who were present. Thus these adults 'saved' the children from a dangerous situation." O. Ivar Lovaas, Benson Schaeffer, and James Q. Simmons, "Building Social Behavior in Autistic Children by Use of Electric Shock," in *Perspectives in Behavior Modification with Deviant Children,* eds. O. Ivar Lovaas and Bradley D. Bucher (Englewood Cliffs, NJ: Prentice-Hall, Inc., 1974), 109.

83. Rimland, "Parents Speak: A Risk/Benefit Perspective on the Use of Aversives," 100. Rimland noted that the program in fact used primarily positive reinforcement—the standard practice in behavior modification programs.

84. Ibid., 101.

85. Katz, "The Kids with the Faraway Eyes," 53.

86. "Parents Speak: Risks and Benefits in the Treatment of Autistic Children," *Journal of Autism and Childhood Schnizophrenia* 8, no. 1 (1978): 99–113. See especially Ann Jepson, "Ethical Use of Aversives," 104–5; and Nancy Mc-Clung, "Risk/Benefit?" 107–8.

87. Kenneth Laureys with Roy Morgan, "Abuse of Aversive Therapy Opposed by NSAC," *The Advocate* (Jan./Feb. 1986): 6–7.

88. Schopler wrote that "some older Board members will remember that the psychoanalysts argued that people with autism are essentially normal and need only psychotherapy. The ASA today seems to want to go them one better by suggesting they only need normal experiences. This seems to bring us full cycle for denying their special problems and needs." "Letter to the Editor," *The Advocate* 20, no. 4 (Winter 1988). Donald Cohen was concerned that language regarding avoiding "physical side effects" of therapies might be construed as arguing against the use of medications in treatment, and that in many cases, routine activities could elicit "emotional stress." See Donald J. Cohen, letter to Edward Ritvo, August 31, 1988, second of two folders marked "ASA, NSAC," Box 1, ACC 92-M-41, Lettick Papers. On the contemporary incarnation of Division TEACCH, see http://www.teacch.com/.

89. Marcia Datlow Smith, "Response to Dr. Rimland's *Don't Ban Aversives,*" *The Advocate* 20, no. 4 (Winter 1988): 14.

90. Marcia Datlow Smith and Bernard Rimland, "Pro and Con Arguments Regarding the ASA Resolution on the Use of Aversives," *The Advocate* 20, no. 4 (Winter 1988).

91. Katz, "The Kids with the Faraway Eyes," 53.

92. Park (2001, 77).

93. Lovaas's first report on the use of reinforcers in training children with autism was a paper presented in 1964, with Gilbert Freitag, the teacher hired, with little success, by the New Haven school system. The experience of the parents in New Haven only serves to underscore the point that laboratory techniques were difficult to translate into less formal settings, and using them successfully in homes and schools possibly required different forms of expertise. Probably the earliest account of Lovaas's work in this area was O. I. Lovaas, G. Freitag, M. I. Kinder, et al., "Experimental Studies in Childhood Schizophrenia—Establishment of Social Reinforcers" (paper delivered at Western Psychological Association, Portland, OR, April, 1964). Another study was published in 1966 on the acquisition of language: O. I. Lovaas. J. P. Berberich, B. F. Perloff, and B. Schaeffer, "Acquisition of Imitative Speech by Schizophrenic Children," *Science* 151, no. 3711 (1966): 705–7.

94. O. Ivar Lovaas, Robert Koegel, James Q. Simmons, and Judith Stevens Long, "Some Generalization and Follow-Up Measures on Autistic Children in Behavior Therapy," *Journal of Applied Behavior Analysis* 6, no. 1 (1973): 131–66.

95. O. Ivar Lovaas, "Parents as Therapists," in *Autism: A Reappraisal of Concepts and Treaments,* eds. Michael Rutter and Eric Schopler (New York: Plenum Press, 1978): 366–78, 371.

96. Ibid., 376–77.

97. O. Ivar Lovaas, "Behavioral Treatment and Normal Educational and Intellectual Functioning in Young Autistic Children," *Journal of Consulting and Clinical Psychology* 55, no. 1 (1987): 3–9

98. Eric Schopler, "Ask the Editor: Will Your Journal Support Parents Advocating for Intensive Behavior Therapy (the Lovaas Method) as an Entitlement under Part H of the Individuals with Disabilities Education Act?" *Journal of Autism and Developmental Disorders* 28, no. 1 (1998): 91–92.

99. Eric Schopler, Andrew Short, and Gary Mesibov, "Relation of Behavioral Treatment to 'Normal Functioning': Comment on Lovaas," *Journal of Consulting and Clinical Psychology* 57, no. 1 (1989): 162–64.

100. They thought that the children selected were higher-functioning than most children with autism and that children were placed in the control group because of the severity of their problems or because their parents were unable to participate fully in the treatment, meaning that the control and experimental group had different selection criteria. Ibid., 163. Lovaas responded that entirely arbitrary subject selection had been impossible because of parent

protests and that they had used the best available outcome measures. O. Ivar Lovaas, Tristram Smith, and John J. McEachin, "Clarifying Comments on the Young Autism Study: Reply to Schopler, Short and Mesibov," *Journal of Consulting and Clinical Psychology* 57, no. 1 (1989): 165–67, 165.

101. Schopler, Short, and Mesibov, "Relation of Behavioral Treatment to 'Normal Functioning': Comment on Lovaas," 164.

102. Schopler and Reichler (1971).

103. Gary Mesibov recalled this in his two obituaries for Schopler. Gary B. Mesibov, "A Tribute to Eric Schopler," *Journal of Autism and Developmental Disorders* 36, no. 8 (2006): 967–70; Gary B. Mesibov, "Eric Schopler (1927–2006)," *American Psychologist* 62, no. 3 (2006): 250.

104. Gary Mesibov assumed the directorship of the program after Schopler partially retired in 1993. On the structure of the experimental program, see Schopler and Reichler (1971, 90–98). On the basic premises of Division TEACCH, see Lee M. Marcus, Margaret Lansing, Carol E. Andrews, and Eric Schopler, "Improvement of Teaching Effectiveness in Parents of Autistic Children," *Journal of the American Academy of Child Psychiatry* 17, no. 4 (1978): 625–39; Eric Schopler, Gary B. Mesibov, and Kathy Hearsey, "Structured Teaching in the TEACCH System," in *Learning and Cognition in Autism,* eds. Erich Schopler and Gary B. Mesibov (New York: Plenum Press, 1995): 243–68.

105. Eric Schopler, "Toward Reducing Behavior Problems in Autistic Children," *Journal of Autism and Childhood Schizophrenia* 6, no. 1 (1976): 1–13, 10.

106. Schopler and Reichler (1971, 92). Lovaas explains how he emphasized the idea of a "work-contract" in O. Ivar Lovaas, "Parents as Therapists," 372. For Schopler's focus on parental control in contrast to Lovaas, see Eric Schopler, "Changing Parental Involvement in Behavioral Treatment," in Michael Rutter and Eric Schopler, eds., *Autism: A Reappraisal of Concepts and Treatment* (New York: Plenum Press, 1978), 416.

107. Schopler and Reichler (1971, 92).

108. Ibid., 93

109. Lee M. Marcus, Margaret Lansing, Carol E. Andrews, and Eric Schopler, "Improvement of Teaching Effectiveness in Parents of Autistic Children," *Journal of the American Academy of Child Psychiatry* 17, no. 4 (1978): 625–39, 627. Kozloff's program was based on social exchange theory. Kozloff (1998, 55–95).

110. Schopler and Reichler (1971, 93, 99).

111. Eric Schopler, "Changing Parental Involvement in Behavioral Treatment," 414.

112. Gerald R. Patterson, R. A. Littman, and W. C. Hinsey, "Parental Effectiveness as Reinforcers in the Laboratory and Its Relation to Child Rearing Practices and Adjustment in the Classroom," *Journal of Personality* 32, no. 2 (1964): 180–99; G. R. Patterson, R. Jones, J. Whittier, and Mary A. Wright, "A Behavior Modification Technique for a Hyperactive Child," *Behaviour Research and Therapy* 2, no. 2–4 (1965): 217–26. O'Dell refers to behavioral techniques

as a "technology" throughout his review, which called for the training of parents in multiple domains. O'Dell (1974, 430). Examples of books that encouraged parents of typically developing children to try behavioral techniques included Gerald R. Patterson, *Families: Applications of Social Learning to Family Life* (Champaign, IL: Research Press, 1971) and Wesley C. Becker, *Parents Are Teachers: A Child Management Program* (Champaign, IL: Research Press, 1971).

113. O. Ivar Lovaas, Robert Koegel, James Q. Simmons, and Judith Stevens Long, "Some Generalization and Follow-Up Measures on Autistic Children in Behavior Therapy," *Journal of Applied Behavior Analysis* 6, no. 1 (1973): 131–66. The comments of reviewers summarized by the journal following the article criticized Lovaas et al.'s argument that children who were institutionalized fared considerably less well on follow-up than those who stayed at home and received treatment from their parents, noting that "many factors" could account for differences between the two groups.

114. O'Dell (1974, 418, 430).

115. The first "systematic application of operant conditioning" as a treatment for autism was probably that of Marian K. DeMyer and C. B. Fester, according to Edward K. Morris, Charryse M. Fouquette, Nathaniel G. Smith, and Deborah E. Altus, "A History of Applied Behavior Analysis in the Treatment of Autism: Fathers, Originators, and Founders" (poster presented at the meeting of the International Society for the History of the Behavioral and Social Sciences, Toronto, Canada, June 26–29, 2008). Morris et al. note that this was not an example of ABA, the first use of which is rightly attributed to other researchers. See "Teaching New Social Behavior to Schizophrenic Children," *Journal of the American Academy of Child and Adolescent Psychiatry* 1, no. 3 (1962): 443–61; and C. B. Ferster and Marian K. DeMyer, "A Method for the Experimental Analysis of the Behavior of Autistic Children," *American Journal of Orthopsychiatry* 32, no. 1 (1962): 89–98.

116. Vey Michael Nordquist and Robert G. Wahler, "Naturalistic Treatment of an Autistic Child," *Journal of Applied Behavior Analysis* 6, no. 1 (1973): 79–87, 79, 85; O'Dell (1974, 418).

117. Benjamin L. Moore and Jon S. Bailey, "Social Punishment in the Modification of a Pre-School Child's 'Autistic-Like' Behavior with a Mother as Therapist," *Journal of Applied Behavior Analysis* 6, no. 3 (1973): 497–507; Margaret Wulbert, "The Generalization of Newly Acquired Behaviors by Parents and Child Across Three Different Settings: A Study of an Autistic Child," *Journal of Abnormal Child Psychology* 2, no. 2 (1974): 87–98.

118. Gep Coletti and Sandra L. Harris, "Behavior Modification in the Home: Siblings as Behavior Modifiers, Parents as Observers," *Journal of Abnormal Child Psychology* 5, no. 1 (1977): 21–30, 29.

119. Moore and Bailey, "Social Punishment in the Modification of a Pre-School Child's 'Autistic-Like' Behavior with a Mother as Therapist," 498.

120. James Fisher (2007) has described some of these memoirs as part of the literary genre of "conversion narratives," where the search for a child with autism's lost selfhood takes the form of a religious journey with a recovery as the goal. I am interested in a parallel set of claims about love and expertise that are compatible with the types of narrative structure that Fisher has aptly identified, and that are present even in memoirs that do not conform to the structure of a conversion narrative.

121. Kaufman (1976, 29–31).

122. Ibid., 39.

123. Ibid., 63.

124. Ibid., 63.

125. Ibid., 96.

126. Ibid., 143. In addition to writing several books about their techniques, Barry and Suzi (now Samahria) Kaufman now offer a range of services and instruction to families of children with disabilities at the Option Institute, where their son Raun is a facilitator.

127. Observers of the program at a later date noted that "Option states that no behavior is judged, yet in practice some behaviors are deliberately misinterpreted, or almost ignored, while others are welcomed and acted upon enthusiastically." Rita Jordan and Stuart Powell, "Reflections of the Option Method as a Treatment for Autism," *Journal of Autism and Developmental Disorders* 23, no. 4 (1993): 682–85, 684.

128. Barron and Barron (2002, 227–28).

129. Greenfeld (1986, 39).

130. Ibid., 79–83, 322.

131. Maurice (1993, 56–57).

132. Ibid., 104, 128.

133. Rapp (1999, 3, 146); Park (2001, 10).

134. Mechanic and Rochefort (1990).

135. A 2001 study by the National Academies of Science found that intensive behavioral therapies for autism were generally effective, and that the specific type of intervention mattered less than the number of hours of therapy received per week, ideally at least twenty-five hours. *Educating Children with Autism*, Commission on Behavioral and Social Sciences and Education (CBASSE; The National Academies Press, 2001). At least one self-advocate has testified in court against behavioral therapies. See Michelle Dawson, "The Misbehaviour of Behaviourists: Ethical Challenges to the Autism-ABA Industry," http://www.sentex.net/~nexus23/naa_aba.html; and Michelle Dawson, "An Autistic Victory: the True Meaning of the Auton Decision," http://www.sentex.net/~nexus23/naa_vic.html. For a description of one family's struggles to implement a behavioral therapy program, see Susan Sheehan, "The Autism Fight," *New Yorker*, December 1, 2003.

136. Leiter (2004) describes how parents contested their position as targets of professional authority, succeeding in changing the terminology used in Early Intervention programs but not the distribution of power within the programs.
137. Rimland (1972, 573).
138. Milt Freudenheim, "Battling Insurers over Autism Treatment," *New York Times*, December 21, 2004.
139. Jane Gross, "Continuing Education: A Master's in Self-Help," *New York Times*, April 20, 2008.
140. There are different reported ranges for the cost of a year of behavioral therapy. Benedict Carey, in "To Treat Autism, Parents Take a Leap of Faith" (*New York Times,* December 27, 2004), reported $40,000–$60,000. An article in the APA *Monitor* (Lea Winerman, "Effective Education for Autism," http://www.apa.org/monitor/dec04/autism.html), reported $40,000–$80,000.
141. The National School Board Association, quoted in Linda Greenhouse, "Legal Victory for Families of Disabled Students," *New York Times*, May 22, 2007.

Interlude

1. The term was probably first used in print by Judy Singer (1999), who says that she coined the term in 1997.
2. Charlton (1998). I have also referred to Shapiro (1994) for the history of the disability rights movement, and Lennard Davis's (2006) essay on the emergence of the concept of normality in the nineteenth century.
3. A number of scholars have written about the neurodiveristy movement from a social science perspective. For summaries of claims made by self-advocates (and thoughtful analyses and critiques of the movement), see Orsini (2009) and Ortega (2009).
4. Durbin-Westby (2010); Robertson (2010).
5. Bagatell (2010, 36).
6. On the invention of the "moral idiot" and "moral imbecile" and associated treatment programs during the latter half of the nineteenth century, see Trent (1994, 20–23).
7. The act was originally the Education for All Handicapped Act, PL 94-142, of 1975. On the growth of advocacy groups for parents of children with cognitive disabilities and a history of the theories that have been applied to the education of children with cognitive disabilities, see Trent (1994).
8. Landsman (2009, 99).
9. Bruno Bettelheim and Emmy Sylvester, "Notes on the Impact of Parental Occupations: Some Cultural Determinants of Symptom Choice in Emotionally Disturbed Children," *American Journal of Orthopsychiatry* 20, no. 4 (1950): 785–95.

10. Sandra L. Harris, "The Family and the Autistic Child: A Behavioral Perspective," in "The Family with Handicapped Members," special issue, *Family Relations* 33 no. 1 (1984): 127–34, 132; Lisa A. Osborne, Louise McHugh, Jo Saunders, and Phil Reed, "Parenting Stress Reduces the Effectiveness of Early Teaching Interventions for Autistic Spectrum Disorders," *Journal of Autism and Developmental Disorders* 38, no. 6 (2008): 1092–1103; Richard P. Hastings and Emma Johnson, "Stress in U.K. Families Conducting Intensive Home-Based Behavioral Intervention for Their Young Child," *Journal of Autism and Developmental Disorders* 31, no. 3 (2001): 327–36, 328.

11. Interestingly, a child's need for support in daily activities or his or her level of intellectual disability seems to have little to do with parents' reported stress. Annette Estes, Jeffrey Munson, Geraldine Dawson, Elizabeth Koehler, et al., "Parenting Stress and Psychological Functioning among Mothers of Preschool Children with Autism and Developmental Delay," *Autism* 13, no. 4 (2009): 375–87, 383; Patricia A. Rao and Deborah C. Beidel, "The Impact of Children with High-Functioning Autism on Stress, Sibling Adjustment, and Family Functioning," *Behavior Modification* 33, no. 4 (2009): 437–51.

12. David E. Gray, "Perceptions of Stigma: The Parents of Autistic Children," *Sociology of Health and Illness* 15, no. 1 (1993): 102–20, 111.

13. Estes et al., "Parenting Stress and Psychological Functioning among Mothers of Preschool Children with Autism and Developmental Delay," 376.

14. Specifically, stress was associated with "regulatory problems" (e.g., problems managing sleep, eating, and emotions), and "externalizing behavior," which can include hyperactivity, explosive outbursts, or aggression. Naomi Ornstein Davis and Alice S. Carter, "Parenting Stress in Mothers and Fathers of Toddlers with Autism Spectrum Disorders: Associations with Child Characteristics," *Journal of Autism and Developmental Disorders* 38, no. 7 (2008): 1278–91. One study did find that maternal stress, in particular, was related to a child's level of social skills. Mary J. Baker-Ericzen, Lauren Brookman-Frazee, and Aubyn Stahmer, "Stress Levels and Adaptability of Toddlers With and Without Autism Spectrum Disorders," *Research and Practice for Persons with Severe Disabilities* 30, no. 4 (2005): 194–204, 201.

15. Gray (1993).

16. Gray (1994) found parents using a variety of strategies, including religion and activism, to cope with stress. Ryan and Cole (2009, 51) write that "activism, then, may be a mechanism for expressing, in a 'selfless' way, the mothers' aspirations and needs."

17. Landsman (2003, 1950).

18. Schopler and Mesibov (1984, 7).

19. E. James Anthony, "Editorial Query," *Journal of Autism and Childhood Schizophrenia* 4, no. 2 (1974): 93. This particular entry was brought to my attention through a reference in Eyal, Hart, Onculer, Oren, et al. (2010, 181).

20. Mary S. Akerley, "Parents Speak: Introduction," *Journal of Autism and Childhood Schizophrenia* 4, no. 4 (1974): 347.

21. Ibid., 347; Margaret A. Dewey and Margaret P. Everard, "The Near-Normal Autistic Adolescent," *Journal of Autism and Childhood Schizophrenia* 4, no. 4 (1974): 348–56, 351. The article was written by a "correspondence panel of parents and professionals from the British and American National Society for Autistic Children" who exchanged observations via airmail (348).

22. Eric Schopler introduced the article, noting that "parents' use of behavior modification techniques predates that of the behavioral scientists, and no doubt has played a part in the scientific formulation." David Park, "Parents Speak: Operant Conditioning of a Speaking Autistic Child," *Journal of Autism and Childhood Schizophrenia* 4, no. 2 (1974): 189–91.

23. David Park and Philip Youderian, "Light and Number: Ordering Principles in the World of an Autistic Child," *Journal of Autism and Childhood Schizophrenia* 4, no. 4 (1974): 313–23.

24. Ruth Christ Sullivan, "Poems on Autism: Beyond Research Data," *Journal of Autism and Childhood Schizophrenia* 7, no. 4 (1977): 397–407.

25. Ruth Christ Sullivan, "Hunches on Some Biological Factors in Autism," *Journal of Autism and Developmental Disorders* 5, no. 2 (1975): 177–84.

26. Ruth Christ Sullivan, "Why Do Autistic Children…?" *Journal of Autism and Developmental Disorders* 10, no. 2 (1980): 231–41.

27. Mary S. Akerley, introduction to Henry A. Beyer, "Parents Speak: Changes in the Parent–Child Legal Relationship—What They Mean to the Clinician and Researcher," *Journal of Autism and Childhood Schizophrenia* 7, no. 1 (1977): 83–108.

28. Mr. and Mrs. M. Fields, "Parents Speak: The Relationship Between Problem Behaviors and Food Allergies: One Family's Story" and comments by Charles H. Banov, Linus Pauling, and Morris A. Lipton, *Journal of Autism and Childhood Schizophrenia* 6, no. 1 (1976): 75–91.

29. Mary S. Akerley, "Springing the Tradition Trap," *Journal of Autism and Childhood Schizophrenia* 5, no. 4 (1975): 373–80, 376, 379.

30. "Springing the Tradition Trap Continued," *Journal of Autism and Childhood Schizophrenia* 6, no. 1 (1976): 93–100. Stella Chess wrote that "I find myself in substantial agreement with the points made by Ms. Akerley. Since a number of children with autism or strong autistic features come to me for evaluation, after having been seen by others, I have duplicated in my clinical experience her examples of subjective and insufficiently substantiated interpretations of symbolic meanings of the children's behavior—interpretations which have been of little help as a guide to management" (94). William Goldfarb wrote that "Ms. Akerley's 'traditional' psychiatrist can probably be better described as incompetent and he would not survive in most of our therapeutic programs" (98). Leon Eisenberg was the only respondent who seconded Aker-

ley's call for "the therapist to become a social advocate," although Stella
Chess saw "no principled professional objection to involvement in community activity and education regarding children's needs of any kind" (97, 95).

31. Kenneth L. Lichstein and Laura Schreibman, "Employing Electric Shock with
Autistic Children: A Review of the Side Effects," *Journal of Autism and Child-
hood Schizophrenia* 6, no. 2 (1976): 163–73; Mary S. Akerley, "Parents Speak:
Reactions to Employing Electric Shock with Autistic Children (Introduc-
tion)," *Journal of Autism and Childhood Schizophrenia* 6, no. 3 (1976): 289;
"Parents Speak: Comments," *Journal of Autism and Childhood Schizophrenia*
6, no. 3 (1976): 290–94; Kenneth L. Lichstein, "Reply to Reader Comments on
'Employing Electric Shock with Autistic Children,'" *Journal of Autism and
Childhood Schizophrenia* 7, no. 3 (1977); "Parents Speak: Comments," *Journal
of Autism and Childhood Schizophrenia* 7, no. 2 (1977): 199–202.

32. Nancy McClung, "Risk/Benefit," in Ruth Christ Sullivan, "Risks and Benefits in the Treatment of Autistic Children," *Journal of Autism and Childhood
Schizophrenia* 8, no. 1 (1978): 111–13, 108.

33. Dan Torisky and Connie Torisky, "Parents Speak: Sex Education and Sexual
Awareness Building for Autistic Children and Youth: Some Viewpoints and
Considerations," *Journal of Autism and Developmental Disorders* 15, no. 2
(1985): 213–27. This was the only column edited by the Toriskys and the last
"Parents Speak" column featured in the journal. The Toriskys wrote, "In
modifying this behavior, it is we who must forget that this is the emotionally charged subject of sexual behavior, and treat this educational process
in much the same manner that we deal with table manners, how to cross
the street, or what to say to the waiter in the restaurant." Dan and Connie
Torisky, "Response," *Journal of Autism and Developmental Disorders* 15, no.
2 (1985): 221–23, 222.

34. "It addresses problems that parents (and truly concerned professionals) talk
about when they are speaking with their hearts: *Who* will care for our severely handicapped children when we're gone?" Ruth Christ Sullivan, "Parents Speak: Needs of the Older Child," (Introduction), *Journal of Autism and
Childhood Schizophrenia* 7, no. 3 (1977): 287–88, 287.

35. Katharine Sangree Stokes, "Planning for the Future of a Severely Handicapped Autistic Child," *Journal of Autism and Childhood Schizophrenia* 7,
no. 3 (1977): 288–98, 289.

36. Ibid., 291.

37. Leonard G. Berger, "Working within the System (Response to Katharine
Sangree Stokes, "Planning for the Future of a Severely Handicapped Autistic Child")," *Journal of Autism and Childhood Schizophrenia* 7, no. 3 (1977),
299–301, 301.

38. Clara Claiborne Park, "The Limits of Normalization (Response to Katharine
Sangree Stokes, "Planning for the Future of a Severely Handicapped Autis-

tic Child")," *Journal of Autism and Childhood Schizophrenia* 7, no. 3 (1977): 301–2, 302.

39. Mesibov explained that normalization was developed by Wolfensberger (1972) as a principle to guide the design of programs for individuals diagnosed with mental retardation, but it began to be applied to autism as well. The concept was incorporated into law in the 1975 Education for All Handicapped Children Act's requirement that educators provide the "least restrictive environment" possible. A "Parents Speak" column on the concept of normalization included comments from both professionals and parents and ran in conjunction with the article by Gary Mesibov, "Implications of the Normalization Principle for Psychotic Children," *Journal of Autism and Childhood Schizophrenia* 6, no. 4 (1976): 360–65; Mary S. Akerley, "Parents Speak: Introduction," *Journal of Autism and Childhood Schizophrenia* 6, no. 4 (1976): 359.

40. "Responses" to Gary Mesibov, "Implications of the Normalization Principle for Psychotic Children," *Journal of Autism and Childhood Schizophrenia* 6, no. 4 (1976): 365–72, especially James P. Chapman, "Normalization a Philosophy, Not a Treatment Strategy," 365–66.

41. Ruth Christ Sullivan (with contributions from Corinne Fredricks, O. Ivar Lovaas, Norris G. Haring, Amy L. Lettick, Eric Schopler, Robert J. Reichler, Donald J. Cohen, Sheridan Neimark, Ellen L. Wike, Anne M. Donnellan, and Gary W. LaVigna), "What Does Deinstitutionalization Mean for Our Children?" *Journal of Autism and Developmental Disorders* 11, no. 3 (1981): 347–56.

42. Amy Lettick, "Letter to the Editor: Dissent from NSAC Deinstitutionalization Resolution," *Journal of Autism and Developmental Disorders* 12, no. 1 (1982): 95–96; Ruth Christ Sullivan, "What Does Deinstitutionalization Mean for Our Children?" 350–51.

43. This is also true of contemporary parents of children with disabilities. Landsman (2005, 139) writes that "mothers' understandings, fitting neatly into neither the medical nor the social model but steeped in the everyday experience of interdependency, may yet converge with efforts within disability studies to reexamine the identity of disability and create a more inclusive world."

44. Landsman (2005, 138).

45. Deborah Barnbaum (2008, 204–7) argues that "autistic integrity" is violated by efforts to cure autism in adults, but she spends very little time discussing the ethics of treatments that may ameliorate but not cure autism.

46. Landsman (2009, 212).

47. Barnbaum (2008, 161) refers to the concept of a child's right to an "open future" to argue for the ethical acceptability of a genetic test used to prevent autism. Landsman's (2009, 183–87) findings suggest that parents may reference their child's future as they consider treatment options, but that other

factors, including social pressures to provide treatments, also figure in their considerations.

48. Landsman (2009, 213); Shakespeare (2006).

49. Bruno Betteheim. "Training the Child-Care Worker in a Residential Setting," *American Journal of Orthopsychiatry* 36, no. 4 (1966): 694–705, 705.

50. Patricia Howlin, Susan Goode, Jane Hutton, and Michael Rutter, "Adult Outcome for Children with Autism," *Journal of Child Psychology and Psychiatry* 45, no. 2 (2004): 212–29.

51. As Landsman (2009, 213) argues, their understanding that dependence is consistent with human dignity allows them to move beyond existing theoretical models of disability.

Part Two
Chapter 4

1. "At the time I was born, we had no idea autism ran in the family." Zaks (2010).

2. Stacey (2003, 254–55).

3. Jeremy Veenstra-VanderWeele, Susan L. Christian, and Edwin H. Cook Jr., "Autism as a Paradigmatic Complex Genetic Disorder," *Annual Review of Genomics and Human Genetics* 5 (2004): 379–405, 379.

4. Uta Frith (1991, 32) affirmed Hans Asperger's comment that many scientists could wish that they had a "dash" of autism.

5. Herbert (2005a).

6. Lindee (2005, 2).

7. A number of studies exist on the history of research in molecular biology and genetics, as well as the markets for and ideological stakes involved in genetics research in the present. This discussion was informed in particular by Doyle (1997), Haraway (1997b), Keller (1995, 2000), Kay (2000), and Lindee (2005).

8. Conrad (1999, 236).

9. Keller (2000, 10).

10. Lindee (2005, 2) explains how lay knowledge about genetic disorders is incorporated into published, authoritative knowledge about the disorders.

11. Government-funded autism research takes place at a number of sites. The NIH funds the Collaborative Programs of Excellence in Autism (CPEAs) through member institutes, as well as the Studies to Advance Autism Research and Treatment Centers Program (STAART) network, in addition to individual researcher grants, through funding provided in the Children's Health Act of 2000. A joint NIH and CDC program called Centers of Excellence for Autism and Developmental Disabilities Research and Epidemiology (CADDRE) is devoted to epidemiological research. The 2006 Combating Autism Act authorized Congress to appropriate $860 million in funding over

five years to autism research, although individual pieces of legislation must be passed to actually provide the funds. As part of the 2007 Defense Appropriations Act, the Department of Defense began funding autism research in order to attempt to help military families that have children with autism, with an emphasis on developing treatments.

12. Sunder Rajan (2003).

13. Jonathan Sebat, quoted in Nikhil Swaminathan, "Autism Risk May Lie in Fragile Areas of Genetic Code," *Scientific American*, March 16, 2007. Attempts have been made to develop a "unified theory" that will tie together sporadic cases of autism with the far less common inherited cases. See Xiaoyue Zhao, Anthony Leotta, Vlad Kustanovich, Clara Lajonchere, et al., "A Unified Genetic Theory for Sporadic and Inherited Autism," *Proceedings of the National Academy of Science* 104, no. 31 (July 2007): 12831–36.

14. "The Child Is Father," *Time*, July 25, 1960.

15. Rimland (1964, 38).

16. Rosenberg (1992).

17. Michael Rutter and Lawrence Bartak, "Causes of Infantile Autism: Some Considerations from Recent Research," *Journal of Autism and Childhood Schizophrenia* 1, no. 1 (1971): 20–32, 24

18. Adams (2005, 214).

19. Rutter and Bartak, "Causes of Infantile Autism," 25.

20. D. R. Hanson and I. I. Gottesman, "The Genetics, If Any, of Infantile Autism and Childhood Schizophrenia," *Journal of Autism and Childhood Schizophrenia* 6, no. 3 (1976): 209–34.

21. Susan Folstein and Michael Rutter, "Infantile Autism: A Genetic Study of 21 Twin Pairs," *Journal of Child Psychology and Psychiatry* 18, no. 4 (1977): 297–321, 308, 298, 304. Also see Susan Folstein and Michael Rutter, "Genetic Influences and Infantile Autism," *Nature* 265, no. 5596 (February 1977): 726–28.

22. M. Mary Konstantareas, "Early Developmental Backgrounds of Autistic and Mentally Retarded Children: Future Research Directions," *Psychiatric Clinics of North America* 9, no. 4 (1986): 671–88.

23. Susan E. Folstein and Joseph Piven, "Etiology of Autism: Genetic Influences," *Pediatrics* 87, no. 5, pt. 2 (1991): 767–73. The two twin studies are E. R. Ritvo, B. J. Freeman, A. Mason-Brothers, A. Mo, et al., "Concordance for the Syndrome of Autism in 40 Pairs of Afflicted Twins," *American Journal of Psychiatry* 142 (1985): 74–77; and S. Steffenberg, C. Gillberg, and L Holmgren, "A Twin Study of Autism in Denmark, Finland, Iceland, Norway, and Sweden," *Journal of Child Psychology and Psychiatry* 30, no. 3 (1986): 405–16.

24. These have included the serotonin transporter gene, the reelin gene (which is involved in neuronal migration), dopamine-related genes, and MECP2, the gene found in the majority of girls with Rett syndrome, another pervasive developmental disorder. See Janine A. Lamb, Jeremy R. Parr, Anthony J. Bailey, and Anthony P. Monaco, "Autism: In Search of Susceptibility Genes," *Neu-*

roMolecular Medicine 2, no. 1 (2002): 11–28, 19. Candidate gene approaches are also discussed in Jeremy Veenstra-VanderWeele and Edwin H. Cook Jr., "Molecular Genetics of Autism Spectrum Disorder," *Molecular Psychiatry* 9, no. 9 (2004): 819–32.

25. Catherine Lord, Bennett L. Leventhal, and Edwin H. Cook Jr., "Quantifying the Phenotype in Autism Spectrum Disorders," *American Journal of Medical Genetics* 105, no. 1 (2001): 36–38, 37. The ADI-R was published in 1994, the ADOS in 1999. On the use of the "broader autism phenotype" in genetic studies, see Susan E. Folstein, Erica Bisson, Susan L. Santangelo, and Joseph Piven, "Finding Specific Genes That Cause Autism: A Combination of Approaches Will Be Needed to Maximize Power," *Journal of Autism and Developmental Disorders* 28, no. 5 (1998): 439–45; Geraldine Dawson, Sara Webb, Bernard D. Schellenberg, Stephen Dager, et al., "Defining the Broader Phenotype of Autism: Genetic, Brain, and Behavioral Perspectives," *Development and Psychopathology* 14, no. 3 (2002): 581–611; and Thomas H. Wassink, Linda M. Brzustowicz, Christopher W. Bartlett, and Peter Szatmari, "The Search for Autism Disease Genes," *Mental Retardation and Developmental Disabilities Research Reviews* 10, no. 4 (2004): 272–83.

26. L. B. Jorde, S. J. Hasstedt, E. R. Ritvo, A. Mason-Brothers, et al., "Complex Segregation Analysis of Autism," *American Journal of Human Genetics* 49, no. 5 (1991): 932–38.

27. Susan E. Folstein and Beth Rosen-Sheidley, "Genetics of Autism: Complex Aetiology for a Heterogeneous Disorder," *Nature Reviews Genetics* 2, no. 12 (2001): 943–55.

28. Ibid., 953.

29. Wassink et al., "The Search for Autism Disease Genes," 272, 281.

30. The authors cited a concordance rate of 60 percent–91 percent for monozygotic twins "depending on whether a narrow or broad phenotype is considered," which by the conclusion of the article was transformed into "the less than 10% of variance that is not genetic." Veenstra-VanderWeele et al., "Autism as a Paradigmatic Complex Genetic Disorder," 380, 396.

31. Laurena A. Weiss, Yiping Shen, Joshua M. Korn, Dan E. Arking, et al. "Association between Microdeletion at 16p11.2 and Autism," *New England Journal of Medicine* 358, no. 7 (2008): 667–75.

32. Lamb et al., "Autism: In Search of Susceptibility Genes," 13.

33. Hedgecoe (2001). Bumiller (2009, 878) has also noted the similarities between the rhetoric of scientists involved in autism genetics and Hedgecoe's observation that Alzheimer's researchers have capitalized on the "complex nature" of the disorder to justify continued research despite unpromising results.

34. Jonathan Sebat, B. Lakshmi, Dheeraj Malhotra, Jennifer Troge, et al., "Strong Association of De Novo Copy Number Mutations with Autism," *Science* 316, no. 445 (2007): 445–49. The Autism Genome Project Consortium, "Mapping Autism Risk Loci Using Genetic Linkage and Chromosomal Rearrange-

ments," *Nature Genetics* 39, no. 3 (2007): 319–28, used a combination of methods, including a genome scan of multiplex families and analysis of copy number variations. A study that used families with high rates of intermarriage to identify genes related to learning in association with autism cases was Eric M. Morrow, Seung-Yun Yoo, Steven W. Flavell, Tae-Kyung Kim, et al., "Identifying Autism Loci and Genes by Tracing Recent Shared Ancestry," *Science* 321, no. 218 (2008): 218–23.

35. Conrad (1999, 236); John N. Constantino, Clara Lajonchere, Marin Lutz, Teddi Gray, et al., "Autistic Social Impairment in the Siblings of Children with Pervasive Developmental Disorders," *American Journal of Psychiatry* 163, no. 2 (2006): 294–96.

36. A genetics education site sponsored by NAAR included the identification of Rett syndrome on its timeline, "A Look at the Genetics of Autism," although it is not clear that the two disorders are related by anything but their shared features of impaired communication and interaction. http://www.exploringautism .org/history/index.htm.

37. Ruthie E. Amir, Ignatia B. Van den Veyver, Mimi Wan, Charles Q. Tran, et al., "Rett Syndrome Is Caused by Mutations in X-linked *MECP2*, Encoding Methyl-CpG-Binding Protein 2," *Nature Genetics* 23 (1999): 185–88.

38. Andreas Rett, "Uber ein eigenartiges hirnatrophisches Syndrom bei Hyperammonamie im Kindesaler," *Wiener Medizinische Wochenschrift* 116 (1966): 723–26, cited in Neumarker (2003).

39. Ruthie E. Amir, Ignatia B. Van den Veyver, Rebecca Schultz, Denise M. Malicki, et al., "Influence of Mutation Type and X Chromosome Inactivation on Rett Syndrome Phenotypes," *Annals of Neurology* 47, no. 5 (2000): 670–79.

40. "Mouse with Rett Syndrome May Provide Model for Testing Treatments, Understanding Disorder," (NIH News Release), National Institute of Child Health and Human Development, July 29, 2002.

41. This research is described in Mona D. Shahbazian, Juan I. Young, Lisa A. Yuva-Paylor, Corinne M. Spencer, et al., "Mice with Truncated MeCP2 Recapitulate Many Rett Syndrome Features and Display Hyperacetylation of Histone H3," *Neuron* 35, no. 2 (2002): 243–54.

42. This was not only a feature of the public presentation of this research. In the publication reporting the creation of a mouse model for Rett syndrome, the extraordinary recapitulation of symptoms in the mouse was also emphasized. Ibid., 246. A video of the Rett syndrome mice can be found at http:// www.hhmi.org/biointeractive/neuroscience/rett_mouse.html.

43. "It is difficult to comprehend how dysfunction of this protein, which might be predicted to cause derepression of hundreds or thousands of genes, leads to primarily neurological phenotypes. To investigate this paradox and understand the disease mechanism, animal models should prove useful." Shahbazian et al., "Mice with Truncated MeCP2 Recapitulate Many Rett Syndrome Features," 243.

44. Amir et al., "Influence of Mutation Type and X Chromosome Inactivation on Rett Syndrome Phenotypes," 671.

45. Claudia Dreifus, "A Conversation with Huda Zoghbi: Researchers Toil with Genes on the Fringe of a Cure," *New York Times*, March 22, 2005.

46. The exact figure was $2,246,817. Antonio Regalado, "Wealth Effect: A Hedge-Fund Titan's Millions Stir Up Research into Autism—James Simons Taps Big Stars from Outside Field to Find a Genetic Explanation—Three Personal DNA Tests," *Wall Street Journal*, December 15, 2005.

47. Simons's growing conviction that genetics research was the key to autism was given support when, according to Simons, he discovered that James Watson was of the same opinion when they met at a dinner party. Ibid.

48. Jacky Guy, Jian Gan, Jim Selfridge, Stuart Cobb, et al., "Reversal of Neurological Defects in a Mouse Model of Rett Syndrome," *Science* 315, no. 5815 (2007): 1143–47.

49. The precise phrasing is "Our data show that developmental absence of MeCP2 does not irreversibly damage neurons, suggesting that RTT is not strictly a neurodevelopmental disorder." Ibid., 1145.

50. The generalization to other autism spectrum disorders (accomplished by emphasizing the status of RTT as an autism spectrum disorder) was reflected in the press release on the research "Reversal of Symptoms in an Autism Spectrum Disorder: Rett Syndrome is Reversed in Genetic Mouse Model," Rett Syndrome Research Foundation, http://www.rsrf.org/reversal_experiment/index.html; and a video, *Families Comment on the Experiment*. Both were posted on the Rett Syndrome Research Foundation Web site. The International Rett Syndrome Association and the Rett Syndrome Research Foundation merged in 2007 to form the International Rett Syndrome Foundation; the Web site is no longer active.

51. Nikhil Swaminathan, "Reversal of Fortune: Researchers Erase Symptoms of Rett Syndrome," *ScientificAmerican.com* (February 8, 2007), http://www.scientificamerican.com/article.cfm?id=reversal-of-fortune-resea.

52 Jacqueline N. Crawley, "Designing Mouse Behavioral Tasks Relevant to Autistic-Like Behaviors," *Mental Retardation and Developmental Disabilities Research Reviews* 10, no. 4 (2004): 248–58.

53. Chang-Hyuk Kwon, Bryan W. Luikart, Jing Zhou, Sharon A. Matheny, et al., "Pten Regulates Neuronal Arborization and Social Interaction in Mice," *Neuron* 50, no. 3 (2006), 377–88; and commentary, Joy M. Greer and Anthony Wynshaw-Boris, "*Pten* and the Brain: Sizing Up Social Interaction," *Neuron* 50, no. 3 (2006): 343–44.

54. David G. Amaral, Margaret D. Bauman, and C. Mills Schumann, "The Amygdala and Autism: Implications from Non-Human Primate Studies," *Genes, Brain and Behavior* 2, no. 5 (2003): 295–302.

55. See, for instance, Margaret Bauman and Thomas L. Kemper, "Histoanatomic Observations of the Brain in Early Infantile Autism," *Neurology* 35,

no. 6 (1985): 866–74; Margaret Bauman, "Microscopic Neuroanatomic Ab-
normalities in Autism," *Pediatrics*, 87, no. 5 (1991): 791–96; Margaret Bau-
man, "Brief Report: Neuroanatomic Observations of the Brain in Pervasive
Developmental Disorders," *Journal of Autism and Developmental Disorders*
26, no. 2 (1996): 199–203; and Margaret L. Bauman and Thomas L. Kemper,
"Observations on the Purkinje Cells in the Cerebellar Vermis in Autism,"
Journal of Neuropathology and Experimental Neurology 55, no. 5 (1996): 613.
On reconsiderations of the results, Elizabeth R. Whitney, Thomas L. Kemper,
Margaret L. Bauman, Douglas L. Rosene, et al., "Cerebellar Purkinje Cells are
Reduced in a Subpopulation of Autistic Brains: A Stereological Experiment
Using Calbindin D28k," *The Cerebellum* 7, no. 3 (2008): 406–16.

56. Nouchine Hadjikhani, Robert M. Joseph, Josh Snyder, and Helen Tager-
Flusberg, "Anatomical Differences in the Mirror Neuron System and Social
Cognition Network in Autism," *Cerebral Cortex* 16, no. 9 (2006): 1276–82, 1276.

57. Baron-Cohen (1997).

58. Eric Courchesne, "Brain Development in Autism: Early Overgrowth Followed by Premature Arrest of Growth," *Mental Retardation and Developmental Disabilities Research Reviews* 10, no. 2 (2004): 106–11; Martha R. Herbert, David A. Ziegler, Nikos Makris, Pauline A. Filipek, et al., "Localization
of White Matter Volume Increase in Autism and Developmental Language
Disorder," *Annals of Neurology* 55, no. 4 (2004): 530–40.

59. Martha R. Herbert, "Large Brains in Autism: The Challenge of Pervasive Ab-
normality," *Neuroscientist* 11, no. 5 (2005): 417–40. On changing programs in
brain imaging research in autism, see Herbert (2004).

60. Diana I. Vargas, Caterina Nascimbene, Chitra Krishnan, Andrew W. Zimmerman, et al., "Neuroglial Activation and Neuroinflammation in the Brain
of Patients with Autism," *Annals of Neurology* 57, no. 1 (2005): 67–81.

61. J. L. R. Rubenstein and M. M. Merzenich, "Model of Autism: Increased Ratio
of Excitation/Inhibition in Key Neural Systems," *Genes, Brain and Behavior*
2, no. 5 (2003): 255–67; Rajesh K. Kana, Timothy A. Keller, Nancy J. Min-
shew, and Marcel Adam Just, "Inhibitory Control in High-Functioning Autism: Decreased Activation and Underconnectivity in Inhibition Networks,"
Biological Psychiatry 62, no. 3 (2007): 198–206.

62. Simon Baron-Cohen and Matthew Belmonte, "Autism: A Window onto the
Development of the Social and Analytic Brain," *Annual Review of Neuroscience* 28 (2005): 109–26.

63. Matthew K. Belmonte, Greg Allen, Andrea Beckel-Mitchener, Lisa M. Bou-
langer, et al., "Autism and Abnormal Development of Brain Connectivity,"
Journal of Neuroscience 24, no. 42 (2004): 9228–31.

64. Matthew K. Belmonte, Edwin H. Cook Jr., George M. Anderson, John L. R.
Rubenstein, et al., "Autism as a Disorder of Neural Information Processing:
Directions for Research and Targets for Therapy," *Molecular Psychiatry* 9,
no. 7 (2004), 646–63.

65. The Autism Tissue Program was founded by the National Alliance for Autism Research. Brains are kept at the Harvard Brain Tissue Resource Center. Information on brain donations on the LADDERS Web site can be found at http://www.ladders.org/pages/Brain-Donations.html. The Autism Tissue Program Web site is located at http://www.autismtissueprogram.org/site/c.nlKUL7MQIsG/b.5183271/k.BD86/Home.htm.

66. On the iconic power of images of brains, especially those that seem to bring the visible differences of disordered brains into sharp relief, see Dumit (2003).

67. Their suggestions are taken up by sociologists and psychologists, for instance Christopher Badcock (2004), who follows Simon Baron-Cohen in viewing autism as an extreme of male cognitive characteristics.

68. Quotes are from a CAN fundraising pamphlet, sent December 2003 (Los Angeles, CA: Cure Autism Now).

69. Rebecca Muhle, Stephanie V. Trentacoste, and Isabelle Rapin. "The Genetics of Autism," *Pediatrics* 113, no. 5 (2004): e472–86, e473.

70. From the CAN Web site, http://www.cureautismnow.org/about/index.jsp (accessed August 4, 2005; no longer available).

71. On the range of strategies used by HIV/AIDS treatment activists, see Epstein (1995, 1996). For an account of the founding of the Pediatric AIDS Foundation, see Elizabeth Glaser (1991). Elizabeth Kilpatrick at CAN mentioned the connection during an interview in June 2003.

72. On the importance of families in driving research into familial dysautonomia, and the centrality of their experiential knowledge in the process of caregiving, see Lindee (2005, 156–87).

73. These normative practices are described by Merton (1973). On deviations from these norms in the practice of scientific work, see Mulkay (1976).

74. Aaron Zitner. "Whose DNA Is It, Anyway?" *LA Times*, July 18, 2003. In another account, there were six researchers, but the general terms of the account are the same. See Allan Coukell, "You Can Hurry Science," *Proto: Massachusetts General Hospital Dispatches from the Frontiers of Medicine* (Winter 2006), http://protomag.com/assets/you-can-hurry-science.

75. This came to over 800 samples from individuals with autism spectrum disorders, or over 1,000 samples including family members. Daniel H. Geschwind, Janice Sowinski, Catherine Lord, Portia Iversen, et al., "The Autism Genetic Resource Exchange: A Resource for the Study of Autism and Related Neuropsychiatric Conditions," *American Journal of Human Genetics* 69, no. 2 (2001): 463–66. General information on AGRE is available at www.agre.org. My information also comes from a visit to CAN/AGRE headquarters in August 2003 and an interview with Portia Iverson in November 2002.

76. CAN press release, http://www.cureautismnow.org/site/apps/nl/content2.asp?c=bhLOK2PILuF&b=1289185&ct=2676321&tr=y&auid=1771171 (accessed May 18, 2007; no longer available).

77. In this sense, AGRE functioned as a kind of "obligatory passage point" through which CAN became "indispensable" for other researchers because it succeeded in incorporating their interests. On the concept of the "obligatory passage point" in actor-network theory see Callon (1987). Heath, Rapp, and Taussig (2004, 164) make a similar point regarding Sharon and Patrick Terry's work to "insure their status as obligatory passage points," by assembling a collection of biological materials and family pedigrees, and by using intellectual property rights to the PXE gene identified in 2000 to compel researchers to follow rules of data-sharing.

78. Although it is difficult to draw a causal line from AGRE to the NIH's decision, Shestack and Iverson's work was arguably a precedent for this type of data-sharing, as one of the first advocacy efforts concerned specifically with sharing biological materials. Nelkin and Andrews (2001, 40–41) suggest that their approach was unique at the time. However, Iverson and Shestack were not the first activists to use their positions as parents and access to materials to manage the behavior of scientists—in addition to Sharon and Patrick Terry's work through PXE International, parent members of DEBRA (founded in 1979) assembled a tissue bank in order to promote research on epidermolysis bullosa. For descriptions of these organizations and other strategies for "organizing access" to genetic material, see Taussig (2005, 232) and Heath, Rapp, and Taussig (2004). On the revised NIH rules, see Charles Jennings, "Universities Unnerved by Revised Rules for Sharing NIH Research," *Nature* 430, no. 7003 (August 2004): 953. For "Final NIH Statement on Sharing Research Data" dated February 26, 2003, see http://grants.nih.gov/grants/guide/notice-files/NOT-OD-03-032.html.

79. NAAR staff member, interview, August 26, 2003.

80. For information on the structure of the program, see National Alliance for Autism Research, "NAAR Autism Genome Project: Frequently Asked Questions," http://www.autismspeaks.org/inthenews/naar_archive/largest_autism_genetics.php.

81. NAAR used a two-tiered review process for proposals, with a first review carried out by a board of advisors, after which a "lay review committee" consisting of members of the board of trustees who were parents or family members of people with autism reviewed the proposals again. CAN maintained similar provisions for input from parents, although the members of their Scientific Review Council were required *both* to have scientific degrees and be parents of people with autism. Alycia Halladay (associate director of research and programs, NAAR), personal communication, December 27, 2005; Therese Finazzo (grants officer, CAN), personal communication, January 6, 2006.

82. These included the Centers for Professional Excellence in Autism (CPEA), the International Molecular Genetic Study of Autism Consortium (IMGSAC), the Autism Genetics Cooperative (AGC), the Collaborative Programs of Excellence in Autism Research (CPEA), and AGRE. National Alliance for

Autism Research. "NAAR Autism Genome Project: Fact Sheet," www .autismspeaks.org/docs/agp1a.pdf. Four institutes of the NIH were involved: the National Institute of Mental Health (NIMH), National Institute of Child Health and Human Development (NICHD), National Institute of Neurological Disorders and Stroke (NINDS), and National Institute of Deafness and Other Communication Disorders (NIDCD).

83. NAAR, "Autism Speaks and the National Alliance for Autism Research (NAAR) Complete Merger" (press release, 2005), http://www.autismspeaks .org/press/autism_speaks_naar_merger.php; CAN, "Autism Speaks and Cure Autism Now Complete Merger: Combined Operations of Leading Autism Organizations Will Lead to Enhanced Research, Treatment and Advocacy Programs" (press release), http://www.autismspeaks.org/press/autism_speaks _can_complete.php).

84. Francesca Happe, Angelica Ronald, and Robert Plomin, "Time to Give Up on a Single Explanation for Autism," *Nature Neuroscience* 9, no. 10 (2006): 1218–20.

85. Autism Speaks, "Autism FAQ: NAAR Autism Genome Project: Frequently Asked Questions" (July 19, 2004), http://www.autismspeaks.org/inthenews/ naar_archive/largest_autism_genetics.php.

86. "Everything changed with the introduction of the Affymetrix GeneChip® Mapping 10K Array. It finally gave researchers the ability to see these tiny little genetic changes that will ultimately help them figure out what happens to the DNA of those affected with autism." Autism Speaks, "Autism FAQ: NAAR Autism Genome Project: Frequently Asked Questions"; The Autism Genome Project Consortium, "Mapping Autism Risk Loci Using Genetic Linkage and Chromosomal Rearrangements."

87. For instance, a program at the MIND Institute, an organization founded by parents at the University of California, Davis, aims to develop tests for "prospective parents." See Diana Hu-Lince, David W. Craig, Matthew J. Huentelman, and Dietrich A. Stephan, "The Autism Genome Project: Goals and Strategies," *American Journal of Pharmacogenomics* 5, no. 4 (2005): 233–46.

88. Art Caplan, "Would You Have Allowed Bill Gates to Be Born? Advances in Genetic Testing Pose Tough Questions," msnbc.com, http://www.msnbc.msn .com/id/7899821.

89. On the possibility that stories about "changelings," fairy children hidden in typical families, are historical accounts of autism, see Lorna Wing and David Potter, "The Epidemiology of Autistic Spectrum Disorders: Is the Prevalence Rising?" *Mental Retardation and Developmental Disabilities Research Reviews* 8, no. 3 (2002): 151–61, 151.

90. http://www.gettingthewordout.org/ (accessed May 27, 2007; no longer available).

91. Amy Harmon. "Finding Out: Adults and Autism: An Answer, but Not a Cure, for A Social Disorder," *New York Times*, April 29, 2004.

92. Rapp (2000); Rapp and Ginsburg (2001).

93. Of course, adults with autism are not a homogeneous group, and some identify as activists while resisting the notion that they can speak for other people with autism. In particular, see Durbin-Westby (2010).

94. Martijn Dekker, "On Our Own Terms: Emerging Autistic Culture" (online essay), http://trainland.tripod.com/martijn.htm (accessed October 14, 2004; no longer available); Jim Sinclair, "Autism Network International: The Development of a Community and Its Culture," http://www.autreat.com/History _of_ANI.html.

95. http://www.gettingthewordout.org/home.php (accessed December 26, 2005; no longer available). For a description of a later protest against a 2007 NYU "public service campaign," which served as a rallying point for the neurodiversity movement, see Kras (2010).

96. http://www.autistics.org/.

97. Although the site was initially published anonymously, Baggs later began writing a blog, including videos that make her identity clear as the author of the Web site.

98. Jim Sinclair, "Don't Mourn for Us," originally published in the Autism Network International newsletter, *Our Voice* 1, no. 3 (1993), based on a presentation given at the 1993 International Conference on Autism, Toronto, Canada, http://www.autreat.com/dont_mourn.html.

99. Ibid. Ian Hacking (2009b, 57) has taken the alien metaphor seriously in an essay on its use by both self-advocates and others, noting that the cognitive differences characteristic of autism make autistic ways of inhabiting the world appear truly "alien" to neurotypical humans. Bridging this difference may require effort on both sides of relationships.

100. Phil Schwartz, "Wearing Two Hats: On Being a Parent and On the Spectrum Myself." The article first appeared in the MAAP newsletter, vol. 2 (2004), http://www.grasp.org/new_art.htm. Schwartz is not the only person to reflect on the experience of parenthood on the autism spectrum. Another notable account is Prince-Hughes (2005). Also see the description of parents recognizing autism in themselves after their child was diagnosed in Harmon, "Finding Out."

101. Kristin Bumiller (2008, 971–72; 2009, 882) writes that spokespeople for neurodiversity not only are clear that "autistic differences are genetic variations found in the general population," but also that many "readily subscribe to" Simon Baron-Cohen's theory about autism as an example of the "extreme male brain."

102. See, for instance, the Autism Acceptance Project, a parent-run organization online at http://www.taaproject.com/, as well as Gernsbacher (2006).

103. Autreat orientation materials, quoted in Jim Sinclair, "Autism Network International: The Development of a Community and Its Culture," http://www .autreat.com/History_of_ANI.html.

104. Joyce Davidson (2009, 795–97, 802) describes how a distinctive autistic culture has emerged through online communities.

105. See, for instance, Adams (2005, 191).
106. Happe, Ronald, and Plomin, "Time to Give Up on a Single Explanation for Autism."
107. Asperger (1944/1991, 41).
108. Leon Eisenberg, "The Fathers of Autistic Children," *American Journal of Orthopsychiatry* 27, no. 4 (1957): 715–24, 721.
109. Bruno Bettelheim and Emmy Sylvester, "Notes on the Impact of Parental Occupations: Some Cultural Determinants of Symptom Choice in Emotionally Disturbed Children," *American Journal of Orthopsychiatry* 20, no. 4 (1950): 785–95; Simon Baron-Cohen, Sally Wheelwright, Carol Stott, Patrick Bolton, and Ian Goodyer, "Is There a Link between Engineering and Autism?" *Autism* 1, no. 1 (1997): 101–9; Ralph Adolphs, Michael L. Spezio, and Morgan Parlier, "Distinct Face-Processing Strategies in Parents of Autistic Children," *Current Biology* 18, no. 14 (2008): 1090–93.
110. Steve Silberman, "Is There an Epidemic of Autism in the Silicon Valley?" *Wired* (December 2001).
111. Rapp (2000).
112. "The field of complex genetics is replete with many researchers and reviewers who want to promote their overly focused interest in one method at the exclusion of others. However, it is essential that the restricted interests of patients with autism not be reflected in overly restrictive genetic approaches if we are to better understand the genetics of autism in the most expeditious and thorough manner." Veenstra-VanderWeele et al., "Autism as a Paradigmatic Complex Genetic Disorder," 379.
113. See, for instance, studies that link elevated levels of certain metabolites in children with autism to genetic polymorphisms, such as S. Jill James, Stepan Melnyk, Stefanie Jernigan, Mario A. Cleves, et al., "Metabolic Endophenotype and Related Genotypes are Associated with Oxidative Stress in Children with Autism," *American Journal of Medical Genetics Part B: Neuropsychiatric Genetics* 141, no. 8 (2006): 947–56. This work was based on findings of elevated levels of biomarkers associated with oxidative stress in children with autism versus controls, a finding that could be interpreted as evidence that environmental factors combined with genetic factors affect the clinical manifestations of autism. See S. Jill James, Paul Cutler, Stepan Melnyk, Stefanie Jernigan, et al., "Metabolic Biomarkers of Increased Oxidative Stress and Impaired Methylation Capacity in Children with Autism," *American Journal of Clinical Nutrition* 80, no. 6 (2004): 1611–17. Current studies such as the Early Autism Risk Longitudinal Investigation (EARLI) Study and the Autism Birth Cohort (The ABC Project) aim to correlate a range of environmental factors, including substances to which mothers were exposed, with genetic variations and autism symptoms. The EARLI Study, based at multiple U.S. sites, tracks pregnant women who already have a child with an autism spectrum disorder. See http://www.earlistudy.org/ and http://www.abc.columbia

.edu/Home.html. Thanks to Martine Lappe for educating me about current developments in this area.

114. See Jennifer Singh's (2010, 162, 134–47) discussion of the ethical implications of research on copy number variations (CNVs) in autism, one of which has revealed a link between some cases of autism and cancer risk, meaning that children must be more closely monitored for signs of the disease. Singh's dissertation also brings the history of genetic research on autism to the present, including an insightful discussion of the politics of scientific and public investment in genome-wide association studies.

115. For instance, Tyler Cowen writes that "I refer to autistics as the 'infovores' of modern society and I argue that along many dimensions we as a society are working hard to mimic their abilities at ordering and processing information. Tyler Cowen, "Autism as Academic Paradigm," *Chronicle of Higher Education*, August 13, 2009, http://chronicle.com/article/Autism-as-Academic-Paradigm/47033/.

116. "This trend in the science of autism is consistent [with], if not due to, political lobbying and independent funding of U.S. advocacy groups." Singh, Illes, Lazzeroni, and Hallmayer (2009, 793).

117. On the questions raised by seeing ourselves as "simultaneously biological things and human persons—when 'the biological' is fundamentally plastic," see Landecker (2005).

Chapter 5

1. Jack Zimmerman, in McCandless (2003, preface).

2. These surveys are most frequently conducted by groups troubled by the rate of complementary and alternative medicine (CAM) use. See Susan E. Levy, David S. Mandell, Stephanie Merhar, Richard F. Ittenbach, et al., "Use of Complementary and Alternative Medicine among Children Recently Diagnosed with Autistic Spectrum Disorder," *Journal of Developmental and Behavioral Pediatrics* 24, no. 6 (2003): 418–23, which reported a rate of 30 percent; and Susan L. Hyman and Susan E. Levy, "Introduction: Novel Therapies in Developmental Disorders—Hope, Reason, and Evidence," *Mental Retardation and Developmental Disabilities Research Reviews* 11, no. 2 (2005): 107–9. A survey of 112 families of children with an autism spectrum disorder found a rate of use of CAM of 74 percent, using a broad definition of CAM. See Ellen Hanson, Leslie A Kalish, Emily Bunce, Christine Curtis, et al., "Use of Complementary and Alternative Medicine among Children Diagnosed with Autism Spectrum Disorder," *Journal of Autism and Developmental Disorders* 37, no. 4 (2007): 628–36.

3. Helen H. L. Wong and Ronald G. Smith, "Patterns of Complementary and Alternative Medical Therapy Use in Children Diagnosed with Autism Spec-

trum Disorders," *Journal of Autism and Developmental Disorders* 36, no. 7 (2006): 901–9; Vanessa A. Green, Keenan A Pituch, Jonathan Itchon, Aram Choi, et al., "Internet Survey of Treatments Used by Parents of Children with Autism," *Research in Developmental Disabilities* 27, no. 1 (2006): 70–84.

4. This observation has been made by a number of researchers, but I am drawing mainly on Martha Herbert's ideas, for example, Herbert (2011).

5. "FDA Approves the First Drug to Treat Irritability Associated with Autism, Risperdal." (October 6, 2006), http://www.fda.gov/NewsEvents/Newsroom/PressAnnouncements/2006/ucm108759.htm. Also see Benjamin Chavez, Mapy Chavez-Brown, and Jose A. Rey, "Role of Risperidone in Children with Autism Spectrum Disorder," *The Annals of Pharmacotherapy* 40, no. 5 (2006): 909–16.

6. Benedict Carey, "Autism Therapies Still a Mystery, But Parents Take a Leap of Faith," *New York Times*, December 27, 2004.

7. Jennifer Levitz, "Desperate Parents Seek Autism's Cure," *Providence Journal*, August 27, 2005.

8. Gardner Harris and Anahad O'Connor, "On Autism's Cause, It's Parents vs. Research," *New York Times*, June 25, 2005.

9. Emily Shartin, "Difficult Choices. Variety of Treatments Face Parents of Autistic Children," *Boston Globe*, January 25, 2004.

10. James Mulick, quoted in Jeff Grabmeier, "As Autism Diagnoses Grow, So Do Number of Fad Treatments, Researchers Say," *Research News,* Ohio State University (August 20, 2007), http://researchnews.osu.edu/archive/fadaut.htm. Similar views were expressed in Jane Brody, "Trying Anything and Everything for Autism," *New York Times*, January 20, 2009.

11. American Academy of Pediatrics Committee on Children with Disabilities, "Counseling Families Who Choose Complementary and Alternative Medicine for Their Child with Chronic Illness or Disability," *Pediatrics* 107, no. 3 (2001): 598–601. On CAM as a means of "stress reduction," see Hanson et al., "Use of Complementary and Alternative Medicine among Children Diagnosed with Autism Spectrum Disorder," 634. A 2003 survey of CAM use in autism noted correctly that these treatments are often used to address "associated medical difficulties that standard treatments do not address," but did not linger on the possibility that such treatments might "affect autism-specific behaviors," despite parental beliefs. Their main concern was that if practitioners appeared dismissive, parents might avoid standard treatments. Levy et al., "Use of Complementary and Alternative Medicine among Children Recently Diagnosed with Autistic Spectrum Disorder," 418, 422.

12. On the potential risks of elimination diets, see Georgianne L. Arnold, Susan L. Hyman, Robert A. Mooney, and Russell S. Kirby, "Plasma Amino Acids Profiles in Children with Autism: Potential Risk of Nutritional Deficiencies," *Journal of Autism and Developmental Disorders* 33, no. 4 (2003): 449–54; and on concerns about the lack of evidence supporting biomedical interven-

tions, see Susan E. Levy and Susan L. Hyman, "Novel Treatments for Autistic Spectrum Disorders," *Mental Retardation and Developmental Disabilities Research Reviews* 11, no. 2 (2005): 131–42, 132.

13. Hanson et al., "Use of Complementary and Alternative Medicine Among Children Diagnosed with Autism Spectrum Disorder," 631–32. A second survey likewise found an association between both maternal and paternal education level and CAM use. Wong and Smith, "Patterns of Complementary and Alternative Medical Therapy Use in Children Diagnosed with Autism Spectrum Disorders," 907.

14. Adams (2005, 61).

15. Schreibman (2005, 7).On the practice of demarcating between science and nonscience as an "ideological style" adopted in scientists' public statements, see Gieryn (1983).

16. Schreibman (2005, 7, 10–12). Levy and Hyman write that "it is ironic that the intervention for treatment of children with Autistic Spectrum Disorders that has been most carefully studied is an alternative, off-label treatment that gained in popularity prior to adequate scientific scrutiny." Levy and Hyman, "Novel Treatments for Autistic Spectrum Disorders," 132.

17. Schreibman (2005, 4, 7).

18. Fitzpatrick (2009, xvi). Also see Roy Richard Grinker, "Review of *Defeating Autism: A Damaging Delusion*," *International Journal of Epidemiology*, 38, no. 5 (2009): 1415–17.

19. This chapter is based on fieldwork conducted from 2002 to 2008 at Defeat Autism Now! conferences and through interviews with practitioners and researchers who either use biomedical treatments or conduct research related to biomedical frameworks for understanding autism. I have referred to ARI/Defeat Autism Now! by name because it is a unique organization that would be immediately identifiable if I used a pseudonym. Because my fieldwork ended in 2008, my descriptions should not be taken as documentation of current ARI/Defeat Autism Now! recommendations or practices. In this discussion, I occasionally employ the abbreviation DAN! in favor of spelling out "Defeat Autism Now!" because this is the conventional spoken usage at conferences, although the abbreviation never appears in ARI's official materials. The organization dropped the Defeat Autism Now! name in 2011, but I have retained it because it was current at the time of my fieldwork.

20. For example, Levy and Hyman, "Novel Treatments for Autistic Spectrum Disorders," 132, who reference the "DAN!™ approach" as an example of "biological treatments" in general. Others sites that promote biomedical interventions include Autism One conferences and Talk About Curing Autism (TACA).

21. Patricia Morris Buckley, "Dr. Bernard Rimland Is Autism's Worst Enemy," *San Diego Jewish Journal*, October 2002; Bernard Rimland, quoted in Noel Osment, "Keying In on the Secret of Autism: Father Is Devoted to His Son, and

to Finding an Answer," *San Diego Union*, July 10, 1988. At one Defeat Autism Now! conference (Fall 2002, San Diego), Rimland told a joke that fell—resoundingly—flat. After a moment of embarrassed silence, the audience erupted in laughter, realizing that his inability to deliver the joke was in fact the joke itself.

22. Buckley, "Dr. Bernard Rimland is Autism's Worst Enemy"; Osment, "Keying In on the Secret of Autism."

23. The diagnosis was later confirmed by their pediatrician. Bernard Rimland, "The History of the Autism Research Institute and the Defeat Autism Now! (DAN!) Project," in Edelson and Rimland (2003, 13).

24. Rimland (1972).

25. Osment, "Keying In on the Secret of Autism"; Alan O. Ross, review of *Infantile Autism: The Syndrome and Its Implications for a Neural Theory of Behavior* (Appleton-Century-Crofts, 1964), *American Journal of Mental Deficiency* 69, no. 4 (1965): 592–93.

26. Rimland, "The History of the Autism Research Institute and the Defeat Autism Now! (DAN!) Project," 14. For the *Autism Research Review International,* see index of volumes 1 to 18, http://www.autism.com/ari/newsletter/index_a.asp.

27. See "Appendix: Suggested Diagnostic Check List" in Rimland (1964, 219). The checklist included questions about gut problems, reactions to "bright lights, bright colors, unusual sounds," "unusual cravings" for foods, loss of verbal skills after acquiring them, and fine motor coordination, along with more conventional diagnostic measures for autism. "Form E-2," a parent assessment of pharmaceutical therapies, biomedical treatments and special diets, has been produced and collated by ARI since 1967. They report that they have collected over 40,000 of these forms, designed to contrast the efficacy of a variety of treatments. Also see http://www.autism.com/pro_parentratings.asp, "Parent Ratings of Behavioral Effects of Biomedical Interventions," updated March 2009.

28. Williams (1956/1998, 5) drew on Archibald Garrod's idea of "chemical individuality" and "genetotrophic diseases" caused by interactions among genetic variation, unique nutritional needs, and environment leading to functional deficiencies. Murphy (2000, 101–3) describes how the idea of "biochemical individuality" was also important for clinicians developing the field of clinical ecology in the 1960s.

29. The two doctors treating Down syndrome were Ruth Harrell and Henry Turkel. Bernard Rimland, "Vitamin and Mineral Supplementation as a Treatment for Autistic and Mentally Retarded Persons" (presentation to the President's Committee on Mental Retardation, Washington, DC, September 20, 1984), 5.

30. Megadoses are defined as doses above the nutritional requirements for an average person. Bernard Rimland, "The History of the Autism Research Institute and the Defeat Autism Now! (DAN!) Project," 15.

31. Turkel's study was repudiated in a one-page critique in the *Journal of the American Medical Association*, while a 1981 paper by Harrell was the subject

of a negative policy statement by the American Academy of Pediatrics. Rimland, "Vitamin and Mineral Supplementation as a Treatment for Autistic and Mentally Retarded Persons."

32. Rimland (1976, 200).

33. Pauling offered to answer questions from physicians wary of supporting their patients' participation in a Vitamin B6 study. Letter from Bernard Rimland to vitamin study participants, December 8, 1968, Institute for Child Behavior Research, San Diego, CA. The letter includes contact information for Linus Pauling in the Chemistry Department at the University of California, San Diego. Folder marked "Rimland, B." Box 2, ACC 92-M-41, Lettick Papers. Also see Rimland, "The History of the Autism Research Institute and the Defeat Autism Now! (DAN!) Project," 16; and Bernard Rimland. "The Effect of High Dosage Levels of Certain Vitamins on the Behavior of Children with Severe Mental Disorders," in *Orthomolecular Psychiatry*, eds. D. R. Hawkins and Linus Pauling (San Francisco: W. H. Freeman, 1973).

34. Rimland (1976, 203). Rimland's work on subtyping also dates from this period. See Bernard Rimland, "The Differentiation of Childhood Psychosis: An Analysis of Checklists of 2,218 Psychotic Children," *Journal of Autism and Childhood Schizophrenia* 1, no. 2 (1971): 161–74.

35. Facilitated communication (FC) was developed by Rosemary Crossley as a way to help people with dyspraxia caused by disorders like cerebral palsy to communicate. Rimland argued that Douglas Biklen's later claims about the capabilities of children with autism were exaggerated and needed to be subjected to testing in "Facilitated Communication: A Light at the End of the Tunnel?" *Autism Research Review International* 7, no. 3 (1993): 3; and Stephen M. Edelson, Bernard Rimland, Carol Lee Berger, and Donald Billings, "Evaluation of a Mechanical Hand-Support for Facilitated Communication," *Journal of Autism and Developmental Disorders* 28, no. 2 (1998): 153–57. For a critical review of facilitated communication studies since see Mark P. Mostert, "Facilitated Communication Since 1995: A Review of Published Studies," *Journal of Autism and Developmental Disorders* 31, no. 3 (2001): 287–313.

36. Rimland, "The History of the Autism Research Institute and the Defeat Autism Now! (DAN!) Project,"18.

37. Ibid., 16. Presenters at Defeat Autism Now! conferences continue to emphasize this point. During a talk at the spring 2005 Defeat Autism Now! conference (Quincy, MA, April 14–17, 2005), Sidney Baker described listening to parents as an "ethos" that involved being conscious of the fact that there are "two people in the room," and he spoke movingly of the need to learn to "translate" the intuitions of parents into "technical language."

38. Bernard Rimland and Sidney M. Baker, "Brief Report: Alternative Approaches to the Development of Effective Treatments for Autism, *Journal of Autism and Developmental Disorders* 26, no. 2 (1996): 237–41, 240.

39. Benedict Carey, "Bernard Rimland, 78, Scientist Who Revised View of Autism, Dies," *New York Times*, November 28, 2006.

40. Stephen M. Edelson, "Following the Vision of Dr. Rimland," *Autism Research Review International* 20, no. 3 (2006).

41. Valerie Paradiz, with an introduction by Stephen Edelson, "When the Twain Shall Meet: Biomed and Self-Advocacy," *Autism Research Review International* 24, no. 2 (September 2010): 3, 7. Paradiz, a self-advocate and parent, is married to ARI's director, Stephen Edelson. She writes that "many of us are practicing biomedical approaches without even knowing that we are, simply by avoiding foods we know make us feel bad."

42. Stephen M. Edelson and Jane Johnson, "Moving Forward in 2011," *Autism Research Review International* 24, no. 4 (2010): 3, 7.

43. Adams (2005, 178).

44. For instance, one study conducted by a researcher affiliated with Defeat Autism Now! found abnormally high levels of plasma B6 in children with autism compared to controls (neither group was taking supplements at the time). The researchers hypothesized that the raised levels might have been due to a polymorphism in the enzyme that modifies B6 into its biochemically active form; supplementation of further B6 might bring the intracellular concentration to a level at which the enzyme would be activated. James B. Adams, Frank George, and T. Audhya, "Abnormally High Plasma Levels of Vitamin B6 in Children with Autism Not Taking Supplements Compared to Controls Not Taking Supplements," *Journal of Alternative and Complementary Medicine* 12, no. 1 (2006): 59–63.

45. Sudhir Gupta, "Immunological Treatments for Autism," *Journal of Autism and Developmental Disorders* 30, no. 5 (2000): 475–79. "Dysregulation" can refer to either overactive or underactive immune functioning. A number of parents report chronic ear infections in their children, even prior to their diagnoses. See, for instance, Debbie Bayliss, "Dillon's Story," and Karyn Seroussi, "We Rescued Our Child from Autism," in Edelson and Rimland (2003, 92–96, 299–305).

46. See "Treatment Options for Mercury/Metal Toxicity in Autism and Related Developmental Disabilities: Consensus Position Paper," Autism Research Institute (February 2005), http://www.autism.com/pro_mercurydetox.asp.

47. See, for instance, Harumi Jyonouchi, Sining Sun, and Hoa Le, "Proinflammatory and Regulatory Cytokine Production Associated with Innate and Adaptive Immune Responses in Children with Autism Spectrum Disorders and Developmental Regression," *Journal of Neuroimmunology* 120, no. 1–2 (2001): 170–79; S. Jill James, Paul Cutler, Stepan Melnyk, Stefanie Jernigan, et al., "Metabolic Biomarkers of Increased Oxidative Stress and Impaired Methylation Capacity in Children with Autism," *American Journal of Clinical Nutrition* 80, no. 6 (2004): 1611–17; Diana L. Vargas, Caterina Nascinbene,

Chitra Krishnan, Andrew W. Zimmerman, et al., "Neuroglial Activation and Neuroinflammation in the Brain of Patients with Autism," *Annals of Neurology* 57, no. 1 (2005): 67–81; and Theodore Page, "Metabolic Approaches to the Treatment of Autism Spectrum Disorders," *Journal of Autism and Developmental Disorders* 30, no. 5 (2000): 463–69.

48. A number of studies support the conclusion that children with autism have trouble removing toxic substances from their bodies, including heavy metals. See Amy S. Holmes, Mark F. Blaxill, and Boyd E. Haley, "Reduced Levels of Mercury in First Baby Haircuts of Autistic Children," *International Journal of Toxicology* 22, no. 4 (2003): 277–85; Janet K. Kern, Bruce D. Grannemann, and Madhukar H. Trivedi, "Sulfhydryl-Reactive Metals in Autism," *Journal of Toxicology and Environmental Health, Part A* 70, no. 8 (2007): 715–21.

49. Katie, a parent, quoted in Pangborn and Baker (2005, 17).

50. Chart and explanation by Brenda Kerr, http://www.autism.com/ind_trackprogress.asp. See Murphy (2000, 114–18) on how sufferers from multiple chemical sensitivity (MCS) similarly track their own symptoms and correlate them with minute changes in their environments.

51. Hays (1998).

52. Adams (2005, 188–89).

53. Christina Adams, "Guest Blog: I Am an Autism Mom," http://blog.washingtonpost.com/onbalance/2006/06/guest_blog_i_am_an_autism_mom.html>.

54. The secretin discussion group, founded in 1999, became inactive as of June 23, 2000, and readers were encouraged to join ABMD. While ABMD was founded as a forum for parents to discuss using infusions of the pancreatic hormone secretin as a treatment for autism, many members of ABMD were also once members of the "St. John's" list, which one former participant described as a kind of "big city" for autism. There were discussions of many biomedical treatments, as well as participants with autism diagnoses.

55. Seroussi (2003); Hamilton (2000).

56. Lewis (1998); Edelson and Rimland (2003).

57. The most recent edition includes an extensive additional literature review and discussion by Teresa Binstock, an independent researcher diagnosed with Asperger syndrome who is active in the Defeat Autism Now! community and widely respected by both parents and practitioners. McCandless (2003).

58. Jack Zimmerman, in McCandless (2003, 194).

59. Hamilton (2000).

60. Amy S. Holmes, "My Son, the King of Metals," in Edelson and Rimland (2003, 185).

61. Autism Research Institute, "Defeat Autism Now! U.S. Clinicians," http://www.autism.com/pro_danlists_results.asp?list=US&type=1.

62. Scott Bono, "Top Ten List" (presentation given at the spring Defeat Autism Now! conference, Quincy, MA, April 14–17, 2005), cited with permission.

63. Robert Tinnell and Craig A. Taillefer, "The Chelation Kid, Episode 107," http://www.webcomicsnation.com/taillefer/chelation_kid/series.php?view=single&ID=49934.

64. One doctor whom I spoke with will not see patients until they have run a battery of allergy and metabolic tests. She maintains that she needs these as a baseline, along with the requirement that a child be entirely gluten-free and casein-free before starting any other therapy.

65. Susan Costen Owens, posting on St. John's List for Autism and Developmental Delay on July 6, 1997, AUTISM@MAELSTROM.STJOHNS.EDU, quoted with permission of author.

66. While Herbert (2009) is not a Defeat Autism Now! doctor, her description of some autism cases as possibly involving "chronic dynamic" processes that may lend themselves to intervention is an excellent description of how this model can apply to research programs.

67. Letter from Susan Costen Owens to Jonathan Shestack, dated 1997 (shared by author and quoted with permission).

68. Jon Pangborn and Sidney Baker both use the phrase "biochemically unique" in talks and presentations and may be implicitly or explicitly referencing Williams (1956/1998, 201) on differences in vitamin requirements between individuals.

69. Although I thought about my dilemma at the time in terms of trust in a very mundane sense, my uncertainty regarding who could be relied on to provide valid information consistent with experimentally supported evidence is also very much part of the modern experience of scientific knowledge. Shapin and Schaffer's (1989) and Shapin's (1994; 1999, 492) work on the problem of trust and witnessing in the creation of modern science is my reference point here, as well as Haraway's (1997a, 23–39) discussion of how Shapin's descriptions relate to feminist science studies.

70. Starr (1982).

71. Murphy (2000, 109) notes similar attitudes in the efforts of MCS sufferers to manage their "personal ecology" and create chemical-free "safe" homes.

72. On the career of the concept of "objectivity" in science, from visual metaphor to moral achievement, see Daston and Galison (1992).

73. Ross, review of *Infantile Autism*.

74. Molly Helt, Elizabeth Kelley, Marcel Kinsbourne, Juhi Pandey, et al., "Can Children with Autism Recover? If So, How?" *Neuropsychology Review* 18, no. 4 (2008) 339–66.

75. Prussing, Sobo, Walker, and Kurtin (2005, 593) observe that this is the case for some parents of children with Down syndrome, who see "CAM as a means of maximizing personal potential," and part of their role as "authoritative advocates and service coordinators for their children."

76. Jill Neimark, "Autism: It's Not Just in the Head," *Discover* (April 2007): 75.

77. Timothy Buie, Daniel B. Campbell, George G. Fuchs, Glenn T. Furuta, et al., "Evaluation, Diagnosis, and Treatment of Gastrointestinal Disorders in

Individuals with ASDs: A Consensus Report," *Pediatrics* 125 Suppl. (January 2010): S1–18. This consensus report did not affirm the existence of unique gastrointestinal symptoms in individuals with ASDs but did acknowledge that further research was warranted.

78. Andrew J. Wakefield, Simon H. Murch, A. Anthony, J. Linnell, et al., "Ileal-Lymphoid-Nodular Hyperplasia, Non-Specific Colitis, and Pervasive Developmental Disorder in Children," *Lancet* 351, no. 9103 (1998): 637–41.

79. Timothy Buie, "Gastrointestinal Issues Encountered in Autism," in *The Neurobiology of Autism* (2nd ed.), eds. Margaret L. Bauman and Thomas L. Kemper (Baltimore, MD: Johns Hopkins University Press, 2004), 103–17.

80. He cited Michael Gershon's (1998) arguments in *The Second Brain*, a book that emphasizes gut-brain connections while remaining firmly situated in neurology—the objective of the book is to describe the gut nervous system rather than theorize how gut pathology might affect neurological functioning indirectly.

81. Timothy Buie, "Processing and Pain in the Gut and Brain" (talk given at the spring Defeat Autism Now! conference, Quincy, MA, April 14–17, 2005).

82. For examples of posturing and self-injury connected to GI pain, see Arthur Krigsman, "Gastrointestinal Pathology in Autism: Description and Treatment," *Medical Veritas* 4 (2007): 1528–36, 1531, 1532. Also see Andrew J. Wakefield, Carol Stott, and Arthur Krigsman, "Getting It Wrong," *Archives of Disease in Childhood* 93, no. 10 (2008): 905–6.

83. The bias toward the brain in autism is even more specific: researchers have focused almost exclusively on the central nervous system, overlooking signs of autonomic nervous system dysfunction in autism, including sleep disorders, difficulty regulating temperature, and gut disturbances. Xue Ming, Peter O. O. Julu, Michael Brimacombe, Susan Connor, and Mary L. Daniels, "Reduced Cardiac Parasympathetic Activity in Children with Autism," *Brain & Development* 27, no. 7 (2005): 509–16.

84 Martha Herbert, personal communication, September 19, 2010. For further development of these concepts see Herbert (forthcoming).

85. Erving Goffman (1959) suggested that medical identities can be understood as a kind of "costume drama" in terms of the role-playing necessary and the specific requirements for attire and equipment. These roles are compromised when practitioners choose to abandon sources of their authority, for instance by admitting their ignorance about causes of certain illnesses. Paul Wolpe (1990, 1994) describes holistic medicine's proposal of an alternative framework for understanding pathology as a form of "medical heresy" that leads to an "ideological battle" in which the orthodoxy's responses can range from cooptation to isolation and outright suppression.

86. Parents have sometimes gone on to coauthor papers with researchers. For example, Sydney Finegold attributed his research program on gut microbiology to the observations and research of Ellen Bolte, the mother of a child with au-

tism. Bolte contacted Feingold while trying to find a doctor to treat her child with vancomycin, an antibiotic, based on her hypothesis that some of her son's symptoms were due to neurotoxins produced by gut flora. Both publications resulting from this research listed Bolte as a coauthor. See Sydney M. Finegold, Denise Molitoris, Yuli Song, Chengxu Liu, et al., "Gastrointestinal Microflora Studies in Late-Onset Autism," *Clinical Infectious Diseases* 35 Suppl. 1 (2002): S6–16; and R. H. Sandler, Sydney M. Finegold, Ellen R. Bolte, Cathleen P. Buchanan, et al., "Short-Term Benefit from Oral Vancomycin Treatment of Regressive-Onset Autism," *Journal of Child Neurology* 15, no. 7 (2000): 429–35.

87. Again, I am using the term "partial" here in Donna Haraway's (1991, 183–201) sense, to mean situated in particular bodies and necessarily incomplete, but also passionate and committed.

88. However, even stabilizing psychiatric categories requires work and is often market-driven. Lakoff (2005, 18–42).

89. Francesca Happe, Angelica Ronald, and Robert Plomin, "Time to Give Up on a Single Explanation for Autism," *Nature Neuroscience* 9, no. 10 (2006): 1218–20. Happe et al. argue that both behavioral and neurological impairments in autism suggest that multiple, independent features may be involved to a different degree in different individuals, although they still consider autism primarily in genetic terms, where behavioral features are potentially separable and attributable to different genes. On Herbert's comments, see Jill Neimark, "Autism: It's Not Just in the Head," *Discover* (April 2007); and Herbert (2005a, 2009, forthcoming).

90. Fromm (1956, 93).

91. Ibid., 103

Chapter 6

1. See the 2003 version of the autism research matrix, which uses risk designations to identify projects that are either more or less likely to be completed in the short or long-term, http://iacc.hhs.gov/reports/2006/evaluating-progress-autism-matrix-nov17.shtml#research-matrix.

2. Announcement for IACC full committee meeting, November 21, 2008. Online at: http://www.nimh.nih.gov/research-funding/scientific-meetings/recurring-meetings/iacc/events/2008/november/iacc-full-committee-meeting.shtml.

3. Brian Vastag, "Congressional Autism Hearings Continue: No Evidence MMR Vaccine Causes Disorder," *Journal of the American Medical Association* 285, no. 20 (2001): 2567–69.

4. There is also published research on the toxicity of thimerosal solution to neural cells in vitro: David S. Baskin, Hop Ngo, and Vladimir V. Didenko,

"Thimerosal Induces DNA Breaks, Capase-3 Activation, Membrane Damage, and Cell Death in Cultured Human Neurons and Fibroblasts," *Toxicological Sciences* 74, no. 2 (2003): 361–68.

5. The study, when it was completed, found no association between the MMR vaccine and autism. Mady Hornig, Thomas Briese, Timothy Buie, Margaret Bauman, et al., "Lack of Association between Measles Virus Vaccine and Autism with Enteropathy: A Case-Control Study," *PLoS ONE* 3, no. 9 (2008): e3140–40, http://www.plosone.org/article/info:doi/10.1371/journal.pone.0003140 .

6. W. Ian Lipkin, presentation at The Autism Summit Conference: Developing a National Agenda, Session on Epidemiological and Environmental Research, Washington, DC, November 19–20, 2003.. The official title for Lipkin's grant was the Pandora's Box Project.

7. Singh, Hallmayer, and Iles (2007, 157) write that "despite a relatively long and intricate history of autism, millions of dollars of funding and thousands of papers in the peer-reviewed literature to explore causes, symptoms and possibilities for intervention, the selective reporting of the press was in sharp contrast to the focus of research and funding," in particular, the emphasis in the press on environmental causes and on vaccines in particular.

8. Durbach (2002).

9. Ibid., 59; Durbach (2005, 114–17).

10. Durbach (2005, 44–46 and 61).

11. Lesli Mitchell, "Secrets and Lies: Is the Astonishing Rise in Autism a Medical Mystery or a Pharmaceutical Shame?" *Salon.com,* August 2, 2000, http://archive.salon.com/mwt/feature/2000/08/02/autism/index.html.

12. Johnston (2004, 279).

13. The treatment guide (Pangborn and Baker 2005, 49–55; 60–64) largely refrains from offering explicit input on detoxification therapies (it details one option), but it does direct readers to a 2005 consensus statement on mercury toxicity and treatment options, including various methods of chelation, available at the ARI Web site. "Treatment Options for Mercury/Metal Toxicity in Autism and Related Developmental Disabilities: Consensus Position Paper" (February 2005), http://www.autism.com/pro_mercurydetox.asp.

14. The first season of the ABC television program *Eli Stone* featured an episode (aired on January 31, 2008) in which a parent sued a vaccine maufacturer for compensation for her son's injury and subsequent autism due to the use of a preservative called "mercuritol" in a flu vaccine. A January 8, 2009, episode of another ABC drama, *Private Practice,* painted a very different picture when a child died of measles because his mother refused to have him vaccinated, believing that an older child had developed autism as a result of the MMR vaccine he received.

15. Mitchell, "Secrets and Lies."

16. Concerns relating to the more familiar form of mercury, methylmercury or organic mercury, are also current in the parent community and public dis-

course. In particular, parents consider the methylmercury accumulated in placental blood as a result of fish consumption and environmental mercury a source of possible cumulative effects.

17. In particular, the researchers claimed that the children showed a characteristic set of bowel changes termed ileo-colonic lymphoid-nodular hyperplasia, an enlargement of the intestinal lymph nodes that by itself is not necessarily pathological, but which seemed to be associated with (or at least occur in conjunction with) physical discomfort and active gut irritation in these children. Andrew J. Wakefield, Simon H. Murch, A. Anthony, J. Linnell, et al., "Ileal-Lymphoid-Nodular Hyperplasia, Non-Specific Colitis, and Pervasive Developmental Disorder in Children" *Lancet* 351, no. 9103 (1998): 637–41.

18 Anders Ekbom, Peter Daszak. Wolfgang Kraaz, and Andrew J. Wakefield, "Crohn's Disease After In-Utero Measles Virus Exposures," *Lancet* 348, no. 9026 (1996): 515–17.

19. Jo Revill, "Scientist's Warning Prompts Fears over Measles Vaccine," *Evening Standard*, February 26, 1998.

20. Kamran Abbasi, "Man, Mission, Rumpus," *British Medical Journal* 322, no. 7281 (2001): 306; Brian Deer, "Secrets of the MMR Scare: How the Measles Crisis Was Meant to Make Money," *British Medical Journal* 342 (2011): c5258.

21. "Reid Calls for Probe into MMR Report," *Mail on Sunday*, February 22, 2004. The editor of the *Lancet* wrote that "had we appreciated the full context in which the work reported in the 1998 *Lancet* paper by Wakefield and colleagues was done, publication would not have taken place the way it did." Richard Horton, "The Lessons of MMR," *The Lancet* 363, no. 9411 (2004): 747–49.

22. Brian Deer, "Revealed: MMR Research Scandal," *Sunday Times*, February 22, 2004; Glenn Frankel, "Charismatic Doctor at Vortex of Vaccine Dispute: Experts Argue over Findings, but Specialist Sees Possible MMR Link to Autism," *Washington Post*, July 11, 2004. The Legal Aid Fund serves to provide legal services in the U.K. to those who cannot afford them. It is now called the Community Legal Service Fund and is run by the Community Legal Services Commission, which replaced the Legal Aid Board. See http://www.clsdirect.org .uk/legalhelp/clscharges.jsp.

23 However, the only research article Wakefield produced after 2006 was withdrawn before publication by the journal *Neurotoxicology* for unspecified reasons (a version of the article was published a year later, without Wakefield listed as a coauthor). For earlier work, see Andrew J. Wakefield, "Enterocolitis in Children with Developmental Disorders," *American Journal of Gastroenterology* 95, no. 9 (2000): 2285–95; Andrew J. Wakefield, "Enterocolitis, Autism and Measles Virus," *Molecular Psychiatry* 7 Suppl. 2 (2002): S44–46; and H. Kawashima, T. Mori, Y. Kashiwagi, K. Takekuma, et al., "Detection and Sequencing of Measles Virus from Peripheral Mononuclear Cells from

Patients with Inflammatory Bowel Disease and Autism," *Digestive Diseases and Sciences* 45, no. 4 (2000): 723–29.

24. See, for instance, testimony reproduced in Neil Z. Miller, *Vaccines, Autism and Childhood Disorders: Crucial Data That Could Save Your Child's Life* (Santa Fe, New Mexico: New Atlantean Press, 2003); and Abbasi, "Man, Mission, Rumpus," 306.

25. James A. Wright and Clare Polack, "Understanding Variation in Measles-Mumps-Rubella Immunization Coverage—A Population-Based Study," *European Journal of Public Health* 16, no. 2 (2006): 137–42; Press Association, "MMR Doctor 'Failed to Act in Interests of Children,'" *Guardian*, January 20, 2010.

26. The *Lancet* editors pointed in particular to the facts that children had not been "consecutively referred" to Wakefield's clinic as had originally been reported, and that the study had not been approved by the "local ethics committee." The Editors of the *Lancet*, "Retraction—Ileal-Lymphoid-Nodular Hyperplasia, Non-Specific Colitis, and Pervasive Developmental Disorder in Children," *Lancet* 375, no. 9713 (2010): 455. See also Gardiner Harris, "Journal Retracts 1998 Paper Linking Autism to Vaccines," *New York Times*, February 2, 2010.

27. The council also barred one colleague of Wakefield's, John Walker-Smith, but cleared another, Simon Murch. John F. Burns, "British Medical Council Bars Doctor Who Linked Vaccine with Autism," *New York Times,* May 25, 2010. The council referenced the fact that Wakefield had paid healthy children for blood samples at his son's birthday party. The interview with Wakefield quoted in the article above aired on NBC's *Today* show on May 24, 2010.

28. Brian Deer, "Secrets of the MMR Scare: How the Case against the MMR Vaccine was Fixed," *British Medical Journal* 342 (2011): c5347; Deer, "Secrets of the MMR Scare: How the Measles Crisis Was Meant to Make Money," c5258.

29. Jane E. Libbey, Thayne L. Sweeten, William M. McMahon, and Robert S. Fujinami, "Autistic Disorder and Viral Infections," *Journal of NeuroVirology* 11, no. 1 (2005): 1–10.

30. Vijendra K. Singh, Sheren X. Lin, and Victor C. Yang, "Serological Association of Measles Virus and Human Herpesvirus-6 with Brain Autoantibodies in Autism," *Clinical Immunology and Immunopathology* 98 (1998): 105–8; Vijendra K. Singh, Sheren X. Lin, Elizabeth Newell, and Courtney Nelson, "Abnormal Measles-Mumps-Rubella Antibodies and CNS Autoimmunity in Children with Autism," *Journal of Biomedical Science* 9, no. 4 (2002): 359–64.

31. Harumi Jyonouchi, Sining Sun, and Hoa Le, "Proinflammatory and Regulatory Cytokine Production Associated with Innate and Adaptive Immune Responses in Children with Autism Spectrum Disorders and Developmental Regression," *Journal of Neuroimmunology* 120, no. 1–2 (2001): 170–79.

32. The study did not draw any explicit connections to vaccines. Diana L. Vargas, Caterina Nascimbene, Chitra Krishnan, Andrew W. Zimmerman, et al.,

"Neuroglial Activation and Neuroinflammation in the Brain of Patients with Autism," *Annals of Neurology* 57, no. 1 (2005): 67–81. Markers of inflammation were unexpectedly absent in samples of serum and cerebrospinal fluid. Andrew W. Zimmerman, Jarumi Jyonouchi, Anne M. Comi, Susan L. Connors, et al., "Cerebrospinal Fluid and Serum Markers of Inflammation in Autism," *Pediatric Neurology* 33, no. 3 (2005).

33. The coauthors who retracted their interpretation stated that "further evidence has been forthcoming in studies from the Royal Free Centre for Paediatric Gastroenterology and other groups to support and extend these findings." Simon Murch, Andrew Anthony, David H. Casson, Mohsin Malik, et al., "Retraction of an Interpretation," *Lancet* 363, no. 9411 (2004): 750.

34. Murch et al., "Retraction of an Interpretation," 750. The *Lancet's* later decision to retract the article in its entirety in February 2010 effectively overrode the earlier, partial, retraction.

35. A. J. Wakefield, "Autistic Enterocolitis: Is It a Histopathological Entity?" *Histopathology* 50, no. 3 (2007): 380–84.

36 However, the study did find elevated rates of regression among children who also had GI disturbances, suggesting an association between the two. Mady Hornig, Thomas Briese, Timothy Buie, Margaret L. Bauman, et al., "Lack of Association between Measles Virus Vaccine and Autism with Enteropathy: A Case-Control Study," *PLoS ONE* 3, no. 9 (2008): e3140–50. An earlier study failed to find measles virus in the immune cells of children with autism. Yasmin D'Souza, Eric Fombonne, and Brian J. Ward, "No Evidence of Persisting Measles Virus in Peripheral Blood Mononuclear Cells From Children with Autism Spectrum Disorder," *Pediatrics*, 118, no. 4 (2006): 1664–75.

37. Baker (2008, 246).

38. Arthur Allen, "The Not-So-Crackpot Autism Theory," *New York Times* Magazine, November 10, 2002. Allen quotes Neal Halsey, head of the Hopkins Institute for Vaccine Safety and a prominent supporter of childhood immunizations, on the growth of his own concerns regarding thimerosal during a June 1999 visit to the FDA.

39. These incidents included industrial pollution that contaminated fish in Japan, leading to outbreaks of Minamata disease in the 1950s and 1960s, and an episode in 1971–1972 in which thousands of people in Iraq consumed bread made from grain treated with a methylmercury fungicide. National Research Council (2000). On the poisoning in Iraq, see T. W. Clarkson, L Amin-Zaki, and S. K. Al-Tikriti, "An Outbreak of Methylmercury Poisoning due to Consumption of Contaminated Grain," *Federation Proceedings* 35, no. 12 (1976): 2395-99.

40. See National Research Council (2000); Daniel A. Axelrad, David C. Bellinger, Louise M. Ryan, and Tracey J. Woodruff, "Dose-Response Relationship of Prenatal Mercury Exposure and IQ: An Integrative Analysis of Epidemiologic Data," *Environmental Health Perspectives* 115, no. 4 (2007): 609–15;

Philippe Grandjean, Pal Weihe, Roberta F. White, Frodi Debes, et al., "Cognitive Deficit in 7-Year-Old Children with Prenatal Exposure to Methylmercury," *Neurotoxicology and Teratology* 19, no. 6 (1997): 417–28.

41. National Research Council (2000, 72); Raymond F. Palmer, Stephen Blanchard, Zachary Stein, David Mandell, et al., "Environmental Mercury Release, Special Education Rates, and Autism Disorder: An Ecological Study of Texas," *Health Place* 12, no. 2 (2006): 203–9.

42. See the FDA Web site, "Mercury Levels in Commercial Fish and Shellfish," http://www.cfsan.fda.gov/~frf/sea-mehg.html, and their "Advisory on Mercury in Seafood," http://www.cfsan.fda.gov/~dms/admehg3.html.

43. Baker (2008, 246).

44. SafeMinds, Sensible Action for Ending Mercury-Induced Neurological Disorders Web site, http://www.safeminds.org/. Generation Rescue, founded by J. B. and Lisa Handley, has also been a vocal proponent of these views since its founding in 2005—the actress Jenny McCarthy is its most visible member. Generation Rescue Web site, http://www.generationrescue.org/.

45. Sally Bernard, Lyn Redwood, Albert Enayati, and Teresa Binstock, "Autism: A Novel Form of Mercury Poisoning?" *Medical Hypotheses* 56, no. 4 (2001): 472–81.

46. Karin B. Nelson and Margaret L. Bauman, "Thimerosal and Autism?" *Pediatrics* 111, no. 3 (2003): 674–79. Nelson and Bauman argued that there was no epidemiological evidence of a connection and that the biological (as opposed to behavioral) signs of methylmercury toxicity were very different from autism. The two authors discuss the *Medical Hypotheses* piece as well as a later article, in which the group made an even more emphatic case for the thimerosal-autism hypothesis, Sally Bernard, Albert Enayati, H. Roger, Teresa Binstock, et al., "The Role of Mercury in the Pathogenesis of Autism," *Molecular Psychiatry* 7 Suppl. 2 (2002): S42–43.

47. Kirby (2005, 141–44).

48. Arthur Allen, "The Not-So-Crackpot Autism Theory."

49. "On average, for each 1,000 lb. of environmentally released mercury, there was a 3% increase in the rate of special education services and a 61% increase in the rate of autism." Palmer et al., "Environmental Mercury Release, Special Education Rates, and Autism Disorder," 203–9; Thomas M. Burbacher, Danny D. Shen, Noelle Liberato, Kimberly S. Grant, et al., "Comparison of Blood and Brain Mercury Levels in Infant Monkeys Exposed to Methylmercury or Vaccines Containing Thimerosal," *Environmental Health Perspectives* 113, no. 8 (2005): 1015–21.

50. Damani K. Parran, Angela Barker, and Marion Ehrich, "Effects of Thimerosal on NGF Signal Transduction and Cell Death in Neuroblastoma Cells," *Toxicological Sciences* 86, no. 1 (2005): 132–40. Also see Baskin et al., "Thimerosal Induces DNA Breaks, Caspase-3 Activation, Membrane Damage, and Cell Death in Cultured Human Neurons and Fibroblasts,": 361–68.

51. Parran et al., "Effects of Thimerosal on NGF Signal Transduction and Cell Death in Neuroblastoma Cells," 132–40; Ramuel R. Goth, Ruth A. Chu, Gennady Cherednichenko, and Issac N. Pessah, "Uncoupling of ATP-Mediated Calcium Signaling and Dysregulated Interleukin-6 Secretion in Dendritic Cells by Nanomolar Thimerosal," *Environmental Health Perspectives* 114, no. 7 (2006): 1083–91.

52. Investigators have found evidence of increased oxidative stress in children with autism and possible evidence of impaired DNA methylation. DNA methylation plays a central role in neural development and regulation. S. Jill James, Paul Cutler, Stepan Melnyk, Stefanie Jernigan, et al., "Metabolic Biomarkers of Increased Oxidative Stress and Impaired Methylation Capacity in Children with Autism," *American Journal of Clinical Nutrition* 80, no. 6 (2004): 1611–17; Janet K. Kern and Anne M. Jones, "Evidence of Toxicity, Oxidative Stress, and Neuronal Insult in Autism," *Journal of Toxicology and Environmental Health, Part B* 9, no. 6 (2006): 485–99; S. Jill James, Stepan Melnyk, Stefanie Jernigan, Mario A. Cleves, et al., "Metabolic Endophenotype and Related Genotypes Are Associated with Oxidative Stress in Children with Autism," *American Journal of Medical Genetics Part B: Neuropsychiatric Genetics* 141, no. 8 (2006): 947–56.

53. Kenneth P. Stoller, "Autism as a Minamata Disease Variant: Analysis of a Pernicious Legacy," *Medical Veritas* 3 (2006): 772–80; M. Waly, H. Olteanu, R. Banerjee, S.-W. Choi, et al., "Activation of Methionine Synthase by Insulin-Like Growth Factor-1 and Dopamine: A Target for Neurodevelopmental Toxins and Thimerosal," *Molecular Psychiatry* 9, no. 4 (2004): 358–70.

54. S. Jill James, William Slikker, Stepan Melnyk, Elizabeth New, et al., "Thimerosal Neurotoxicity Is Associated with Glutathione Depletion: Protection with Glutathione Precursors," *NeuroToxicology* 26, no. 1 (2004): 1–8.

55. M. Hornig, D. Chian, and W. I. Lipkin, "Neurotoxic Effects of Postnatal Thimerosal Are Mouse Strain Dependent." *Molecular Psychiatry* 9, no. 9 (2004): 1–13.

56. Anshu Agrawal, Poonam Kaushal, Sudhanshu Agrawal, Sastry Gollapudi, et al., "Thimerosal Induces TH2 Responses via Influencing Cytokine Secretion by Human Dendritic Cells," *Journal of Leukocyte Biology* 81, no. 2 (2007): 474–82.

57. Thomas H. Maugh II, "Study Finds Genetic Link Between Autism, Vaccines," *LA Times*, June 9, 2004. Researchers were unable to reproduce the study—see Robert F. Berman, Isaac N. Pessah, Peter R. Mouton, Deepak Mav, et al., "Low-Level Neonatal Thimerosal Exposure: Further Evaluation of Altered Neurotoxic Potential in SJL Mice," *Toxicological Sciences*, 101, no. 2 (2008): 294–309.

58. Studies that found lower levels of mercury in the hair of autistic children are Amy S. Holmes, Mark F. Blaxill, and Boyd E. Haley, "Reduced Levels of Mercury in First Baby Haircuts of Autistic Children," *International Journal of Toxicology* 22, no. 4 (2003): 277–85; and Janet K. Kern, Bruce D.

Grannemann, Madhukar H. Trivedi, and James B. Adams, "Sulfhydryl-Reactive Metals in Autism," *Journal of Toxicology and Environmental Health Part A* 70, no. 8 (2007): 715–21. The latter article found that children with autism may sequester not only mercury, but also lead, arsenic, and cadmium. Another article argued that the differences between children with autism and their typically developing siblings in levels of hair mercury was not significant. P. Gail Williams, Joseph H. Hersh, AnnaMary Allard, and Lonnie L. Sears, "A Controlled Study of Mercury Levels in Hair Samples of Children with Autism as Compared to Their Typically Developing Siblings," *Research in Autism Spectrum Disorders* 2, no. 1 (2008): 170–75.

59. "Treatment Options for Mercury/Metal Toxicity in Autism and Related Developmental Disabilities: Consensus Position Paper," Autism Research Institute (February, 2005), http://www.autism.com/pro_mercurydetox.asp; Karen Kane and Virginia Linn, "Boy Dies During Autism Treatment," *Pittsburgh Post-Gazette*, August 25, 2005, http://www.post-gazette.com/pg/05237/559756.stm; M. J. Brown, T. Willis, B. Omalu, and R. Leiker, "Deaths Resulting from Hypocalcemia after Administration of Edetate Disodium: 2003–2005," *Pediatrics* 118, no. 2: e534–36. At the time, there was speculation that some of the confusion may have resulted from the similarities between the brand names of the two substances, Versenate (edetate calcium disodium) and Endrate (edetate disodium).

60. Karen Kane, "Drug Error, Not Chelation Therapy, Killed Boy, Expert Says," *Pittsburgh Post-Gazette*, January 18, 2006, http://www.post-gazette.com/pg/06018/639721.stm.

61. National Institute of Mental Health (NIMH),"New NIMH Program Launches Autism Trials," NIMH (September 7, 2006), http://www.nimh.nih.gov/science-news/2006/new-nimh-research-program-launches-autism-trials.shtml; Carla K. Johnson, "Fringe Autism Treatment Could Get Federal Study," *Associated Press Archive*, July 8, 2008.

62. Ibid.; Erik Stokstad, "Stalled Trial for Autism Highlights Dilemma for Alternative Treatments," *Science* 321, no. 5887 (July 2008): 326; Carla K. Johnson, "U.S. Researchers Call Off Controversial Autism Study," *Associated Press Archive*, September 18, 2008.

63. Other groups have produced results that call into question the idea that children with autism have higher heavy metal burdens than typically developing controls, for example, Sarah E. Soden, Jennifer A. Lowry, Carol B. Garrison, and Gary S. Wasserman, "24-Hour Provoked Urine Excretion Test for Heavy Metals in Children with Autism and Typically Developing Controls, A Pilot Study," *Clinical Toxicology* 45, no. 5 (2007): 476–81.

64. See Congressman Dan Burton's Web site, http://www.house.gov/burton/. Burton has been a strong advocate of investigations into both the use of thimerosal and the MMR vaccine, starting with testimony as committee chairman to the House of Representatives Committee on Government Reform on

"Autism: Present Challenges, Future Needs. Why the Increased Rates?" April 6, 2000. A number of parents testified at the hearing, as well as Drs. Andrew Wakefield, Bernard Rimland, Vigendra K. Singh, and Mary Megson, among others. See transcripts included in Miller, *Vaccines, Autism and Childhood Disorders*. Also see Rep. Dave Weldon, "Before the Institute of Medicine" (comments), Institute of Medicine, February 9, 2004, www.iom.edu/~/media/Files/Activity%20Files/.../IOMWeldonFinal2904.pdf.

65. Robert F. Kennedy Jr., "Deadly Immunity: Robert F. Kennedy Jr. Investigates the Government Cover-Up of a Mercury/Autism Scandal," *Rolling Stone*, June 20, 2005, http://www.rollingstone.com/politics/story/7395411/deadly _immunity/ (no longer available); Kirby (2005).

66. Offit (2008, 149–53).

67. Carole Gan, "Four Dads' Passion Leads to New University-Based Institute for Treating Autism and Other Disorders: Team Effort and Relentless Drive Makes Parents' Vision a Reality" (press release, March 19, 1999), http://www .ucdmc.ucdavis.edu/news/MIND_Inst.html.

68. Immunization Safety Review Committee, *Immunization Safety Review: Vaccines and Autism* (Washington, DC: National Academies Press, May 17, 2004).

69. Both the National Vaccine Information Center and SafeMinds immediately issued press releases claiming that the IOM report was biased and incomplete and had ignored evidence in support of the mercury–autism hypothesis.

70. Kathleen Stratton, Alicia Gable, and Marie C. McCormick, eds., *Immunization Safety Review: Thimerosal-Containing Vaccines and Neurodevelopmental Disorders*. (Washngton, D.C.: National Academies Press, October 1, 2001); Kathleen Stratton, Alicia Gable, Padma Shetty, and Marie McCormick, eds., *Immunization Safety Review: Measles-Mumps-Rubella Vaccine and Autism* (Washington, DC: National Academies Press, April 23, 2001).

71. SafeMinds obtained the meeting's transcript through the Freedom of Information Act and posted it, correspondence following the meeting, and their own analysis and summary, "Analysis and Critique of the CDC's Handling of the Thimerosal Exposure Assessment Based on Vaccine Safety Datalink (VSD) Information (October 2003)," on their Web site, http://www.safeminds .org/government-affairs/foia/simpsonwood.html. For the particular points mentioned, see p. 38 as well as Kirby (2005, 168–74).

72. Offit (2008, 91–94).

73. Eric Fombonne, Rita Zakarian, Andrew Bennett, Linyan Meng, et al., "Pervasive Developmental Disorders in Montreal, Quebec, Canada: Prevalence and Links with Immunizations," *Pediatrics* 118, no. 1 (2006): 139–50. Other important studies have been B. Taylor, E. Miller, R. Lingam, N. Andrews, et al.,"Measles, Mumps, and Rubella Vaccination and Bowel Problems or Developmental Regression in Children with Autism: Population Study, *British Medical Journal* 324, no. 7334 (2002): 393–96; and Kreesten Meldgaard Madsen, Anders Hviid, Mogens Vestergaard, Diana Schendel, et al., "A

Population-Based Study of Measles, Mumps, and Rubella Vaccination and Autism," *New England Journal of Medicine* 347, no. 19 (2002): 1477–82; and the study discussed at Simpsonwood, Thomas Verstraeten, Robert L. Davis, Frank DeStefano, Tracy A. Lieu, et al., "Safety of Thimerosal-Containing Vaccines: A Two-Phased Study of Computerized Health Maintenance Organization Databases," *Pediatrics* 112, no. 5 (2003): 1039–48. A metananalysis of studies on autism and MMR vaccine also found no association: Kumanan Wilson, Ed Mills, Cory Ross, Jessie McGowan, et al., "Association of Autistic Spectrum Disorder and the Measles, Mumps and Rubella Vaccine: A Systematic Review of Current Epidemiological Evidence," *Archives of Pediatric and Adolescent Medicine* 157, no.7 (2003): 628–34. A more recent study also took prenatal exposure into account, finding no association. Cristofer S. Price, William W. Thompson, Barbara Goodson, Eric S. Weintraub, et al., "Prenatal and Infant Exposure to Thimerosal from Vaccines and Immunoglobulins and Risk of Autism," *Pediatrics* 126, no. 4 (2010): 656–64.

74. As Epstein (1996) has documented, similar disputes played out around trials of medications for HIV/AIDS, in which patient advocates had very different ideas from investigators about what constituted "good science" in a clinical trial.

75. The National Immunization Program was responsible for overseeing immunization coverage and monitoring safety through the Immunization Safety Branch. In 2005, the Immunization Safety Branch, now the Immunization Safety Office (ISO), was moved to a different branch of the CDC. Nevertheless, a "mismatch in resources" remains, encouraging doubts about the CDC's commitment to vaccine safety—the NCIRD (formerly the National Immunization Program) receives about $3 billion in funds per year, while the ISO was getting about $20 millon as of 2008. Louis Z. Cooper, Heidi J. Larson, and Samuel L. Katz, "Protecting Public Trust in Immunization," *Pediatrics* 122, no. 1 (2008): 149–53, 152.

76. The requirement for post-market monitoring was a provision of the National Childhood Vaccine Injury Act, PL 99-660. The VAERS database was established in cooperation with the FDA and the VSD in cooperation with several HMOs.

77. Johnston (2004) describes a television segment that showed a mother attempting to navigate the forms and paperwork required to file a report, suggesting that the system is anything but streamlined.

78. American Academy of Pediatrics, "Study Fails to Show a Connection between Thimerosal and Autism" (press release).

79. See, for instance, the exchange about a 2003 article, Mark R. Geier and David A. Geier, "Neurodevelopmental Disorders after Thimerosal-Containing Vaccines: A Brief Communication," *Experimental Biology and Medicine* 228, no. 6 (2003): 660–64; Joshua R. Mann, "Questions About Thimerosal Remain," *Experimental Biology and Medicine* 228 (2003): 991–92; and David A. Geier

and Mark R. Geier, "Response to Comments by J. R. Mann," *Experimental Biology and Medicine* 228, no. 9 (2003): 993–94.

80. "Joint Statement on the Use of the CDC's Vaccine Safety Datalink for Thimerosal Investigations," CAN-Alert listserv, November 3, 2003.

81. R. Lingam, A. Simmons, N. Andrews, E. Miller, et al., "Prevalence of Autism and Parentally Reported Triggers in a North East London Population," *Archives of Disease in Childhood* 88, no. 8 (2003): 666–70, 668–69. The authors suggest that some parents changed their accounts of the onset of their child's autism to reflect developmental regression only after Wakefield's first public statements about the MMR vaccine. The article dates this phenomenon to August 1997, seven months before the press conference regarding the *Lancet* study, but close in time to some other reports of statements by Wakefield, e.g., Louise McKee, "New MMR Studies Revive Crohn's and Autism Fears," *Pulse*, August 2, 1997.

82. Kathy Blanco, "Story of Ryan and Stacy Blanco," in Edelson and Rimland (2003, 105).

83. Jason Rowe and Angelene Rowe, "Love Never Fails," in Edelson and Rimland (2003, 279).

84. Tory Mead and George Mead, "Through a Glass Darkly," in Edelson and Rimland (2003, 251).

85. Kathy Blanco, "Story of Ryan and Stacy Blanco," in Edelson and Rimland (2003, 108).

86. Dianne Doggett, "A Very Tough Kid," in Edelson and Rimland (2003, 145).

87. For instance, Murphy (2000) and Brown et al. (2001).

88. Vijendra K. Singh, "Letter to the Editor: Thimerosal is Unrelated to Autoimmune Autism," *Pediatric Allergy and Immunology* 18, no. 1 (2007): 89.

89. Her words were, "Thank goodness for the vaccine court." Bernadine Healy, "Fighting the Vaccine-Autism War," *U.S. News and World Report*, April 10, 2008, http://health.usnews.com/articles/health/brain-and-behavior/2008/04/10/fighting-the-autism-vaccine-war.html.

90. Gardiner Harris, "Opening Statements in Case on Autism and Vaccinations," *New York Times*, June 12, 2007.

91. Johnston (2004). The VICP is administered jointly by the Department of Health and Human Services, the U.S. Court of Federal Claims, and the Department of Justice. The hearing process requires a substantial contribution from each member organization, and even then requires a degree of streamlining, such as the Special Masters, in order to function. Information on the program can be found at http://www.cdc.gov/nip/vacsafe/.

92. The figure is from the Health Resources and Services Administration, part of the Department of Health and Human Services, which administers the VICP. Online at http://hrsa.gov/vaccinecompensation/omnibusproceeding.htm.

93. For instance, in the Cedillo case see U.S. Court of Federal Claims, *Theresa Cedillo and Michael Cedillo, as Parents and Natural Guardians of Michelle*

Cedillo, Petitioners v. Secretary of Health and Human Services, Respondent, Docket No. 98-916V, June 19, 2007, 1364, 1649–51. Also see the dispute over dating the presence of autistic symptoms for Jordan King and William Mead: *Fred and Mylinda King, Parents of Jordan King, a Minor, Petitioners v. Secretary of Health and Human Services, Respondent,* Docket No. 03-584V; and *George and Victoria Mead, Parents of William P. Mead, a Minor, Petitioners v. Secretary of Health and Human Services, Respondent,* Docket No. 03-215V, May 30, 2008, 4221–44. In the Cedillo case, the parents were reluctant to release the complete videotapes rather than excerpts to the respondent's experts, citing privacy concerns, until the Special Master assigned to the case required that they produce the tapes. George L. Hastings, "Ruling on Respondent's 'Motion for Production'" in *Cedillo v. Secretary of Health and Human Services,* filed May 10, 2007. Transcripts for all referenced cases can be found at http://www.uscfc.uscourts.gov/omnibus-autism-proceeding.

94. *Cedillo v. Secretary of Health and Human Services,* 2879.
95. This was David Amaral, director of the MIND Institute at the University of California, Davis, and Peter Hotez, president of the Sabin Vaccine Institute, on the radio program *Talk of the Nation,* June 14, 2007.
96. Rachel Heathcock, "Measles Outbreaks in London, United Kingdom—A Preliminary Report," *Eurosurveillance* 13, no. 15 (2008): 18829.
97. Sugarman (2007, 1277). Cases utilizing scientific evidence delivered by expert witnesses require that the science used reflect the consensus of the scientific community in addition to being testable and relevant to the case at hand. Specifically, under the *Daubert* standard, the testimony of an expert witness must be both "relevant" and "reliable," where reliability is defined in terms of standards that include testability, consensus of the scientific community, and rates of errors. For a thorough discussion of the standards for evidence in federal cases, see Jasanoff (1997).
98. Mark Blaxill, "Something Is Rotten in Denmark," unpublished presentation (May 18, 2004), http://www.safeminds.org/research/commentary.html.
99. *Cedillo v. Secretary of Health and Human Services,* 14.
100. *King and Mead v. Secretary of Health and Human Services,* 72.
101. *King and Mead v. Secretary of Health and Human Services,* 60. The full quote reads "What has no place here are experts at the margins of legitimate science who present untested theories, untested hypothesis [sic], speculation, conjecture, logical fallacies based on post hoc ergo propter hoc reasoning."
102. *King v. Secretary of Health and Human Services* and *Mead vs. Health and Human Services,* 56–57.
103. *King v. Secretary of Health and Human Services* and *Mead vs. Health and Human Services,* 4368–69.
104. Poling's parents are not convinced that she in fact had an underlying disorder, but the court chose to agree with the theory that proposed an underlying disorder as the source of Poling's illness. Gardiner Harris, "Deal in Autism Case Fu-

els Debate on Vaccine," *New York Times*, March 8, 2008; Marie McCullough, "Autism Theory Gains Support: Conceding a Rare Vaccine Tie," *Philadelphia Inquirer*, May 28, 2008, http://www.philly.com/inquirer/home_top_stories/20080529_Autism_theory_gains_support.html. Commentators cautioned that it was unlikely that the same mechanism applied to many other cases. Paul Offit, "Inoculated Against Facts," *New York Times*, March 31, 2008.

105. Donald G. McNeil Jr., "Court Says Vaccine Not to Blame for Autism," *New York Times*, February 12, 2009.

106. In the course of the proceedings, the Petitioners' Steering Committee (representing the families) concluded that the information relevant to the MMR-only theory had been presented as part of the joint theory and elected to present cases for only the first two theories. The decision on the part of the petitioners to not seek review of the decisions brought hearings on the second theory to an end, although an appeal on the *Cedillo* case remained pending. On the decisions, see Office of Special Masters, In Re: Claims for Vaccine Injuries Resulting in Autism Spectrum Disorder or a Similar Neurodevelopmental Disorder, *Various Petitioners v. Health and Human Services, Respondent,* Autism Update, March 25, 2010; and on the decision to not seek review, see Office of Special Masters, In Re: Claims for Vaccine Injuries Resulting in Autism Spectrum Disorder or a Similar Neurodevelopmental Disorder, *Various Petitioners v. Health and Human Services, Respondent,* Autism Update, May 20, 2010. For a summary, see Donald G. McNeil Jr., "3 Rulings Find No Link to Vaccines and Autism," *New York Times*, March 12, 2010.

107. George L. Hastings Jr., decision in *Cedillo v. Secretary of Health and Human Services*, 173.

108 *Cedillo v. Secretary of Health and Human Services,* 15; Offit (2008, 160).

109. It follows that educational efforts often focus on perceived "misunderstandings" on the part of parents. See, for instance, a 2008 presentation by a nurse who serves on an advisory committee for the CDC: Patricia Stinchfield, "Effectively Addressing Parents' Concerns about Immunizations," presentation at the Centers for Disease Control and Prevention Vaccine Safety Netconference (June 12, 2008), www.cdc.gov/vaccines/ed/ciinc/downloads/June_08/Stinchfield.ppt; and Hobson-West (2003, 278). Hobson-West writes that "in a horrific irony, proponents argue, the success of vaccination undermines itself."

110. Brownlie and Howson (2005, 224, 233, 235).

111. Hobson-West (2003, 278); Senier (2008, 219–20).

112. Casiday (2007, 1065); Hobson-West (2007, 211).

113. The full quote reads, "The process of education and learning is more important than the eventual decision and that trust, (or at least blind faith) is constructed as itself a source of risk." Hobson-West (2007, 209, 211–12).

114. Kaufman (2010, 22–24).

115. Casiday (2007, 1067).

116. Brownlie and Howson (2006, 439).

117. Senier (2008, 225).
118. Hobson-West (2007, 203–4); Blume (2006, 637, 640).
119. "Editorial: Silencing Debate over Autism," *Nature Neuroscience* 10, no. 5 (2007): 531.
120. Irva Hertz-Picciotto and Lora Delwiche, "The Rise in Autism and the Role of Age at Diagnosis," *Epidemiology* 20, no. 1 (2009): 84–90.
121. See, for instance, a 2008 study that investigates a possible association between regression and gastrointestinal issues. Maria D. Valicenti-McDermott, Kathryn McVicar, Herbert J. Cohen, Barry K. Wershil, et al., "Gastrointestinal Symptoms in Children with an Autism Spectrum Disorder and Language Regression," *Pediatric Neurology* 39, no. 6 (2008): 392–98. Other studies have looked at the relationship between developmental regression and the severity of autistic symptoms, for instance, A.-A. S. Meilleur and E. Fombonne, "Regression of Language and Non-Language Skills in Pervasive Developmental Disorders," *Journal of Intellectual Disability Research* 53, no. 2 (2009): 115–24.
122. Martha Herbert, "Learning from the Autism Catastrophe: Key Leverage Points," *Alternative Therapies* 14, no. 6 (2008): 28–30.
123. Herbert (2010). A special issue of the *American Journal of Biochemistry and Biotechnology* featured articles on a number of candidate factors in the etiology of autism, including infections, mercury, immune dysfunction, and mitochondrial disorders. Of particular interest were Teresa A. Evans, Sandra L. Siedlak, Liang Lu, Xiaoming Fu, et al., "The Autistic Phenotype Exhibits a Remarkably Localized Modification of Brain Protein by Products of Free Radical-Induced Lipid Oxidation," *American Journal of Biochemistry and Biotechnology* 4, no. 2 (2008): 61–72; and Matthew P. Anderson, Brian S. Hooker, and Martha R. Herbert, "Bridging from Cells to Cognition in Autism Pathophysiology: Biological Pathways to Defective Brain Function and Plasticity," *American Journal of Biochemistry and Biotechnology* 4, no. 2 (2008): 167–76.

Conclusion

1. For instance, "There comes a point in every great mystery when a confusing set of clues begins to narrow." Sandra Blakeslee, "Focus Narrows in Search for Autism's Cause," *New York Times*, February 8, 2005.
2. For example, Sally J. Rogers, "What Are Infant Siblings Teaching Us about Autism in Infancy?" *Autism Research* 2, no. 3 (2003): 125–37; and Lonnie Zwaigenbaum, Susan Bryson, Catherine Lord, Sally Rogers, et al., "Clinical Assessment and Management of Toddlers with Suspected Autism Spectrum Disorder: Insights from Studies of High-Risk Infants," *Pediatrics* 123, no. 5 (2009): 1383–91.

3. In using "syncretic," I am thinking of Lawrence Cohen's (1995) use of the term. While Cohen described the parallel application of incommensurate medical belief systems within modern medical practice in India, I am extending the argument to biomedicine in the United States by observing that it contains multiple, often contradictory, belief systems. Just because behaviorism and genetics are both used by psychiatric professionals, it does not mean that the assumptions that they make about the origins and treatment of disease, or the motivations behind human behavior, are entirely compatible.

4. Haraway (1997a, 128).

5. Hacking (1983, 136).

6. For instance, I cowrote an editorial for *GeneWatch*, the Journal of the Council for Responsible Genetics, with Martha Herbert, in which we argued that genetics was overemphasized and overfunded in the search for autism's causes, and another article with Jeffrey Brosco, a developmental pediatrician, in which we argued that clinicians need to remember how important parental insights have been in developing better understandings of autism and new treatment strategies.

7. Forsythe (1999); Nader (1972).

8. Rabinow and Lowy, quoted in Blume (2000, 142).

9. Ibid., 141–43.

10. Blume (2000, 139, 162).

11. Osteen (2008, 8).

12. One excellent example of research that explicitly asked autistic adults for guidance is Chamak, Bonniau, Jaunay, and Cohen (2008).

13. Eric Schopler made much the same point in criticizing those who claimed that psychogenic theories offered more prospects for improvement—many "organically involved" patients improved while those suffering from "habits formed early in life" might not do so well. Eric Schopler, "The Stress of Autism as Ethology," *Journal of Autism and Childhood Schizophrenia*, 3, no. 4 (1974): 193–96, 195.

14. Park (2001, 201, 10).

15. Landecker (2005) expresses a similar idea when she asks, "What is the social and cultural task of being biological entitities—being simultaneously biological things and human persons—when 'the biological' is fundamentally plastic?"

Adams, Christina. 2005. *A Real Boy: A True Story of Autism, Early Intervention, and Recovery*. New York: Berkeley Books.

Amsterdamska, Olga, and Anja Hiddinga. 2004, August. "Negotiating Classifications: Autism in the DSM." Paper given at the Society for Social Studies of Science, Paris, France.

Apple, Rima D. 1995. "Constructing Mothers: Scientific Motherhood in the Nineteenth and Twentieth Centuries." *Social History of Medicine* 8 (2): 161–78.

———. 2006. *Perfect Motherhood: Science and Childrearing in America*. New Brunswick, NJ: Rutgers University Press.

Ariès, Philip. 1962. *Centuries of Childhood: A Social History of Family Life*. Trans. Robert Baldick. New York: Vintage Books.

Aronowitz, Robert. 1998. *Making Sense of Illness: Science, Society, and Disease*. Cambridge, UK: Cambridge University Press.

Asperger, Hans. 1991/1944. "'Autistic Psychopathy' in Childhood." In *Autism and Asperger Syndrome,* ed. Uta Frith, 37–92.Cambridge, UK: Cambridge University Press.

Badcock, Christopher. 2004. "Mentalism and Mechanism: The Twin Modes of Human Cognition." In *Evolutionary Psychology, Public Policy and Personal Decisions,* eds. Charles Crawford and Catherine Salmon, 99–116. Mahwah, NJ: Lawrence Erlbaum Associates.

Bagatell, Nancy. 2010. "From Cure to Community: Transforming Notions of Autism." *Ethos: Journal of the Society for Psychological Anthropology* 38 (1): 33–55.

Baker, Jeffrey P. 2008. "Mercury, Vaccines, and Autism: One Controversy, Three Histories." *American Journal of Public Health* 98 (2): 244–53.

Barnbaum, Deborah. 2008. *The Ethics of Autism: Among Them, But Not Of Them*. Bloomington, IN: Indiana University Press.

Baron-Cohen, Simon. 1997. *Mindblindness: An Essay on Autism and Theory of Mind*. Cambridge, MA: MIT Press.

———. 2003. *The Essential Difference: The Truth about the Male and Female Brain*. New York: Basic Books.

Barron, Judy, and Sean Barron. 2002. *There's a Boy in Here: Emerging From the Bonds of Autism.* New York: Simon and Schuster.

Belmonte, Matthew K. 2008. "Human, but More So: What the Autistic Brain Tells Us about the Process of Narrative." In *Autism and Representation.,* ed. Mark Osteen, 166–79. New York: Routledge.

Bérubé, Michael. 1996. *Life as We Know It: A Father, a Family, and an Exceptional Child.* New York: Pantheon Books.

Bettelheim, Bruno. 1943. "Individual and Mass Behavior in Extreme Situations." *Journal of Abnormal and Social Psychology* 38 (4): 417–52.

———. 1950. *Love Is Not Enough: The Treatment of Emotionally Disturbed Children.* Glencoe, IL: The Free Press.

———. 1959. "Joey: A 'Mechanical Boy.'" *Scientific American* 200 (3): 116–20.

———. 1967. *The Empty Fortress: Infantile Autism and the Birth of the Self.* New York: The Free Press.

———. 1974. *A Home for the Heart.* New York: Knopf.

———. 1987. *A Good Enough Parent: A Book on Child-Rearing.* New York: Knopf.

Blume, Stuart. 2000. "Land of Hope and Glory: Exploring Cochlear Implantation in the Netherlands." *Science, Technology and Human Values* 25 (2): 139–66.

———. 2006. "Anti-Vaccination Movements and their Interpretations." *Social Science and Medicine* 62 (3): 628–42.

Bourdieu, Pierre. 1975/1999. "The Specificity of the Scientific Field and the Social Conditions of the Progress of Reason." In *The Science Studies Reader,* ed. Mario Biagioli, 31–50. New York: Routledge.

———. 1984. *Distinction: A Social Critique of the Judgment of Taste.* Trans. Richard Nice. Cambridge, MA: Harvard University Press.

Braslow, Joel. 1996. "The Influence of a Biological Therapy on Physicians' Narratives and Interrogations: The Case of General Paralysis of the Insane and Malaria Fever Therapy, 1910–1950," *Bulletin of the History of Medicine.* 70 (4): 577–608.

Brown, Phil, Stephen Zavestoski, Sabrina McCormick, Meadow Linder, Joshua Mandelbaum, and Theo Luebke. 2001. "A Gulf of Difference: Disputes over Gulf War–Related Illnesses." *Journal of Health and Social Behavior* 42 (3): 235–57.

Brown, Phil, Stephen Zavestoski, Sabrina McCormick, Brian Mayer, Rachel Morello-Frosch, and Rebecca Gasior Altman. 2004. "Embodied Health Movements: New Approaches to Social Movements in Health," *Sociology of Health and Illness* 26 (1): 50–80.

Brownlie, Julie, and Alexandra Howson. 2005. "'Leaps of Faith' and MMR: An Empirical Study of Trust." *Sociology* 39 (2): 221–239.

———. 2006. "'Between the Demands of Trust and Government': Health Practitioners, Trust and Immunisation Work." *Social Science & Medicine* 62 (2): 433–43.

Buchanan, Roderick D. 2003. "Legislative Warriors: American Psychiatrists, Psychologists, and Competing Claims over Psychotherapy in the 1950s." *Journal of the History of the Behavioral Sciences* 39 (3): 225–49.

Bumiller, Kristin. 2008. "Quirky Citizens: Autism, Gender, and Reimagining Disability," *Signs: Journal of Women in Culture and Society* 33 (4): 967–91.

———. 2009. "The Geneticization of Autism: From New Reproductive Technologies to the Conception of Genetic Normalcy." *Signs: Journal of Women in Culture and Society* 34 (4): 875–99.

Callon, Michel. 1987. "Some Elements of a Sociology of Translation: Domestication of the Scallops and the Fishermen of St. Brieuc Bay." In *Power, Action and Belief: A New Sociology of Knowledge,* ed. John Law, 196–223. London: Routledge and Kegan Paul.

Casiday, Rachel Elizabeth. 2007. "Children's Health and the Social Theory of Risk: Insights from the British Measles, Mumps and Rubella (MMR) Controversy." *Social Science & Medicine* 65 (5): 1059–70.

Chamak, Brigitte. 2008. "Autism and Social Movements: French Parents' Associations and International Autistic Individuals' Organisations." *Sociology of Health and Illness* 30 (1): 76–96.

Chamak, Brigitte, Beatrice Bonniau, Emmanuel Jaunay, and David Cohen. 2008. "What Can We Learn about Autism from Autistic Persons?" *Psychotherapy and Psychosomatics* 77 (5): 271–79.

Charlton, James. 1998. *Nothing About Us Without Us: Disability Oppression and Empowerment.* Berkeley: University of California Press.

Clifford, Stacy A. 2006. "The Politics of Autism: Expanding the Location of Care." Master's thesis, Ohio University.

Cohen, Lawrence. 1995. "The Epistemological Carnival: Meditations on Disciplinary Intentionality and Ayurveda." In *Knowledge and the Scholarly Medical Traditions,* ed. Don Bates, 320–43. Cambridge, UK: Cambridge University Press.

Conrad, Peter. 1999. "A Mirage of Genes," *Sociology of Health & Illness.* 21 (2): 228–41.

Cowan, Ruth Schwartz. 1983. *More Work for Mother: The Ironies of Household Technology from the Open Hearth to the Microwave.* New York: Basic Books.

Daley, Tamara. 2002. "Diagnostic Conceptualization of Autism among Indian Psychiatrists, Psychologists, and Pediatricians." *Journal of Autism and Developmental Disorders* 32 (1): 531–50.

———. 2004. "From Symptom Recognition to Diagnosis: Children with Autism in Urban India," *Social Science & Medicine* 58 (7): 1323--35.

Daston, Lorraine. 1992. "Objectivity and the Escape from Perspective." *Social Studies of Science* 22 (4): 597–618.

Daston, Lorraine, and Peter Galison. 1992. "The Image of Objectivity." *Representations* 40 (1): 81–128

Davidson, Joyce. 2008. "Autistic Culture Online: Virtual Communication and Cultural Expression on the Spectrum." *Social and Cultural Geography* 9 (7): 791–806.

Davis, Lennard. 2006. "Constructing Normalcy: the Bell Curve, the Novel, and the Invention of the Disabled Body in the 19th Century." *Disability Studies Reader*, 2nd ed. New York: Routledge.

de Chadarevian, Soraya. 2002. *Designs for Life: Molecular Biology after World War II*. Cambridge, UK: Cambridge University Press.

Didion, Joan. 1979/1990. *The White Album*. New York: Farrar, Straus and Giroux.

Doyle, Richard. 1997. *On Beyond Living: Rhetorical Transformations of the Life Sciences*. Palo Alto, CA: Stanford University Press.

Dumit, Joseph. 2000. "When Explanations Rest: "Good-Enough" Brain Science and the New Socio-Medical Disorders." In *Living and Working With the New Medical Technologies,* eds. Margaret Lock, Alberto Cambrosio, and Allan Young, 209–32.. Cambridge, UK: Cambridge University Press.

———. 2003. *Picturing Personhood: Brain Scans and Biomedical Identity*. Princeton, NJ: Princeton University Press.

Dundes, Alan. 1991. "Bruno Bettelhem's Uses of Enchantment and Abuses of Scholarship." *The Journal of American Folklore* 104 (411): 74–83.

Durbach, Nadja. 2002. "Class, Gender, and the Conscientious Objector to Vaccination, 1898–1907." *The Journal of British Studies* 41 (1): 58–83.

———. 2005. *Bodily Matters: The Anti-Vaccination Movement in England, 1853–1907*. Durham, NC: Duke University Press.

Durbin-Westby, Paula C. 2010. "Cultural Commentary: 'Public Law 109-416 Is Not Just About Scientific Research': Speaking Truth to Power at Interagency Autism Coordinating Committee Meetings." *Disability Studies Quarterly* 30 (1).

Edelson, Steven, and Bernard Rimland, eds. 2003. *Treating Autism: Parent Stories of Hope and Success*. San Diego, CA: Autism Research Institute.

Eliot, Stephen. 2002. *Not the Thing I Was: Thirteen Years at Bruno Bettelheim's Orthogenic School*. New York: St. Martin's Press.

Epstein, Steven. 1995. "The Construction of Lay Expertise: AIDS Activism and the Forging of Credibility in the Reform of Clinical Trials." *Science, Technology, & Human Values*. Special Issue: Constructivist Perspectives on Medical Work: Medical Practices and Science and Technology Studies. 20 (4): 408–37.

———. 1996. *Impure Science: AIDS, Activism and the Politics of Knowledge*. Berkeley: University of California Press.

Eyal, Gil, Brendan Hart, Emine Onculer, Neta Oren, and Natasha Rossi. 2010. *The Autism Matrix*. Cambridge, UK: Polity Press.

Fees, Craig. 1998. "'No Foundation All the Way Down the Line': History, Memory and 'Milieu Therapy' From the View of a Specialist Archive in Britain." *Therapeutic Communities: The International Journal for Therapeutic and Specialist Organizations* 19 (2): 167–78.

Feinstein, Noah. 2006, November. "Silenced by Science? Parents of Autistic Children Finding Their Voice." Paper presented at the Society for Social Studies of Science, Vancouver, BC.

Ferguson, Phil. 1996. "Mental Retardation Historiography and the Culture of Knowledge." *Disability Studies Quarterly* 16 (3): 18–31.

Fischer, Michael M. J. 1999. "Emergent Forms of Life: Anthropologies of Late or Postmodernities." *Annual Review of Anthropology* 28: 455–78.

———. 2000. "Calling the Future(s) with Ethnographic and Historiographic Legacy Disciplines: STS@the_Turn_[ ]ooo.mit.edu." In *Late Editions 8: Zeroing in on the Year 2000: The Final Edition*, ed. George E. Marcus, 218–302. Chicago: University of Chicago Press.

Fisher, David James. 1991. "Homage to Bettelheim (1903-1990)." *Psychohistory Review* 19 (2): 255–61.

Fisher, James. 2007. "No Search, No Subject? Autism and the American Conversion Narrative." In *Autism and Representation,* ed. Mark Osteen, 51-64. New York: Routledge.

Fitzpatrick, Michael. 2009. *Defeating Autism: A Damaging Delusion.* New York: Routledge.

Fleck, Ludwik. 1979. *Genesis and Development of a Scientific Fact.* Chicago: University of Chicago Press.

Forsythe, Diana E. 1999. "Ethics and Politics of Studying Up in Technoscience." *Anthropology of Work Review* 20 (1): 6–11.

Frankfurt, Harry. 2006. *Taking Ourselves Seriously & Getting It Right.* Palo Alto, CA: Stanford University Press.

Frith, Uta. 1989/2003. *Autism: Explaining the Enigma.* Malden, MA: Blackwell Publishers.

———. 1991. "Asperger and His Syndrome." In *Autism and Asperger Syndrome,* ed. Uta Frith, 1–36. Cambridge: Cambridge University Press.

Fromm, Erich. 1956. *The Art of Loving.* New York: Harper and Row.

Gernsbacher, Morton Ann. 2006. "Toward a Behavior of Reciprocity." *Journal of Developmental Processes* 1: 138–52

Gershon, Michael. 1998. *The Second Brain: The Scientific Basis of Gut Instinct and a Groundbreaking New Understanding of Nervous Disorders of the Stomach and Intestine.* New York: HarperCollins.

Gibbon, Sahra. 2007. *Breast Cancer Genes and the Gendering of Knowledge: Science and Citizenship in the Cultural Context of the "New" Genetics.* Houndmills, UK: Palgrave Macmillan.

Gieryn, Thomas F. 1983. "Boundary-Work and the Demarcation of Science from Non-Science: Strains and Interests in Professional Ideologies." *American Sociological Review* 48 (6): 781–95.

Gifford, Sanford. 1991. "The American Reception of Psychoanalysis." In *1915, The Cultural Moment: The New Politics, The New Woman, The New Art, and the*

New Theater in America, eds. Adele Heller and Lois Rudnick, 128–45. New Brunswick: Rutgers University Press.

Gilligan, Carol. 1982. *In a Different Voice: Psychological Theory and Women's Development.* Cambridge, MA: Harvard University Press.

Glaser, Elizabeth, with Laura Palmer. 1991. *In the Absence of Angels: A Hollywood Family's Courageous Story.* New York: Berkeley Books.

Goffman, Erving. 1959. *The Presentation of Self in Everyday Life.* New York: Doubleday.

Grant, Julia. 1998. *Raising Baby by the Book: The Education of American Mothers.* New Haven, CT: Yale University Press.

Gray, David E. 1993. "Negotiating Autism: Relations Between Parents and Treatment Staff." *Social Science & Medicine* 36 (8): 1037–46.

———. 1994. "Coping with Autism: Stresses and Strategies." *Sociology of Health and Illness* 16 (3): 275–300.

Greenfeld, Josh. 1970. *A Child Called Noah.* New York: Pocket Books.

———. 1978. *A Place for Noah.* San Diego, CA: Harcourt Brace Jovanovich.

———. 1986. *A Client Called Noah.* New York: Henry Holt and Company.

Grinker, Roy Richard. 2008. *Unstrange Minds: Remapping the World of Autism.* New York: Basic Books.

Grob, Gerald. 1994. *The Mad among Us: A History of the Care of America's Mentally Ill.* Cambridge, MA: Harvard University Press.

Hacking, Ian. 1983. *Representing and Intervening: Introductory Topics in the Philosophy of Natural Science.* Cambridge, UK: Cambridge University Press.

———. 1998. *Rewriting the Soul: Multiple Personality and the Sciences of Memory.* Princeton, NJ: Princeton University Press.

———. 1999. "Making Up People." In *The Science Studies Reader*, ed. Mario Biagioli, 161–71. New York: Routledge.

———. 2007. "Kinds of People: Moving Targets." *Proceedings of the British Academy* 151: 285–318.

———. 2009a. "How We Have Been Learning to Talk About Autism: A Role for Stories." *Metaphilosophy* 40 (3–4): 499–516.

———. 2009b. "Humans, Aliens, and Autism." *Daedalus* 138 (3): 44–59.

Haddon, Mark. 2004. *The Curious Incident of the Dog in the Night-Time.* New York: Vintage.

Hale, Nathan G. 1978. "From Bergasse XIX to Central Park West: The Americanization of Psychoanalysis, 1919–1940." *Journal of the History of the Behavioral Sciences* 14 (4): 299–315.

Hamilton, Lynn. 2000. *Facing Autism: Giving Parents Reasons for Hope and Guidance for Help.* Colorado Springs, CO: Waterbrook Press.

Happe, Francesca. 1994. *Autism: An Introduction to Psychological Theory.* Cambridge, MA: Harvard University Press.

Haraway, Donna. 1989. *Primate Visions: Gender, Race, and Nature in the World of Modern Science.* New York: Routledge.

———. 1991. *Simians, Cyborgs, and Women: The Reinvention of Nature*. New York: Routledge.

———. 1997a. "enlightenment@science_wars.com: A Personal Reflection on Love and War," *Social Text* 50 (The Politics of Sport): 123–29.

———. 1997b. *Modest_Witness@Second_Millenium.FemaleMan©_Meets_Onco-Mouse™: Feminism and Technoscience*. New York and London: Routledge.

Hays, Sharon. 1996. *The Cultural Contradictions of Motherhood*. New Haven, CT: Yale University Press.

Heath, Deborah, Rayna Rapp, and Karen-Sue Taussig. 2004. "Genetic Citizen-ship." In *A Companion to the Anthropology of Politics,* eds. David Nugent and Joan Vincent, 152–67. Malden, MA: Blackwell Publishing.

Hedgecoe, Adam. 2001. "Schizophrenia and the Narrative of Enlightened Geneti-cization." *Social Studies of Science* 31 (6): 875–911.

Henry, Jules. 1971. *Pathways to Madness*. New York: Random House.

Herbert, Martha R. 2004. "Neuroimaging in Disorders of Social and Emotional Functioning: What Is the Question?" *Journal of Child Neurology* 19 (10): 772–84.

———. 2005a. "Autism: A Brain Disorder, or a Disorder that Affects the Brain?" *Clinical Neuropsychiatry* 2 (6): 354–79.

———. 2005b. "Autism Biology and the Environment." *San Francisco Medicine* 78 (8): 13–16.

———. 2009. "Autism: The Centrality of Active Pathophysiology and the Shift from Static to Chronic Dynamic Encephalopathy." In *Autism: Oxidative Stress, Inflammation, and Immune Abnormalities*, eds. Abha Chauhan, Ved Chauhan, and W. Ted Brown, 343–87. Boca Raton, FL: Taylor & Francis/CRC Press.

———. 2010. "Contributions of the Environment and Environmentally Vulner-able Physiology to Autism Spectrum Disorders." *Current Opinions in Neurol-ogy* 23 (2): 103–10.

———. 2011. "A Whole Body Systems Approach to ASD." In *The Neuropsychology of Autism*, ed. Deborah A. Fein, 499–510. Oxford, UK: Oxford University Press.

Herman, Ellen. 1995. *The Romance of American Psychology: Political Culture in the Age of Experts*. Berkeley, CA: University of California Press.

Hobson-West, Pru. 2003. "Understanding Vaccination Resistance: Moving Be-yond Risk." *Health, Risk & Society* 5 (3): 273–83.

———. 2007. "'Trusting Blindly Can Be the Biggest Risk of All': Organised Re-sistance to Childhood Vaccination in the UK." *Sociology of Health & Illness* 29 (2): 198–215.

Houston, Rab A., and Uta Frith. 2000. *Autism in History: The Case of Hugh Blair of Borgue*. Oxford, UK: Blackwell Publishing Limited.

Iverson, Portia. 2006. *Strange Son: Two Mothers, Two Sons, and the Quest to Un-lock the Hidden World of Autism*. New York: Riverhead Hardcover.

Jacobsen, Kurt, ed. 2004. *Maverick Voices: Conversations with Political and Cultural Rebels*. Oxford, UK: Rowman & Littlefield Publishers.

Jasanoff, Sheila. 1997. *Science at the Bar: Science and Technology in American Law*. Cambridge, MA: Harvard University Press.

Johnson, Carol, and Julia Crowder. 1994. *Autism: From Tragedy to Triumph*. Boston: Branden Books.

Johnston, Robert D. 2004. "Contemporary Anti-Vaccination Movements in Historical Perspective." In *The Politics of Healing: Histories of Twentieth-Century Alternative Medicine in North America,* ed. Robert D. Johnston, 259–86. New York: Routledge.

Jurecic, Ann. 2006. "Mindblindness: Autism, Writing, and the Problem of Empathy," *Literature and Medicine* 25 (1): 1–23.

Kanner, Leo. 1943. "Autistic Disturbances of Affective Contact." *Nervous Child* 2: 217–50.

———. 1971. "Follow-Up Study of Eleven Autistic Children Originally Reported in 1943." *Journal of Autism and Childhood Schizophrenia* 1 (2): 119–45.

———. 1973. *Childhood Psychosis: Initial Studies and New Insights*. Washington, DC: V. H. Winston & Sons.

Kaufman, Barry Neil. 1976. *Son-Rise*. New York: Warner Books.

Kaufman, Sharon. 2010. "Regarding the Rise in Autism: Vaccine Safety Doubt, Conditions of Inquiry, and the Shape of Freedom." *Ethos: Journal of the Society for Psychological Anthropology* 38 (1): 8–32.

Kay, Lily E. 1993. *The Molecular Vision of Life: Caltech, the Rockefeller Foundation, and the Rise of the New Biology*. New York: Oxford University Press.

———. 2000. *Who Wrote the Book of Life?: A History of the Genetic Code*. Stanford, CA: Stanford University Press.

Keller, Evelyn Fox. 1983. *A Feeling for the Organism: The Life and Work of Barbara McClintock*. New York: Henry Holt and Co.

———. 1992. *Secrets of Life/Secrets of Death: Essays on Language, Gender, and Science*. New York: Routledge.

———. 1995. *Refiguring Life: Metaphors of Twentieth-Century Biology*. New York: Cambridge University Press.

———. 2000. *The Century of the Gene*. Cambridge, MA: Harvard University Press.

———. 2007. "Whole Bodies, Whole Persons? Cultural Studies, Psychoanalysis, and Biology." In *Subjectivity: Ethnographic Investigations*, eds. Joao Biehl, Byron Good, and Arthur Kleinman, 352–61. Berkeley: University of California Press.

Kennett, Jeanette. 2002. "Autism, Empathy, and Moral Agency," *The Philosophical Quarterly* 52 (208): 340–57.

Kephart, Newell C. 1960. *The Slow Learner in the Classroom*. Columbus, OH: Charles E. Merrill Publishing Company.

Kirby, David. 2005. *Evidence of Harm: Mercury in Vaccines and the Autism Epidemic—A Medical Controversy*. New York: St. Martin's Press.

Kirk, Stuart A., and Herb Kutchins, 1992. *The Selling of DSM: The Rhetoric of Science in Psychiatry*. New York: Aldine de Gruyter.

Kittay, Eva Feder. 1999. *Love's Labor: Essays on Women, Equality, and Dependency*. New York: Routledge.

———. 2001. "When Caring is Just and Justice is Caring: Justice and Mental Retardation." *Public Culture* 13 (3): 557–79.

Kozloff, Martin A. 1973/1998. *Reaching the Autistic Child: A Parent Training Program*. Cambridge, MA: Brookline Books.

Kramer, Peter. 1993/1997. *Listening to Prozac: The Landmark Book about Antidepressants and the Remaking of the Self*, rev. ed. New York: Penguin Books.

Kras, Joseph F. 2010. "The 'Ransom Notes' Affair: When the Neurodiversity Movement Came of Age." *Disability Studies Quarterly* 30 (1). http://www.dsq-sds.org/article/view/1065/1254.

Kroll-Smith, J. Stephen, and H. Hugh Floyd. 2000. *Bodies in Protest: Environmental Illness and the Struggle over Medical Knowledge*. New York: NYU Press.

Kuhn, Roland, and Charles H. Cahn. 2004. "Eugen Bleuler's Concepts of Psychopathology." *History of Psychiatry* 15 (3): 361–66.

Kutchins, Herb, and Stuart A. Kirk. 1997. *Making Us Crazy: DSM, the Psychiatric Bible and the Creation of Mental Disorder*. New York: Free Press.

Ladd-Taylor, Molly, and Lauri Umansky, eds. 1998. *"Bad" Mothers: The Politics of Blame in Twentieth-Century America*. New York: New York University Press.

Lakoff, Andrew. 2005. *Pharmaceutical Reason: Knowledge and Value in Global Psychiatry*. Cambridge, UK: Cambridge University Press.

Landecker, Hannah. 2005. "Living Differently in Time: Plasticity, Temporality and Cellular Biotechnologies." *Culture Machine: Generating Research in Culture and Theory*. http://culturemachine.tees.ac.uk/Cmach/Backissues/j007/Articles/landecker.htm.

Landsman, Gail. 2003. "Emplotting Children's Lives: Developmental Delay vs. Disability." *Social Science and Medicine* 56 (9): 1947–60.

———. 2005. "Mothers and Models of Disability." *Journal of Medical Humanities* 26 (2/3): 121–39.

Landsman, Gail Heidi. 2009. *Reconstructing Motherhood and Disability in the Age of "Perfect" Babies*. New York: Routledge.

Lane, Harlan. 1979. *The Wild Boy of Aveyron*. Harvard University Press.

Latour, Bruno. 1988. *The Pasteurization of France*. Trans. Alan Sheridan and John Law. Cambridge, MA: Harvard University Press.

Leiter, Valerie. 2004. "Parental Activism, Professional Dominance, and Early Childhood Disablity." *Disability Studies Quarterly* 24 (2). http://www.dsq-sds.org/article/view/483/660.

Lemov, Rebecca. 2005. *World as Laboratory: Experiments with Mice, Mazes, and Men*. New York: Hill and Wang.

Lettick, Amy L. 1979a. *Benhaven Then and Now*. New Haven, CT: Benhaven Press.

Lettick, Amy L. 1979b. *Benhaven at Work, May through August, 1978.* New Haven, CT: Benhaven Press.

Lewis, Lisa. 1998. *Special Diets for Special Kids: Understanding and Implementing Special Diets to Aid in the Treatment of Autism and Related Developmental Disorders.* Arlington, TX: Future Horizons.

Lindee, Susan. 2005. *Moments of Truth in Genetic Medicine.* Baltimore, MD: Johns Hopkins University Press.

Lovaas, O. Ivar. 1977. *The Autistic Child: Language Development through Behavior Modification.* New York: Irvington Publishers.

———. 1981. *Teaching Developmentally Disabled Children: The ME Book.* Austin, TX: Pro-Ed.

Luhrmann, Tanya. 2000. *Of Two Minds: An Anthropologist Looks at American Psychiatry.* New York: Vintage Books.

Lunbeck, Elizabeth. 1994. *The Psychiatric Persuasion: Knowledge, Gender and Power in Modern America.* Princeton, NJ: Princeton University Press.

Lyons, Tom Wallace. 1983. *The Pelican and After.* Richmond, VA: Prescott, Durrell, and Company.

MacIntyre, Alasdair. 1999. *Dependent Rational Animals* Peru, IL: Open Court Publishing Company.

Marcus, George. 1998. *Ethnography through Thick and Thin.* Princeton, NJ: Princeton University Press.

Marcus, George, and Michael M. J. Fischer. 1986. *Anthropology as Cultural Critique: An Experimental Moment in the Human Sciences.* Chicago: University of Chicago Press.

Matthews, Fred. 1967. "The Americanization of Sigmund Freud: Adaptations of Psychoanalysis before 1917." *Journal of American Studies* 1: 39–62.

Maurice, Catherine. 1993. *Let Me Hear Your Voice: A Family's Triumph over Autism.* New York: Fawcett Columbine.

McCandless, Jacquelyn. 2003. *Children with Starving Brains: A Medical Treatment Guide for Autism Spectrum Disorder.* Bramble Books.

Mechanic, David, and David A. Rochefort 1990. "Deinstitutionalization: An Appraisal of Reform." *Annual Review of Sociology* 16: 301–27.

Merton, Robert K. 1942/1973. "The Normative Structure of Science." In *The Sociology of Science,* ed N. W. Storer, 267–78. Chicago: University of Chicago Press.

Moon, Elizabeth. 2003. *The Speed of Dark.* New York: Ballantine Books.

Mulkay, Michael. 1976. "Norms and Ideology in Science." *Social Science Information* 15 (45): 637–56.

Murphy, Michelle. 2000. "The 'Elsewhere within Here' and Environmental Illness; or, How to Build Yourself a Body in a Safe Space," *Configurations* 8 (1): 87–120.

Murray, Stuart. 2008. *Representing Autism: Culture, Narrative, Fascination.* Liverpool, UK: Liverpool University Press.

Nader, Laura. 1972. "Up the Anthropologist: Perspectives Gained from Studying Up." In *Reinventing Anthropology,* ed. Dell H. Hymes, 284–311. New York: Pantheon Books.

Nadesan, Majia Holmer. 2005. *Constructing Autism: Unravelling the "Truth" and Understanding the Social.* New York: Routledge.

National Research Council (NRC). 2000. *Toxicological Effects of Methylmercury.* Washington, DC: National Academies Press.

Nelkin, Dorothy, and Lori Andrews. 2001. *Body Bazaar: The Market for Human Tissue in the Biotechnology Age.* New York: Crown Books.

Nelkin, Dorothy, and Lawrence Tancredi. 1994. *Dangerous Diagnostics: The Social Power of Biological Information.* Chicago: University of Chicago Press.

Neumärker, K. J. 2003. "Leo Kanner: His Years in Berlin, 1906–24. The Roots of Autistic Disorder." *History of Psychiatry* 14 (2): 205–18.

Nichols, Shana, with Gina Marie Moravcik and Samara Pulver Tentenbaum. 2009. *Girls Growing Up on the Autism Spectrum: What Parents and Professionals Should Know about the Pre-Teen and Teenage Years.* London: Jessica Kingsley Publishers.

Noll, Steven. 1995. *Feeble-Minded in Our Midst: Institutions for the Mentally Retarded in the South, 1900–1940.* Chapel Hill, NC: University of North Carolina Press.

Nussbaum, Martha. 2006. *Frontiers of Justice: Disability, Nationality, Species Membership.* Cambridge, MA: Belknap Press.

Ochs, Elinor, and Olga Solomon. 2010. "Autistic Sociality." *Ethos: Journal of the Society for Psychological Anthropology* 38 (1): 69–92.

O'Dell, Stan. 1974. "Training Parents in Behavior Modification: A Review." *Psychological Bulletin* 81 (7): 418–33.

Offit, Paul A. 2008. *Autism's False Prophets: Bad Science, Risky Medicine, and the Search for a Cure.* New York: Columbia University Press.

Oppenheim, Rosalind. 1974. *Effective Teaching Methods for Autistic Children.* Springfield, IL: Charles C. Thomas.

Orsini, Michael. 2009. "Contesting the Autistic Subject: Biological Citizenship and the Autism/Autistic Movement." In *Critical Interventions in the Ethics of Healthcare: Challenging the Principle of Autonomy in Bioethics,* eds. Stuart Murray and Dave Holmes, 115–30. Farnham, Surrey, UK: Ashgate.

Ortega, Francisco. 2009. "The Cerebral Subject and the Challenge of Neurodiversity." *BioSocieties* 4 (4): 425–45.

Osteen, Mark. 2008. "Autism and Representation: A Comprehensive Introduction." In *Autism and Representation,* ed. Mark Osteen, 1–48. New York: Routledge.

Pangborn, Jon, and Sidney Baker. 2005. *Autism: Effective Biomedical Treatments. Have We Done Everything We Can for this Child? Individuality in an Epidemic,* 2nd ed. San Diego, CA: Autism Research Institute.

Park, Clara Claiborne. 1967. *The Siege: A Family's Journey into the World of an Autistic Child.* Boston, MA: Little, Brown, and Co.

Park, Clara Claiborne. 1985. Review of *Autism: Nightmare without End*, by Dorothy Johnson Beavers. *Journal of Autism and Developmental Disorders* 15 (1): 113–19.

———. 2001. *Exiting Nirvana: A Daughter's Life with Autism*. Boston: Back Bay Books.

Park, Melissa. 2008. "Making Scenes: Imaginative Practices of a Child with Autism in a Sensory Integration-Based Therapy Session," *Medical Anthropology Quarterly* 22 (3): 234–56.

Pollak, Richard. 1997. *The Creation of Dr. B: A Biography of Bruno Bettelheim*. New York: Simon and Schuster.

Pressman, Jack D. 1998. *Last Resort: Psychosurgery and the Limits of Medicine*. Cambridge, UK: Cambridge University Press.

Prince-Hughes, Dawn. 2005. *Expecting Teryk: An Exceptional Path to Parenthood*. Athens, OH: Swallow Press.

Prussing, Erica, Elisa J. Sobo, Elizabeth Walker, and Paul S. Kurtin. 2005. "Between 'Desperation' and Disability Rights: A Narrative Analysis of Complementary/Alternative Medicine Use by Parents for Children with Down Syndrome." *Social Science and Medicine* 60 (3): 587–98.

Rabinow, Paul. 1996. "Artificiality and Enlightenment: From Sociobiology to Biosociality." In *Essays on the Anthropology of Reason*, 91–111. Princeton, NJ: Princeton University Press.

Raines, Theron. 2002. *Rising to the Light: A Portrait of Bruno Bettelheim*. New York: Knopf.

Rapp, Rayna. 1999. *Testing Women, Testing the Fetus: The Social Impact of Amniocentesis in America*. New York: Routledge.

———. 2000. "Extra Chromosomes and Blue Tulips: Medico-Familial Interpretations." In *Living and Working with the New Medical Technologies: Intersections of Inquiry*, eds. Margaret Lock, Allan Young, and Alberto Cambrosio, 184–207. Cambridge, UK: Cambridge University Press.

Rapp, Rayna, and Faye Ginsburg. 2001. "Enabling Disability: Rewriting Kinship, Reimagining Citizenship." *Public Culture* 13 (3): 533–56.

Rimland, Bernard. 1964. *Infantile Autism: The Syndrome and Its Implications for a Neural Theory of Behavior*. New York: Meredith Publishing Company.

———. 1972. "Operant Conditioning: Breakthrough in the Treatment of Mentally Ill Children." In *Readings on the Exceptional Child: Research and Theory*, 2nd ed., eds. E. P. Traff and P. Himelstein, 573–86. New York: Appleton-Century-Crofts.

———. 1976. "Psychological Treatment versus Megavitamin Therapy." In *Modern Therapies: Noted Practitioners Describe Twelve Different Types of Therapy and the Problems Each Can Help You Solve*, eds. Virginia Binder, Arnold Binder, and Bernard Rimland, 150–65. Englewood Cliffs, NJ: Prentice-Hall.

Roazen, Paul. 1992. "The Rise and Fall of Bruno Bettelheim." *The Psychohistory Review* 20 (3): 221–50.

Robertson, Scott Michael. 2010. "Neurodiversity, Quality of Life, and Autistic Adults: Shifting Research and Professional Focuses onto Real-Life Challenges." *Disability Studies Quarterly* 30 (1). http://www.dsq-sds.org/article/view/1069/1234.

Rose, Hilary. 1983. "Hand, Brain and Heart: A Feminist Epistemology for the Natural Sciences." *Signs* 9 (1): 73–90.

———. 1994. *Love, Power and Knowledge: Towards a Feminist Transformation of the Sciences.* Bloomington and Indianapolis: Indiana University Press.

Rose, Nikolas. 2007. *The Politics of Life Itself: Biomedicine, Power, and Subjectivity in the Twenty-First Century.* Princeton, NJ: Princeton University Press.

Rosenberg, Charles. 1979/1992. "The Therapeutic Revolution: Medicine, Meaning and Social Change in Nineteenth-Century America." In *Explaining Epidemics and Other Studies in the History of Medicine,* 9–31. Cambridge, UK: Cambridge University Press.

Rosenberg, Charles E. 2002. "The Tyranny of Diagnosis: Specific Entities and Individual Experience." *Milbank Quarterly* 80 (2): 237–60.

Rosenberg, Charles, and Janet Golden, eds. 1992. *Framing Disease: Studies in Cultural History.* New Brunswick, NJ: Rutgers University Press.

Rosenhan, David L. 1973. "On Being Sane in Insane Places." *Science* 179 (4070): 250–58.

Ryan, Sara, and Katherine Runswick Cole. 2009. "From Advocate to Activist? Mapping the Experiences of Mothers of Children on the Autism Spectrum." *Journal of Applied Research on Intellectual Disabilities* 22 (1): 43–53.

Sanders, Jacquelyn Seevak. 1989. *A Greenhouse for the Mind.* Chicago and London: University of Chicago Press.

———. 1996. "Autism at the Orthogenic School and in the Field at Large, 1951–1985" *Residential Treatment for Children & Youth.* 14 (2): 1–18

Sanders, Jacquelyn. 2005. "Architecture at the Sonia Shankman Orthogenic School at the University of Chicago." *The Annual of Psychoanalysis* 33: 285–95.

Schopler, Eric, and Gary B. Mesibov. 1984. "Professional Attitudes toward Parents: a Forty-Year Progress Report." In *The Effects of Autism on the Family,* eds. Eric Schopler and Gary Mesibov, 3–17. New York, Plenum Press.

Schopler, Eric, and Robert Reichler. 1971. "Parents as Cotherapists in the Treatment of Psychotic Children." *Journal of Autism and Childhood Schizophrenia* 1 (1): 87–102.

Schreibman, Laura. 2005. *The Science and Fiction of Autism.* Cambridge, MA: Harvard University Press.

Senier, Laura. 2008. "'It's Your Most Precious Thing': Worst-Case Thinking, Trust, and Parental Decision Making about Vaccinations." *Sociological Inquiry* 78 (2): 207–29.

Seroussi, Karen. 2003. *Unraveling the Mystery of Autism and Pervasive Developmental Disorders: A Mother's Story of Research and Recovery.* New York: Simon & Schuster.

Severson, Katherine DeMaria, James Arnt Aune, and Denise Jodlowski. 2008. "Bruno Bettelheim, Autism, and the Rhetoric of Scientific Authority." In *Autism and Representation,* ed. Mark Osteen, 65–77. New York: Routledge.

Shaked, Michal. 2005. "The Social Trajectory of Illness: Autism in the Ultraorthodox Community in Israel." *Social Science and Medicine* 61 (10): 2190–2230

Shaked, Michal, and Yoram Bilu. 2006. "Grappling with Affliction: Autism in the Jewish Ultraorthodox Community in Israel." *Culture, Medicine, and Psychiatry* 30 (1): 1–27.

Shakespeare, Tom. 2006. "The Social Model of Disability." In *The Disability Studies Reader,* 2nd ed., ed. Lennard Davis, 197–204. New York: Routledge.

Shapin, Steven. 1994. *A Social History of Truth: Civility and Science in Seventeenth-Century Century England.* Chicago: University of Chicago Press.

———. 1999. "The House of Experiment in Seventeenth-Century England." In *The Science Studies Reader,* ed. Mario Biagioli, 479–504. New York: Routledge.

Shapin, Steven, and Simon Schaffer. 1989. *Leviathan and the Air-Pump: Hobbes, Boyle, and the Experimental Life.* Princeton, NJ: Princeton University Press.

Shapiro, Joseph P. 1994. *No Pity: People with Disabilities Forging a New Civil Rights Movement.* New York: Times Books.

Singer, Judy. 1999. "Why Can't You Be Normal for Once in Your Life? From a 'Problem with No Name' to the Emergence of a New Category of Difference." In *Disability Discourse,* eds. Mairian Corker and Sally French, 59–67. Buckingham, UK: Open University Press.

Singh, Jennifer. 2010. "Autism Spectrum Disorders: Parents, Scientists, and the Interpretations of Genetic Knowledge." Ph.D. diss., University of California, San Francisco.

Singh, Jennifer, Joachim Hallmayer, and Judy Illes. 2007. "Interacting and Paradoxical Forces in Neuroscience and Society." *Nature.* 8 (2): 153–60.

Singh, Jennifer, Judy Illes, Laura Lazzeroni, and Joachim Hallmayer. 2009. "Trends in U.S. Autism Research Funding." *Journal of Autism and Developmental Disorders* 39 (5): 788–95.

Solomon, Olga. 2010. "What a Dog Can Do: Children with Autism and Therapy Dogs in Social Interaction," *Ethos: Journal of the Society for Psychological Anthropology* 38 (1): 143–66.

Stacey, Patricia. 2003. *The Boy Who Loved Windows: Opening the Heart and Mind of a Child Threatened with Autism.* Cambridge, MA: Da Capo Press.

Starr, Paul. 1982. *The Social Transformation of American Medicine: The Rise of a Sovereign Profession and the Making of a Vast Industry.* New York: Basic Books.

Stearns, Peter N. 2003. *Anxious Parents: A History of Modern Childrearing in America.* New York: New York University Press.

Stevenson, Sheryl. 2008. "(M)Othering and Autism: Maternal Rhetorics of Self-Revision." In *Autism and Representation,* ed. Mark Osteen, 197–211. New York: Routledge.

Sugarman, Stephen D. 2007. "Cases in Vaccine Court—Legal Battles over Vaccines and Autism." *New England Journal of Medicine* 357 (13): 1275–77.

Sunder Rajan, Kaushik. 2003. "Genomic Capital: Public Cultures and Market Logics of Corporate Biotechnology." *Science as Culture*. 12 (1): 87–121.

Sutton, Nina. 1996. *Bettelheim: A Life and a Legacy*. New York: Basic Books.

Taussig, Karen-Sue. 2005. "The Molecular Revolution in Medicine: Promise, Reality, and Social Organization." In *Complexities: Beyond Nature & Nurture*, eds. Susan McKinnon and Sydel Silverman, 223–47. Chicago: University of Chicago Press.

Tinbergen, Niko, and Elisabeth A. Tinbergen. 1983. *'Autistic' Children: New Hope for a Cure*. London, UK: Allen & Unwin.

Tomes, Nancy. 1981. "A Generous Confidence: Thomas Story Kirkbride's Philosophy of Asylum Construction and Management." In *Madhouses, Mad-Doctors and Madmen: The Social History of Psychiatry in the Victorian Era*, ed. Andrew Scull, 120–43. Philadelphia: University of Pennsylvania Press.

Trent, James. 1994. *Inventing the Feeble Mind: A History of Mental Retardation in the United States*. Berkeley: University of California Press.

Wajcman, Judy. 1991. *Feminism Confronts Technology*. University Park, PA: Penn State University Press.

Waltz, Mitzi, and Paul Shattock. 2004. "Autistic Disorder in Nineteenth-Century London," *Autism*. 8 (1): 7–20.

Warren, Frank. 1984. "The Role of the National Society in Working with Families." In *The Effects of Autism on the Family*, ed. Eric Schopler, 99–115. New York: Plenum Press.

Williams, Roger. 1956/1998. *Biochemical Individuality: The Basis for the Genetotrophic Concept*. New Canaan, CT: Keats Publishing.

Wing, Lorna. 1993. "The Definition and Prevalence of Autism: A Review." *European Child and Adolescent Psychiatry* 2 (2): 61–74.

———. 2001. *The Autistic Spectrum: A Parents' Guide to Understanding and Helping Your Child*. Berkeley, CA: The Ulysses Press.

Wolfensberger, Wolf. 1972. *The Principle of Normalization in Human Services*. Toronto, Ontario, Canada: National Institute on Mental Retardation.

Wolff, Sula. 2004. "The History of Autism." *European Journal of Child and Adolescent Psychiatry* 13 (4): 201–8.

Wolpe, Paul Root. 1990. "The Holistic Heresy: Strategies of Ideological Challenge in the Medical Profession." *Social Science and Medicine* 31 (8): 913–23.

———. 1994. "The Dynamics of Heresy in a Profession." *Social Science & Medicine* 39 (9): 1133–48.

Zaks, Zosia. 2010. "Cultural Commentary: I Have Asperger Syndrome, and I Am a Parent." *Disability Studies Quarterly* 30 (1). http://www.dsq-sds.org/article/view/1057/1243.

Zelan, Karen. 1993. "*Bruno Bettelheim* (1903–1990)," *Prospects: The Quarterly Review of Comparative Education* 23 (1/2): 85–100.

Zelizer, Viviana. 1985. *Pricing the Priceless Child: The Changing Social Value of Children*. New York: Basic Books.

INDEX

ABA. *See* applied behavior analysis

Adams, Christina, 179–80

ADI. *See* Autism Diagnostic Interview

ADOS. *See* Autism Diagnostic Observation Schedule

adults with autism, 234; children of, 162, 286n100; medical problems of, 177; neurodiversity movement among, 234–35, 286nn97–104; self-advocacy by, 7, 11, 15, 125–26, 136, 161–64, 286n88; writings of, 161–62, 249n83, 286nn97–98, 295n57. *See also* self-advocacy movements

advocacy activities, 14–18, 23–24, 49–54; for biomedical treatments, 167–96; biosociality in, 16–18, 142–43, 184–85, 193–96, 240nn50–52, 241n57; for educational rights, 127; embrace of autistic culture in, 143; genetic citizenship debates in, 16–17, 23–24, 241nn57, 59; for genetic research, 149–52, 155–60; internet spaces of, 180–81, 207; for mental patients' rights, 122; moral personhood debates in, 7, 11, 125–26, 143; neurodiversity debates in, 125, 155, 161–65, 176, 234–35, 273nn1, 3, 286n87; parent roles in, 15–16, 23–24, 53–54, 121–23, 267nn66–67, 273n7; political economy of, 17–18, 49–54, 242n62; on vaccines, 200–203, 206–7. *See also* names of specific organizations, e.g. Autism Society of America; self-advocacy movements

affective practices. *See* love

Aichhorn, August, 69, 79

AIDS research, 156–57

Akerley, Mary S., 130–32, 276n30

Allen, Woody, 254n5

allergies/immune dysfunction, 47, 164, 188–92, 204–5

alternative practices. *See* biomedical treatments

Alzheimer's disease, 149, 280n33

amateur therapists. *See* parents' treatment activities

American Academy of Pediatrics, 216

American Psychiatric Association. See *Diagnostic and Statistical Manual of Mental Disorders*

Amsterdamska, Olga, 242n60

amygdala, 153, 155

animal models, 149–53, 209, 281nn42–43

antiviral medication, 178

apoptosis, 208–9

applied behavior analysis (ABA), 95, 108–9, 114, 121, 123–24, 172–73, 267n75. *See also* behavior modification techniques

ARI. *See* Autism Research Institute

Asperger, Hans, 37, 44–45, 50–51, 163, 243n25, 247n64, 278n4

Asperger syndrome, 12, 21, 37, 160, 243n25; diagnostic markers for, 50–52; gendered context of, 44–46, 247n64; self-advocacy in, 52, 161–64

autism (definitions), 2–3, 48–49, 107, 237n4

Autism Biomedical Discussion Group (ABMD), 180–81, 295n54

Autism Birth Cohort (the ABC Project), 288n113

Autism Diagnostic Interview (ADI), 54–55, 59, 60, 194, 252n116

Autism Diagnostic Interview–Revised (ADI–R), 57, 148, 280n25

Autism Diagnostic Observation Schedule (ADOS), 54–57, 59, 60, 148, 194, 252nn116, 119, 280n25

enterocolitis, 189, 203–5, 300n17. *See also* gastrointestinal symptoms
environmental toxins, 176–78, 199, 227, 295n50; chelation treatments for, 135–36, 178–79, 191, 210–12, 219, 295n48; common diseases resulting from, 218; ethanol and lead as, 209; ethylmercury as, 198–99, 202–3, 206–12; genetic impacts of, 165, 288n113; mercury as, 202–3, 206–7, 302n39, 303nn46, 49, 304n58; methyl-mercury as, 206, 208, 299n16, 302n39; oxidative stress and neuroinflammation from, 204–5, 228, 302n32, 304n51, 311n123; sequestration levels of, 304n58, 305n63; thimerosal as, 198–99, 202, 206–12. *See also* vaccines
epidemiological surveys, 47–48
epistemological practices, 5–7
Erikson, Erik, 69
ethical debates, 233–36; on aversive techniques, 110–12, 114, 120, 132, 268nn82–83; on genetics and neurodiversity, 125, 155, 160–65, 177, 273nn1, 3, 286nn87, 97–104; intermingling with parental love of, 9, 125–27, 130–37, 225–26, 277n43, 278n51; on moral personhood, 7–12, 127, 134–35, 239nn25, 28, 273n1, 277nn43, 45, 47
ethylene diamine tetraacetic acid (EDTA), 210, 304n59
ethylmercury, 198–99, 202–3, 206–12
etiology debates, 41–47, 59–60, 141–66, 169, 245n47, 311n123; Bettelheim's psychogenic theory in, 38–39, 41–42, 61–73, 145–46; brain structure studies in, 44, 59–60, 89, 112–13, 153–55, 245–46nn53–54; chronic disease theory of autism in, 209–12, 218–19, 228; environmental causes in, 24, 47, 176–79, 197–228, 295nn48, 50; genetic possibilities in, 43, 46, 60, 90, 245n52; historical views on, 37–41; link with schizophrenia in, 39–41, 244n35, 249n87; Rimland's neurogenic theory in, 41–43, 106, 145; vaccines in, 24, 176, 197–228
Eval, Gil, 248n79
evaluation. *See* diagnosis of autism
Evidence of Harm (Kirby), 207–8, 211
evolution of autism, 2–3

facilitated communication, 174–75, 293n35
Facing Autism (Hamilton), 181
familial links. *See* genetic relations of autism

Feinstein, Noah, 239n34
feminist scholarship, 6–7, 233
Fenichel, Carl, 39
Ferguson, Phil, 240n40
Finegold, Sydney, 297n86
Fischer, Michael M. J., 242n63
Fisher, Barbara Loe, 201
Fisher, James, 272n120
Fitzpatrick, Michael, 171
Fleck, Ludwik, 241n55
Folstein, Susan, 43, 147
Food and Drug Administration (FDA), 169, 198
food sensitivities, 175, 177, 180, 188–91
Ford Foundation, 82
Fragile X syndrome, 149
Frankfurt, Harry, 10
Fredricks, Corinne, 133
Freitag, Gilbert, 104–5, 269n93
Freud, Anna, 61, 64, 69
Freud, Sigmund: Americanized ego psychology of, 74; Bettelheim's theoretical basis in, 69; on cure through love, 3, 61, 238n6
Frith, Uta, 22, 50, 243n25, 246n54, 278n4
Fromm, Erich, 10, 195–96

Garrod, Archibald, 292n28
gastrointestinal symptoms, 47, 188–92, 228, 296n77, 297nn80, 83; following immunization, 203–5, 300n17; in regressive autism, 302n36, 311n121
Gates, Bill, 160
Gay, Peter, 69
Geier, Mark and David, 216
gendered contexts: in Asperger syndrome diagnosis, 44–45, 247nn61–62; in autism diagnosis, 6, 247n64, 284n67, 286n101; of caring labor, 6–7, 84–85, 238nn18, 20; in comorbidity of autism and mental retardation, 44; in responses to mercury, 207; in Rett syndrome, 150, 279n24
Generation Rescue, 207, 303n44
genetic relations of autism, 141–66, 176; affected-sibling-pair research of, 144, 147–48, 149, 279n13; environmental contexts of, 165, 288n113; in etiology debates, 43, 46, 60, 90, 245n52; familial traits in, 145–46, 149, 160–61, 163–64, 172, 280n34, 288n112; fears related to, 160; genetic citizenship in, 16–17, 23–24, 241nn57, 59;